Christopher Marlowe's
TAMBURLAINE
PART ONE AND PART TWO
Text and Major Criticism

Copyright © 1974 by the Bobbs-Merrill Company, Inc.
Printed in the United States of America
First Printing

Library of Congress Cataloging in Publication Data

Marlowe, Christopher, 1564–1593.
    Christopher Marlowe's Tamburlaine.

    Bibliography: p.
        1. Timur, the Great, 1336–1405—Drama.
2. Marlowe, Christopher, 1564–1593. Tamburlaine
the Great. I. Ribner, Irving, ed. II. Title.
III. Title: Tamburlaine.
PR2669.A1   1974   822′.3   73–7938
ISBN 0–672–53061–9
ISBN 0–672–63061–3 (pbk.)

Christopher Marlowe's

TAMBURLAINE PART ONE AND PART TWO

Text and Major Criticism

Marlowe, Christopher
"   *[Tamburlaine the Great]*

Edited by Irving Ribner

THE ODYSSEY PRESS
A Division of
THE BOBBS-MERRILL COMPANY, INC., PUBLISHERS
Indianapolis · New York

Contents

CONTENTS

Foreword

It is difficult to imagine that the late Irving Ribner's professional career spanned less than a quarter of a century. Many would no doubt be content to acknowledge even half of his accomplishments as a full life's work. Professor Ribner edited not only *The Complete Plays of Christopher Marlowe* (1963), but also *The Complete Works of William Shakespeare* (1966–71). (Curiously, he edited *King John* on two separate occasions, an unusual accomplishment of which he was immensely proud.) In addition, he edited Tourner's *The Atheist's Tragedy* for the Revels' Plays Series, compiled a useful bibliography of Tudor and Stuart drama, was co-editor of an anthology of poetry, served as an editor of the *Tulane Drama Review,* and prepared separate "text and major criticism" collections for four individual Marlowe plays, a series of which this present volume is a part.

As a scholar-critic, Professor Ribner's accomplishments were no less impressive. He contributed essays to commemorative volumes, including those celebrating the four-hundredth anniversaries of the births of Marlowe and Shakespeare. He published articles in respected journals that covered almost every aspect of English Renaissance literature. His seminal study, *The English History Play in the Age of Shakespeare* (1957; revised edition, 1965), is a remarkably rich essay which for the first time fully traces the growth of historical drama. His critical studies include *Patterns in Shakespearean Tragedy* (1960) and *Jacobean Tragedy: The Quest for Moral Order* (1962). After preparing his edition of Shakespeare, he found time to write *William Shakespeare: An Introduction to His Life, Times, and Theater.*

Professor Ribner was a native of New York City. After teaching for many years at Tulane, and then at the University of Delaware, he returned home, in a sense, when he accepted a position at Stony Brook in 1968. During the four years that followed, his undergraduate Shakespeare course became a local institution; the large enrollments for "Ribner's Shakespeare" testify to his abilities as teacher and lecturer. His graduate seminars enabled him to share his prodigious learning in a more informal setting. Members of the last seminar he taught met at his secluded and comfortable home, where the genial atmosphere was usually enhanced by a fire roaring on the hearth, hot coffee, and occasional glasses of wine. Rarely did so productive an exchange of ideas occur under such pleasant circumstances.

Despite his many accomplishments, Professor Ribner never grew complacent about his work. He possessed a profound curiosity, and was constantly reevaluating his materials. At the time of his death in the early summer of 1972, he was working on a study of Shakespeare's development as a dramatist in relation to the literary and dramatic circles in which he functioned. Even in this unfinished work one may observe the manner in which Professor Ribner brought his finest powers of intellect to bear on a nexus of facts and theories about Shakespeare. He exhibited an uncanny ability to grasp and synthesize disparate ideas and to render them with utmost clarity. These qualities of mind are surely demonstrated in the following pages.

I should like to thank the Bobbs-Merrill editors, Jared Carter and James Chiplis, for their assistance with the manuscript. I am especially grateful to Mrs. Roslyn Ribner for her support during a most difficult time, and for her unwavering faith in the efforts to publish this volume.

Kenneth Friedenreich

State University of New York
at Stony Brook
Spring, 1973

Preface

When Christopher Marlowe came down to London after taking his M.A. at Cambridge in March of 1587, he may well have brought with him an early draft of a play about *Tamburlaine*. He must have completed the play very soon after his arrival, for by the beginning of 1588 both parts were being acted by the Lord Admiral's Men and were being so enthusiastically received by the London audience that they gave rise to a host of imitations and have often been regarded as the plays which ushered in the greatest age of the English drama. When the two parts were printed together in a black-letter octavo in 1590, Marlowe's name did not appear upon the title page, but such omission was not unusual in Elizabethan play publication, and there can be no serious question as to his authorship. Not only is this verified by contemporary allusions to the play, but the style is such as we can attribute to no other writer.

The career of Tamburlaine, or Timur Khan (1336–1405), the Mongolian conqueror who had defeated the Turks at Ankara in 1402 and thus unwittingly become the savior of Christian Europe, was a favorite Renaissance subject, and Marlowe might have read of him in many places. In the library of his Cambridge college was the Latin *Magni Tamerlanis Scythiarum Imperatoris Vita* (1553), which we may be sure he consulted. At Cambridge also in Marlowe's time was the scholar Richard Knolles, already engaged upon his massive *Historie of the Turkes* which was to be published in 1603. It is very likely that the two men knew one another, and it is possible that it was Knolles who first aroused

Marlowe's interest in Islamic history, for he seems to have consulted a draft of Knolles' work in manuscript. Marlowe probably read the account in Thomas Fortescue's *The Forest, or Collection of Histories,* itself translated from the Spanish of Pedro Mexia's *Silva de Varia Lection* (1542) with the help of a French version by Claude Gruget. This version also formed the basis of an account of Tamburlaine in George Whetsone's *The English Mirror,* whose publication in 1586 may have inspired Marlowe with the idea for his play and which may well have been his most immediate source.

Marlowe himself referred to the second part of *Tamburlaine* as an afterthought occasioned by the great popularity of the first part, and this has been the usual view, although some recent critics have argued that the two plays make an integral unit and must have been conceived of together. It is nevertheless clear that when Marlowe came to write his second part he had fairly well exhausted his historical sources, and thus most of the play is his own invention, although the Olympia-Theridamas episode is borrowed from Ariosto's *Orlando Furioso,* and the perfidy of King Sigismund of Hungary is based upon actual historical events which led up to the battle of Varna in 1444. Marlowe probably read of these in the *Rerum Ungaricarum decades quator* (1543) of Antonius Bonfinius and the *Chronicorum Turcicorum tomi duo* (1578) of Philippus Lonicerus. For much of his military detail he seems to have used *The Practice of Fortification* by Paul Ive, which was not published until 1589, but which there is good reason to believe that Marlowe was able to consult in manuscript. For the geography of both parts of *Tamburlaine* he consulted a great new atlas of the world, the *Theatrum Orbis Terrarum* of Abraham Ortelius, published at Antwerp in 1570.

There were many other places where Marlowe might have read of Tamburlaine, for his career furnished a favorite source for moral *exempla,* both for those writers who saw in him a pattern of tyranny and cruelty, and for those who saw in him an illustration of the highest potential of human aspiration. Humanist historians had glorified Tamburlaine as a man who could bend fortune to his will and who could at last be conquered only by death. This view may have come to Marlowe through Petrus Perondinus, and he may have encountered it as well in Louis

LeRoy's *La Vicissitude ou Variété des Choses en l'Universe,* which he may well have read in the French edition of 1575. What was to be an extremely popular English translation of this work by Robert Ashley did not appear until 1594, when Marlowe was already dead.

The diversity in historical accounts of Tamburlaine may be found reflected in the many conflicting critical reactions which Marlowe's play has generated. Although few would question its greatness as a work of art, it has not been easy to define the precise nature of this greatness, and there has been little agreement as to the play's structure, its meaning, or its moral implications. The present volume is designed to offer a sampling of the most significant approaches to the play, including as many points of view as possible. A final essay by Kenneth Friedenreich reviews the history of the play's critical reception, so that the essays included in this collection may be seen in a fuller perspective.

The standard old-spelling edition of *Tamburlaine* is in *The Works of Christopher Marlowe,* edited by C. F. Tucker Brooke (London, 1910). A modern spelling edition by Una M. Ellis-Fermor appeared in the six volume edition of *The Works and Life of Christopher Marlowe* under the general editorship of R. H. Case (London, 1930–33). The text of *Tamburlaine* and the Textual Notes in the present volume are reprinted from *The Complete Plays of Christopher Marlowe,* published by the Odyssey Press (New York, 1963). Except where indicated, direct quotations from Marlowe's plays have been made to conform with this edition.

Irving Ribner

State University of New York
at Stony Brook
Spring 1972

Tamburlaine

the Great.

Who, from a Scythian Shephearde, by his rare and woonderfull Conquests, became a most puissant and migh-
tye Monarque.

And (for his tyranny, and terrour in
Warre)was tearmed,

The Scourge of God.

Deuided into two Tragicall Dis-
courses, as they were sundrie times
shewed vpon Stages in the Citie
of London.

By the right honozable the Lozd
Admyzall, his seruantes.

Now first, and newlie published.

LONDON.

Printed by Richard Ihones: at the signe
of the Rose and Crowne neere Hol-
berne Bridge. 1590.

TO THE GENTLEMEN READERS AND OTHERS THAT TAKE PLEASURE IN READING HISTORIES:

Gentlemen and courteous readers whosoever, I have here published in print for your sakes the two tragical discourses of the Scythian shepherd Tamburlaine, that became so great a conqueror and so mighty a monarch. My hope is that they will be now no less acceptable unto you to read after your serious affairs and studies than they [5 have been lately delightful for many of you to see, when the same were showed in London upon stages. I have purposely omitted and left out some fond and frivolous gestures, digressing and, in my poor opinion, far unmeet for the matter, which I thought might seem more tedious unto the wise than any way else to be regarded, though haply [10 they have been of some vain, conceited fondlings greatly gaped at, what times they were showed upon the stage in their graced deformities. Nevertheless, now to be mixtured in print with such matter of worth, it would prove a disgrace to so honorable and stately a history. Great folly were it in me to commend unto your wisdoms either the [15 eloquence of the author that writ them or the worthiness of the matter itself. I therefore leave unto your learned censures both the one and the other and myself, the poor printer of them, unto your most courteous and favorable protection, which if you vouchsafe to accept, you shall evermore bind me to employ what travel and service [20 I can to the advancing and pleasuring of your excellent degree.

Yours, most humble at commandment,

R[ICHARD] J[ONES], Printer

THE TWO TRAGICAL DISCOURSES OF MIGHTY TAMBURLAINE, THE SCYTHIAN SHEPHERD, ETC.

TAMBURLAINE THE GREAT: PART ONE

THE PLAYERS

Mycetes, King of Persia
Cosroe, his brother
Meander ⎫
Theridamas ⎪
Ortygius ⎬ Persian lords
Ceneus ⎪
Menaphon ⎭
Tamburlaine, A Scythian
   Shepherd

Teschelles ⎫
Usumcasane ⎭ his followers

Bajazeth, Emperor of the Turks
King of Fez
King of Morocco
King of Argier

King of Arabia
Soldan of Egypt
Governor of Damascus

Agydas ⎫
Magnetes ⎭ Median lords

Capolin, an Egyptian
Philemus
Bashaws, Lords, Citizens, Moors,
   Soldiers and Attendants
Zenocrate, daughter of the Soldan
   of Egypt
Anippe, her maid
Zabina, wife of Bajazeth
Ebea, her maid
Virgins of Damascus

THE SCENE
Africa and Asia

THE PROLOGUE

From jigging veins of rhyming mother wits,
And such conceits as clownage keeps in pay,
We'll lead you to the stately tent of war,
Where you shall hear the Scythian Tamburlaine
Threat'ning the world with high astounding **terms**   **5**
And scourging kingdoms with his **conquering sword.**
View but his picture in this **tragic glass,**
And then applaud his **fortunes as you please.**

3

[*Enter*] *Mycetes, Cosroe, Meander, Theridamas, Ortygius,*
Ceneus, [Menaphon,] with others.

Mycetes.   Brother Cosroe, I find myself agrieved,
Yet insufficient to express the same,
For it requires a great and thund'ring speech.
Good brother, tell the cause unto my lords;
I know you have a better wit than I.   5
Cosroe.   Unhappy Persia, that in former age
Hast been the seat of mighty conquerors,
That in their prowess and their policies
Have triumphed over Afric and the bounds
Of Europe, where the sun dares scarce appear   10
For freezing meteors and congealèd cold,
Now to be ruled and governed by a man
At whose birthday Cynthia with Saturn joined,
And Jove, the sun, and Mercury denied
To shed their influence in his fickle brain!   15
Now Turks and Tartars shake their swords at thee,
Meaning to mangle all thy provinces.
Mycetes.   Brother, I see your meaning well enough,
And through your planets I perceive you think
I am not wise enough to be a king.   20
But I refer me to my noblemen
That know my wit and can be witnesses.
I might command you to be slain for this.
Meander, might I not?
Meander.   Not for so small a fault, my sovereign lord.   25
Mycetes.   I mean it not, but yet I know I might.
Yet live; yea live; Mycetes wills it so.
Meander, thou, my faithful counsellor,
Declare the cause of my conceivèd grief,
Which is, God knows, about that Tamburlaine,   30
That, like a fox in midst of harvest-time,
Doth prey upon my flocks of passengers,
And, as I hear, doth mean to pull my plumes.
Therefore 'tis good and meet for to be wise.
Meander.   Oft have I heard your majesty complain   35

I,i.

2 *insufficient* unable.

8 *policies* statecraft, diplomacy. See
Introduction, p. xxxi.

13–15 *birthday . . . brain* The personality of Mycetes is explained in 16th
century astrological terms. Cynthia (the
moon) was a traditional symbol of change

and fickleness, Saturn of stupidity. The
magnanimity of Jove, the artistic nature
of Apollo (the sun) and the wit of Mercury have had no share in his composition.

16 *thee* i.e., Persia.

32 *passengers* travelers.

Of Tamburlaine, that sturdy Scythian thief
That robs your merchants of Persepolis,
Treading by land unto the Western Isles,
And in your confines with his lawless train
Daily commits uncivil outrages,   40
Hoping, misled by dreaming prophecies,
To reign in Asia, and with barbarous arms
To make himself the monarch of the East.
But ere he march in Asia or display
His vagrant ensign in the Persian fields,   45
Your grace hath taken order by Theridamas,
Charged with a thousand horse, to apprehend
And bring him captive to your highness' throne.
Mycetes. Full true thou speak'st, and like thyself, my lord,
Whom I may term a Damon for thy love.   50
Therefore 'tis best, if so it like you all,
To send my thousand horse incontinent
To apprehend that paltry Scythian.
How like you this, my honorable lords?
Is it not a kingly resolution?   55
Cosroe. It cannot choose, because it comes from you.
Mycetes. Then hear thy charge, valiant Theridamas,
The chiefest captain of Mycetes' host,
The hope of Persia, and the very legs
Whereon our state doth lean, as on a staff   60
That holds us up and foils our neighbor foes.
Thou shalt be leader of this thousand horse,
Whose foaming gall, with rage and high disdain,
Have sworn the death of wicked Tamburlaine.
Go frowning forth, but come thou smiling home,   65
As did Sir Paris with the Grecian dame.
Return with speed; time passeth swift away.
Our life is frail, and we may die today.

---

36 *Scythian* The name Scythia has been applied to different areas at different times. The Greek historian, Herodotus, writes of Scythians as nomadic people who lived in southeastern Europe between the Carpathian mountains and the river Don. Later Scythia comes to refer to a large area in northern and central Asia. The historical Tamburlaine was a Mongol, born at Samarkand in Turkestan, and Marlowe's Scythia, according to the maps of Ortelius to which the dramatist referred (see Introduction, p. xxii), was an area on the north shore of the Black Sea, west of Crimea.

37 *Persepolis* the ancient capital of Persia on the Araxis river, some ruins of which still survive.

38 *Western Isles* Britain.

45 *vagrant ensign* nomadic banner.

47 *Charged with* placed in command of.

50 *Damon* with Pythias, a traditional symbol of friendship.

52 *incontinent* at once.

56 *choose* be otherwise.

66 *Grecian dame* i.e., Helen of Troy, stolen from her husband, Menelaus, by the Trojan prince, Paris.

Theridamas. Before the moon renew her borrowed light,
　　Doubt not, my lord and gracious sovereign,   70
　　But Tamburlaine and that Tartarian rout
　　Shall either perish by our warlike hands
　　Or plead for mercy at your highness' feet.
Mycetes. Go, stout Theridamas; thy words are swords,
　　And with thy looks thou conquerest all thy foes.   75
　　I long to see thee back return from thence,
　　That I may view these milk-white steeds of mine
　　All loaden with the heads of killèd men,
　　And from their knees even to their hoofs below
　　Besmeared with blood; that makes a dainty show.   80
Theridamas. Then now, my lord, I humbly take my leave.

　　　　　　　　　　　　　　　　　　　　　　　Exit.

Mycetes. Theridamas, farewell ten thousand times.
　　Ah, Menaphon, why stay'st thou thus behind
　　When other men press forward for renown?
　　Go, Menaphon, go into Scythia,   85
　　And foot by foot follow Theridamas.
Cosroe. Nay, pray you let him stay. A greater [task]
　　Fits Menaphon than warring with a thief.
　　Create him prorex of Africa,
　　That he may win the Babylonians' hearts,   90
　　Which will revolt from Persian government
　　Unless they have a wiser king than you.
Mycetes. Unless they have a wiser king than you?
　　These are his words; Meander, set them down.
Cosroe. And add this to them: that all Asia   95
　　Lament to see the folly of their king.
Mycetes. Well, here I swear by this my royal seat—
Cosroe. You may do well to kiss it then. [*Aside.*]
Mycetes. Embossed with silk as best beseems my state,
　　To be revenged for these contemptuous words.   100
　　O, where is duty and allegiance now?
　　Fled to the Caspian or the ocean main?
　　What, shall I call thee brother? No, a foe,
　　Monster of nature, shame unto thy stock,
　　That dar'st presume thy sovereign for to mock.   105
　　Meander come. I am abused, Meander.

　　　　　　　　　　　　　　Exit [Mycetes with his train].

　　　　　　　　　　　Cosroe and Menaphon remain.
Menaphon. How now, my lord? What, mated and amazed
　　To hear the king thus threaten like himself?

---

71 *Tartarian* used interchangeably with Scythian by Marlowe. Tartary in the maps of Ortelius covered a wide area of central and northern Asia. The Tartar or Mongol empire had, in fact, extended into Europe to include a part of Russia. 78 *loaden* laden.　89 *prorex* viceroy. 107 *mated* confounded.

Cosroe.   Ah, Menaphon, I pass not for his threats.
  The plot is laid by Persian noblemen   110
  And captains of the Median garrisons
  To crown me emperor of Asia.
  But this it is that doth excruciate
  The very substance of my vexèd soul:
  To see our neighbors that were wont to quake   115
  And tremble at the Persian monarch's name
  Now sits and laughs our regiment to scorn;
  And that which might resolve me into tears,
  Men from the farthest equinoctial line
  Have swarmed in troops into the Eastern India,   120
  Lading their ships with gold and precious stones,
  And made their spoils from all our provinces.
Menaphon.   This should entreat your highness to rejoice,
  Since Fortune gives you opportunity
  To gain the title of a conqueror   125
  By curing of this maimèd empery.
  Afric and Europe bordering on your land
  And continent to your dominions,
  How easily may you with a mighty host
  Pass into Græcia, as did Cyrus once,   130
  And cause them to withdraw their forces home,
  Lest you subdue the pride of Christendom.
                    [*Trumpets sound within.*]
Cosroe.   But, Menaphon, what means this trumpet's sound?
Menaphon.   Behold, my lord, Ortygius and the rest
  Bringing the crown to make you emperor!   135
    Enter Ortygius and Ceneus, bearing a crown, with others.
Ortygius.   Magnificent and mighty prince Cosroe,
  We, in the name of other Persian states
  And commons of this mighty monarchy,
  Present thee with th'imperial diadem.
Ceneus.   The warlike soldiers and the gentlemen,   140
  That heretofore have filled Persepolis
  With Afric captains taken in the field,
  Whose ransom made them march in coats of gold,
  With costly jewels hanging at their ears

109 *pass* care.
117 *regiment* rule, authority.
118 *resolve* dissolve.
119 *equinoctial line* equator.
124 *Fortune* the goddess Fortuna, who with her wheel provided a common classical and medieval symbol of the uncertainty of worldly things.
126 *empery* empire. This is one of Marlowe's favorite words.

128 *continent to* bordering upon.
130 *Græcia* the Greek settlements in Asia Minor. *Cyrus* the elder, the son of Cambises, was the founder of the Persian empire who conquered these Greek settlements.
132 *pride of Christendom* Byzantium or Constantinople.
137 *states* noblemen.

And shining stones upon their lofty crests,   145
Now living idle in the wallèd towns,
Wanting both pay and martial discipline,
Begin in troops to threaten civil war
And openly exclaim against the king.
Therefore, to stay all sudden mutinies,   150
We will invest your highness emperor,
Whereat the soldiers will conceive more joy
Than did the Macedonians at the spoil
Of great Darius and his wealthy host.

Cosroe.   Well, since I see the state of Persia droop   155
And languish in my brother's government,
I willingly receive th'imperial crown
And vow to wear it for my country's good,
In spite of them shall malice my estate.

Ortygius.   And in assurance of desired success,   160
We here do crown thee monarch of the East,
Emperor of Asia and of Persia,
Great lord of Media and Armenia,
Duke of Africa and Albania,
Mesopotamia and of Parthia,   165
East India and the late discovered isles,
Chief lord of all the wide, vast Euxine Sea,
And of the ever-raging Caspian lake.
Long live Cosroe, mighty emperor!

Cosroe.   And Jove may never let me longer live   170
Than I may seek to gratify your love,
And cause the soldiers that thus honor me
To triumph over many provinces;
By whose desires of discipline in arms
I doubt not shortly but to reign sole king,   175
And with the army of Theridamas,
Whither we presently will fly, my lords,
To rest secure against my brother's force.

Ortygius.   We knew, my lord, before we brought the crown,
Intending your investion so near   180
The residence of your despised brother,
The lords would not be too exasperate
To injure or suppress your worthy title.
Or if they would, there are in readiness
Ten thousand horse to carry you from hence   185

153-154 *Macedonians . . . host* Alexander the Great, son of Philip of Macedon, defeated the Emperor Darius and his Persian army in 333 B.C. at the Battle of Issus.

159 *malice* bear malice towards.

166 *late discovered isles* a possible reference to America.

167 *Euxine Sea* Black Sea.

170 *Jove may never* i.e., may Jove never.

180 *investion* investiture.

182 *exasperate* exasperated.

In spite of all suspected enemies.
Cosroe.　I know it well, my lord, and thank you all.
Ortygius.　Sound up the trumpets, then. God save the king!

　　　　　　　　　　　　　　　　　Exeunt.

　　　　　　　　　　　　　　　　　　　　　　　　　I,ii.
[Enter] Tamburlaine leading Zenocrate, [with] Techelles,
Usumcasane, [Magnetes, Agydas and] other Lords and Soldiers,
laden with treasure.

Tamburlaine.　Come lady, let not this appall your thoughts;
　　The jewels and the treasure we have ta'en
　　Shall be reserved, and you in better state
　　Than if you were arrived in Syria,
　　Even in the circle of your father's arms,　　　　　　5
　　The mighty Soldan of Egyptia.
Zenocrate.　Ah, shepherd, pity my distressèd plight—
　　If, as thou seem'st thou art so mean a man—
　　And seek not to enrich thy followers
　　By lawless rapine from a silly maid,　　　　　　　10
　　Who, travelling with these Median lords
　　To Memphis from my uncle's country of Media,
　　Where all my youth I have been governèd,
　　Have passed the army of the mighty Turk,
　　Bearing his privy signet and his hand　　　　　　15
　　To safe conduct us thorough Africa.
Magnetes.　And since we have arrived in Scythia,
　　Besides rich presents from the puissant Cham,
　　We have his highness' letters to command
　　Aid and assistance if we stand in need.　　　　　20
Tamburlaine.　But now you see these letters and commands
　　Are countermanded by a greater man,
　　And through my provinces you must expect
　　Letters of conduct from my mightiness,
　　If you intend to keep your treasure safe,　　　　25
　　But since I love to live at liberty,
　　As easily may you get the Soldan's crown

I,ii.

3 *reserved* safeguarded. *better state* greater honors.

6 *Soldan of Egyptia* None of the wives of the historical Tamburlaine was daughter to the Sultan of Egypt. His chief wife seems to have been a Tartar princess.

10 *silly* childlike, harmless.

15 *hand* signed guarantee of safe-conduct.

18 *Cham* Tartar emperor.

26 *at liberty* with liberality, bounteously.

As any prizes out of my precinct.
For they are friends that help to wean my state,
Till men and kingdoms help to strengthen it,   30
And must maintain my life exempt from servitude.
But tell me, madam, is your grace betrothed?
Zenocrate.   I am, my lord, for so you do import.
Tamburlaine.   I am a lord, for so my deeds shall prove,
And yet a shepherd by my parentage.   35
But, lady, this fair face and heavenly hue
Must grace his bed that conquers Asia
And means to be a terror to the world,
Measuring the limits of his empery
By east and west, as Phœbus doth his course.   40
Lie here, ye weeds that I disdain to wear!
             [*He removes his shepherd's clothes to
                  reveal his armor beneath them.*]
This complete armor and this curtle-axe
Are adjuncts more beseeming Tamburlaine.
And madam, whatsoever you esteem
Of this success and loss unvaluèd,   45
Both may invest you empress of the East.
And these, that seem but silly country swains,
May have the leading of so great an host
As with their weight shall make the mountains quake,
Even as when windy exhalations,   50
Fighting for passage, tilt within the earth.
Techelles.   As princely lions when they rouse themselves,
Stretching their paws and threatening herds of beasts,
So in his armor looketh Tamburlaine.
Methinks I see kings kneeling at his feet,   55
And he with frowning brows and fiery looks
Spurning their crowns from off their captive heads.
Usumcasane.   And making thee and me, Techelles, kings,
That even to death will follow Tamburlaine.
Tamburlaine.   Nobly resolved, sweet friends and followers!   60
These lords perhaps do scorn our estimates,
And think we prattle with distempered spirits,
But since they measure our deserts so mean,
That in conceit bear empires on our spears,
Affecting thoughts co-equal with the clouds,   65
They shall be kept our forcèd followers,

28 *precinct* province or administrative unit.
29 *wean my state* nurture my greatness, help it to grow.
40 *Phœbus* the sun, Apollo.
41 *weeds* garments.

45 *success* event, i.e., her capture. *unvaluèd* of little value.
47 *these* i.e., his followers. *silly* simple, lowly.
62 *prattle* speak idly.
64 *conceit* imagination.
65 *Affecting* indulging themselves with.

Till with their eyes they view us emperors.
Zenocrate.   The gods, defenders of the innocent,
  Will never prosper your intended drifts,
  That thus oppress poor friendless passengers.   70
  Therefore at least admit us liberty,
  Even as thou hop'st to be eternizèd
  By living Asia's mighty emperor.
Agydas.   I hope our lady's treasure and our own
  May serve for ransom of our liberties.   75
  Return our mules and empty camels back,
  That we may travel into Syria,
  Where her betrothèd lord, Alcidamus,
  Expects th'arrival of her highness' person.
Magnetes.   And wheresoever we repose ourselves,   80
  We will report but well of Tamburlaine.
Tamburlaine.   Disdains Zenocrate to live with me?
  Or you, my lords, to be my followers?
  Think you I weigh this treasure more than you?
  Not all the gold in India's wealthy arms   85
  Shall buy the meanest soldier in my train.
  Zenocrate, lovelier than the love of Jove,
  Brighter than is the silver Rhodope,
  Fairer than whitest snow on Scythian hills,
  Thy person is more worth to Tamburlaine   90
  Than the possession of the Persian crown,
  Which gracious stars have promised at my birth.
  A hundred Tartars shall attend on thee,
  Mounted on steeds swifter than Pegasus.
  Thy garments shall be made of Median silk,   95
  Enchased with precious jewels of mine own,
  More rich and valurous than Zenocrate's.
  With milk-white harts upon an ivory sled,
  Thou shalt be drawn amidst the frozen pools,
  And scale the icy mountains' lofty tops,   100
  Which with thy beauty will be soon resolved.
  My martial prizes, with five hundred men
  Won on the fifty-headed Volga's waves,
  Shall all we offer to Zenocrate,

69 *drifts* purposes.
70 *passengers* travelers.
73 *living* living to become.
88 *silver Rhodope* a snow-capped mountain range in Thrace, regarded by the Greeks as sacred to Dionysius and famous for silver mines.
94 *Pegasus* the famous winged horse of Greek mythology which had sprung from the blood of the gorgon, Medusa.

96 *enchased* adorned. The term was applied usually to the embellishing of metal with jewels and not to the embroidery of silk, as it is here. See note to *Dido* I,i,101.
97 *valurous* valuable.
101 *resolved* melted.
103 *fifty-headed Volga* the delta of the Volga river, with its many streams and tributaries.

And then myself to fair Zenocrate.   105
Techelles.   What now? In love?
Tamburlaine.   Techelles, women must be flatterèd.
But this is she with whom I am in love.
                              Enter a Soldier.
Soldier.   News, news!
Tamburlaine.   How now? What's the matter?   110
Soldier.   A thousand Persian horsemen are at hand,
Sent from the king to overcome us all.
Tamburlaine.   How now, my lords of Egypt and Zenocrate?
Now must your jewels be restored again,
And I that triumphed so be overcome?   115
How say you lordings? Is not this your hope?
Agydas.   We hope yourself will willingly restore them.
Tamburlaine.   Such hope, such fortune, have the thousand horse.
Soft ye, my lords and sweet Zenocrate,
You must be forcèd from me ere you go.   120
A thousand horsemen! We five hundred foot!
An odds too great for us to stand against.
But are they rich? And is their armor good?
Soldier.   Their plumèd helms are wrought with beaten gold,
Their swords enamelled, and about their necks   125
Hangs massy chains of gold down to the waist,
In every part exceeding brave and rich.
Tamburlaine.   Then shall we fight courageously with them,
Or look you I should play the orator?
Techelles.   No; cowards and faint-hearted runaways   130
Look for orations when the foe is near.
Our swords shall play the orators for us.
Usumcasane.   Come, let us meet them at the mountain foot,
And with a sudden and an hot alarm
Drive all their horses headlong down the hill.   135
Techelles.   Come, let us march.
Tamburlaine.   Stay Techelles; ask a parley first.
                              The Soldiers enter.
Open the mails; yet guard the treasure sure.
Lay out our golden wedges to the view,
That their reflections may amaze the Persians,   140
And look we friendly on them when they come.
But if they offer word or violence,
We'll fight, five hundred men-at-arms to one,
Before we part with our possession.
And 'gainst the general we will lift our swords,   145
And either lance his greedy thirsting throat,
Or take him prisoner, and his chain shall serve
For manacles till he be ransomed home.

138 *mails* trunks.

Techelles.   I hear them come. Shall we encounter them?
Tamburlaine.   Keep all your standings, and not stir a foot;   150
  Myself will bide the danger of the brunt.
                Enter Theridamas, with others.
Theridamas.   Where is this Scythian, Tamburlaine?
Tamburlaine.   Whom seek'st thou, Persian? I am Tamburlaine.
Theridamas.   Tamburlaine! A Scythian shepherd so embellishèd
  With nature's pride and richest furniture!   155
  His looks do menace heaven and dare the gods.
  His fiery eyes are fixed upon the earth
  As if he now devised some stratagem,
  Or meant to pierce Avernus' darksome vaults
  To pull the triple-headed dog from hell.   160
Tamburlaine.   Noble and mild this Persian seems to be,
  If outward habit judge the inward man.
Techelles.   His deep affections make him passionate.
Tamburlaine.   With what a majesty he rears his looks!
  In thee, thou valiant man of Persia,
  I see the folly of thy emperor.   165
  Art thou but captain of a thousand horse,
  That by characters graven in thy brows,
  And by thy martial face and stout aspect,
  Deserv'st to have the leading of an host?
  Forsake thy king and do but join with me,   170
  And we will triumph over all the world.
  I hold the Fates bound fast in iron chains,
  And with my hand turn Fortune's wheel about,
  And sooner shall the sun fall from his sphere   175
  Then Tamburlaine be slain or overcome.
  Draw forth thy sword, thou mighty man-at-arms,
  Intending but to raze my charmèd skin,
  And Jove himself will stretch his hand from heaven
  To ward the blow and shield me safe from harm.   180
  See how he rains down heaps of gold in showers,
  As if he meant to give my soldiers pay;
  And as a sure and grounded argument
  That I shall be the monarch of the East,
  He sends this Soldan's daughter, rich and brave,   185
  To be my queen and portly emperess.
  If thou wilt stay with me, renownèd man,

155 *furniture* equipment.
159 *Avernus* a dark volcanic lake supposed to lead to the underworld.
160 *triple-headed dog* Cerberus, who guarded the gates of the underworld.
163 *affections* emotions.
173 *Fates* See note to *Dido*, III,ii,3.
175 *sun . . . sphere* The sun was conceived, in the Ptolemaic astronomy which Marlowe uses, to move in an orbit or sphere about the earth.
186 *portly* stately. *emperess* empress. Here and elsewhere I have retained the original spelling for the sake of the meter.

And lead thy thousand horse with my conduct,
Besides thy share of this Egyptian prize,
Those thousand horse shall sweat with martial spoil   190
Of conquered kingdoms and of cities sacked.
Both we will walk upon the lofty clifts,
And Christian merchants, that with Russian stems
Plough up huge furrows in the Caspian Sea,
Shall vail to us as lords of all the lake.   195
Both we will reign as consuls of the earth,
And mighty kings shall be our senators.
Jove sometimes maskèd in a shepherd's weed,
And by those steps that he hath scaled the heavens,
May we become immortal like the gods.   200
Join with me now in this my mean estate—
I call it mean because, being yet obscure,
The nations far removed admire me not—
And when my name and honor shall be spread
As far as Boreas claps his brazen wings,   205
Or fair Boötes sends his cheerful light,
Then shalt thou be competitor with me,
And sit with Tamburlaine in all his majesty.
Theridamas.   Not Hermes, prolocutor to the gods,
Could use persuasions more pathetical.   210
Tamburlaine.   Nor are Apollo's oracles more true
Than thou shalt find my vaunts substantial.
Techelles.   We are his friends, and if the Persian king
Should offer present dukedoms to our state,
We think it loss to make exchange for that   215
We are assured of by our friend's success.
Usumcasane.   And kingdoms at the least we all expect,
Besides the honor in assured conquests,
Where kings shall crouch unto our conquering swords
And hosts of soldiers stand amazed at us,   220
When with their fearful tongues they shall confess
These are the men that all the world admires.
Theridamas.   What strong enchantments tice my yielding soul!
Ah, these resolvèd noble Scythians!
But shall I prove a traitor to my king?   225

188 *conduct* direction.
192 *clifts* cliffs.
193 *stems* ships.
195 *vail* lower their topsails as a
token of respect.
198 *maskèd . . . weed* disguised himself as a shepherd.
201 *estate* condition.
205 *as . . . wings* to the farthest
reaches of the North.
206 *Boötes* a northern constellation,

known also as the bear, containing the
bright star, Arcturus.
207 *competitor* partner.
209 *prolocutor to* spokesman or messenger for; Hermes was the god of
eloquence.
210 *pathetical* moving.
214 *offer . . . state* i.e., offer to make
us dukes.
223 *tice* entice.
224 *resolvèd* determined.

Tamburlaine.　No, but the trusty friend of Tamburlaine.
Theridamas.　Won with thy words and conquered with thy looks,
　I yield myself, my men, and horse to thee,
　To be partaker of thy good or ill,
　As long as life maintains Theridamas.　　　　　230
Tamburlaine.　Theridamas, my friend, take here my hand,
　Which is as much as if I swore by heaven
　And called the gods to witness of my vow.
　Thus shall my heart be still combined with thine,
　Until our bodies turn to elements,　　　　　235
　And both our souls aspire celestial thrones.
　Techelles and Casane, welcome him.
Techelles.　Welcome, renownèd Persian, to us all.
Usumcasane.　Long may Theridamas remain with us.
Tamburlaine.　These are my friends in whom I more rejoice　　　240
　Than doth the king of Persia in his crown;
　And by the love of Pylades and Orestes,
　Whose statues we adore in Scythia,
　Thyself and them shall never part from me
　Before I crown you kings in Asia.　　　　　245
　Make much of them, gentle Theridamas,
　And they will never leave thee till the death.
Theridamas.　Nor thee, nor them, thrice-noble Tamburlaine,
　Shall want my heart to be with gladness pierced,
　To do you honor and security.　　　　　250
Tamburlaine.　A thousand thanks, worthy Theridamas.
　And now, fair madam and my noble lords,
　If you will willingly remain with me,
　You shall have honors as your merits be,
　Or else you shall be forced with slavery.　　　　　255
Agydas.　We yield unto thee, happy Tamburlaine.
Tamburlaine.　For you then, madam, I am out of doubt.
Zenocrate.　I must be pleased perforce. Wretched Zenocrate!

　　　　　　　　　　　　　　　　Exeunt.

234 *still* forever.
235 *elements* i.e., earth, air, fire, and water.
236 *aspire* aspire to.
242 *Pylades and Orestes* When Orestes returned to Argos, his faithful friend, Pylades, accompanied him, and after Orestes had slain his mother, Clytem-nestra, and was pursued by the Furies, Pylades shared the exile and suffering of his friend.
248 *Nor . . . them* neither to thee nor to them.
249 *want* be found lacking.
250 *security* protection.

II,i.

[Enter] Cosroe, Menaphon, Ortygius, Ceneus, with other
Soldiers.

Cosroe. Thus far are we towards Theridamas
And valiant Tamburlaine, the man of fame,
The man that in the forehead of his fortune
Bears figures of renown and miracle.
But tell me, that hast seen him, Menaphon,   5
What stature wields he, and what personage?
Menaphon. Of stature tall, and straightly fashionèd,
Like his desire, lift upwards and divine,
So large of limbs, his joints so strongly knit,
Such breadth of shoulders as might mainly bear   10
Old Atlas' burden. 'Twixt his manly pitch,
A pearl more worth than all the world is placed,
Wherein by curious sovereignty of art
Are fixed his piercing instruments of sight,
Whose fiery circles bear encompassèd   15
A heaven of heavenly bodies in their spheres,
That guides his steps and actions to the throne
Where honor sits invested royally.
Pale of complexion, wrought in him with passion,
Thirsting with sovereignty, with love of arms,   20
His lofty brows in folds do figure death,
And in their smoothness amity and life.
About them hangs a knot of amber hair,
Wrappèd in curls, as fierce Achilles' was,
On which the breath of heaven delights to play,   25
Making it dance with wanton majesty.
His arms and fingers, long and sinewy,
Betokening valor and excess of strength—
In every part proportioned like the man
Should make the world subdued to Tamburlaine.   30
Cosroe. Well hast thou portrayed in thy terms of life
The face and personage of a wondrous man.
Nature doth strive with Fortune and his stars
To make him famous in accomplished worth,
And well his merits show him to be made   35

II,i.

3-4 *man . . . miracle* It was a part of
Moslem belief that Allah wrote the destiny of a man in secret signs upon his
forehead.
10 *mainly* with strength.
11 *Old Atlas' burden* See note to *Dido*,
I,i,99. *pitch* the width of his shoulders.
12 *pearl* i.e., his head.
15-17 *Whose . . . throne* i.e., within

his eyes there shines a constellation of
such propitious stars as might cause
him to attain the throne. (All human
events were believed to be influenced
by the stars.)
21 *in folds* when furrowed.
26 *wanton* careless.
31 *of life* vivid.

His fortune's master and the king of men,
That could persuade, at such a sudden pinch,
With reasons of his valor and his life,
A thousand sworn and overmatching foes.
Then, when our powers in points of swords are joined,   40
And closed in compass of the killing bullet,
Though strait the passage and the port be made
That leads to palace of my brother's life,
Proud is his fortune if we pierce it not.
And when the princely Persian diadem   45
Shall overweigh his weary witless head
And fall, like mellowed fruit, with shakes of death,
In fair Persia noble Tamburlaine
Shall be my regent and remain as king.

Ortygius.   In happy hour we have set the crown   50
Upon your kingly head, that seeks our honor
In joining with the man ordained by heaven
To further every action to the best.

Ceneus.   He that with shepherds and a little spoil
Durst, in disdain of wrong and tyranny,   55
Defend his freedom 'gainst a monarchy,
What will he do supported by a king,
Leading a troop of gentlemen and lords,
And stuffed with treasure for his highest thoughts?

Cosroe.   And such shall wait on worthy Tamburlaine.   60
Our army will be forty thousand strong,
When Tamburlaine and brave Theridamas
Have met us by the river Araris;
And all conjoined to meet the witless king
That now is marching near to Parthia,   65
And with unwilling soldiers faintly armed,
To seek revenge on me and Tamburlaine,
To whom, sweet Menaphon, direct me straight.

Menaphon.   I will, my lord.

Exeunt.

*

[*Enter*] *Mycetes, Meander, with other Lords and Soldiers.*   II,ii.
Mycetes.   Come, my Meander, let us to this gear.
I tell you true, my heart is swoll'n with wrath

---

42 *port* entrance.
63 *river Araris* probably the river
Araxis which flowed through Armenia
to the Caspian Sea.

65 *Parthia* an Asian kingdom, south-
east of the Caspian Sea.
II,ii.
1 *gear* business.

On this same thievish villain, Tamburlaine,
And of that false Cosroe, my traitorous brother.
Would it not grieve a king to be so abused   5
And have a thousand horsemen ta'en away?
And—which is worse—to have his diadem
Sought for by such scald knaves as love him not?
I think it would. Well then, by heavens I swear,
Aurora shall not peep out of her doors,   10
But I will have Cosroe by the head
And kill proud Tamburlaine with point of sword.
Tell you the rest, Meander; I have said.
Meander.   Then, having passed Armenian deserts now,
And pitched our tents under the Georgian hills,   15
Whose tops are covered with Tartarian thieves
That lie in ambush, waiting for a prey,
What should we do but bid them battle straight
And rid the world of those detested troops,
Lest, if we let them linger here a while,   20
They gather strength by power of fresh supplies.
This country swarms with vile outrageous men
That live by rapine and by lawless spoil,
Fit soldiers for the wicked Tamburlaine.
And he that could with gifts and promises   25
Inveigle him that led a thousand horse,
And make him false his faith unto his king,
Will quickly win such as are like himself.
Therefore cheer up your minds; prepare to fight.
He that can take or slaughter Tamburlaine   30
Shall rule the province of Albania.
Who brings that traitor's head, Theridamas,
Shall have a government in Media,
Beside the spoil of him and all his train.
But if Cosroe—as our spials say,   35
And as we know—remains with Tamburlaine,
His highness' pleasure is that he should live
And be reclaimed with princely lenity.
                    [*Enter a Spy.*]
Spy.   An hundred horsemen of my company,
Scouting abroad upon these champion plains,   40
Have viewed the army of the Scythians,
Which make reports it far exceeds the king's.
Meander.   Suppose they be in number infinite,
Yet being void of martial discipline,

---

8 *scald* scurvy, contemptible.   27 *false* betray.
10 *Aurora* goddess of the dawn.   35 *spials* spies.
22 *outrageous* fierce, likely to commit   40 *champion* level.
outrages.

All running headlong after greedy spoils,   45
And more regarding gain than victory,
Like to the cruel brothers of the earth,
Sprung of the teeth of dragons venomous,
Their careless swords shall lance their fellows' throats
And make us triumph in their overthrow.   50
Mycetes.   Was there such brethren, sweet Meander, say,
That sprung of teeth of dragons venomous?
Meander.   So poets say, my lord.
Mycetes.   And 'tis a pretty toy to be a poet.
Well, well, Meander, thou art deeply read,   55
And having thee, I have a jewel sure.
Go on, my lord, and give your charge, I say.
Thy wit will make us conquerors today.
Meander.   Then, noble soldiers, to entrap these thieves
That live confounded in disordered troops,   60
If wealth or riches may prevail with them,
We have our camels laden all with gold,
Which you that be but common soldiers
Shall fling in every corner of the field,
And while the base-born Tartars take it up,   65
You, fighting more for honor than for gold,
Shall massacre those greedy-minded slaves;
And when their scattered army is subdued,
And you march on their slaughtered carcasses,
Share equally the gold that bought their lives,   70
And live like gentlemen in Persia.
Strike up the drum and march courageously.
Fortune herself doth sit upon our crests.
Mycetes.   He tells you true, my masters; so he does.
Drums, why sound ye not when Meander speaks?   75
                                        Exeunt.

                                                            II,iii.
[*Enter*] *Cosroe, Tamburlaine, Theridamas, Techelles, Usum-
           casane, Ortygius, with others.*
Cosroe.   Now, worthy Tamburlaine, have I reposed
In thy approvèd fortunes all my hope.
What think'st thou, man, shall come of our attempts?
For even as from assurèd oracle,

47–48 *cruel . . . venomous* When Cad-   one another until only five were left,
mus killed the dragon sacred to Mars,   and these founded the city of Thebes.
he sowed the teeth, and from the earth   54 *toy* idle pastime.
sprang armed soldiers who destroyed

I take thy doom for satisfaction.   5
Tamburlaine.   And so mistake you not a whit, my lord,
For fates and oracles [of] heaven have sworn
To royalize the deeds of Tamburlaine,
And make them blessed that share in his attempts.
And doubt you not but, if you favor me   10
And let my fortunes and my valor sway
To some direction in your martial deeds,
The world will strive with hosts of men-at-arms
To swarm unto the ensign I support.
The host of Xerxes, which by fame is said   15
To drink the mighty Parthian Araris,
Was but a handful to that we will have.
Our quivering lances shaking in the air
And bullets like Jove's dreadful thunderbolts,
Enrolled in flames and fiery smoldering mists,   20
Shall threat the gods more than Cyclopian wars;
And with our sun-bright armor, as we march
We'll chase the stars from heaven and dim their eyes
That stand and muse at our admirèd arms.
Theridamas.   You see, my lord, what working words he hath,   25
But when you see his actions top his speech,
Your speech will stay or so extol his worth
As I shall be commended and excused
For turning my poor charge to his direction.
And these, his two renownèd friends, my lord,   30
Would make one thrust and strive to be retained
In such a great degree of amity.
Techelles.   With duty and with amity we yield
Our utmost service to the fair Cosroe.
Cosroe.   Which I esteem as portion of my crown.   35
Usumcasane and Techelles both,
When she that rules in Rhamnrs' golden gates
And makes a passage for all prosperous arms
Shall make me solely emperor of Asia,
Then shall your meeds and valors be advanced   40

II,iii.

5 *doom* judgment, opinion. *satisfaction* certainty.

15 *Xerxes* King of Persia, who invaded Greece with the greatest army ever assembled in ancient times (more than two million men, according to Herodotus, although this must be an exaggeration) and was repulsed by the Spartans at Thermopylae.

16 *Parthian Araris* See note at II,i,63. The legend is told by Herodotus, who calls the river Araxis, referring probably to the river Oxus.

21 *Cyclopian wars* Marlowe is identifying the Cyclops with those Titans who warred against Jove. See note to *Dido*, I,i,147.

25 *working words* speech with power to create action.

26 *top* exceed.

37 *she . . . gates* Nemesis, the goddess of revenge. See note to *Dido*, III, ii,20.

To rooms of honor and nobility.
Tamburlaine.　Then haste, Cosroe, to be king alone,
　That I with these my friends and all my men
　May triumph in our long expected fate.
　The king, your brother, is now hard at hand;　　　　　45
　Meet with the fool, and rid your royal shoulders
　Of such a burden as outweighs the sands
　And all the craggy rocks of Caspea.
　　　　　　[Enter a Messenger.]
Messenger.　My lord, we have discoverèd the enemy
　Ready to charge you with a mighty army.　　　　　50
Cosroe.　Come, Tamburlaine, now whet thy wingèd sword,
　And lift thy lofty arm into the clouds,
　That it may reach the king of Persia's crown
　And set it safe on my victorious head.
Tamburlaine.　See where it is, the keenest curtle-axe　　　　　55
　That e'er made passage thorough Persian arms.
　These are the wings shall make it fly as swift
　As doth the lightning or the breath of heaven,
　And kill as sure as it swiftly flies.
Cosroe.　Thy words assure me of kind success.　　　　　60
　Go, valiant soldier, go before and charge
　The fainting army of that foolish king.
Tamburlaine.　Usumcasane and Techelles, come.
　We are enough to scar the enemy,
　And more than needs to make an emperor.　　　　　65
　　　　　　　　　　　[Exeunt.]

　　　　　　　　　　　　　　　II,iv.
　[Enter Soldiers] to the battle and [then exeunt]. Mycetes comes
　　　out alone with his crown in his hand, offering to hide it.
Mycetes.　Accursed be he that first invented war!
　They knew not—ah, they knew not, simple men—
　How those were hit by pelting cannon shot
　Stand staggering like a quivering aspen leaf
　Fearing the force of Boreas' boisterous blasts.　　　　　5
　In what a lamentable case were I,
　If nature had not given me wisdom's lore,
　For kings are clouts that every man shoots at,
　Our crown the pin that thousands seek to cleave.

---

41 *rooms* places.
48 *Caspea* the Caspian Sea.

II,iv.
5 *Boreas* the north wind.

8–9 *kings . . . cleave* The metaphor is drawn from archery. Clouts are targets. To cleave the pin is to split the nail in the center of the target which holds it in place.

Therefore in policy I think it good   10
To hide it close—a goodly stratagem,
And far from any man that is a fool.
So shall not I be known, or if I be,
They cannot take away my crown from me.
Here will I hide it in this simple hole.   15

Enter Tamburlaine.

Tamburlaine. What, fearful coward! Straggling from the camp,
When kings themselves are present in the field?
Mycetes. Thou liest.
Tamburlaine. Base villain, dar'st thou give the lie?
Mycetes. Away! I am the king. Go! Touch me not!   20
Thou break'st the law of arms unless thou kneel
And cry me, 'Mercy, noble king!'
Tamburlaine. Are you the witty king of Persia?
Mycetes. Ay, marry, am I. Have you any suit to me?
Tamburlaine. I would entreat you to speak but three wise words. 25
Mycetes. So I can, when I see my time.
Tamburlaine. Is this your crown?
Mycetes. Ay. Didst thou ever see a fairer?

[He hands him the crown.]

Tamburlaine. You will not sell it, will ye?
Mycetes. Such another word, and I will have thee executed.   30
Come, give it me.
Tamburlaine. No; I took it prisoner.
Mycetes. You lie; I gave it you.
Tamburlaine. Then 'tis mine.
Mycetes. No; I mean I let you keep it.   35
Tamburlaine. Well, I mean you shall have it again.
Here, take it for a while; I lend it thee
Till I may see thee hemmed with armèd men.
Then shalt thou see me pull it from thy head;
Thou art no match for mighty Tamburlaine.   40

[Exit.]

Mycetes. O gods, is this Tamburlaine the thief?
I marvel much he stole it not away.

Sound trumpets to the battle, and he runs in.

II,v.

[Enter] Cosroe, Tamburlaine, Theridamas, Menaphon, Mean-
der, Ortygius, Techelles, Usumcasane, with others.
Tamburlaine. Hold thee, Cosroe; wear two imperial crowns.
Think thee invested now as royally,
Even by the mighty hand of Tamburlaine,

As if as many kings as could encompass thee,
With greatest pomp, had crowned thee emperor.   5
Cosroe.   So do I, thrice renownèd man at arms,
And none shall keep the crown but Tamburlaine.
Thee do I make my regent of Persia
And general lieutenant of my armies.
Meander, you that were our brother's guide   10
And chiefest counsellor in all his acts,
Since he is yielded to the stroke of war,
On your submission we with thanks excuse
And give you equal place in our affairs.
Meander.   Most happy emperor, in humblest terms   15
I vow my service to your majesty,
With utmost virtue of my faith and duty.
Cosroe.   Thanks, good Meander. Then, Cosroe, reign
And govern Persia in her former pomp.
Now send embassage to thy neighbor kings,   20
And let them·know the Persian king is changed
From one that knew not what a king should do
To one that can command what 'longs thereto.
And now we will to fair Persepolis
With twenty thousand expert soldiers.   25
The lords and captains of my brother's camp
With little slaughter take Meander's course,
And gladly yield them to my gracious rule.
Ortygius and Menaphon, my trusty friends,
Now will I gratify your former good   30
And grace your calling with a greater sway.
Ortygius.   And as we ever aimed at your behoof,
And sought your state all honor it deserved,
So will we with our powers and our lives
Endeavor to preserve and prosper it.   35
Cosroe.   I will not thank thee, sweet Ortygius;
Better replies shall prove my purposes.
And now, Lord Tamburlaine, my brother's camp
I leave to thee and to Theridamas,
To follow me to fair Persepolis.   40
Then will we march to all those Indian mines
My witless brother to the Christians lost,
And ransom them with fame and usury.
And till thou overtake me, Tamburlaine,
Staying to order all the scattered troops,   45
Farewell, lord regent and his happy friends.
I long to sit upon my brother's throne.

II,v.
  32 *behoof* profit.

Menaphon. Your majesty shall shortly have your wish,
  And ride in triumph through Persepolis.
                    Exeunt [all except] Tamburlaine, Techelles,
                        Theridamas, [and] Usumcasane.
Tamburlaine. And ride in triumph through Persepolis!   50
  Is it not brave to be a king, Techelles?
  Usumcasane and Theridamas,
  Is it not passing brave to be a king,
  And ride in triumph through Persepolis?
Techelles. O, my lord, 'tis sweet and full of pomp.   55
Usumcasane. To be a king is half to be a god.
Theridamas. A god is not so glorious as a king.
  I think the pleasure they enjoy in heaven
  Can not compare with kingly joys in earth:
  To wear a crown enchased with pearl and gold,   60
  Whose virtues carry with it life and death;
  To ask and have, command and be obeyed;
  When looks breed love, with looks to gain the prize,
  Such power attractive shines in princes' eyes.
Tamburlaine.   Why say, Theridamas, wilt thou be a king?   65
Theridamas.   Nay; though I praise it, I can live without it.
Tamburlaine.   What says my other friends? Will you be kings?
Techelles.   Ay, if I could, with all my heart, my lord.
Tamburlaine.   Why, that's well said, Techelles; so would I.
  And so would you, my masters, would you not?   70
Usumcasane.   What then, my lord?
Tamburlaine. Why then, Casane, shall we wish for aught
  The world affords in greatest novelty
  And rest attemptless, faint and destitute?
  Methinks we should not. I am strongly moved,   75
  That if I should desire the Persian crown,
  I could attain it with a wondrous ease;
  And would not all our soldiers soon consent,
  If we should aim at such a dignity?
Theridamas. I know they would with our persuasions.   80
Tamburlaine. Why then, Theridamas, I'll first assay
  To get the Persian kingdom to myself;
  Then thou for Parthia; they for Scythia and Media;
  And if I prosper, all shall be as sure
  As if the Turk, the Pope, Afric and Greece   85
  Came creeping to us with their crowns apace.
Techelles. Then shall we send to this triumphing king,
  And bid him battle for his novel crown?
Usumcasane. Nay, quickly then, before his room be hot.

---

60 *enchased* See note at I,ii,96.   75 *moved* inwardly convinced.
73 *in greatest novelty* no matter how
rare.

Tamburlaine.   'Twill prove a pretty jest, in faith, my friends.   90
Theridamas.   A jest to charge on twenty thousand men?
  I judge the purchase more important far.
Tamburlaine.   Judge by thyself, Theridamas, not me,
  For presently Techelles here shall haste
  To bid him battle ere he pass too far   95
  And lose more labor than the game will quite.
  Then shalt thou see the Scythian Tamburlaine
  Make but a jest to win the Persian crown.
  Techelles, take a thousand horse with thee,
  And bid him turn him back to war with us,   100
  That only made him king to make us sport.
  We will not steal upon him cowardly,
  But give him warning and more warriors.
  Haste thee, Techelles; we will follow thee.

  [Exit Techelles.]

  What saith Theridamas?
Theridamas.   Go on, for me.   105

                                Exeunt.

                                                    II,vi.
[*Enter*] *Cosroe, Meander, Ortygius, Menaphon, with other
                      Soldiers.*
Cosroe.   What means this devilish shepherd to aspire
  With such a giantly presumption,
  To cast up hills against the face of heaven,
  And dare the force of angry Jupiter?
  But as he thrust them underneath the hills,   5
  And pressed out fire from their burning jaws,
  So will I send this monstrous slave to hell,
  Where flames shall ever feed upon his soul.
Meander.   Some powers divine, or else infernal, mixed
  Their angry seeds at his conception,   10
  For he was never sprung of human race,
  Since with the spirit of his fearful pride,
  He dares so doubtlessly resolve of rule,
  And by profession be ambitious.
Ortygius.   What god, or fiend, or spirit of the earth,   15

92 *purchase* what will be gained.
96 *quite* requite, repay.

II,vi.

3 *cast . . . heaven* i.e., as did the
Titans who warred against Jove.
5 *them* i.e., the Titans. Jupiter did
not thrust the rebellious Titans beneath
the hills. It was Typhœus he imprisoned
beneath Mt. Ætna. See note to *Dido,*
IV,i,19.
13 *doubtlessly* without fear or hesita-
tion. *resolve of* determine to.

Or monster turnèd to a manly shape,
Or of what mold or mettle he be made,
What star or state soever govern him,
Let us put on our meet encountering minds,
And in detesting such a devilish thief,   20
In love of honor and defense of right
Be armed against the hate of such a foe,
Whether from earth, or hell, or heaven he grow.
Cosroe. Nobly resolved, my good Ortygius,
And since we all have sucked one wholesome air,   25
And with the same proportion of elements
Resolve, I hope we are resembled,
Vowing our loves to equal death and life.
Let's cheer our soldiers to encounter him,
That grievous image of ingratitude,
That fiery thirster after sovereignty,   30
And burn him in the fury of that flame
That none can quench but blood and empery.
Resolve, my lords and loving soldiers, now
To save your king and country from decay.   35
Then strike up, drum; and all the stars that make
The loathsome circle of my dated life,
Direct my weapon to his barbarous heart,
That thus opposeth him against the gods
And scorns the powers that govern Persia.   40

                                                [*Exeunt.*]

II,vii.
*Enter [Soldiers] to the battle, and [then exit]. After the battle
enter Cosroe, wounded, Theridamas, Tamburlaine, Techelles,
Usumcasane, with others.*
Cosroe. Barbarous and bloody Tamburlaine,
Thus to deprive me of my crown and life!
Treacherous and false Theridamas,
Even at the morning of my happy state,
Scarce being seated in my royal throne,   5
To work my downfall and untimely end!
An uncouth pain torments my grievèd soul,
And death arrests the organ of my voice,
Who, entering at the breach thy sword hath made,
Sacks every vein and artier of my heart.   10

---

27 *Resolve* are decomposed (when we   **II,vii.**
die).   10 *artier* artery.

Bloody and insatiate Tamburlaine!
Tamburlaine.   The thirst of reign and sweetness of a crown,
That caused the eldest son of heavenly Ops
To thrust his doting father from his chair,
And place himself in the imperial heaven,   15
Moved me to manage arms against thy state.
What better precedent than mighty Jove?
Nature, that framed us of four elements
Warring within our breasts for regiment,
Doth teach us all to have aspiring minds.   20
Our souls, whose faculties can comprehend
The wondrous architecture of the world
And measure every wandering planet's course,
Still climbing after knowledge infinite,
And always moving as the restless spheres,   25
Wills us to wear ourselves and never rest,
Until we reach the ripest fruit of all,
That perfect bliss and sole felicity,
The sweet fruition of an earthly crown.
Theridamas.   And that made me to join with Tamburlaine,   30
For he is gross and like the massy earth
That moves not upwards, nor by princely deeds
Doth mean to soar above the highest sort.
Techelles.   And that made us, the friends of Tamburlaine,
To lift our swords against the Persian king.   35
Usumcasane.   For as when Jove did thrust old Saturn down,
Neptune and Dis gained each of them a crown,
So do we hope to reign in Asia,
If Tamburlaine be placed in Persia.
Cosroe.   The strangest men that ever nature made!   40
I know not how to take their tyrannies.
My bloodless body waxeth chill and cold,
And with my blood my life slides through my wound;
My soul begins to take her flight to hell
And summons all my senses to depart.   45
The heat and moisture which did feed each other,
For want of nourishment to feed them both,
Is dry and cold; and now doth ghastly death
With greedy talents gripe my bleeding heart

13–14 *eldest . . . chair*   Jupiter, the
son of Saturn and Ops, with his mother's
aid deposed his father and made himself king of the gods.

15 *imperial*   The 1590 'Emperiall' may
be read also as 'empyreal.' There seems
to have been little distinction in Marlowe's time between the two words.

37 *Neptune and Dis*   the brothers of

Jove, gods of the ocean and underworld
respectively.

46–48 *The heat . . . cold*   i.e., since
his blood, consisting of the qualities of
heat and moisture, is departing, what
remains is cold and dryness, the composition, according to medieval cosmology,
of the earth.

49 *talents*   talons.

And like a harpy tires on my life.   50
Theridamas and Tamburlaine, I die—
And fearful vengeance light upon you both!
          [*He dies. Tamburlaine*] *takes the crown and puts it on.*
Tamburlaine.   Not all the curses which the Furies breathe
Shall make me leave so rich a prize as this.
Theridamas, Techelles, and the rest,   55
Who think you now is king of Persia?
All.   Tamburlaine! Tamburlaine!
Tamburlaine.   Though Mars himself, the angry god of arms,
And all the earthly potentates conspire
To dispossess me of this diadem,   60
Yet will I wear it in despite of them,
As great commander of this eastern world,
If you but say that Tamburlaine shall reign.
All.   Long live Tamburlaine, and reign in Asia!
Tamburlaine.   So; now it is more surer on my head   65
Than if the gods had held a parliament,
And all pronounced me king of Persia.

                                                            [*Exeunt.*]

                                                                III,i.
     [*Enter*] *Bajazeth, the Kings of Fez, Morocco,* **and** *Argier, with
                     others, in great pomp.*
Bajazeth.   Great kings of Barbary and my portly bassoes,
We hear the Tartars and the eastern thieves,
Under the conduct of one Tamburlaine,
Presume a bickering with your emperor,
And thinks to rouse us from our dreadful siege   5
Of the famous Grecian Constantinople.
You know our army is invincible;
As many circumcisèd Turks we have,
And warlike bands of Christians renièd,
As hath the ocean or the Terrene sea   10
Small drops of water when the moon begins
To join in one her semicircled horns.

---

50 *harpy* one of the mythological birds with heads of women, long claws, and faces pale with hunger. *tires* preys.
53 *Furies* See note to *Dido,* II,i,230.

III,i.

1 *bassoes* bashaws, or pashas. Marlowe prefers this archaic form through-out *Tamburlaine,* and I have retained it in the text, although not in the stage directions.
9 *Christians renièd* apostates.
10 *Terrene sea* Mediterranean.
11–12 *moon . . . horns* i.e., when the moon is full and therefore the tides are high.

Yet would we not be braved with foreign power,
Nor raise our siege before the Grecians yield
Or breathless lie before the city walls.   15
King of Fez. Renownèd emperor and mighty general,
What if you sent the bassoes of your guard
To charge him to remain in Asia,
Or else to threaten death and deadly arms
As from the mouth of mighty Bajazeth?   20
Bajazeth. Hie thee, my basso, fast to Persia.
Tell him thy lord, the Turkish emperor,
Dread lord of Afric, Europe, and Asia,
Great king and conqueror of Græcia,
The ocean, Terrene, and the coal-black sea,   25
The high and highest monarch of the world,
Wills and commands—for say not I entreat—
Not once to set his foot in Africa
Or spread his colors in Græcia,
Lest he incur the fury of my wrath.   30
Tell him I am content to take a truce,
Because I hear he bears a valiant mind;
But if, presuming on his silly power,
He be so mad to manage arms with me,
Then stay thou with him—say, I bid thee so—   35
And if, before the sun have measured heaven
With triple circuit, thou regreet us not,
We mean to take his morning's next arise
For messenger he will not be reclaimed,
And mean to fetch thee in despite of him.   40
Bashaw. Most great and puissant monarch of the earth,
Your basso will accomplish your behest
And show your pleasure to the Persian,
As fits the legate of the stately Turk.
                                        Exit Bashaw.
King of Argier. They say he is the king of Persia;   45
But if he dare attempt to stir your siege,
'Twere requisite he should be ten times more,
For all flesh quakes at your magnificence.
Bajazeth. True, Argier, and tremble at my looks.
King of Morocco. The spring is hindered by your smothering host, 50
For neither rain can fall upon the earth,
Nor sun reflex his virtuous beams thereon,
The ground is mantled with such multitudes.
Bajazeth. All this is true as holy Mahomet,
And all the trees are blasted with our breaths.   55
King of Fez. What thinks your greatness best to be achieved

---

24 *Græcia* See note at I,i,130.   33 *silly* childlike, of little strength.

In pursuit of the city's overthrow?
Bajazeth.   I will the captive pioners of Argier
  Cut off the water that by leaden pipes
  Runs to the city from the mountain Carnon.   60
  Two thousand horse shall forage up and down,
  That no relief or succor come by land,
  And all the sea my galleys countermand.
  Then shall our footmen lie within the trench,
  And with their cannons mouthed like Orcus' gulf,   65
  Batter the walls, and we will enter in;
  And thus the Grecians shall be conquerèd.

                                           Exeunt.

*

          [Enter] Agydas, Zenocrate, Anippe, with others.   III,ii
Agydas.   Madam Zenocrate, may I presume
  To know the cause of these unquiet fits
  That work such trouble to your wonted rest?
  'Tis more than pity such a heavenly face
  Should by heart's sorrow wax so wan and pale,   5
  When your offensive rape by Tamburlaine,
  Which of your whole displeasures should be most,
  Hath seemed to be digested long ago.
Zenocrate.   Although it be digested long ago,
  As his exceeding favors have deserved,   10
  And might content the queen of heaven as well
  As it hath changed my first-conceived disdain;
  Yet, since, a farther passion feeds my thoughts
  With ceaseless and disconsolate conceits,
  Which dyes my looks so lifeless as they are,   15
  And might, if my extremes had full events,
  Make me the ghastly counterfeit of death.
Agydas.   Eternal heaven sooner be dissolved,
  And all that pierceth Phœbe's silver eye,
  Before such hap fall to Zenocrate!   20
Zenocrate.   Ah, life and soul, still hover in his breast,
  And leave my body senseless as the earth,
  Or else unite you to his life and soul,
  That I may live and die with Tamburlaine!

III,ii.

58 *pioners* trench-diggers.
63 *countermand* control.
65 *Orcus' gulf* the mouth of hell.
Orcus was one of several Greek names
for Hades.

6 *rape* seizure.
11 *queen of heaven* Juno.
13 *since* since that time.
16 *extremes* violent passions. *events*
expression in action.

Enter, [behind,] Tamburlaine, with Techelles, and others.

Agydas. With Tamburlaine? Ah, fair Zenocrate,   25
    Let not a man so vile and barbarous,
    That holds you from your father in despite
    And keeps you from the honors of a queen,
    Being supposed his worthless concubine,
    Be honored with your love, but for necessity.   30
    So, now the mighty Soldan hears of you,
    Your highness needs not doubt but in short time
    He will, with Tamburlaine's destruction,
    Redeem you from this deadly servitude.
Zenocrate. Leave to wound me with these words,   35
    And speak of Tamburlaine as he deserves.
    The entertainment we have had of him
    Is far from villainy or servitude,
    And might in noble minds be counted princely.
Agydas. How can you fancy one that looks so fierce,   40
    Only disposed to martial stratagems?
    Who, when he shall embrace you in his arms,
    Will tell how many thousand men he slew,
    And, when you look for amorous discourse,
    Will rattle forth his facts of war and blood,   45
    Too harsh a subject for your dainty ears.
Zenocrate. As looks the sun through Nilus' flowing stream,
    Or when the morning holds him in her arms,
    So looks my lordly love, fair Tamburlaine;
    His talk much sweeter than the Muses' song   50
    They sung for honor 'gainst Pierides,
    Or when Minerva did with Neptune strive;
    And higher would I rear my estimate
    Than Juno, sister to the highest god,
    If I were matched with mighty Tamburlaine.   55
Agydas. Yet be not so inconstant in your love,
    But let the young Arabian live in hope,
    After your rescue to enjoy his choice.
    You see, though first the king of Persia,
    Being a shepherd, seemed to love you much,   60
    Now, in his majesty, he leaves those looks,
    Those words of favor, and those comfortings,
    And gives no more than common courtesies.
Zenocrate. Thence rise the tears that so distain my cheeks,
    Fearing his love through my unworthiness.   65

---

47 *Nilus* the river Nile.

50–51 *Muses' song . . . Pierides* The nine daughters of Pierus, King of Emathia in Macedonia, were given the names of the Muses by their father, but when they entered a singing contest with the actual Muses were defeated and transformed into birds.

52 *Minerva . . . strive* They struggled for control of the government of Athens.

65 *Fearing* fearing the loss of.

Tamburlaine goes to her, and takes her away lovingly by the
hand, looking wrathfully on Agydas, and says nothing. [Exeunt
all except Agydas.]

Agydas. Betrayed by fortune and suspicious love,
Threat'nèd with frowning wrath and jealousy,
Surprised with fear of hideous revenge,
I stand aghast; but most astonièd
To see his choler shut in secret thoughts,   70
And wrapt in silence of his angry soul.
Upon his brows was portrayed ugly death,
And in his eyes the fury of his heart,
That shine as comets, menacing revenge,
And casts a pale complexion on his cheeks.   75
As when the seaman sees the Hyadès
Gather an army of Cimmerian clouds,
(Auster and Aquilon with wingèd steeds,
All sweating, tilt about the watery heavens,
With shivering spears enforcing thunder-claps,   80
And from their shields strike flames of lightning)
All-fearful folds his sails and sounds the main,
Lifting his prayers to the heavens for aid
Against the terror of the winds and waves,
So fares Agydas for the late-felt frowns   85
That sent a tempest to my daunted thoughts
And makes my soul divine her overthrow.
    Enter Techelles with a naked dagger, [and Usumcasane.]
Techelles.   See you, Agydas, how the king salutes you.
He bids you prophesy what it imports.
Agydas.   I prophesied before, and now I prove   90
The killing frowns of jealousy and love.
He needed not with words confirm my fear,
For words are vain where working tools present
The naked action of my threatened end.
It says, Agydas, thou shalt surely die,   95
And of extremities elect the least.
More honor and less pain it may procure,
To die by this resolvèd hand of thine
Than stay the torments he and heaven have sworn.
Then haste, Agydas, and prevent the plagues   100
Which thy prolongèd fates may draw on thee.
Go wander free from fear of tyrant's rage,
Removèd from the torments and the hell

---

69 *astonièd* astonished.
76 *Hyadès* a constellation of seven stars
which would bring rain if they rose at
the same time as the sun.
77 *Cimmerian* black. The Cimmerii,
a mythical people mentioned by Homer,
lived in total darkness.
78 *Auster* the southwest wind. *Aquilon*
the north wind.
99 *stay* wait for.

Wherewith he may excruciate thy soul,
And let Agydas by Agydas die,   105
And with this stab slumber eternally.   [*He stabs himself.*]
Techelles.   Usumcasane, see how right the man
  Hath hit the meaning of my lord the king.
Usumcasane.   Faith and, Techelles, it was manly done;
  And, since he was so wise and honorable,   110
  Let us afford him now the bearing hence,
  And crave his triple-worthy burial.
Techelles.   Agreed, Casane; we will honor him.
                        [*Exeunt, bearing out the body.*]

                                                              III,iii.
      [*Enter*] *Tamburlaine, Techelles, Usumcasane, Theridamas,* [a]
                Bashaw, Zenocrate, [*Anippe,*] *with others.*
Tamburlaine.   Basso, by this thy lord and master knows
  I mean to meet him in Bithynia.
  See how he comes! Tush, Turks are full of brags
  And menace more than they can well perform.
  He meet me in the field and fetch thee hence!   5
  Alas, poor Turk, his fortune is too weak
  T'encounter with the strength of Tamburlaine.
  View well my camp, and speak indifferently:
  Do not my captains and my soldiers look
  As if they meant to conquer Africa?   10
Bashaw.   Your men are valiant, but their number few,
  And cannot terrify his mighty host.
  My lord, the great commander of the world,
  Besides fifteen contributory kings,
  Hath now in arms ten thousand janissaries,   15
  Mounted on lusty Mauritanian steeds,
  Brought to the war by men of Tripoli;
  Two hundred thousand footmen that have served
  In two set battles fought in Græcia;
  And for the expedition of this war,   20
  If he think good, can from his garrisons
  Withdraw as many more to follow him.
Techelles.   The more he brings, the greater is the spoil,
  For when they perish by our warlike hands,
  We mean to set our footmen on their steeds   25

III,iii.
  2 *Bithynia* a district in Asia Minor   8 *indifferently* without bias.
south of the Black Sea.   15 *janissaries* Turkish infantrymen.

And rifle all those stately janissars.

Tamburlaine.   But will those kings accompany your lord?

Bashaw.   Such as his highness please; but some must stay
   To rule the provinces he late subdued.

Tamburlaine.   Then fight courageously; their crowns are yours.   30
   This hand shall set them on your conquering heads,
   That made me emperor of Asia.

Usumcasane.   Let him bring millions infinite of men,
   Unpeopling Western Africa and Greece,
   Yet we assure us of the victory.   35

Theridamas.   Even he, that in a trice vanquished two kings
   More mighty than the Turkish emperor,
   Shall rouse him out of Europe and pursue
   His scattered army till they yield or die.

Tamburlaine.   Well said, Theridamas! Speak in that mood,   40
   For 'will' and 'shall' best fitteth Tamburlaine,
   Whose smiling stars gives him assurèd hope
   Of martial triumph, ere he meet his foes.
   I that am termed the scourge and wrath of God,
   The only fear and terror of the world,   45
   Will first subdue the Turk, and then enlarge
   Those Christian captives which you keep as slaves,
   Burdening their bodies with your heavy chains,
   And feeding them with thin and slender fare,
   That naked row about the Terrene sea,   50
   And, when they chance to breathe and rest a space,
   Are punished with bastones so grievously
   That they lie panting on the galley's side,
   And strive for life at every stroke they give.
   These are the cruel pirates of Argier,   55
   That damnèd train, the scum of Africa,
   Inhabited with straggling runagates,
   That make quick havoc of the Christian blood.
   But, as I live, that town shall curse the time
   That Tamburlaine set foot in Africa.   60

     Enter Bajazeth with his Bashaws and Contributory Kings,
         [Zabina, and Ebea].

Bajazeth.   Bassoes and janissaries of my guard,
   Attend upon the person of your lord,
   The greatest potentate of Africa.

Tamburlaine.   Techelles and the rest, prepare your swords;
   I mean t'encounter with that Bajazeth.   65

Bajazeth.   Kings of Fez, Morocco, and Argier,
   He calls me Bajazeth, whom you call lord!
   Note the presumption of this Scythian slave!

---

52 *bastones* cudgels.   57 *runagates* vagabonds, deserters.
55 *Argier* Algeria.

I tell thee, villain, those that lead my horse
Have to their names titles of dignity,　　　　　　70
And dar'st thou bluntly call me Bajazeth?
Tamburlaine. And know thou, Turk, that those which lead my horse
Shall lead thee captive thorough Africa,
And dar'st thou bluntly call me Tamburlaine?
Bajazeth. By Mahomet my kinsman's sepulcher,　　　75
And by the holy Alcoran I swear,
He shall be made a chaste and lustless eunuch,
And in my sarell tend my concubines;
And all his captains, that thus stoutly stand,
Shall draw the chariot of my emperess,　　　　　80
Whom I have brought to see their overthrow.
Tamburlaine. By this my sword that conquered Persia,
Thy fall shall make me famous through the world.
I will not tell thee how I'll handle thee,
But every common soldier of my camp　　　　　85
Shall smile to see thy miserable state.
King of Fez. What means the mighty Turkish emperor
To talk with one so base as Tamburlaine?
King of Morocco. Ye Moors and valiant men of Barbary,
How can ye suffer these indignities?　　　　　90
King of Argier. Leave words, and let them feel your lances' points,
Which glided through the bowels of the Greeks.
Bajazeth. Well said, my stout contributory kings.
Your threefold army and my hugy host
Shall swallow up these base-born Persians.　　　95
Techelles. Puissant, renowned, and mighty Tamburlaine,
Why stay we thus prolonging all their lives?
Theridamas. I long to see those crowns won by our swords,
That we may reign as kings of Africa.
Usumcasane. What coward would not fight for such a prize?　　　100
Tamburlaine. Fight all courageously, and be you kings.
I speak it, and my words are oracles.
Bajazeth. Zabina, mother of three braver boys
Than Hercules, that in his infancy
Did pash the jaws of serpents venomous,　　　105
Whose hands are made to gripe a warlike lance,
Their shoulders broad, for complete armor fit,
Their limbs more large and of a bigger size
Than all the brats y-sprung from Typhon's loins,
Who, when they come unto their father's age,　　　110
Will batter turrets with their manly fists—

78 *sarell* harem.
94 *hugy* huge.
105 *pash* crush, dash to pieces.
109 *hrats . . . loins* Typhon or Typhœus (see note to *Dido*, IV,i,19) was
the father of the harpies (see note at
II,vii,50) as well as of the cruel winds.

Sit here upon this royal chair of state,
And on thy head wear my imperial crown,
Until I bring this sturdy Tamburlaine
And all his captains bound in captive chains.   115
Zabina.   Such good success happen to Bajazeth!
Tamburlaine.   Zenocrate, the loveliest maid alive,
    Fairer than rocks of pearl and precious stone,
    The only paragon of Tamburlaine,
    Whose eyes are brighter than the lamps of heaven   120
    And speech more pleasant than sweet harmony,
    That with thy looks canst clear the darkened sky
    And calm the rage of thundering Jupiter—
    Sit down by her, adornèd with my crown,
    As if thou wert the empress of the world.   125
    Stir not, Zenocrate, until thou see
    Me march victoriously with all my men,
    Triumphing over him and these his kings,
    Which I will bring as vassals to thy feet.
    Till then, take thou my crown, vaunt of my worth,   130
    And manage words with her, as we will arms.
Zenocrate.   And may my love, the king of Persia,
    Return with victory and free from wound!
Bajazeth.   Now shalt thou feel the force of Turkish arms,
    Which lately made all Europe quake for fear.   135
    I have of Turks, Arabians, Moors, and Jews,
    Enough to cover all Bithynia.
    Let thousands die! Their slaughtered carcasses
    Shall serve for walls and bulwarks to the rest;
    And as the heads of Hydra, so my power,   140
    Subdued, shall stand as mighty as before.
    If they should yield their necks unto the sword,
    Thy soldiers' arms could not endure to strike
    So many blows as I have heads for thee.
    Thou know'st not, foolish hardy Tamburlaine,   145
    What 'tis to meet me in the open field,
    That leave no ground for thee to march upon.
Tamburlaine.   Our conquering swords shall marshal us the way
    We use to march upon the slaughtered foe,
    Trampling their bowels with our horses' hoofs,   150
    Brave horses bred on the white Tartarian hills.
    My camp is like to Julius Cæsar's host,
    That never fought but had the victory;
    Nor in Pharsalia was there such hot war
    As these, my followers, willingly would have.   155
    Legions of spirits, fleeting in the air,

140 *Hydra* a hundred-headed monster   154 *Pharsalia* battle in which Julius
killed by Hercules.   Caesar defeated Pompey in 48 B.C.

Direct our bullets and our weapons' points,
And make our strokes to wound the senseless air;
And when she sees our bloody colors spread,
Then Victory begins to take her flight,   160
Resting herself upon my milk-white tent.
But come, my lords, to weapons let us fall;
The field is ours, the Turk, his wife, and all.

                                    Exit with his followers.

Bajazeth.   Come, kings and bassoes, let us glut our swords,
    That thirst to drink the feeble Persians' blood.   165

                                    Exit with his followers.

Zabina.   Base concubine, must thou be placed by me
    That am the empress of the mighty Turk?
Zenocrate.   Disdainful Turkess, and unreverend boss,
    Call'st thou me concubine, that am betrothed
    Unto the great and mighty Tamburlaine?   170
Zabina.   To Tamburlaine, the great Tartarian thief!
Zenocrate.   Thou wilt repent these lavish words of thine
    When thy great basso-master and thyself
    Must plead for mercy at his kingly feet,
    And sue to me to be your advocates.   175
Zabina.   And sue to thee? I tell thee, shameless girl,
    Thou shalt be laundress to my waiting-maid.
    How lik'st thou her, Ebea? Will she serve?
Ebea.   Madam, she thinks perhaps she is too fine,
    But I shall turn her into other weeds   180
    And make her dainty fingers fall to work.
Zenocrate.   Hear'st thou, Anippe, how thy drudge doth talk,
    And how my slave, her mistress, menaceth?
    Both for their sauciness shall be employed
    To dress the common soldiers' meat and drink,   185
    For we will scorn they should come near ourselves.
Anippe.   Yet sometimes let your highness send for them
    To do the work my chambermaid disdains.

                                    They sound the battle within.

Zenocrate.   Ye gods and powers that govern Persia,
    And made my lordly love her worthy king,   190
    Now strengthen him against the Turkish Bajazeth,
    And let his foes, like flocks of fearful roes
    Pursued by hunters, fly his angry looks,
    That I may see him issue conqueror.
Zabina.   Now, Mahomet, solicit God himself,   195
    And make him rain down murdering shot from heaven
    To dash the Scythians' brains, and strike them dead

---

168 *boss* fat woman.   180 *weeds* garments.
175 *advocates* possibly "advocatess" (a
feminine form).

That dare to manage arms with him
That offered jewels to thy sacred shrine
When first he warred against the Christians.   200
               [*They sound within*] *to the battle again.*
Zenocrate.   By this the Turks lie weltering in their blood,
   And Tamburlaine is lord of Africa.
Zabina.   Thou art deceived. I heard the trumpets sound
   As when my emperor overthrew the Greeks
   And led them captive into Africa.   205
   Straight will I use thee as thy pride deserves;
   Prepare thyself to live and die my slave.
Zenocrate.   If Mahomet should come from heaven and swear
   My royal lord is slain or conquerèd,
   Yet should he not persuade me otherwise   210
   But that he lives and will be conqueror.
      [*Enter Bajazeth, pursued by Tamburlaine. They fight briefly
         and*] *Bajazeth is overcome.*
Tamburlaine.   Now, king of bassoes, who is conqueror?
Bajazeth.   Thou, by the fortune of this damnèd foil.
Tamburlaine.   Where are your stout contributory kings?
         Enter Techelles, Theridamas, [and] Usumcasane.
Techelles.   We have their crowns; their bodies strow the field.   215
Tamburlaine.   Each man a crown? Why, kingly fought, i'faith.
   Deliver them into my treasury.
Zenocrate.   Now let me offer to my gracious lord
   His royal crown again, so highly won.
Tamburlaine.   Nay, take the Turkish crown from her, Zenocrate,   220
   And crown me emperor of Africa.
Zabina.   No, Tamburlaine; though now thou gat the best,
   Thou shalt not yet be lord of Africa.
Theridamas.   Give her the crown, Turkess, you were best.
               He takes it from her and gives it [to] Zenocrate.
Zabina.   Injurious villains, thieves, runagates,   225
   How dare you thus abuse my majesty?
Theridamas.   Here, madam, you are empress; she is none.
Tamburlaine.   Not now, Theridamas; her time is past.
   The pillars that have bolstered up those terms
   Are fall'n in clusters at my conquering feet.   230
Zabina.   Though he be prisoner, he may be ransomèd.
Tamburlaine.   Not all the world shall ransom Bajazeth.
Bajazeth.   Ah, fair Zabina, we have lost the field,
   And never had the Turkish emperor
   So great a foil by any foreign foe.   235
   Now will the Christian miscreants be glad,
   Ringing with joy their superstitious bells,

211 *he* i.e., Tamburlaine.   213 *foil* defeat.

And making bonfires for my overthrow.
But ere I die, those foul idolaters
Shall make me bonfires with their filthy bones,   240
For though the glory of this day be lost,
Afric and Greece have garrisons enough
To make me sovereign of the earth again.
Tamburlaine. Those wallèd garrisons will I subdue,
And write myself great lord of Africa.   245
So from the East unto the furthest West
Shall Tamburlaine extend his puissant arm.
The galleys and those pilling brigandines,
That yearly sail to the Venetian gulf
And hover in the Straits for Christians' wrack,   250
Shall lie at anchor in the Isle Asant,
Until the Persian fleet and men-of-war,
Sailing along the oriental sea,
Have fetched about the Indian continent,
Even from Persepolis to Mexico,   255
And thence unto the Straits of Jubalter,
Where they shall meet and join their force in one,
Keeping in awe the Bay of Portingale
And all the ocean by the British shore;
And by this means I'll win the world at last.   260
Bajazeth. Yet set a ransom on me, Tamburlaine.
Tamburlaine. What, think'st thou Tamburlaine esteems thy gold?
I'll make the kings of India, ere I die,
Offer their mines to sue for peace to me,
And dig for treasure to appease my wrath.   265
Come, bind them both, and one lead in the Turk;
The Turkess let my love's maid lead away.
                                        They bind them.
Bajazeth. Ah, villains, dare ye touch my sacred arms?
O Mahomet! O sleepy Mahomet!
Zabina. O cursèd Mahomet, that mak'st us thus   270
The slaves to Scythians rude and barbarous!
Tamburlaine. Come, bring them in, and for this happy conquest
Triumph, and solemnize a martial feast.
                                        Exeunt.

248 *pilling* pillaging.
251 *Isle Asant* Zante, an island off the
northern coast of Peloponnesus (Achaia).

255 *Persepolis to Mexico* i.e., across
the Pacific.
256 *Jubalter* Gibraltar.
258 *Portingale* Biscay.

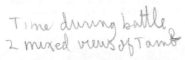

IV,i.

[Enter the] Soldan of Egypt, with three or four Lords, Capolin,
[and a Messenger].

Soldan.   Awake, ye men of Memphis! Hear the clang
   Of Scythian trumpets! Hear the basilisks,
   That roaring shake Damascus' turrets down!
   The rogue of Volga holds Zenocrate,
   The Soldan's daughter, for his concubine,   5
   And with a troop of thieves and vagabonds,
   Hath spread his colors to our high disgrace,
   While you, faint-hearted base Egyptians,
   Lie slumbering on the flowery banks of Nile,
   As crocodiles that unaffrighted rest   10
   While thundering cannons rattle on their skins.
Messenger.   Nay, mighty Soldan, did your greatness see
   The frowning looks of fiery Tamburlaine,
   That with his terror and imperious eyes
   Commands the hearts of his associates,   15
   It might amaze your royal majesty.
Soldan.   Villain, I tell thee, were that Tamburlaine
   As monstrous as Gorgon, prince of hell,
   The Soldan would not start a foot from him.
   But speak, what power hath he?   20
Messenger.   Mighty lord,
   Three hundred thousand men in armor clad,
   Upon their prancing steeds, disdainfully
   With wanton paces trampling on the ground;
   Five hundred thousand footmen threatening shot,   25
   Shaking their swords, their spears, and iron bills,
   Environing their standard round, that stood
   As bristle-pointed as a thorny wood;
   Their warlike engines and munition
   Exceed the forces of their martial men.   30
Soldan.   Nay, could their numbers countervail the stars,
   Or ever-drizzling drops of April showers,
   Or withered leaves that autumn shaketh down,
   Yet would the Soldan by his conquering power
   So scatter and consume them in his rage,   35
   That not a man should live to rue their fall.
Capolin.   So might your highness, had you time to sort
   Your fighting men and raise your royal host,
   But Tamburlaine by expedition
   Advantage takes of your unreadiness.   40

IV,i.

2 *basilisks* large cannons.   31 *countervail* equal in number.
18 *monstrous* unnatural. *Gorgon* Dem-   39 *expedition* speedy action.
ogorgon, a devil.

Soldan.   Let him take all th'advantages he can.
  Were all the world conspired to fight for him,
  Nay, were he devil, as he is no man,
  Yet in revenge of fair Zenocrate,
  Whom he detaineth in despite of us,   45
  This arm should send him down to Erebus,
  To shroud his shame in darkness of the night.
Messenger.   Pleaseth your mightiness to understand,
  His resolution far exceedeth all.
  The first day when he pitcheth down his tents,   50
  White is their hue, and on his silver crest
  A snowy feather spangled-white he bears,
  To signify the mildness of his mind
  That, satiate with spoil, refuseth blood;
  But when Aurora mounts the second time,   55
  As red as scarlet is his furniture;
  Then must his kindled wrath be quenched with blood,
  Not sparing any that can manage arms;
  But if these threats move not submission,
  Black are his colors, black pavilion;   60
  His spear, his shield, his horse, his armor, plumes,
  And jetty feathers menace death and hell;
  Without respect of sex, degree, or age,
  He razeth all his foes with fire and sword.
Soldan.   Merciless villain, peasant ignorant   65
  Of lawful arms or martial discipline!
  Pillage and murder are his usual trades.
  The slave usurps the glorious name of war.
  See Capolin, the fair Arabian king,
  That hath been disappointed by this slave   70
  Of my fair daughter and his princely love,
  May have fresh warning to go war with us,
  And be revenged for her disparagement.

                                              [*Exeunt.*]

                                                        IV,ii.
  [*Enter*] *Tamburlaine, Techelles, Theridamas, Usumcasane,*
  Zenocrate, Anippe, two Moors drawing Bajazeth in his cage,
              and his Wife, [*Zabina*] *following him.*
Tamburlaine.   Bring out my footstool.
                          They take Bajazeth out of the cage.

---

46 *Erebus* the son of Chaos and the
brother of Night, whose name came to
signify the dark region between Earth
and Hades.

55 *Aurora mounts* The dawn comes
up.
56 *furniture* military equipment (tent
and dress, etc.).

Bajazeth. Ye holy priests of heavenly Mahomet,
That, sacrificing, slice and cut your flesh,
Staining his altars with your purple blood,
Make heaven to frown and every fixèd star   5
To suck up poison from the moorish fens,
And pour it in this glorious tyrant's throat!
Tamburlaine. The chiefest god, first mover of that sphere
Enchased with thousands ever-shining lamps,
Will sooner burn the glorious frame of heaven   10
Than it should so conspire my overthrow.
But, villain, thou that wishest this to me,
Fall prostrate on the low disdainful earth,
And be the footstool of great Tamburlaine,
That I may rise into my royal throne.   15
Bajazeth. First shalt thou rip my bowels with thy sword
And sacrifice my heart to death and hell,
Before I yield to such a slavery.
Tamburlaine. Base villain, vassal, slave to Tamburlaine,
Unworthy to embrace or touch the ground   20
That bears the honor of my royal weight,
Stoop, villain, stoop! Stoop, for so he bids
That may command thee piecemeal to be torn,
Or scattered like the lofty cedar trees
Struck with the voice of thundering Jupiter.   25
Bajazeth. Then, as I look down to the damnèd fiends,
Fiends, look on me; and thou, dread god of hell,
With ebon scepter strike this hateful earth,
And make it swallow both of us at once!
        Tamburlaine gets up upon him [and in]to his chair.
Tamburlaine. Now clear the triple region of the air,   30
And let the majesty of heaven behold
Their scourge and terror tread on emperors.
Smile stars that reigned at my nativity,
And dim the brightness of their neighbor lamps;
Disdain to borrow light of Cynthia,   35
For I, the chiefest lamp of all the earth,
First rising in the east with mild aspect,
But fixèd now in the meridian line,
Will send up fire to your turning spheres
And cause the sun to borrow light of you.   40
My sword struck fire from his coat of steel,
Even in Bithynia, when I took this Turk,
As when a fiery exhalation,
Wrapped in the bowels of a freezing cloud,
Fighting for passage, makes the welkin crack   45

IV,ii.
  7 *glorious* vaunting, boastful.

  35 *Cynthia* the moon.
  45 *welkin* world.

And casts a flash of lightning to the earth.
But ere I march to wealthy Persia,
Or leave Damascus and th'Egyptian fields,
As was the fame of Clymene's brain-sick son
That almost brent the axle-tree of heaven,   50
So shall our swords, our lances, and our shot
Fill all the air with fiery meteors.
Then, when the sky shall wax as red as blood,
It shall be said I made it red myself,
To make me think of naught but blood and war.   55
Zabina.   Unworthy king, that by thy cruelty
Unlawfully usurpest the Persian seat,
Dar'st thou, that never saw an emperor
Before thou met my husband in the field,
Being thy captive, thus abuse his state,   60
Keeping his kingly body in a cage,
That roofs of gold and sun-bright palaces
Should have prepared to entertain his grace?
And treading him beneath thy loathsome feet,
Whose feet the kings of Africa have kissed?   65
Techelles.   You must devise some torment worse, my lord,
To make these captives rein their lavish tongues.
Tamburlaine.   Zenocrate, look better to your slave.
Zenocrate.   She is my handmaid's slave, and she shall look
That these abuses flow not from her tongue.   70
Chide her, Anippe.
Anippe.   Let these be warnings for you then, my slave,
How you abuse the person of the king;
Or else I swear to have you whipped stark naked.
Bajazeth.   Great Tamburlaine, great in my overthrow,   75
Ambitious pride shall make thee fall as low,
For treading on the back of Bajazeth,
That should be horsèd on four mighty kings.
Tamburlaine.   Thy names and titles and thy dignities
Are fled from Bajazeth and remain with me,   80
That will maintain it against a world of kings.
Put him in again.
                              [*They put him into the cage.*]
Bajazeth.   Is this a place for mighty Bajazeth?
Confusion light on him that helps thee thus.
Tamburlaine.   There, whiles he lives, shall Bajazeth be kept,   85
And where I go be thus in triumph drawn;
And thou, his wife, shalt feed him with the scraps

---

49 *Clymene's brain-sick son* Phaëthon, son of Apollo and Clymene, who drove the chariot of his father, the sun, but was unable to control the horses.   50 *brent* burned. *axle-tree of heaven* the axis of the universe on which all of the heavenly spheres were believed to turn.   60 *state* royal position.

My servitors shalt bring thee from my board,
For he that gives him other food than this
Shall sit by him and starve to death himself.   90
This is my mind, and I will have it so.
Not all the kings and emperors of the earth,
If they would lay their crowns before my feet,
Shall ransom him or take him from his cage.
The ages that shall talk of Tamburlaine,   95
Even from this day to Plato's wondrous year,
Shall talk how I have handled Bajazeth.
These Moors, that drew him from Bithynia
To fair Damascus, where we now remain,
Shall lead him with us wheresoe'er we go.   100
Techelles, and my loving followers,
Now may we see Damascus' lofty towers,
Like to the shadows of Pyramidès
That with their beauties graced the Memphian fields.
The golden stature of their feathered bird,   105
That spreads her wings upon the city walls,
Shall not defend it from our battering shot.
The townsmen mask in silk and cloth of gold,
And every house is as a treasury;
The men, the treasure, and the town is ours.   110
Theridamas.   Your tents of white now pitched before the gates,
And gentle flags of amity displayed,
I doubt not but the governor will yield,
Offering Damascus to your majesty.
Tamburlaine.   So shall he have his life, and all the rest.   115
But if he stay until the bloody flag
Be once advanced on my vermilion tent,
He dies, and those that kept us out so long.
And when they see me march in black array,
With mournful streamers hanging down their heads,   120
Were in that city all the world contained,
Not one should 'scape, but perish by our swords.
Zenocrate.   Yet would you have some pity for my sake,
Because it is my country's and my father's.
Tamburlaine.   Not for the world, Zenocrate, if I have sworn.   125
Come, bring in the Turk.

                                        Exeunt.

96 *Plato's wondrous year* a time when the irregularities in the universe caused by the movement of planets are all regularized, all being in the same position at the end of the year as at the beginning. This concept, which Plato refers to in his *Timæus,* was commonplace in medieval and Renaissance thought.

105 *stature* statue. *bird* the ibis, a bird sacred to the Egyptians.

IV,iii.

[Enter] Soldan, [King of] Arabia, Capolin, with streaming
colours; and Soldiers.

Soldan. Methinks we march as Meleager did,
  Environèd with brave Argolian knights,
  To chase the savage Calydonian boar,
  Or Cephalus, with lusty Theban youths,
  Against the wolf that angry Themis sent   5
  To waste and spoil the sweet Aonian fields.
  A monster of five hundred thousand heads,
  Compact of rapine, piracy, and spoil,
  The scum of men, the hate and scourge of God,
  Raves in Egyptia and annoyeth us.   10
  My lord, it is the bloody Tamburlaine,
  A sturdy felon, and a base-bred thief,
  By murder raisèd to the Persian crown,
  That dares control us in our territories.
  To tame the pride of this presumptuous beast,   15
  Join your Arabians with the Soldan's power;
  Let us unite our royal bands in one
  And hasten to remove Damascus' siege.
  It is a blemish to the majesty
  And high estate of mighty emperors,   20
  That such a base usurping vagabond
  Should brave a king or wear a princely crown.
King of Arabia. Renownèd Soldan, have ye lately heard
  The overthrow of mighty Bajazeth
  About the confines of Bithynia?   25
  The slavery wherewith he persecutes
  The noble Turk and his great emperess?
Soldan. I have, and sorrow for his bad success.
  But, noble lord of great Arabia,
  Be so persuaded that the Soldan is   30
  No more dismayed with tidings of his fall,
  Than in the haven when the pilot stands
  And views a stranger's ship rent in the winds
  And shiverèd against a craggy rock.
  Yet in compassion of his wretched state,   35
  A sacred vow to heaven and him I make,

IV,iii.

1 *Meleager* a Greek hero who slew the
giant boar which laid waste his native
Calydon.

2 *Argolian* of Argos.

4 *Cephalus* a hunter beloved by Eos,
the dawn, and possessed of a spear which
never missed its mark.

5 *Themis* daughter of Uranus and
Gea and married to Zeus; stands for order and justice in the universe. She is
the mother of the nymphs.

6 *Aonian* Greek.

Confirming it with Ibis' holy name,
That Tamburlaine shall rue the day, the hour,
Wherein he wrought such ignominious wrong
Unto the hallowed person of a prince,   40
Or kept the fair Zenocrate so long,
As concubine, I fear, to feed his lust.
King of Arabia.   Let grief and fury hasten on revenge.
Let Tamburlaine for his offences feel
Such plagues as heaven and we can pour on him.   45
I long to break my spear upon his crest
And prove the weight of his victorious arm;
For fame, I fear, hath been too prodigal
In sounding through the world his partial praise.
Soldan.   Capolin, hast thou surveyed our powers?   50
Capolin.   Great emperors of Egypt and Arabia,
The number of your hosts united is
A hundred and fifty thousand horse,
Two hundred thousand foot, brave men-at-arms,
Courageous and full of hardiness,   55
As frolic as the hunters in the chase
Of savage beasts amid the desert woods.
King of Arabia.   My mind presageth fortunate success,
And, Tamburlaine, my spirit doth foresee
The utter ruin of thy men and thee.   60
Soldan.   Then rear your standards; let your sounding drums
Direct our soldiers to Damascus' walls.
Now, Tamburlaine, the mighty Soldan comes
.And leads with him the great Arabian king
To dim thy baseness and obscurity,   65
Famous for nothing but for theft and spoil;
To raze and scatter thy inglorious crew
Of Scythians and slavish Persians.

Exeunt.

*

IV,iv.

The banquet [is set out] and to it come Tamburlaine, all in
scarlet, [Zenocrate], Theridamas, Techelles, Usumcasane,
[Bajazeth], the Turk, [drawn in his cage, Zabina], with others.
Tamburlaine.   Now hang our bloody colors by Damascus,
Reflexing hues of blood upon their heads,
While they walk quivering on their city walls,
Half dead for fear before they feel my wrath.

37 *Ibis' holy name* See note at IV,ii.   47 *prove* test.
105.

Then let us freely banquet and carouse 5
Full bowls of wine unto the god of war,
That means to fill your helmets full of gold,
And make Damascus' spoils as rich to you
As was to Jason Colchos' golden fleece.
And now, Bajazeth, hast thou any stomach? 10
Bajazeth. Ay, such a stomach, cruel Tamburlaine, as I could willingly
feed upon thy blood-raw heart.
Tamburlaine. Nay, thine own is easier to come by. Pluck out that, and
'twill serve thee and thy wife. Well, Zenocrate, Techelles, and the
rest, fall to your victuals. 15
Bajazeth. Fall to, and never may your meat digest!
Ye Furies, that can mask invisible,
Dive to the bottom of Avernus' pool,
And in your hands bring hellish poison up,
And squeeze it in the cup of Tamburlaine! 20
Or, wingèd snakes of Lerna, cast your stings,
And leave your venoms in this tyrant's dish!
Zabina. And may this banquet prove as ominous
As Progne's to th'adulterous Thracian king
That fed upon the substance of his child. 25
Zenocrate. My lord, how can you suffer these
Outrageous curses by these slaves of yours?
Tamburlaine. To let them see, divine Zenocrate,
I glory in the curses of my foes,
Having the power from the imperial heaven 30
To turn them all upon their proper heads.
Techelles. I pray you, give them leave, madam; this speech is a goodly
refreshing to them.
Theridamas. But, if his highness would let them be fed, it would do
them more good. 35
Tamburlaine. Sirrah, why fall you not to? Are you so daintily brought
up, you cannot eat your own flesh?
Bajazeth. First, legions of devils shall tear thee in pieces.
Usumcasane. Villain, knowest thou to whom thou speakest?
Tamburlaine. Oh, let him alone. Here; eat, sir; take it from my [40
sword's point, or I'll thrust it to thy heart.
　　　　　[Bajazeth] takes [the food,] and stamps upon it.

IV,iv.

9 *Jason* Greek hero who with his Argonauts journeyed to Colchos in quest of the golden fleece.

10 *stomach* (1) appetite (2) anger (since choler was produced in the stomach).

18 *Furies* See note to *Dido*, II,i,230.

19 *Avernus' pool* See note at I,ii,159.

21 *Lerna* region near Argos where Hercules killed the Hydra, a nine-headed monster.

24-25 *Progne . . . child* After Tereus, king of Thrace, had ravished Philomela, her sister, Progne, sought vengeance upon the king, her husband, by murdering their child, Itys, and tricking Tereus into eating the body.

30 *imperial* See note at II,vii,15.

Theridamas.   He stamps it under his feet, my lord.

Tamburlaine.   Take it up, villain, and eat it, or I will make thee slice
the brawns of thy arms into carbonadoes and eat them.

Usumcasane.   Nay, 'twere better he killed his wife, and then she   [45
shall be sure not to be starved, and he be provided for a month's
victual beforehand.

Tamburlaine.   Here is my dagger. Dispatch her while she is fat, for if
she live but a while longer, she will fall into a consumption with
fretting, and then she will not be worth the eating.   50

Theridamas.   Dost thou think that Mahomet will suffer this?

Techelles.   'Tis like he will, when he cannot let it.

Tamburlaine.   Go to; fall to your meat. What, not a bit? Belike he
hath not been watered to-day; give him some drink.

> *They give [Bajazeth] water to drink, and he flings*
> *it on the ground.*

Fast, and welcome, sir, while hunger make you eat. How now,   [55
Zenocrate, doth not the Turk and his wife make a goodly show at a
banquet?

Zenocrate.   Yes, my lord.

Theridamas.   Methinks 'tis a great deal better than a consort of music.

Tamburlaine.   Yet music would do well to cheer up Zenocrate.   [60
Pray thee tell, why art thou so sad? If thou wilt have a song, the
Turk shall strain his voice. But why is it?

Zenocrate.   My lord, to see my father's town besieged,
The country wasted, where myself was born,
How can it but afflict my very soul?   65
If any love remain in you, my lord,
Or if my love unto your majesty
May merit favor at your highness' hands,
Then raise your siege from fair Damascus' walls,
And with my father take a friendly truce.   70

Tamburlaine.   Zenocrate, were Egypt Jove's own land,
Yet would I with my sword make Jove to stoop.
I will confute those blind geographers
That make a triple region in the world,
Excluding regions which I mean to trace,   75
And with this pen reduce them to a map,
Calling the provinces, cities, and towns,
After my name and thine, Zenocrate.
Here at Damascus will I make the point
That shall begin the perpendicular.   80

44 *brawns* muscles. *carbonadoes* thin
strips of meat (like rashers of bacon).
52 *let* hinder.
55 *while* until.
59 *consort* company of musicians.

74 *triple region* i.e., Asia, Africa, and
Europe.
76 *this pen* i.e., his sword.
79–80 *Here . . . perpendicular* The
sense of this difficult passage is that

And wouldst thou have me buy thy father's love
With such a loss? Tell me, Zenocrate.
Zenocrate.   Honor still wait on happy Tamburlaine;
Yet give me leave to plead for him, my lord.
Tamburlaine.   Content thyself; his person shall be safe,   85
And all the friends of fair Zenocrate,
If with their lives they will be pleased to yield,
Or may be forced to make me emperor;
For Egypt and Arabia must be mine.
   Feed, you slave; thou mayst think thyself happy to be fed   [90
from my trencher.   [*To Bajazeth.*]
Bajazeth.   My empty stomach, full of idle heat,
Draws bloody humors from my feeble parts,
Preserving life by hasting cruel death.
My veins are pale, my sinews hard and dry,   95
My joints benumbed; unless I eat, I die.
Zabina.   Eat, Bajazeth. Let us live in spite of them, looking some happy
power will pity and enlarge us.
Tamburlaine.   Here, Turk; wilt thou have a clean trencher?
Bajazeth.   Ay, tyrant, and more meat.   100
Tamburlaine.   Soft, sir, you must be dieted; too much eating will make
you surfeit.
Theridamas.   So it would, my lord, 'specially having so small a walk
and so little exercise.
                    Enter a second course of crowns.
Tamburlaine.   Theridamas, Techelles, and Casane, here are the   [105
cates you desire to finger, are they not?
Theridamas.   Ay, my lord, but none save kings must feed with these.
Techelles.   'Tis enough for us to see them, and for Tamburlaine only
to enjoy them.
Tamburlaine.   Well, here is now to the Soldan of Egypt, the King   [110
of Arabia, and the Governor of Damascus. Now, take these three
crowns, and pledge me, my contributory kings. I crown you here,
Theridamas, King of Argier; Techelles, King of Fez; and Usumcasane,
King of Morocco. How say you to this, Turk? These are not your
contributory kings.   115
Bajazeth.   Nor shall they long be thine, I warrant them.
Tamburlaine.   Kings of Argier, Morocco, and of Fez,
You that have marched with happy Tamburlaine
As far as from the frozen place of heaven

Tamburlaine will make Damascus the
center of the new world he will create
by making its meridian the first meridian. It will, in other words, occupy the
position on the map which Greenwich,
England occupies today.

83 *still* forever.
97 *looking* hoping that.
99 *trencher* flat wooden dish.
106 *cates* delicacies.

Unto the wat'ry morning's ruddy bower,   120
And thence by land unto the torrid zone,
Deserve these titles I endow you with
By valor and by magnanimity.
Your births shall be no blemish to your fame,
For virtue is the fount whence honor springs,   125
And they are worthy she investeth kings.
Theridamas.   And since your highness hath so well vouchsafed,
If we deserve them not with higher meeds
Than erst our states and actions have retained,
Take them away again, and make us slaves.   130
Tamburlaine.   Well said, Theridamas. When holy Fates
Shall 'stablish me in strong Egyptia,
We mean to travel to th'antarctic pole,
Conquering the people underneath our feet,
And be renowned as never emperors were.   135
Zenocrate, I will not crown thee yet,
Until with greater honors I be graced.

                                        [*Exeunt.*]

                                                        V,i.
[*Enter*] *the Governor of Damascus with three or four Citizens,*
    and four Virgins with branches of laurel in their hands.
Governor.   Still doth this man, or rather god of war,
Batter our walls and beat our turrets down;
And to resist with longer stubbornness
Or hope of rescue from the Soldan's power,
Were but to bring our wilful overthrow,   5
And make us desperate of our threat'nèd lives.
We see his tents have now been alterèd
With terrors to the last and cruel'st hue.
His coal-black colors, everywhere advanced,
Threaten our city with a general spoil;   10
And if we should with common rites of arms
Offer our safeties to his clemency,
I fear the custom proper to his sword,
Which he observes as parcel of his fame,
Intending so to terrify the world,   15
By any innovation or remorse
Will never be dispensed with till our deaths.
Therefore, for these our harmless virgins' sakes,

                        V,i.

124 *births* humble origins.   14 *parcel of* an essential part of.
126 *they* they that.   16 *innovation* alteration.

Whose honors and whose lives rely on him,
Let us have hope that their unspotted prayers,   20
Their blubbered cheeks, and hearty humble moans
Will melt his fury into some remorse,
And use us like a loving conqueror.
First Virgin.   If humble suits or imprecations—
Uttered with tears of wretchedness and blood   25
Shed from the heads and hearts of all our sex,
Some made your wives, and some your children—
Might have entreated your obdurate breasts
To entertain some care of our securities
Whiles only danger beat upon our walls,   30
These more than dangerous warrants of our death
Had never been erected as they be,
Nor you depend on such weak helps as we.
Governor.   Well, lovely virgins, think our country's care,
Our love of honor, loath to be enthralled   35
To foreign powers and rough imperious yokes,
Would not with too much cowardice or fear,
Before all hope of rescue were denied,
Submit yourselves and us to servitude.
Therefore, in that your safeties and our own,   40
Your honors, liberties, and lives were weighed
In equal care and balance with our own,
Endure as we the malice of our stars,
The wrath of Tamburlaine and power of wars,
Or be the means the overweighing heavens   45
Have kept to qualify these hot extremes,
And bring us pardon in your cheerful looks.
Second Virgin.   Then here, before the majesty of heaven
And holy patrons of Egyptia,
With knees and hearts submissive we entreat   50
Grace to our words and pity to our looks
That this device may prove propitious,
And through the eyes and ears of Tamburlaine
Convey events of mercy to his heart.
Grant that these signs of victory we yield   55
May bind the temples of his conquering head
To hide the folded furrows of his brows,
And shadow his displeasèd countenance
With happy looks of ruth and lenity.
Leave us, my lord, and loving countrymen.   60
What simple virgins may persuade, we will.
Governor.   Farewell, sweet virgins, on whose safe return
Depends our city, liberty, and lives.

Exeunt [all except the Virgins].

21 *blubbered* tear-stained.   54 *events* results.

V,ii.

[*Enter*] *Tamburlaine, Techelles, Theridamas, Usumcasane,*
   with others; Tamburlaine all in black, and very melancholy.
Tamburlaine.   What, are the turtles frayed out of their nests?
   Alas, poor fools, must you be first shall feel
   The sworn destruction of Damascus?
   They know my custom; could they not as well
   Have sent ye out when first my milk-white flags,   5
   Through which sweet Mercy threw her gentle beams,
   Reflexing them on your disdainful eyes,
   As now when fury and incensèd hate
   Flings slaughtering terror from my coal-black tents,
   And tells for truth submissions comes too late?   10
First Virgin.   Most happy king and emperor of the earth,
   Image of honor and nobility,
   For whom the powers divine have made the world
   And on whose throne the holy Graces sit,
   In whose sweet person is comprised the sum   15
   Of nature's skill and heavenly majesty,
   Pity our plights! O, pity poor Damascus!
   Pity old age, within whose silver hairs
   Honor and reverence evermore have reigned.
   Pity the marriage-bed, where many a lord,   20
   In prime and glory of his loving joy,
   Embraceth now with tears of ruth and blood
   The jealous body of his fearful wife,
   Whose cheeks and hearts, so punished with conceit
   To think thy puissant never-stayèd arm   25
   Will part their bodies and prevent their souls
   From heavens of comfort yet their age might bear,
   Now wax all pale and withered to the death,
   As well for grief our ruthless governor
   Have thus refused the mercy of thy hand,   30
   Whose scepter angels kiss and Furies dread,
   As for their liberties, their loves, or lives.
   Oh, then, for these, and such as we ourselves,
   For us, for infants, and for all our bloods,

V,ii.

Although the virgins remain on stage
and no change of place is indicated, I
have followed the 1590 direction, *Actus
5 Scæna 2*, in indicating a new scene
here.

1 *turtles frayed* frightened turtle-
doves.

2 *fools* helpless ones.

14 *Graces* three daughters of Jupiter
(Euphrosyne, Aglaia, and Thalia) who
lend their charms to whatever elevates
man, poetry in particular; for they live
in harmony with the Muses on Mt.
Olympus.

24 *conceit* foreboding.

31 *Furies* See note to *Dido*, II,i,230.

That never nourished thought against thy rule,   35
Pity, O pity, sacred emperor,
The prostrate service of this wretched town;
And take in sign thereof this gilded wreath,
Whereto each man of rule hath given his hand,
And wished, as worthy subjects, happy means   40
To be investers of thy royal brows
Even with the true Egyptian diadem.
Tamburlaine.   Virgins, in vain ye labor to prevent
That which mine honor swears shall be performed.
Behold my sword; what see you at the point?   45
First Virgin.   Nothing but fear and fatal steel, my lord.
Tamburlaine.   Your fearful minds are thick and misty then,
For there sits Death; there sits imperious Death,
Keeping his circuit by the slicing edge.
But I am pleased you shall not see him there.   50
He now is seated on my horsemen's spears,
And on their points his fleshless body feeds.
Techelles, straight go charge a few of them
To charge these dames and show my servant, Death,
Sitting in scarlet on their armèd spears.   55
Virgins.   Oh, pity us!
Tamburlaine.   Away with them, I say, and show them Death.
                                        They take them away.
I will not spare these proud Egyptians,
Nor change my martial observations
For all the wealth of Gihon's golden waves,   60
Or for the love of Venus, would she leave
The angry god of arms and lie with me.
They have refused the offer of their lives;
And know my customs are as peremptory
As wrathful planets, death or destiny.   65
                         Enter Techelles.
What, have your horsemen shown the virgins Death?
Techelles.   They have, my lord, and on Damascus' walls
Have hoisted up their slaughtered carcasses.
Tamburlaine.   A sight as baneful to their souls, I think,
As are Thessalian drugs or mithridate.   70
But go, my lords, put the rest to the sword.
                         Exeunt [all except Tamburlaine].

49 *circuit* sphere of action.

52 *fleshless body* Death is conceived of, in the medieval manner, as a skeleton. He is also a judge whose circuit is equal to that reached by the edge of Tamburlaine's sword.

59 *observations* customary practices.

60 *Gihon* one of the traditional four rivers of Eden.

62 *god of arms* i.e., Mars, the beloved of Venus.

70 *mithridate* Although generally used as an antidote against poisons, it is here referred to as a poison itself.

Ah, fair Zenocrate! Divine Zenocrate!
Fair is too foul an epithet for thee,
That in thy passion for thy country's love,
And fear to see thy kingly father's harm,   75
With hair dishevelled wip'st thy watery cheeks;
And, like to Flora in her morning's pride,
Shaking her silver tresses in the air,
Rain'st on the earth resolvèd pearl in showers,
And sprinklest sapphires on thy shining face,   80
Where Beauty, mother to the Muses, sits,
And comments volumes with her ivory pen,
Taking instructions from thy flowing eyes,
Eyes, when that Ebena steps to heaven,
In silence of thy solemn evening's walk,   85
Making the mantle of the richest night,
The moon, the planets, and the meteors, light.
There angels in their crystal armors fight
A doubtful battle with my tempted thoughts
For Egypt's freedom and the Soldan's life,   90
His life that so consumes Zenocrate,
Whose sorrows lay more siege unto my soul
Than all my army to Damascus' walls;
And neither Persians' sovereign nor the Turk
Troubled my senses with conceit of foil   95
So much by much as doth Zenocrate.
What is beauty, saith my sufferings, then?
If all the pens that ever poets held
Had fed the feeling of their masters' thoughts,
And every sweetness that inspired their hearts,   100
Their minds, and muses on admirèd themes;
If all the heavenly quintessence they still
From their immortal flowers of poesy,
Wherein, as in a mirror, we perceive
The highest reaches of a human wit;   105
If these had made one poem's period,
And all combined in beauty's worthiness,
Yet should there hover in their restless heads
One thought, one grace, one wonder, at the least,
Which into words no virtue can digest.   110
But how unseemly is it for my sex,
My discipline of arms and chivalry,

---

74 *passion* sorrow.
77 *Flora* goddess of springtime and flowers.
79 *resolvèd pearl* i.e., tears.
84 *Ebena* There is no such classical deity, and where Marlowe derived the name has been much debated. The sense of the passage (84–87) is that Zenocrate's eyes at evening lend light to the moon, stars, and planets.
95 *conceit of foil* conception of defeat.
102 *still* distill.

My nature, and the terror of my name,
To harbor thoughts effeminate and faint!
Save only that in beauty's just applause,   115
With whose instinct the soul of man is touched;
And every warrior that is rapt with love
Of fame, of valor, and of victory,
Must needs have beauty beat on his conceits.
I thus conceiving and subduing both,   120
That which hath stopped the tempest of the gods,
Even from the fiery-spangled veil of heaven,
To feel the lovely warmth of shepherds' flames
And march in cottages of strowèd weeds,
Shall give the world to note, for all my birth,   125
That virtue solely is the sum of glory,
And fashions men with true nobility.
Who's within there?
                    Enter two or three [Attendants].
Hath Bajazeth been fed to-day?
Attendant. Ay, my lord.   130
Tamburlaine. Bring him forth. And let us know if the town be ran-
sacked.

                              [*Exeunt Attendants.*]

    Enter Techelles, Theridamas, Usumcasane, and others.
Techelles. The town is ours, my lord, and fresh supply
    Of conquest and of spoil is offered us.
Tamburlaine. That's well, Techelles. What's the news?   135
Techelles. The Soldan and the Arabian king together
    March on us with such eager violence
    As if there were no way but one with us.
Tamburlaine. No more there is not, I warrant thee, Techelles.
    *They bring in [Bajazeth], the Turk [in his cage, followed by
                            Zabina].*
Theridamas. We know the victory is ours, my lord,   140
    But let us save the reverend Soldan's life
    For fair Zenocrate that so laments his state.
Tamburlaine. That will we chiefly see unto, Theridamas,
    For sweet Zenocrate, whose worthiness
    Deserves a conquest over every heart.   145
    And now, my footstool, if I lose the field,
    You hope of liberty and restitution.
    Here let him stay, my masters, from the tents,
    Till we have made us ready for the field.

121–124 *That . . . weeds* a very obscure passage which has been much
emended. The sense seems to be that
beauty has eased the fury of the gods
and caused them to assume the guise of
shepherds, as Jove and Apollo did when
courting mortal women.

Pray for us, Bajazeth; we are going.   150
                    Exeunt [all except Bajazeth and Zabina].
Bajazeth.   Go, never to return with victory!
    Millions of men encompass thee about,
    And gore thy body with as many wounds!
    Sharp forkèd arrows light upon thy horse!
    Furies from the black Cocytus lake,   155
    Break up the earth, and with their firebrands
    Enforce thee run upon the baneful pikes!
    Volleys of shot pierce through thy charmèd skin,
    And every bullet dipped in poisoned drugs!
    Or roaring cannons sever all thy joints,   160
    Making thee mount as high as eagles soar!
Zabina.   Let all the swords and lances in the field
    Stick in his breast as in their proper rooms!
    At every pore let blood come dropping forth,
    That lingering pains may massacre his heart   165
    And madness send his damnèd soul to hell!
Bajazeth.   Ah, fair Zabina, we may curse his power,
    The heavens may frown, the earth for anger quake,
    But such a star hath influence in his sword
    As rules the skies and countermands the gods   170
    More than Cimmerian Styx or Destiny.
    And then shall we in this detested guise,
    With shame, with hunger, and with horror—ay,
    Griping our bowels with retorquèd thoughts—
    And have no hope to end our ecstasies.   175
Zabina.   Then is there left no Mahomet, no God,
    No fiend, no fortune, nor no hope of end
    To our infamous, monstrous slaveries?
    Gape earth, and let the fiends infernal view
    A hell as hopeless and as full of fear   180
    As are the blasted banks of Erebus,
    Where shaking ghosts with ever-howling groans
    Hover about the ugly ferryman
    To get a passage to Elysium!
    Why should we live? Oh, wretches, beggars, slaves!   185
    Why live we, Bajazeth, and build up nests
    So high within the region of the air,
    By living long in this oppression,
    That all the world will see and laugh to scorn
    The former triumphs of our mightiness   190

---

155 *Cocytus* a river leading into the
underworld; it was a tributary of Avernus
(see note at I,ii,159).
  171 *Cimmerian* black (see note at III,
ii,77). *Styx* the chief river of Hades.

174 *retorquèd* frustrated, bent and
twisted back upon itself.
  181 *Erebus* See note at IV,i,46.
  183 *ferryman* Charon, who conveyed
the dead across the river Styx.

In this obscure infernal servitude?
Bajazeth.   O life more loathsome to my vexèd thoughts
    Than noisome parbreak of the Stygian snakes,
    Which fills the nooks of hell with standing air,
    Infecting all the ghosts with cureless griefs!   195
    O dreary engines of my loathèd sight,
    That sees my crown, my honor, and my name
    Thrust under yoke and thraldom of a thief,
    Why feed ye still on day's accursèd beams,
    And sink not quite into my tortured soul?   200
    You see my wife, my queen, and emperess,
    Brought up and proppèd by the hand of Fame,
    Queen of fifteen contributory queens,
    Now thrown to rooms of black abjection,
    Smeared with blots of basest drudgery,   205
    And villainess to shame, disdain, and misery.
    Accursèd Bajazeth, whose words of ruth,
    That would with pity cheer Zabina's heart,
    And make our souls resolve in ceaseless tears,
    Sharp hunger bites upon and gripes the root   210
    From whence the issues of my thoughts do break.
    O poor Zabina! O my queen, my queen!
    Fetch me some water for my burning breast,
    To cool and comfort me with longer date,
    That in the shortened sequel of my life   215
    I may pour forth my soul into thine arms
    With words of love, whose moaning intercourse
    Hath hitherto been stayed with wrath and hate
    Of our expressless banned inflictions.
Zabina.   Sweet Bajazeth, I will prolong thy life   220
    As long as any blood or spark of breath
    Can quench or cool the torments of my grief.

                                            She goes out.

Bajazeth.   Now, Bajazeth, abridge thy baneful days,
    And beat thy brains out of thy conquered head,
    Since other means are all forbidden me,   225
    That may be ministers of my decay.
    O highest lamp of ever-living Jove,
    Accursèd day, infected with my griefs,
    Hide now thy stainèd face in endless night,
    And shut the windows of the lightsome heavens.   230
    Let ugly Darkness with her rusty coach
    Engirt with tempests, wrapped in pitchy clouds,
    Smother the earth with never-fading mists,
    And let her horses from their nostrils breathe

193 *parbreak* vomit.   209 *resolve* dissolve.
196 *engines* instruments.

Rebellious winds and dreadful thunder claps,   235
That in this terror Tamburlaine may live,
And my pined soul, resolved in liquid air,
May still excruciate his tormented thoughts!
Then let the stony dart of senseless cold
Pierce through the center of my withered heart,   240
And make a passage for my loathèd life!

> *He brains himself against the cage.*

> *Enter Zabina.*

Zabina.   What do mine eyes behold? My husband dead!
His skull all riven in twain, his brains dashed out!
The brains of Bajazeth, my lord and sovereign!
O, Bajazeth, my husband and my lord!   245
O Bajazeth! O Turk! O emperor!
Give him his liquor? Not I. Bring milk and fire, and my blood I
bring him again. Tear me in pieces. Give me the sword with a ball
of wild-fire upon it. Down with him! Down with him! Go to, my
child. Away, away, away! Ah, save that infant! Save him, save [250
him! I, even I, speak to her. The sun was down—streamers white, red,
black. Here, here, here! Fling the meat in his face! Tamburlaine,
Tamburlaine! Let the soldiers be buried. Hell, death, Tamburlaine,
hell! Make ready my coach, my chair, my jewels. I come, I come, I
come!   255

> *She runs against the cage and brains herself.*

> *[Enter] Zenocrate with Anippe.*

Zenocrate.   Wretched Zenocrate, that livest to see
Damascus' walls dyed with Egyptian blood,
Thy father's subjects and thy countrymen;
Thy streets strowed with dissevered joints of men,
And wounded bodies gasping yet for life;   260
But most accursed, to see the sun-bright troop
Of heavenly virgins and unspotted maids,
Whose looks might make the angry god of arms
To break his sword and mildly treat of love,
On horsemen's lances to be hoisted up,   265
And guiltlessly endure a cruel death.
For every fell and stout Tartarian steed,
That stamped on others with their thundering hoofs,
When all their riders charged their quivering spears,
Began to check the ground and rein themselves,   270
Gazing upon the beauty of their looks.
Ah, Tamburlaine, wert thou the cause of this,
That term'st Zenocrate thy dearest love?
Whose lives were dearer to Zenocrate
Than her own life, or aught save thine own love?   275

263 *god of arms* Mars.   270 *check* stamp **upon.**

But see, another bloody spectacle!
Ah, wretched eyes, the enemies of my heart,
How are ye glutted with these grievous objects,
And tell my soul more tales of bleeding ruth!
See, see, Anippe, if they breathe or no.　　　　　　　280
Anippe.　No breath, nor sense, nor motion in them both.
Ah, madam, this their slavery hath enforced,
And ruthless cruelty of Tamburlaine.
Zenocrate.　Earth, cast up fountains from thy entrails,
And wet thy cheeks for their untimely deaths.　　　　285
Shake with their weight in sign of fear and grief.
Blush heaven, that gave them honor at their birth
And let them die a death so barbarous.
Those that are proud of fickle empery
And place their chiefest good in earthly pomp,　　　290
Behold the Turk and his great emperess!
Ah, Tamburlaine my love, sweet Tamburlaine,
That fights for scepters and for slippery crowns,
Behold the Turk and his great emperess!
Thou, that in conduct of thy happy stars,　　　　295
Sleep'st every night with conquest on thy brows,
And yet wouldst shun the wavering turns of war,
In fear and feeling of the like distress,
Behold the Turk and his great emperess!
Ah, mighty Jove and holy Mahomet,　　　　300
Pardon my love! Oh, pardon his contempt
Of earthly fortune and respect of pity,
And let not conquest, ruthlessly pursued,
Be equally against his life incensed
In this great Turk and hapless emperess!　　　305
And pardon me that was not moved with ruth
To see them live so long in misery!
Ah, what may chance to thee, Zenocrate?
Anippe.　Madam, content yourself, and be resolved,
Your love hath Fortune so at his command,　　　310
That she shall stay and turn her wheel no more,
As long as life maintains his mighty arm
That fights for honor to adorn your head.
　　　　　Enter [Philemus], a Messenger.
Zenocrate.　What other heavy news now brings Philemus?
Philemus.　Madam, your father and th'Arabian king,　　　315
The first affecter of your excellence,
Comes now, as Turnus 'gainst Æneas did,
Armèd with lance into the Egyptian fields,

---

289 *empery* imperial power.
317 *Turnus* the foe of Æneas (see note to *Dido*, I,i,89) whose enmity began when Æneas married Lavinia, who had once been betrothed to Turnus.

Ready for battle 'gainst my lord the king.
Zenocrate.   Now shame and duty, love and fear presents   320
   A thousand sorrows to my martyred soul.
   Whom should I wish the fatal victory,
   When my poor pleasures are divided thus,
   And racked by duty from my cursèd heart?
   My father and my first-betrothèd love   325
   Must fight against my life and present love,
   Wherein the change I use condemns my faith
   And makes my deeds infamous through the world.
   But as the gods, to end the Trojans' toil,
   Prevented Turnus of Lavinia   330
   And fatally enriched Æneas' love,
   So, for a final issue to my griefs,
   To pacify my country and my love,
   Must Tamburlaine by their resistless powers,
   With virtue of a gentle victory,   335
   Conclude a league of honor to my hope;
   Then, as the powers divine have pre-ordained,
   With happy safety of my father's life
   Send like defense of fair Arabia.
      They sound to the battle [within], and Tamburlaine enjoys
      the victory, after [which, the King of] Arabia enters wounded.
King of Arabia.   What cursèd power guides the murdering hands   340
   Of this infamous tyrant's soldiers,
   That no escape may save their enemies,
   Nor fortune keep themselves from victory?
   Lie down Arabia, wounded to the death,
   And let Zenocrate's fair eyes behold   345
   That, as for her thou bear'st these wretched arms,
   Even so for her thou diest in these arms,
   Leaving thy blood for witness of thy love.
Zenocrate.   Too dear a witness for such love, my lord.
   Behold Zenocrate, the cursed object   350
   Whose fortunes never masterèd her griefs.
   Behold her wounded in conceit for thee,
   As much as thy fair body is for me!
King of Arabia.   Then shall I die with full contented heart,
   Having beheld divine Zenocrate,   355
   Whose sight with joy would take away my life,
   As now it bringeth sweetness to my wound,
   If I had not been wounded as I am.
   Ah, that the deadly pangs I suffer now
   Would lend an hour's licence to my tongue,   360
   To make discourse of some sweet accidents
   Have chanced thy merits in this worthless bondage,

352 *conceit* imagination.

And that I might be privy to the state
Of thy deserved contentment and thy love.
But, making now a virtue of thy sight,   365
To drive all sorrow from my fainting soul,
Since death denies me further cause of joy,
Deprived of care, my heart with comfort dies,
Since thy desired hand shall close mine eyes.

[*He dies.*]

Enter Tamburlaine, leading the Soldan; Techelles, Theri-
damas, Usumcasane, with others.

Tamburlaine.   Come, happy father of Zenocrate,   370
A title higher than thy Soldan's name.
Though my right hand have thus enthrallèd thee,
Thy princely daughter here shall set thee free,
She that hath calmed the fury of my sword,
Which had ere this been bathed in streams of blood   375
As vast and deep as Euphrates or Nile.
Zenocrate.   O sight thrice-welcome to my joyful soul,
To see the king my father issue safe
From dangerous battle of my conquering love!
Soldan.   Well met, my only dear Zenocrate,   380
Though with the loss of Egypt and my crown.
Tamburlaine.   'Twas I, my lord, that gat the victory,
And therefore grieve not at your overthrow,
Since I shall render all into your hands,
And add more strength to your dominions   385
Than ever yet confirmed th'Egyptian crown.
The god of war resigns his room to me,
Meaning to make me general of the world.
Jove, viewing me in arms, looks pale and wan,
Fearing my power should pull him from his throne.   390
Where'er I come the Fatal Sisters sweat,
And grisly Death, by running to and fro
To do their ceaseless homage to my sword.
And here in 'Afric, where it seldom rains,
Since I arrived with my triumphant host,   395
Have swelling clouds, drawn from wide-gasping wounds,
Been oft resolved in bloody purple showers,
A meteor that might terrify the earth,
And make it quake at every drop it drinks.
Millions of souls sit on the banks of Styx,   400
Waiting the back-return of Charon's boat;
Hell and Elysium swarm with ghosts of men
That I have sent from sundry foughten fields

386 *confirmed* was confirmed by.   391 *Fatal Sisters* the Fates. See note
                                           to *Dido,* III,ii,3.

To spread my fame through hell and up to heaven.
And see, my lord, a sight of strange import,   405
Emperors and kings lie breathless at my feet.
The Turk and his great empress, as it seems,
Left to themselves while we were at the fight,
Have desperately dispatched their slavish lives;
With them Arabia too hath left his life;   410
All sights of power to grace my victory.
And such are objects fit for Tamburlaine,
Wherein, as in a mirror, may be seen
His honor, that consists in shedding blood
When men presume to manage arms with him.   415
Soldan.   Mighty hath God and Mahomet made thy hand,
Renownèd Tamburlaine, to whom all kings
Of force must yield their crowns and emperies;
And I am pleased with this my overthrow,
If, as beseems a person of thy state,   420
Thou hast with honor used Zenocrate.
Tamburlaine.   Her state and person wants no pomp, you see,
And for all blot of foul unchastity,
I record heaven, her heavenly self is clear.
Then let me find no further time to grace   425
Her princely temples with the Persian crown;
But here these kings that on my fortunes wait,
And have been crowned for provèd worthiness
Even by this hand that shall establish them,
Shall now, adjoining all their hands with mine,   430
Invest her here my Queen of Persia.
What saith the noble Soldan and Zenocrate?
Soldan.   I yield with thanks and protestations
Of endless honor to thee for her love.
Tamburlaine.   Then doubt I not but fair Zenocrate   435
Will soon consent to satisfy us both.
Zenocrate.   Else should I much forget myself, my lord.
Theridamas.   Then let us set the crown upon her head,
That long hath lingered for so high a seat.
Techelles.   My hand is ready to perform the deed,   440
For now her marriage-time shall work us rest.
Usumcasane.   And here's the crown, my lord; help set it on.
Tamburlaine.   Then sit thou down, divine Zenocrate,
And here we crown thee Queen of Persia,
And all the kingdoms and dominions   445
That late the power of Tamburlaine subdued.
As Juno, when the giants were suppressed,
That darted mountains at her brother Jove,

447–448 *Juno . . . Jove* Juno actually   war of the Titans against Jove.
had no part in classical accounts of the

So looks my love, shadowing in her brows
Triumphs and trophies for my victories;   450
Or as Latona's daughter, bent to arms,
Adding more courage to my conquering mind.
To gratify thee, sweet Zenocrate,
Egyptians, Moors, and men of Asia,
From Barbary unto the Western Indie,   455
Shall pay a yearly tribute to thy sire;
And from the bounds of Afric to the banks
Of Ganges shall his mighty arm extend.
And now, my lords and loving followers,
That purchased kingdoms by your martial deeds,   460
Cast off your armor, put on scarlet robes,
Mount up your royal places of estate,
Environèd with troops of noblemen,
And there make laws to rule your provinces.
Hang up your weapons on Alcides' post,   465
For Tamburlaine takes truce with all the world.
Thy first-betrothèd love, Arabia,
Shall we with honor, as beseems, entomb
With this great Turk and his fair emperess.
Then, after all these solemn exequies,   470
We will our rites of marriage solemnise.

                                                    [*Exeunt.*]

451 *Latona's daughter* Diana (whose   465 *Alcides' post* the door post of the
arms were the bow and arrow used for   temple of Hercules (Alcides).
hunting, not for warfare).

TAMBURLAINE THE GREAT: PART TWO

THE PLAYERS

Tamburlaine, King of Persia

Calyphas ⎱
Amyras ⎰ his sons
Celebinus

Theridamas, King of Argier
Techelles, King of Fez
Usumcasane, King of Morocco
Orcanes, King of Natolia
King of Trebizon
King of Soria
King of Jerusalem
King of Amasia
Gazellus, Viceroy of Byron
Uribassa
Sigismund, King of Hungary

Frederick ⎱ lords of Buda and Bo-
Baldwin ⎰   hemia

Callapine, son to Bajazeth, and
    prisoner to Tamburlaine
Almeda, his keeper

Governor of Babylon
Captain of Balsera
His Son
Another Captain
Maximus, Perdicas, Physicians,
    Lords, Citizens, Messengers,
    Soldiers, and Attendants
Zenocrate, wife to Tamburlaine

Olympia, wife to the Captain of
    Balsera

Turkish Concubines

THE SCENE

Asia and Africa

The Second Part of The Bloody Conquests of Mighty Tamburlaine. With his impassionate fury, for the death of his lady and love, fair Zenocrate: his form of exhortation and discipline to his three sons, and the manner of his own death.

Prologue.

THE PROLOGUE

THE general welcomes Tamburlaine received,
When he arrivèd last upon our stage,
Hath made our poet pen his Second Part,
Where death cuts off the progress of his pomp
And murderous Fates throws all his triumphs down.   5
But what became of fair Zenocrate,
And with how many cities' sacrifice
He celebrated her sad funeral,
Himself in presence shall unfold at large.

[Enter] Orcanes, King of Natolia, Gazellus, Viceroy of Byron,
Uribassa, and their train, with drums and trumpets.

Orcanes. Egregious viceroys of these eastern parts,
  Placed by the issue of great Bajazeth,
  And sacred lord, the mighty Callapine,
  Who lives in Egypt prisoner to that slave
  Which kept his father in an iron cage,   5
  Now have we marched from fair Natolia
  Two hundred leagues, and on Danubius' banks
  Our warlike host in complete armor rest,
  Where Sigismund, the king of Hungary,
  Should meet our person to conclude a truce.   10
  What! Shall we parle with the Christian,
  Or cross the stream and meet him in the field?
Gazellus. King of Natolia, let us treat of peace.
  We all are glutted with the Christians' blood,
  And have a greater foe to fight against,   15
  Proud Tamburlaine, that now in Asia,
  Near Guyron's head, doth set his conquering feet
  And means to fire Turkey as he goes.
  'Gainst him, my lord, must you address your power.
Uribassa. Besides, King Sigismund hath brought from Christendom 20
  More than his camp of stout Hungarians—
  Slavonians, Almains, Rutters, Muffs, and Danes,
  That with the halberd, lance, and murdering axe,
  Will hazard that we might with surety hold.
Orcanes. Though from the shortest northern parallel,   25
  Vast Gruntland, compassed with the frozen sea,
  Inhabited with tall and sturdy men,
  Giants as big as hugy Polypheme,
  Millions of soldiers cut the arctic line,
  Bringing the strength of Europe to these arms,   30
  Our Turkey blades shall glide through all their throats,
  And make this champion mead a bloody fen.
  Danubius' stream, that runs to Trebizon,

I,i.

1 *Egregious* distinguished.
17 *Guyron's head* a town on the upper
Euphrates river, northeast of Aleppo.
22 *Slavonians* Slavs. *Almains* Germans.
Rutters horsemen. *Muffs* Swiss.
24 *that* that which.
26 *Gruntland* Greenland. *frozen sea*
Arctic ocean.
28 *hugy* huge. *Polypheme* one of the

Cyclops (see note to *Dido,* I,i,147) who
fell in love with the nymph, Galatea and
who was blinded by Ulysses.
32 *champion mead* level plain.
33–41 *Danubius' . . . argosies.* The waters of the Danube are conceived of
here as flowing from the river mouth in
two currents, the one going across the
Black sea to Trebizond, the other going

Shall carry, wrapped within his scarlet waves,
As martial presents to our friends at home,   35
The slaughtered bodies of these Christians.
The Terrene main, wherein Danubius falls,
Shall by this battle be the bloody sea.
The wandering sailors of proud Italy
Shall meet those Christians, fleeting with the tide,   40
Beating in heaps against their argosies,
And make fair Europe, mounted on her bull,
Trapped with the wealth and riches of the world,
Alight and wear a woeful mourning weed.
Gazellus.   Yet, stout Orcanes, prorex of the world,   45
Since Tamburlaine hath mustered all his men,
Marching from Cairon northward with his camp,
To Alexandria and the frontier towns,
Meaning to make a conquest of our land,
'Tis requisite to parle for a peace   50
With Sigismund, the king of Hungary,
And save our forces for the hot assaults
Proud Tamburlaine intends Natolia.
Orcanes.   Viceroy of Byron, wisely hast thou said.
My realm, the center of our empery,   55
Once lost, all Turkey would be overthrown;
And for that cause the Christians shall have peace.
Slavonians, Almains, Rutters, Muffs, and Danes,
Fear not Orcanes, but great Tamburlaine,
Nor he, but Fortune that hath made him great.   60
We have revolted Grecians, Albanese,
Sicilians, Jews, Arabians, Turks, and Moors,
Natolians, Sorians, black Egyptians,
Illyrians, Thracians, and Bithynians,
Enough to swallow forceless Sigismund,   65
Yet scarce enough t'encounter Tamburlaine.
He brings a world of people to the field:
From Scythia to the oriental plage
Of India, where raging Lantchidol

south to the Mediterranean (Terrene
Main) and then into the Aegean. Each
of these currents will carry the bodies
of Christian soldiers which will beat
against the merchant ships (argosies) of
Christian seamen.
  42 *Europe . . . bull* Europa, daughter of Agenor, king of Phoenicia, was
wooed by Jupiter in the form of a bull.
When she mounted his back, the bull
plunged into the sea and swam with her

to Crete. She gave her name to the continent of Europe.
  44 *weed* garment.
  45 *prorex* viceroy.
  55 *empery* empire.
  59 *Fear* frighten.
  60 *Fortune* See note to *I Tamb.*, I,i,
124.
  61 *revolted* renegade.
  68 *oriental plage* eastern shore.
  69 *Lantchidol* an arm of the Indian
ocean.

Beats on the regions with his boisterous blows,   70
That never seaman yet discoverèd,
All Asia is in arms with Tamburlaine.
Even from the midst of fiery Cancer's tropic
To Amazonia under Capricorn,
And thence as far as Archipelago,   75
All Afric is in arms with Tamburlaine;
Therefore, viceroys, the Christians must have peace.

                                                            I,ii.

> [Enter] *Sigismund, Frederick, Baldwin, and their train, with*
> *drums and trumpets.*

Sigismund.   Orcanes, as our legates promised thee,
We, with our peers, have crossed Danubius' stream
To treat of friendly peace or deadly war.
Take which thou wilt; for, as the Romans used,
I here present thee with a naked sword.   5
Wilt thou have war, then shake this blade at me;
If peace, restore it to my hands again,
And I will sheathe it to confirm the same.
Orcanes.   Stay, Sigismund. Forgett'st thou I am he
That with the cannon shook Vienna walls   10
And made it dance upon the continent,
As when the massy substance of the earth
Quiver about the axle-tree of heaven?
Forgett'st thou that I sent a shower of darts,
Minglèd with powdered shot and feathered steel   15
So thick upon the blink-eyed burghers' heads,
That thou thyself, then County Palatine,
The King of Boheme, and the Austric Duke,
Sent heralds out, which basely on their knees,
In all your names desired a truce of me?   20
Forgett'st thou that to have me raise my siege,
Wagons of gold were set before my tent,
Stamped with the princely fowl that in her wings
Carries the fearful thunderbolts of Jove?
How canst thou think of this and offer war?   25

73–74 *from . . . Capricorn* i.e., from the Canary islands (the center of the Tropic of Cancer) to a region known on ancient maps as *Amazonum regio* around the source of the Nile. Marlowe seems to see this territory as extending below the tropic of Capricorn.

75 *thence . . . Archipelago* northward to the Mediterranean islands.

I,ii.
The 1590 indication of a scene divi-
sion is retained here (*Act. I Scæna* 2.) even though there is no change of place, and Orcanes and his followers are left standing on the stage. Such scene division was common in classical drama and may reflect Marlowe's intention.

13 *axle-tree of heaven* See note to *I Tamb.*, IV,ii,50.

16 *blink-eyed* probably wide-eyed with amazement.

18 *Austric* Austrian.

23 *princely fowl* eagle.

Sigismund. Vienna was besieged, and I was there,
  Then County Palatine, but now a king,
  And what we did was in extremity.
  But now, Orcanes, view my royal host
  That hides these plains and seems as vast and wide   30
  As doth the desert of Arabia
  To those that stand on Badgeth's lofty tower,
  Or as the ocean to the traveler
  That rests upon the snowy Appenines,
  And tell me whether I should stoop so low,   35
  Or treat of peace with the Natolian king.
Gazellus. Kings of Natolia and of Hungary,
  We came from Turkey to confirm a league,
  And not to dare each other to the field.
  A friendly parle might become ye both.   40
Frederick. And we from Europe to the same intent,
  Which if your general refuse or scorn,
  Our tents are pitched, our men stand in array,
  Ready to charge you ere you stir your feet.
Orcanes. So prest are we; but yet, if Sigismund   45
  Speak as a friend, and stand not upon terms,
  Here is his sword; let peace be ratified
  On these conditions specified before,
  Drawn with advice of our ambassadors.
Sigismund. Then here I sheathe it and give thee my hand,   50
  Never to draw it out or manage arms
  Against thyself or thy confederates,
  But whilst I live will be at truce with thee.
Orcanes. But, Sigismund, confirm it with an oath,
  And swear in sight of heaven and by thy Christ.   55
Sigismund. By Him that made the world and saved my soul,
  The Son of God and issue of a maid,
  Sweet Jesus Christ, I solemnly protest
  And vow to keep this peace inviolable.
Orcanes. By sacred Mahomet, the friend of God,   60
  Whose holy Alcoran remains with us,
  Whose glorious body, when he left the world,
  Closed in a coffin mounted up the air
  And hung on stately Mecca's temple roof,
  I swear to keep this truce inviolable.   65
  Of whose conditions and our solemn oaths,
  Signed with our hands, each shall retain a scroll
  As memorable witness of our league.
  Now, Sigismund, if any Christian king

30 *hides* covers.   45 *prest* ready.
32 *Badgeth's lofty tower* Bagdad's tall-
est minaret.

Encroach upon the confines of thy realm,   70
Send word, Orcanes of Natolia
Confirmed this league beyond Danubius' stream,
And they will, trembling, sound a quick retreat;
So am I feared among all nations.
Sigismund. If any heathen potentate or king   75
  Invade Natolia, Sigismund will send
  A hundred thousand horse trained to the war,
  And backed by stout lancèrs of Germany,
  The strength and sinews of the imperial seat.
Orcanes. I thank thee, Sigismund; but, when I war,   80
  All Asia Minor, Africa, and Greece
  Follow my standard and my thundering drums.
  Come, let us go and banquet in our tents.
  I will dispatch chief of my army hence
  To fair Natolia and to Trebizon,   85
  To stay my coming 'gainst proud Tamburlaine.
  Friend Sigismund and peers of Hungary,
  Come, banquet and carouse with us a while,
  And then depart we to our territories.

                                             Exeunt.

      [Enter] Callapine, with Almeda, his keeper.   I,iii.
Callapine. Sweet Almeda, pity the ruthful plight
  Of Callapine, the son of Bajazeth,
  Born to be monarch of the western world,
  Yet here detained by cruel Tamburlaine.
Almeda. My lord, I pity it, and with my heart   5
  Wish your release; but he whose wrath is death,
  My sovereign lord, renownèd Tamburlaine,
  Forbids you further liberty than this.
Callapine. Ah, were I now but half so eloquent
  To paint in words what I'll perform in deeds,   10
  I know thou wouldst depart from hence with me.
Almeda. Not for all Afric; therefore move me not.
Callapine. Yet hear me speak, my gentle Almeda.
Almeda. No speech to that end, by your favor, sir.
Callapine. By Cairo runs—   15
Almeda. No talk of running, I tell you, sir.
Callapine. A little further, gentle Almeda.
Almeda. Well, sir, what of this?
Callapine. By Cairo runs to Alexandria bay
                     I,iii.
86 *stay* await.   3 *western world* Turkish empire.

Darotes' streams, wherein at anchor lies   20
A Turkish galley of my royal fleet,
Waiting my coming to the river side,
Hoping by some means I shall be released;
Which, when I come aboard, will hoist up sail
And soon put forth into the Terrene sea,   25
Where, 'twixt the isles of Cyprus and of Crete,
We quickly may in Turkish seas arrive.
Then shalt thou see a hundred kings and more,
Upon their knees, all bid me welcome home.
Amongst so many crowns of burnished gold,   30
Choose which thou wilt; all are at thy command.
A thousand galleys, manned with Christian slaves,
I freely give thee, which shall cut the Straits,
And bring armadoes from the coasts of Spain,
Fraughted with gold of rich America.   35
The Grecian virgins shall attend on thee,
Skillful in music and in amorous lays,
As fair as was Pygmalion's ivory girl
Or lovely Iö metamorphosèd.
With naked negroes shall thy coach be drawn,   40
And as thou rid'st in triumph through the streets,
The pavement underneath thy chariot wheels
With Turkey carpets shall be coverèd,
And cloth of Arras hung about the walls,
Fit objects for thy princely eye to pierce.   45
A hundred bassoes, clothed in crimson silk,
Shall ride before thee on Barbarian steeds;
And, when thou goest, a golden canopy
Enchased with precious stones, which shine as bright
As that fair veil that covers all the world,   50
When Phœbus, leaping from his hemisphere,
Descendeth downward to th'Antipodes—
And more than this, for all I cannot tell.
Almeda.   How far hence lies the galley, say you?
Callapine.   Sweet Almeda, scarce half a league from hence.   55
Almeda.   But need we not be spièd going aboard?
Callapine.   Betwixt the hollow hanging of a hill

---

20 *Darotes' streams* the Nile from
Cairo to Alexandria, which runs by the
town of Darote.
22 *Waiting* awaiting.
25 *Terrene sea* Mediterranean.
34 *armadoes* warships.
35 *Fraughted* laden.
38 *Pygmalion's ivory girl* Galatea. See
note to *Dido*, II,i,16.
39 *Iö* the daughter of Inachus, king

of Argus, who was loved by Jupiter and
transformed into a heifer out of fear of
Juno.
49 *Enchased* adorned. See note to
Dido, I,i,101.
52 *Antipodes* a small group of islands
in the Western Pacific, among whom the
sun was believed to set.
56 *need we not* shall we not inevitably.

And crooked bending of a craggy rock,
The sails wrapped up, the mast and tacklings down,
She lies so close that none can find her out.   60
Almeda.   I like that well. But tell me, my lord, if I should let you go,
would you be as good as your word? Shall I be made a king for my
labor?
Callapine.   As I am Callapine the emperor,
And by the hand of Mahomet I swear,   65
Thou shalt be crowned a king, and be my mate.
Almeda.   Then here I swear, as I am Almeda,
Your keeper under Tamburlaine the Great,
—For that's the style and title I have yet—
Although he sent a thousand armèd men   70
To intercept this haughty enterprise,
Yet would I venture to conduct your grace
And die before I brought you back again!
Callapine.   Thanks, gentle Almeda. Then let us haste,
Lest time be past and lingering let us both.   75
Almeda.   When you will, my lord, I am ready.
Callapine.   Even straight; and farewell, cursèd Tamburlaine.
Now go I to revenge my father's death.

                                        Exeunt.

                                                        I,iv.
[*Enter*] *Tamburlaine with Zenocrate, and his three sons,*
    Calyphas, Amyras, and Celebinus, with drums and trumpets.
Tamburlaine.   Now, bright Zenocrate, the world's fair eye,
Whose beams illuminate the lamps of heaven,
Whose cheerful looks do clear the cloudy air
And clothe it in a crystal livery,
Now rest thee here on fair Larissa plains,   5
Where Egypt and the Turkish empire parts,
Between thy sons that shall be emperors,
And every one commander of a world.
Zenocrate.   Sweet Tamburlaine, when wilt thou leave these arms
And save thy sacred person free from scathe   10
And dangerous chances of the wrathful war?
Tamburlaine.   When heaven shall cease to move on both the poles,
And when the ground, whereon my soldiers march,

I,iv.

66 *mate* equal.   5 *Larissa* a sea-coast town south of
75 *let* hinder.   Gaza, the present-day El Arish.

Shall rise aloft and touch the hornèd moon,
And not before, my sweet Zenocrate.   15
Sit up, and rest thee like a lovely queen.
So, now she sits in pomp and majesty,
When these, my sons, more precious in mine eyes
Than all the wealthy kingdoms I subdued,
Placed by her side, look on their mother's face.   20
But yet methinks their looks are amorous,
Not martial as the sons of Tamburlaine.
Water and air, being symbolized in one,
Argue their want of courage and of wit;
Their hair, as white as milk, and soft as down—   25
Which should be like the quills of porcupines,
As black as jet, and hard as iron or steel—
Bewrays they are too dainty for the wars;
Their fingers made to quaver on a lute,
Their arms to hang about a lady's neck,   30
Their legs to dance and caper in the air,
Would make me think them bastards, not my sons,
But that I know they issued from thy womb,
That never looked on man but Tamburlaine.
Zenocrate.   My gracious lord, they have their mother's looks, 35
But when they list, their conquering father's heart.
This lovely boy, the youngest of the three,
Not long ago bestrid a Scythian steed,
Trotting the ring, and tilting at a glove,
Which when he tainted with his slender rod,   40
He reined him straight and made him so curvet
As I cried out for fear he should have fall'n.
Tamburlaine.   Well done, my boy! Thou shalt have shield and lance,
Armor of proof, horse, helm, and curtle-axe,
And I will teach thee how to charge thy foe   45
And harmless run among the deadly pikes.
If thou wilt love the wars and follow me,
Thou shalt be made a king and reign with me,
Keeping in iron cages emperors.
If thou exceed thy elder brothers' worth,   50
And shine in complete virtue more than they,
Thou shalt be king before them, and thy seed
Shall issue crownèd from their mother's womb.

21 *amorous* loving, gentle.

23-24 *Water . . . wit* Tamburlaine is explaining the weak temperaments of his sons in terms of the physiology of Marlowe's day. Being overbalanced in the phlegmatic (chiefly water) and sanguine (blood) humours, the boys lack the necessary black bile (chiefly earth) and choler (chiefly fire) which might give them courage and wit.

28 *Bewrays* betrays, reveals.

40 *tainted* struck (a technical term used in tilting).

44 *proof* metal which has been tested.

Celebinus. Yes, father; you shall see me, if I live,
 Have under me as many kings as you,
 And march with such a multitude of men   55
 As all the world shall tremble at their view.
Tamburlaine. These words assure me, boy, thou art my son.
 When I am old and cannot manage arms,
 Be thou the scourge and terror of the world.   60
Amyras. Why may not I, my lord, as well as he,
 Be termed the scourge and terror of the world?
Tamburlaine. Be all a scourge and terror to the world,
 Or else you are not sons of Tamburlaine.
Calyphas. But while my brothers follow arms, my lord, 65
 Let me accompany my gracious mother.
 They are enough to conquer all the world,
 And you have won enough for me to keep.
Tamburlaine. Bastardly boy, sprung from some coward's loins,
 And not the issue of great Tamburlaine!   70
 Of all the provinces I have subdued
 Thou shalt not have a foot, unless thou bear
 A mind courageous and invincible;
 For he shall wear the crown of Persia
 Whose head hath deepest scars, whose breast most wounds, 75
 Which being wroth sends lightning from his eyes,
 And in the furrows of his frowning brows
 Harbors revenge, war, death, and cruelty;
 For in a field, whose superficies
 Is covered with a liquid purple veil   80
 And sprinkled with the brains of slaughtered men,
 My royal chair of state shall be advanced;
 And he that means to place himself therein,
 Must armèd wade up to the chin in blood.
Zenocrate. My lord, such speeches to our princely sons 85
 Dismays their minds before they come to prove
 The wounding troubles angry war affords.
Celebinus. No, madam, these are speeches fit for us,
 For if his chair were in a sea of blood,
 I would prepare a ship and sail to it,   90
 Ere I would lose the title of a king.
Amyras. And I would strive to swim through pools of blood
 Or make a bridge of murdered carcasses,
 Whose arches should be framed with bones of Turks,
 Ere I would lose the title of a king.   95
Tamburlaine. Well, lovely boys, you shall be emperors both,
 Stretching your conquering arms from east to west.
 And, sirrah, if you mean to wear a crown,
 When we shall meet the Turkish deputy

And all his viceroys, snatch it from his head,　　　　100
And cleave his pericranion with thy sword.
Calyphas.　If any man will hold him, I will strike
And cleave him to the channel with my sword.
Tamburlaine.　Hold him, and cleave him too, or I'll cleave thee;
For we will march against them presently.　　　　105
Theridamas, Techelles, and Casane
Promised to meet me on Larissa plains
With hosts apiece against this Turkish crew;
For I have sworn by sacred Mahomet
To make it parcel of my empery.　　　　110
The trumpets sound, Zenocrate; they come.

　　　　　　　　　　　　　　　　　　　　　I,v.

Enter Theridamas, and his train, with drums and trumpets.
Tamburlaine.　Welcome Theridamas, king of Argier.
Theridamas.　My lord, the great and mighty Tamburlaine,
Arch-monarch of the world, I offer here
My crown, myself, and all the power I have,
In all affection at thy kingly feet.　　　　5
Tamburlaine.　Thanks, good Theridamas.
Theridamas.　Under my colors march ten thousand Greeks,
And of Argier and Afric's frontier towns
Twice twenty thousand valiant men-at-arms,
All which have sworn to sack Natolia.　　　　10
Five hundred brigandines are under sail,
Meet for your service on the sea, my lord,
That, launching from Argier to Tripoli,
Will quickly ride before Natolia
And batter down the castles on the shore.　　　　15
Tamburlaine.　Well said, Argier; receive thy crown again.

　　　　Enter Techelles and Usumcasane together.　　I,vi.
Tamburlaine.　Kings of Morocco and of Fez, welcome.
Usumcasane.　Magnificent and peerless Tamburlaine,
I and my neighbor king of Fez have brought,
To aid thee in this Turkish expedition,
A hundred thousand expert soldiers;　　　　5
From Azamor to Tunis near the sea
Is Barbary unpeopled for thy sake,

---

103 *channel* collar bone.

I,v.
　See note at I,ii.
　11 *brigandines* light vessels which could be either sailed or rowed.

I,vi.
　See note at I,ii and I,v.
　6 *Azamor* town in North Africa.

And all the men in armor under me,
Which with my crown I gladly offer thee.
Tamburlaine.   Thanks, king of Morocco; take your crown again.   10
Techelles.   And, mighty Tamburlaine, our earthly god,
   Whose looks make this inferior world to quake,
   I here present thee with the crown of Fez,
   And with an host of Moors trained to the war,
   Whose coal-black faces make their foes retire   15
   And quake for fear, as if infernal Jove,
   Meaning to aid thee in these Turkish arms,
   Should pierce the black circumference of hell,
   With ugly Furies bearing fiery flags,
   And millions of his strong tormenting spirits;   20
   From strong Tesella unto Biledull
   All Barbary is unpeopled for thy sake.
Tamburlaine.   Thanks, king of Fez; take here thy crown again.
   Your presence, loving friends and fellow kings,
   Makes me to surfeit in conceiving joy.   25
   If all the crystal gates of Jove's high court
   Were opened wide, and I might enter in
   To see the state and majesty of heaven,
   It could not more delight me than your sight.
   Now will we banquet on these plains a while,   30
   And after march to Turkey with our camp,
   In number more than are the drops that fall
   When Boreas rents a thousand swelling clouds;
   And proud Orcanes of Natolia
   With all his viceroys shall be so afraid,   35
   That though the stones, as at Deucalion's flood,
   Were turned to men, he should be overcome.
   Such lavish will I make of Turkish blood,
   That Jove shall send his wingèd messenger
   To bid me sheathe my sword and leave the field;   40
   The sun, unable to sustain the sight,
   Shall hide his head in Thetis' watery lap
   And leave his steeds to fair Boötes' charge;
   For half the world shall perish in this fight.
   But now, my friends, let me examine ye;   45
   How have ye spent your absent time from me?
Usumcasane.   My lord, our men of Barbary have marched
   Four hundred miles with armor on their backs,

---

21 *Tesella . . . Biledull*   towns   in
North Africa.
33 *Boreas* the north wind.
36 *Deucalion's flood* See note to *Dido*,
V,i,57.

39 *wingèd messenger* Mercury.
42 *Thetis* See note to *Dido*, I,i,132.
43 *steeds* i.e., of his chariot. *Boötes*
See note to *I Tamb.*, I,ii,206.

And lain in leaguer fifteen months and more;
For, since we left you at the Soldan's court,   50
We have subdued the southern Guallatia
And all the land unto the coast of Spain.
We kept the narrow Strait of Gibraltar,
And made Canaria call us kings and lords;
Yet never did they recreate themselves,   55
Or cease one day from war and hot alarms;
And therefore let them rest a while, my lord.
Tamburlaine.   They shall, Casane, and 'tis time, i'faith.
Techelles.   And I have marched along the river Nile
To Machda, where the mighty Christian priest,   60
Called John the Great, sits in a milk-white robe,
Whose triple mitre I did take by force,
And made him swear obedience to my crown.
From thence unto Cazates did I march,
Where Amazonians met me in the field,   65
With whom, being women, I vouchsafed a league,
And with my power did march to Zanzibar,
The western part of Afric, where I viewed
The Ethiopian sea, rivers and lakes,
But neither man nor child in all the land.   70
Therefore I took my course to Manico,
Where, unresisted, I removed my camp;
And, by the coast of Byather, at last
I came to Cubar, where the negroes dwell,
And, conquering that, made haste to Nubia.   75
There, having sacked Borno, the kingly seat,
I took the king and led him bound in chains
Unto Damascus, where I stayed before.
Tamburlaine.   Well done, Techelles. What saith **Theridamas?**
Theridamas.   I left the confines and the bounds of Afric,   80
And made a voyage into Europe,

---

49 *in leaguer* in camp.
51 *Guallatia* Gualata, a province in North Africa.
54 *Canaria* the Canary islands.
60 *Machda* an Abyssinian town on a tributary of the Nile.
64 *Cazates* a town in *Amazonum regio* (see note at I,i,73–74) where the Nile rises out of the great body of water we today call Lake Victoria.
65 *Amazonians* warlike women supposed to inhabit *Amazonum regio*, although according to Greek legendry they came from the Caucasus and settled in Asia Minor.

67–68 *Zanzibar . . . Afric* Marlowe, following the maps of Ortelius, takes Zanzibar as the entire west coast of Africa.
69 *Ethiopian sea* the ocean separating West Africa from South America.
71–76 *Manico . . . Borno* The campaign of Techelles can actually be followed on the maps of Ortelius. He moved from the province of Manicongo (Manico) to Biafar (Byather), another province whose chief town is Gubar (Cubar) and on to Borno, the chief town of the province of Nubia on Lake Borno.

Where by the river Tyros I subdued
Stoka, Padalia, and Codemia;
Then crossed the sea and came to Oblia
And Nigra Silva, where the devils dance,   85
Which, in despite of them, I set on fire.
From thence I crossed the gulf called by the name
Mare Majore of th'inhabitants.
Yet shall my soldiers make no period
Until Natolia kneel before your feet.   90
Tamburlaine.   Then we will triumph, banquet, and carouse.
Cooks shall have pensions to provide us cates
And glut us with the dainties of the world;
Lachryma Christi and Calabrian wines
Shall common soldiers drink in quaffing bowls,   95
Ay, liquid gold,' when we have conquered him,
Minglèd with coral and with orient pearl.
Come, let us banquet and carouse the whiles.

                         Exeunt.

                             II,i.

[Enter] Sigismund, Frederick, [and] Baldwin, with their train.
Sigismund.   Now say, my lords of Buda and Bohemia,
What motion is it that enflames your thoughts,
And stirs your valors to such sudden arms?
Frederick.   Your majesty remembers, I am sure,
What cruel slaughter of our Christian bloods   5
These heathenish Turks and pagans lately made
Betwixt the city Zula and Danubius;
How through the midst of Varna and Bulgaria,
And almost to the very walls of Rome,
They have, not long since, massacred our camp.   10
It resteth now, then, that your majesty
Take all advantages of time and power

82–90 *Tyros . . . Natolia* The march of Theridamas in Eastern Europe can also be traced on the maps of Ortelius. He moved along the river Dniester (Tyros) which serves as the southern boundary of the province of Podolia (Padalia). He subdued the city of Stoko (Stoka) on the river and the city of Codemia close by it on another stream. Between Codemia and Olbia (Oblia) is an area called the Nigra Silva or Black Forest, but what sea he had to cross here is not clear. From the general region of present-day Odessa he then crossed the Black Sea (Mare Majore) and so passed into Asia Minor.

92 *cates* delicacies.

94 *Lachryma Christi* a sweet wine made in southern Italy.

II,i.

7 *Zula* a city which the maps of Ortelius locate north of the Danube river.

9 *Rome* possibly Roumania.

And work revenge upon these infidels.
Your highness knows, for Tamburlaine's repair,
That strikes a terror to all Turkish hearts,   15
Natolia hath dismissed the greatest part
Of all his army pitched against our power
Betwixt Cutheia and Orminius' mount,
And sent them marching up to Belgasar,
Acantha, Antioch, and Cæsarea,   20
To aid the kings of Soria and Jerusalem.
Now then, my lord, advantage take hereof
And issue suddenly upon the rest,
That in the fortune of their overthrow
We may discourage all the pagan troop   25
That dare attempt to war with Christians.
Sigismund.   But calls not then your grace to memory
The league we lately made with King Orcanes,
Confirmed by oath and articles of peace,
And calling Christ for record of our truths?   30
This should be treachery and violence
Against the grace of our profession.
Baldwin.   No whit, my lord; for with such infidels,
In whom no faith nor true religion rests,
We are not bound to those accomplishments   35
The holy laws of Christendom enjoin;
But as the faith which they profanely plight
Is not by necessary policy
To be esteemed assurance for ourselves,
So what we vow to them should not infringe   40
Our liberty of arms and victory.
Sigismund.   Though I confess the oaths they undertake
Breed little strength to our security,
Yet those infirmities that thus defame
Their faiths, their honors, and their religion   45
Should not give us presumption to the like.
Our faiths are sound, and must be consummate,
Religious, righteous, and inviolate.
Frederick.   Assure your grace, 'tis superstition
To stand so strictly on dispensive faith;   50
And should we lose the opportunity
That God hath given to venge our Christians' death
And scourge their foul blasphemous paganism,

---

14 *repair* return.
18–20 *Betwixt . . . Cæsarea* The passage describes the movement of Orcanes' army through various places in Asia Minor.

35 *accomplishments* performance of obligations.
47 *consummate* perfect, of the highest quality.
50 *dispensive faith* faith which may be set aside by special dispensation.

As fell to Saul, to Balaam, and the rest,
That would not kill and curse at God's command,   55
So surely will the vengeance of the Highest,
And jealous anger of his fearful arm,
Be poured with rigor on our sinful heads,
If we neglect this offered victory.
Sigismund.   Then arm, my lords, and issue suddenly,   60
Giving commandment to our general host,
With expedition to assail the pagan,
And take the victory our God hath given.

                                   Exeunt.

                                                        II,ii.
   [*Enter*] *Orcanes, Gazellus,* [*and*] *Uribassa, with their train.*
Orcanes.   Gazellus, Uribassa, and the rest,
Now we will march from proud Orminius' mount
To fair Natolia, where our neighbor kings
Expect our power and our royal presence,
T'encounter with the cruel Tamburlaine,   5
That nigh Larissa sways a mighty host,
And with the thunder of his martial tools
Makes earthquakes in the hearts of men and heaven.
Gazellus.   And now come we to make his sinews shake
With greater power than erst his pride hath felt.   10
An hundred kings, by scores, will bid him arms,
And hundred thousands subjects to each score;
Which, if a shower of wounding thunderbolts
Should break out of the bowels of the clouds
And fall as thick as hail upon our heads,   15
In partial aid of that proud Scythian,
Yet should our courages and steelèd crests,
And numbers more than infinite of men,
Be able to withstand and conquer him.
Uribassa.   Methinks I see how glad the Christian king   20
Is made for joy of your admitted truce,
That could not but before be terrified
With unacquainted power of our host.
                     Enter a Messenger.

                              II,ii.

54 *Balaam* Marlowe's biblical allusion is somewhat confused, for Balaam was ordered by God not to curse the children of Israel. See Numbers, XXII.
62 *expedition* speed.

2 *Orminius' mount* Mount Horminius in Asia Minor.
6 *Larissa* See note at I,iv,5.
11 *bid him arms* challenge him to combat.

Messenger.   Arm, dread sovereign, and my noble lords!
   The treacherous army of the Christians,   25
   Taking advantage of your slender power,
   Comes marching on us and determines straight
   To bid us battle for our dearest lives.
Orcanes.   Traitors, villains, damnèd Christians!
   Have I not here the articles of peace   30
   And solemn covenants we have both confirmed,
   He by his Christ and I by Mahomet?
Gazellus.   Hell and confusion light upon their heads,
   That with such treason seek our overthrow,
   And cares so little for their prophet Christ!   35
Orcanes.   Can there be such deceit in Christians
   Or treason in the fleshly heart of man,
   Whose shape is figure of the highest God?
   Then if there be a Christ, as Christians say,
   But in their deeds deny him for their Christ,   40
   If he be son to everliving Jove,
   And hath the power of his outstretchèd arm,
   If he be jealous of his name and honor
   As is our holy prophet Mahomet,
   Take here these papers as our sacrifice   45
   And witness of Thy servant's perjury.
               [He tears to pieces the articles of peace.]
   Open, thou shining veil of Cynthia,
   And make a passage from the imperial heaven,
   That He that sits on high and never sleeps,
   Nor in one place is circumscriptible,   50
   But everywhere fills every continent
   With strange infusion of His sacred vigor,
   May, in His endless power and purity,
   Behold and venge this traitor's perjury!
   Thou Christ that art esteemed omnipotent,   55
   If thou wilt prove thyself a perfect God,
   Worthy the worship of all faithful hearts,
   Be now revenged upon this traitor's soul,
   And make the power I have left behind—
   Too little to defend our guiltless lives—   60
   Sufficient to discomfort and confound
   The trustless force of those false Christians.
   To arms, my lords! On Christ still let us cry.
   If there be Christ, we shall have victory.
                                 [Exeunt.]

48 *imperial* See note at *I Tamb.*, II, vii,15 and IV,iv,30.

II,iii.

Sound to the battle, and Sigismund comes out wounded.

Sigismund. Discomfited is all the Christian host,
And God hath thundered vengeance from on high
For my accursed and hateful perjury.
O just and dreadful punisher of sin,
Let the dishonor of the pains I feel   5
In this my mortal well-deservèd wound
End all my penance in my sudden death!
And let this death, wherein to sin I die,
Conceive a second life in endless mercy!

                                       [He dies.]

Enter Orcanes, Gazellus, Uribassa, with others.

Orcanes. Now lie the Christians bathing in their bloods,   10
And Christ or Mahomet hath been my friend.

Gazellus. See here the perjured traitor Hungary,
Bloody and breathless for his villainy.

Orcanes. Now shall his barbarous body be a prey
To beasts and fowls, and all the winds shall breathe   15
Through shady leaves of every senseless tree,
Murmurs and hisses for his heinous sin.
Now scalds his soul in the Tartarian streams
And feeds upon the baneful tree of hell,
That Zoacum, that fruit of bitterness,   20
That in the midst of fire is engraffed,
Yet flourisheth as Flora in her pride,
With apples like the heads of damnèd fiends.
The devils there, in chains of quenchless flame,
Shall lead his soul through Orcus' burning gulf,   25
From pain to pain, whose change shall never end.
What say'st thou yet, Gazellus, to his foil,
Which we referred to justice of his Christ
And to His power, which here appears as full
As rays of Cynthia to the clearest sight?   30

Gazellus. 'Tis but the fortune of the wars, my lord,
Whose power is often proved a miracle.

Orcanes. Yet in my thoughts shall Christ be honorèd,
Not doing Mahomet an injury,
Whose power had share in this our victory;   35
And since this miscreant hath disgraced his faith
And died a traitor both to heaven and earth,

II,iii.

20 *Zoacum* (or *Ezecum*) a tree of hell
described in the thirty-seventh chapter
of the Koran.
22 *Flora* the goddess of springtime and
flowers.

25 *Orcus* the Greek Hades. Marlowe in
this passage fuses Moslem, Christian,
and Greek notions of hell.
27 *foil* disgrace.

We will both watch and ward shall keep his trunk
Amidst these plains for fowls to prey upon.
Go, Uribassa, give it straight in charge.   40
Uribassa. I will, my lord.

                              Exit Uribassa.

Orcanes. And now, Gazellus, let us haste and meet
Our army, and our brother of Jerusalem,
Of Soria, Trebizon, and Amasia,
And happily, with full Natolian bowls   45
Of Greekish wine, now let us celebrate
Our happy conquest and his angry fate.

                                Exeunt.

                                    II,iv.

The arras is drawn, and Zenocrate lies in her bed of state,
[with] Tamburlaine sitting by her, three Physicians about her
bed, tempering potions, [and] Theridamas, Techelles, Usum-
casane and the three sons.

Tamburlaine. Black is the beauty of the brightest day;
The golden ball of heaven's eternal fire,
That danced with glory on the silver waves,
Now wants the fuel that inflamed his beams,
And all with faintness and for foul disgrace,   5
He binds his temples with a frowning cloud,
Ready to darken earth with endless night.
Zenocrate, that gave him light and life,
Whose eyes shot fire from their ivory bowers,
And tempered every soul with lively heat,   10
Now by the malice of the angry skies,
Whose jealousy admits no second mate,
Draws in the comfort of her latest breath,
All dazzled with the hellish mists of death.
Now walk the angels on the walls of heaven,   15
As sentinels to warn th'immortal souls
To entertain divine Zenocrate.
Apollo, Cynthia, and the ceaseless lamps
That gently looked upon this loathsome earth
Shine downwards now no more, but deck the heavens   20
To entertain divine Zenocrate.
The crystal springs, whose taste illuminates
Refinèd eyes with an eternal sight,

II,iv.
   4 *inflamed* filled with flame.   9 *bowers* i.e., places wherein her eyes
                                              are set.

Like trièd silver runs through Paradise
To entertain divine Zenocrate.   25
The cherubins and holy seraphins,
That sing and play before the King of Kings,
Use all their voices and their instruments
To entertain divine Zenocrate.
And in this sweet and curious harmony,   30
The god that tunes this music to our souls
Holds out his hand in highest majesty
To entertain divine Zenocrate.
Then let some holy trance convey my thoughts
Up to the palace of th'imperial heaven,   35
That this my life may be as short to me
As are the days of sweet Zenocrate.
Physicians, will no physic do her good?
First Physician.   My lord, your majesty shall soon perceive,
And if she pass this fit, the worst is past.   40
Tamburlaine.   Tell me, how fares my fair Zenocrate?
Zenocrate.   I fare, my lord, as other empresses,
That, when this frail and transitory flesh
Hath sucked the measure of that vital air
That feeds the body wth his dated health,   45
Wane with enforced and necessary change.
Tamburlaine.   May never such a change transform my love,
In whose sweet being I repose my life,
Whose heavenly presence, beautified with health,
Gives light to Phœbus and the fixèd stars,   50
Whose absence makes the sun and moon as dark
As when, opposed in one diameter,
Their spheres are mounted on the serpent's head,
Or else descended to his winding train.
Live still, my love, and so conserve my life,   55
Or, dying, be the author of my death.
Zenocrate.   Live still, my lord! Oh, let my sovereign live!
And sooner let the fiery element
Dissolve and make your kingdom in the sky,
Than this base earth should shroud your majesty;   60
For, should I but suspect your death by mine,
The comfort of my future happiness
And hope to meet your highness in the heavens,
Turned to despair, would break my wretched breast,
And fury would confound my present rest.   65

35 *imperial* See note at II,ii,48.
45 *dated* limited.
52 *opposed in one diameter* in eclipse, the moon being exactly opposite to the sun, with the earth between them.
53–54 *spheres . . . train* i.e., when, as part of the eclipse, either the head or the tail of the constellation Scorpio (the serpent) falls in the same plane as the earth, sun, and moon. Why Marlowe considers this phenomenon as necessary to an eclipse is not clear.

But let me die, my love; yet let me die;
With love and patience let your true love die.
Your grief and fury hurts my second life.
Yet let me kiss my lord before I die,
And let me die with kissing of my lord.   70
But since my life is lengthened yet a while,
Let me take leave of these my loving sons,
And of my lords, whose true nobility
Have merited my latest memory.
Sweet sons, farewell! In death resemble me,   75
And in your lives your father's excellency.
Some music, and my fit will cease, my lord.

                                            They call [for] music.

Tamburlaine.   Proud fury and intolerable fit,
That dares torment the body of my love
And scourge the scourge of the immortal God!   80
Now are those spheres where Cupid used to sit,
Wounding the world with wonder and with love,
Sadly supplied with pale and ghastly death,
Whose darts do pierce the center of my soul.
Her sacred beauty hath enchanted heaven,   85
And had she lived before the siege of Troy,
Helen, whose beauty summoned Greece to arms
And drew a thousand ships to Tenedos,
Had not been named in Homer's Iliads;
Her name had been in every line he wrote.   90
Or, had those wanton poets, for whose birth
Old Rome was proud, but gazed a while on her,
Nor Lesbia nor Corinna had been named;
Zenocrate had been the argument
Of every epigram or elegy.   95

                                    The music sounds, and she dies.

What, is she dead? Techelles, draw thy sword
And wound the earth, that it may cleave in twain
And we descend into th'infernal vaults,
To hale the Fatal Sisters by the hair
And throw them in the triple moat of hell,   100
For taking hence my fair Zenocrate.
Casane and Theridamas, to arms!
Raise cavalieros higher than the clouds,
And with the cannon break the frame of heaven.
Batter the shining palace of the sun,   105

88 *Tenedos* an island in the Aegean sea to which the Greeks withdrew their fleet in order to make the Trojans think they had departed.

90 *Her* i.e., Zenocrate's.

93 *Lesbia . . . Corinna* ladies cele- brated in the Latin love poetry of Ovid, Horace, and Catullus.

99 *Fatal Sisters* See note to *Dido*, III, ii,3.

103 *cavalieros* mounds on which cannon were placed.

And shiver all the starry firmament,
For amorous Jove hath snatched my love from hence,
Meaning to make her stately queen of heaven.
What god soever holds thee in his arms,
Giving thee nectar and ambrosia,   110
Behold me here, divine Zenocrate,
Raving, impatient, desperate, and mad,
Breaking my steelèd lance, with which I burst
The rusty beams of Janus' temple doors,
Letting out death and tyrannising war,   115
To march with me under this bloody flag!
And, if thou pitiest Tamburlaine the Great,
Come down from heaven, and live with me again!
Theridamas. Ah, good my lord, be patient. She is dead,
And all this raging cannot make her live.   120
If words might serve, our voice hath rent the air;
If tears, our eyes have watered all the earth;
If grief, our murdered hearts have strained forth blood.
Nothing prevails, for she is dead, my lord.
Tamburlaine. For she is dead! Thy words do pierce my soul!   125
Ah, sweet Theridamas, say so no more.
Though she be dead, yet let me think she lives
And feed my mind that dies for want of her.
Where'er her soul be, thou [*to the body*] shalt stay with me,
Embalmed with cassia, ambergris, and myrrh,   130
Not lapped in lead, but in a sheet of gold,
And till I die thou shalt not be interred.
Then in as rich a tomb as Mausolus'
We both will rest and have one epitaph
Writ in as many several languages   135
As I have conquered kingdoms with my sword.
This cursed town will I consume with fire,
Because this place bereft me of my love;
The houses, burnt, will look as if they mourned;
And here will I set up her statue   140
And march about it with my mourning camp,
Drooping and pining for Zenocrate.

                              The arras is drawn.

114 *Janus' temple doors* The doors of
the temple of Janus in Rome stood
open in time of war and were closed in
time of peace.

133 *Mausolus* king of Caria, whose
wife (also his sister) Artemisia built a
costly tomb for him after his death,
called the Mausoleum.

III,i.

Enter the Kings of Trebizon and Soria, one bringing a sword
and another a scepter. [Enter] next [Orcanes, King of] Natolia,
and [the King of] Jerusalem, with the imperial crown. After
[them, enter] Callapine, and after him [Almeda] and other
Lords. Orcanes and [the King of] Jerusalem crown Callapine,
and the other[s] give him the scepter.

Orcanes. Callapinus Cyricelibes, otherwise Cybelius, son and successive
   heir to the late mighty emperor, Bajazeth, by the aid of God and his
   friend Mahomet, Emperor of Natolia, Jerusalem, Trebizon, Soria,
   Amasia, Thracia, Illyria, Carmonia, and all the hundred and thirty
   kingdoms late contributory to his mighty father. Long live [5
   Callapinus, Emperor of Turkey!

Callapine. Thrice worthy kings, of Natolia and the rest,
   I will requite your royal gratitudes
   With all the benefits my empire yields;
   And were the sinews of th'imperial seat   10
   So knit and strengthened as when Bajazeth,
   My royal lord and father, filled the throne,
   Whose cursèd fate hath so dismembered it,
   Then should you see this thief of Scythia,
   This proud usurping king of Persia,   15
   Do us such honor and supremacy,
   Bearing the vengeance of our father's wrongs,
   As all the world should blot our dignities
   Out of the book of base born infamies.
   And now I doubt not but your royal cares   20
   Hath so provided for this cursèd foe,
   That, since the heir of mighty Bajazeth—
   An emperor so honored for his virtues—
   Revives the spirits of true Turkish hearts,
   In grievous memory of his father's shame,   25
   We shall not need to nourish any doubt,
   But that proud Fortune, who hath followed long
   The martial sword of mighty Tamburlaine,
   Will now retain her old inconstancy
   And raise our honors to as high a pitch,   30
   In this our strong and fortunate encounter;
   For so hath heaven provided my escape
   From all the cruelty my soul sustained,
   By this my friendly keeper's happy means,
   That Jove, surcharged wth pity of our wrongs,   35
   Will pour it down in showers on our heads,
   Scourging the pride of cursèd Tamburlaine.

Orcanes. I have a hundred thousand men in arms,
   Some, that in conquest of the perjured Christian,

Being a handful to a mighty host,   40
Think them in number yet sufficient
To drink the river Nile or Euphrates,
And for their power enow to win the world.

King of Jerusalem.   And I as many from Jerusalem,
Judæa, Gaza, and Scalonians' bounds,   45
That on mount Sinai, with their ensigns spread,
Look like the parti-colored clouds of heaven
That show fair weather to the neighbor morn.

King of Trebizon.   And I as many bring from Trebizon,
Chio, Famastro, and Amasia,   50
All bordering on the Mare Major Sea,
Riso, Sancina, and the bordering towns
That touch the end of famous Euphrates,
Whose courages are kindled with the flames
The cursèd Scythian sets on all their towns,   55
And vow to burn the villain's cruel heart.

King of Soria.   From Soria with seventy thousand strong,
Ta'en from Aleppo, Soldino, Tripoli,
And so unto my city of Damascus,
I march to meet and aid my neighbor kings,   60
All which will join against this Tamburlaine
And bring him captive to your highness' feet.

Orcanes.   Our battle then, in martial manner pitched,
According to our ancient use, shall bear
The figure of the semicircled moon,   65
Whose horns shall sprinkle through the tainted air
The poisoned brains of this proud Scythian.

Callapine.   Well, then, my noble lords, for this my friend
That freed me from the bondage of my foe,
I think it requisite and honorable   70
To keep my promise and to make him king,
That is a gentleman, I know, at least.

Almeda.   That's no matter, sir, for being a king, for Tamburlaine
came up of nothing.

King of Jerusalem.   Your majesty may choose some 'pointed time,   75
Performing all your promise to the full.
'Tis naught for your majesty to give a kingdom.

III,i.
43 *enow* enough.
45 *Scalonians* men of Ascalon, often
called Scalona on ancient maps.
51 *Mare Major Sea* Black Sea.
57–59 *From Soria . . . Damascus* The
movement is from Aleppo southward
to the sea coast near Cyprus, passing
Soldino and Tripoli, and then inland
to Damascus.
63–65 *battle . . . moon* The crescent-
shaped battle formation was a favorite
among the ancients.

Callapine. Then will I shortly keep my promise, Almeda.
Almeda. Why, I thank your majesty.

                                           Exeunt.

                                                          III,ii.

[Enter] Tamburlaine, with Usumcasane and his three sons;
four [Attendants] bearing the hearse of Zenocrate, and the
drums sounding a doleful march; the town burning.
Tamburlaine. So, burn the turrets of this cursèd town,
  Flame to the highest region of the air,
  And kindle heaps of exhalations
  That, being fiery meteors, may presage
  Death and destruction to th'inhabitants!   5
  Over my zenith hang a blazing star,
  That may endure till heaven be dissolved,
  Fed with the fresh supply of earthly dregs,
  Threatening a dearth and famine to this land!
  Flying dragons, lightning, fearful thunder-claps,   10
  Singe these fair plains, and make them seem as black
  As is the island where the Furies mask,
  Compassed with Lethe, Styx, and Phlegethon,
  Because my dear Zenocrate is dead.
Calyphas. This pillar, placed in memory of her,   15
  Where in Arabian, Hebrew, Greek, is writ,
  This town, being burnt by Tamburlaine the Great,
  Forbids the world to build it up again.
Amyras. And here this mournful streamer shall be placed,
  Wrought with the Persian and Egyptian arms,   20
  To signify she was a princess born
  And wife unto the monarch of the East.
Celebinus. And here this table as a register
  Of all her virtues and perfections.
Tamburlaine. And here the picture of Zenocrate,   25
  To show her beauty which the world admired;

III,ii.

2-9 *Flame . . . land* i.e., may the flames of the burning town rise as high as the uppermost limit of the atmosphere, believed in Ptolemaic astronomy to be next to the sphere of the moon, and may these flames create meteors which—since meteors traditionally were regarded as signs of coming disasters—might give prophecy of the death and destruction to follow. At the same time, in a direct line over Tamburlaine's head, may a burning star hang, to be kept in flame by the continuing fires of destruction which he will light on earth, and may this star also presage death and famine on earth.

13 *Lethe, Styx and Phlegethon* the rivers of the Greek underworld.

20 *Wrought* embroidered.

Sweet picture of divine Zenocrate,
That, hanging here, will draw the gods from heaven
And cause the stars fixed in the southern arc,
Whose lovely faces never any viewed   30
That have not passed the center's latitude,
As pilgrims travel to our hemisphere,
Only to gaze upon Zenocrate.
Thou shalt not beautify Larissa plains,
But keep within the circle of mine arms;   35
At every town and castle I besiege,
Thou shalt be set upon my royal tent;
And when I meet an army in the field,
Those looks will shed such influence in my camp,
As if Bellona, goddess of the war,   40
Threw naked swords and sulphur balls of fire
Upon the heads of all our enemies.
And now, my lords, advance your spears again.
Sorrow no more, my sweet Casane, now.
Boys, leave to mourn; this town shall ever mourn,   45
Being burnt to cinders for your mother's death.
Calyphas.   If I had wept a sea of tears for her,
It would not ease the sorrows I sustain.
Amyras.   As is that town, so is my heart consumed
With grief and sorrow for my mother's death.   50
Celebinus.   My mother's death hath mortified my mind,
And sorrow stops the passage of my speech.
Tamburlaine.   But now, my boys, leave off and list to me,
That mean to teach you rudiments of war.
I'll have you learn to sleep upon the ground,   55
March in your armor thorough watery fens,
Sustain the scorching heat and freezing cold,
Hunger and thirst, right adjuncts of the war,
And after this, to scale a castle wall,
Besiege a fort, to undermine a town,   60
And make whole cities caper in the air.
Then next, the way to fortify your men,
In champion grounds what figure serves you best,
For which the quinque-angle form is meet,
Because the corners there may fall more flat   65
Whereas the fort may fittest be assailed,

29-32 *stars . . . hemisphere* i.e., the southern stars, seen only by those who have passed below the equator (center's latitude), will travel to the northern half of the globe (hemisphere) in order to see Zenocrate.

34 *Larissa* See note at I,iv,5.

40 *Bellona* Roman goddess of war,

usually regarded as the sister or wife of Mars.

41 *sulphur balls of fire* probably the primitive ancestors of our hand grenades.

63 *champion* level.

64 *quinque-angle form* star-shaped fort

66 *Whereas* where.

And sharpest where th'assault is desperate.
The ditches must be deep, the counterscarps
Narrow and steep, the walls made high and broad,
The bulwarks and the rampires large and strong,   70
With cavalieros and thick counterforts,
And room within to lodge six thousand men.
It must have privy ditches, countermines,
And secret issuings to defend the ditch.
It must have high argins and covered ways   75
To keep the bulwark fronts from battery,
And parapets to hide the musketeers,
Casemates to place the great artillery,
And store of ordnance, that from every flank
May scour the outward curtains of the fort,   80
Dismount the cannon of the adverse part,
Murder the foe, and save the walls from breach.
When this is learned for service on the land,
By plain and easy demonstration
I'll teach you how to make the water mount,   85
That you may dry-foot march through lakes and pools,
Deep rivers, havens, creeks, and little seas,
And make a fortress in the raging waves,
Fenced with the concave of a monstrous rock,
Invincible by nature of the place.   90
When this is done, then are ye soldiers
And worthy sons of Tamburlaine the Great.
Calyphas.   My lord, but this is dangerous to be done;
We may be slain or wounded ere we learn.
Tamburlaine.   Villain, art thou the son of Tamburlaine,   95
And fear'st to die, or with a curtle-axe
To hew thy flesh and make a gaping wound?
Hast thou beheld a peal of ordnance strike
A ring of pikes, minglèd with shot and horse,
Whose shattered limbs, being tossed as high as heaven,   100
Hang in the air as thick as sunny motes,
And canst thou, coward, stand in fear of death?
Hast thou not seen my horsemen charge the foe,
Shot through the arms, cut overthwart the hands,
Dyeing their lances with their streaming blood,   105
And yet at night carouse within my tent,
Filling their empty veins with airy wine,

---

68 *counterscarps* walls of the ditches facing a fort.

70 *rampires* ramparts.

71 *cavalieros* See note at II,iv,103.

75 *argins* earthworks. *covered ways* protected passages between earthworks and counterscarps.

78 *Casemates* vaulted chambers within the ramparts of a fortress.

80 *curtains of the fort* walls connecting the fortress towers.

101 *sunny motes* particles of dust in the sunlight.

That, being concocted, turns to crimson blood,
And wilt thou shun the field for fear of wounds?
View me, thy father, that hath conquered kings,   110
And with his host marched round about the earth,
Quite void of scars and clear from any wound,
That by the wars lost not a dram of blood,
And see him lance his flesh to teach you all.

                                        He cuts his arm.

A wound is nothing, be it ne'er so deep;   115
Blood is the god of war's rich livery.
Now look I like a soldier, and this wound
As great a grace and majesty to me,
As if a chair of gold enamellèd,
Enchased with diamonds, sapphires, rubies,   120
And fairest pearl of wealthy India,
Were mounted here under a canopy,
And I sat down, clothed with the massy robe
That late adorned the Afric potentate,
Whom I brought bound unto Damascus' walls.   125
Come, boys, and with your fingers search my wound,
And in my blood wash all your hands at once,
While I sit smiling to behold the sight.
Now, my boys, what think you of a wound?

Calyphas.   I know not what I should think of it. Methinks 'tis a   [130
    pitiful sight.
Celebinus.   'Tis nothing. Give me a wound, father.
Amyras.   And me another, my lord.
Tamburlaine.   Come, sirrah, give me your arm.
Celebinus.   Here, father, cut it bravely, as you did your own.   135
Tamburlaine.   It shall suffice thou dar'st abide a wound.
My boy, thou shalt not lose a drop of blood
Before we meet the army of the Turk;
But then run desperate through the thickest throngs,
Dreadless of blows, of bloody wounds, and death;   140
And let the burning of Larissa walls,
My speech of war, and this my wound you see,
Teach you, my boys, to bear courageous minds,
Fit for the followers of great Tamburlaine.
Usumcasane, now come let us march   145
Towards Techelles and Theridamas,
That we have sent before to fire the towns,
The towers and cities of these hateful Turks,
And hunt that coward faint-heart runaway,
With that accursèd traitor, Almeda,   150
Till fire and sword have found them at a bay.
Usumcasane.   I long to pierce his bowels with my sword,

124 *Afric potentate* i.e., Bajazeth.

That hath betrayed my gracious sovereign,
That cursed and damnèd traitor, Almeda.
Tamburlaine.   Then let us see if coward Callapine   155
Dare levy arms against our puissance,
That we may tread upon his captive neck,
And treble all his father's slaveries.

                                        Exeunt.

*

     [*Enter*] *Techelles, Theridamas, and their train.*   III,iii.
Theridamas.   Thus have we marched northward from Tamburlaine,
   Unto the frontier point of Soria,
   And this is Balsera, their chiefest hold,
   Wherein is all the treasure of the land.
Techelles.   Then let us bring our light artillery,   5
   Minions, falc'nets, and sakers, to the trench,
   Filling the ditches with the walls' wide breach,
   And enter in to seize upon the gold.
   How say ye, soldiers; shall we not?
Soldiers.   Yes, my lord, yes; come, let's about it.   10
Theridamas.   But stay a while; summon a parle, drum.
   It may be they will yield it quietly,
   Knowing two kings, the friends to Tamburlaine,
   Stand at the walls with such a mighty power.
     [*A*] *Summon*[*s to*] *the battle* [*is sounded*]. [*The*] *Captain, with*
     [*Olympia*], *his wife and* [*their young*] *son* [*appear on the walls*].
Captain.   What require you, my masters?   15
Theridamas.   Captain, that thou yield up thy hold to us.
Captain.   To you! Why, do you think me weary of it?
Techelles.   Nay, captain, thou art weary of thy life
   If thou withstand the friends of Tamburlaine.
Theridamas.   These pioners of Argier in Africa   20
   Even in the cannon's face shall raise a hill
   Of earth and faggots higher than thy fort,
   And over thy argins and covered ways
   Shall play upon the bulwarks of thy hold
   Volleys of ordnance, till the breach be made   25
   That with his ruin fills up all the trench;
   And, when we enter in, not heaven itself
   Shall ransom thee, thy wife, and family.

III,iii.

  3 *Balsera* probably Passera, a town in
Natolia indicated on the maps of Ortelius.
  6 *Minions, falc'nets, and sakers* small
ordnance pieces.

  20 *pioners* trench diggers. *Argier* Algeria.
  23 *argins . . . ways* See note at III.
ii,75.

Techelles.   Captain, these Moors shall cut the leaden pipes
   That bring fresh water to thy men and thee,   30
   And lie in trench before thy castle walls,
   That no supply of victual shall come in,
   Nor [any] issue forth but they shall die;
   And, therefore, captain, yield it quietly.
Captain.   Were you, that are the friends of Tamburlaine,   35
   Brothers to holy Mahomet himself,
   I would not yield it; therefore do your worst.
   Raise mounts, batter, intrench, and undermine,
   Cut off the water, all convoys that can,
   Yet I am resolute; and so, farewell.   40
      [*The Captain, Olympia, and their son retire from the walls.*]
Theridamas.   Pioners, away! And where I struck the stake,
   Intrench with those dimensions I prescribed;
   Cast up the earth towards the castle wall,
   Which, till it may defend you, labor low,
   And few or none shall perish by their shot.   45
Pioners. We will, my lord.
                      Exeunt [*Pioners*].

Techelles.   A hundred horse shall scout about the plains
   To spy what force comes to relieve the hold.
   Both we, Theridamas, will intrench our men,
   And with the Jacob's staff measure the height   50
   And distance of the castle from the trench,
   That we may know if our artillery
   Will carry full point blank unto their walls.
Theridamas.   Then see the bringing of our ordinance
   Along the trench into the battery,   55
   Where we will have gabions of six foot broad,
   To save our cannoneers from musket shot;
   Betwixt which shall our ordnance thunder forth,
   And with the breach's fall, smoke, fire, and dust,
   The crack, the echo, and the soldier's cry,   60
   Make deaf the air and dim the crystal sky.
Techelles.   Trumpets and drums, alarum presently!
   And, soldiers, play the men; the hold is yours!
                         [*Exeunt.*]

38 *intrench* dig trenches.
50 *Jacob's staff* an instrument for measuring heights and distances.
54 *ordinance* Here and elsewhere the archaic spelling of the 1590 text is retained for the sake of the meter.
56 *gabions* great baskets filled with earth, used to steady cannons.

III,iv.

[*Alarms within.*] *Enter the Captain, with Olympia, and* [*their*]
                            son.

Olympia.   Come, good my lord, and let us haste from hence
    Along the cave that leads beyond the foe.
    No hope is left to save this conquered hold.
Captain.   A deadly bullet gliding through my side
    Lies heavy on my heart; I cannot live.   5
    I feel my liver pierced, and all my veins,
    That there begin and nourish every part,
    Manglèd and torn, and all my entrails bathed
    In blood that straineth from their orifex.
    Farewell, sweet wife! Sweet son, farewell! I die.   10
                                     [*He dies.*]
Olympia.   Death, whither art thou gone, that both we live?
    Come back again, sweet Death, and strike us both!
    One minute end our days, and one sepulcher
    Contain our bodies! Death, why com'st thou not?
    Well, this must be the messenger for thee.   15
                            [*She draws a dagger.*]
    Now, ugly Death, stretch out thy sable wings
    And carry both our souls where his remains.
    Tell me, sweet boy, art thou content to die?
    These barbarous Scythians, full of cruelty,
    And Moors, in whom was never pity found,   20
    Will hew us piecemeal, put us to the wheel,
    Or else invent some torture worse than that;
    Therefore die by thy loving mother's hand,
    Who gently now will lance thy ivory throat
    And quickly rid thee both of pain and life.   25
Son.   Mother, dispatch me, or I'll kill myself;
    For think ye I can live and see him dead?
    Give me your knife, good mother, or strike home;
    The Scythians shall not tyrannize on me.
    Sweet mother, strike, that I may meet my father.   30
                            She stabs him, [*and he dies*].
Olympia.   Ah, sacred Mahomet, if this be sin,
    Entreat a pardon of the God of heaven,
    And purge my soul before it come to thee.
            [*She burns the bodies of her husband and son, and
                        then attempts to kill herself.*]

    Enter Theridamas, Techelles, and all their train.
Theridamas.   How now, madam, what are you doing?
Olympia.   Killing myself, as I have done my son,   35

III,iv.
    9 *orifex* orifice.

Whose body, with his father's, I have burnt,
Lest cruel Scythians should dismember him.
Techelles. 'Twas bravely done, and like a soldier's wife.
   Thou shalt with us to Tamburlaine the Great,
   Who, when he hears how resolute thou wert,   40
   Will match thee with a viceroy or a king.
Olympia. My lord deceased was dearer unto me
   Than any viceroy, king, or emperor;
   And for his sake here will I end my days.
Theridamas. But, lady, go with us to Tamburlaine,   45
   And thou shalt see a man greater than Mahomet,
   In whose high looks is much more majesty
   Than from the concave superficies
   Of Jove's vast palace, the imperial orb,
   Unto the shining bower where Cynthia sits,   50
   Like lovely Thetis, in a crystal robe;
   That treadeth fortune underneath his feet
   And makes the mighty god of arms his slave;
   On whom Death and the Fatal Sisters wait
   With naked swords and scarlet liveries;   55
   Before whom, mounted on a lion's back,
   Rhamnusia bears a helmet full of blood
   And strows the way with brains of slaughtered men;
   By whose proud side the ugly Furies run,
   Hearkening when he shall bid them plague the world;   60
   Over whose zenith, clothed in windy air,
   And eagle's wings joined to her feathered breast,
   Fame hovereth, sounding of her golden trump,
   That to the adverse poles of that straight line
   Which measureth the glorious frame of heaven   65
   The name of mighty Tamburlaine is spread;
   And him, fair lady, shall thy eyes behold.
   Come.
Olympia. Take pity of a lady's ruthful tears,
   That humbly craves upon her knees to stay   70
   And cast her body in the burning flame
   That feeds upon her son's and husband's flesh.
Techelles. Madam, sooner shall fire consume us both
   Than scorch a face so beautiful as this,

47–51 *In whose . . . robe* i.e., **in** whose looks there is more majesty than may be found in all of heaven, from the hollow roof (concave superficies) of Jove's palace itself to the bower where the moon (Cynthia) sits, like the sea-deity Thetis, wearing a veil of crystal.
53 *god of arms* Mars.

54 *Fatal Sisters* the Parcae. See note to *Dido*, III,ii,3.
57 *Rhamnusia* Nemesis. See note to *Dido*, III,ii,20.
58 *strows* strews.
59 *Furies* See note to *Dido*, II,i,230.
61 *zenith* crest, or head.
64–65 *adverse . . . heaven* the diameter of the sphere of heaven.

In frame of which nature hath showed more skill   75
Than when she gave eternal chaos form,
Drawing from it the shining lamps of heaven.
Theridamas. Madam, I am so far in love with you
That you must go with us—no remedy.
Olympia. Then carry me, I care not, where you will,   80
And let the end of this my fatal journey
Be likewise end to my accursèd life.
Techelles. No, madam, but the beginning of your joy.
Come willingly, therefore.
Theridamas. Soldiers, now let us meet the general,   85
Who by this time is at Natolia,
Ready to charge the army of the Turk.
The gold, the silver, and the pearl ye got,
Rifling this fort, divide in equal shares:
This lady shall have twice so much again   90
Out of the coffers of our treasury.

                                                    Exeunt.

✱

                                                      III,v.
[*Enter*] *Callapine, Orcanes,* [*the Kings of*] *Jerusalem, Trebizon,*
      and Soria, with their train, Almeda, [*and a Messenger*].
Messenger. Renownèd emperor, mighty Callapine,
God's great lieutenant over all the world,
Here at Aleppo, with an host of men,
Lies Tamburlaine, this king of Persia,
In number more than are the quivering leaves   5
Of Ida's forest, where your highness' hounds
With open cry pursues the wounded stag,
Who means to girt Natolia's walls with siege,
Fire the town, and over-run the land.
Callapine. My royal army is as great as his,   10
That, from the bounds of Phrygia to the sea
Which washeth Cyprus with his brinish waves,
Covers the hills, the valleys and the plains.
Viceroys and peers of Turkey, play the men.
Whet all your swords to mangle Tamburlaine,   15
His sons, his captains, and his followers.
By Mahomet, not one of them shall live.
The field wherein this battle shall be fought
For ever term the Persians' sepulcher,
In memory of this our victory.   20

III,v.
   6 *Ida's forest* probably on Mt. Ida in Crete. See note to *Dido,* III,ii,99.

Orcanes.   Now he that calls himself the scourge of Jove,
  The emperor of the world, and earthly god,
  Shall end the warlike progress he intends
  And travel headlong to the lake of hell,
  Where legions of devils, knowing he must die   25
  Here in Natolia by your highness' hands,
  All brandishing their brands of quenchless fire,
  Stretching their monstrous paws, grin with their teeth
  And guard the gates to entertain his soul.
Callapine.   Tell me, viceroys, the number of your men,   30
  And what our army royal is esteemed.
King of Jerusalem.   From Palestina and Jerusalem,
  Of Hebrews three score thousand fighting men
  Are come, since last we showed your majesty.
Orcanes.   So from Arabia desert, and the bounds   35
  Of that sweet land whose brave metropolis
  Re-edified the fair Semiramis,
  Came forty thousand warlike foot and horse,
  Since last we numbered to your majesty.
King of Trebizon.   From Trebizon in Asia the Less,   40
  Naturalizèd Turks and stout Bithynians
  Came to my bands full fifty thousand more,
  That, fighting, knows not what retreat doth mean,
  Nor e'er return but with the victory,
  Since last we numbered to your majesty.   45
King of Soria.   Of Sorians from Halla is repaired,
  And neighbor cities of your highness' land,
  Ten thousand horse and thirty thousand foot,
  Since last we numbered to your majesty;
  So that the army royal is esteemed   50
  Six hundred thousand valiant fighting men.
Callapine.   Then welcome, Tamburlaine, unto thy death.
  Come, puissant viceroys, let us to the field,
  The Persians' sepulcher, and sacrifice
  Mountains of breathless men to Mahomet,   55
  Who now, with Jove, opens the firmament
  To see the slaughter of our enemies.
     [*Enter*] *Tamburlaine with his three sons, Usumcasane, with*
                              other[*s*].
Tamburlaine.   How now, Casane! See, a knot of kings,
  Sitting as if they were a-telling riddles.
Usumcasane.   My lord, your presence makes them pale and wan.   60
  Poor souls, they look as if their deaths were near.

36–37 *sweet land . . . Semiramis* i.e.,   40 *Asia the Less* Asia **Minor.**
Babylon, whose walls supposedly were   46 *Halla* a town to the southeast of
built by Semiramis.   Aleppo.

Tamburlaine.   Why, so he is, Casane; I am here.
   But yet I'll save their lives and make them slaves.
   Ye petty kings of Turkey, I am come,
   As Hector did into the Grecian camp,   65
   To overdare the pride of Græcia
   And set his warlike person to the view
   Of fierce Achilles, rival of his fame.
   I do you honor in the simile;
   For, if I should, as Hector did Achilles,   70
   The worthiest knight that ever brandished sword,
   Challenge in combat any of you all,
   I see how fearfully ye would refuse,
   And fly my glove as from a scorpion.
Orcanes.   Now thou art fearful of thy army's strength,   75
   Thou wouldst with overmatch of person fight.
   But, shepherd's issue, base born Tamburlaine,
   Think of thy end; this sword shall lance thy throat.
Tamburlaine.   Villain, the shepherd's issue, at whose birth
   Heaven did afford a gracious aspect,   80
   And joined those stars that shall be opposite
   Even till the dissolution of the world,
   And never meant to make a conqueror
   So famous as is mighty Tamburlaine,
   Shall so torment thee and that Callapine,   85
   That, like a roguish runaway, suborned
   That villain there, that slave, that Turkish dog,
   To false his service to his sovereign,
   As ye shall curse the birth of Tamburlaine.
Callapine.   Rail not, proud Scythian. I shall now revenge 90
   My father's vile abuses mine own.
King of Jerusalem.   By Mahomet, he shall be tied in chains,
   Rowing with Christians in a brigandine
   About the Grecian isles to rob and spoil,
   And turn him to his ancient trade again.   95
   Methinks the slave should make a lusty thief.
Callapine.   Nay, when the battle ends, all we will meet
   And sit in council to invent some pain
   That most may vex his body and his soul.

65–68 *As Hector . . . fame* No such episode appears in the *Iliad* of Homer. It does occur, however, in Lydgate's *Troy Book* and in other medieval accounts of the Trojan war.

66 *Græcia* Greece.

74 *glove* i.e., thrown down as a challenge.

80–82 *Heaven . . . world* i.e., heaven never again will cause the stars to come into a relationship similar to that at Tamburlaine's birth, and therefore the world will never see another like him. It was commonly believed that a man's life was determined by the conjunction of stars at his birth.

88 *false* betray.

93 *brigandine* See note at I,v,11.

Tamburlaine. Sirrah Callapine, I'll hang a clog about your neck   [100
  for running away again. You shall not trouble me thus to come and
  fetch you.
    But as for you, viceroy, you shall have bits,
    And, harnessed like my horses, draw my coach;
    And, when ye stay, be lashed with whips of wire.   105
    I'll have you learn to feed on provender
    And in a stable lie upon the planks.
Orcanes. But, Tamburlaine, first thou shalt kneel to us
    And humbly crave a pardon for thy life.
King of Trebizon. The common soldiers of our mighty host   110
    Shall bring thee bound unto the general's tent.
King of Soria. And all have jointly sworn thy cruel death,
    Or bind thee in eternal torments' wrath.
Tamburlaine. Well, sirs, diet yourselves; you know I shall have occa-
    sion shortly to journey you.   115
Celebinus. See, father, how Almeda the jailor looks upon us.
Tamburlaine. Villain, traitor, damnèd fugitive.
    I'll make thee wish the earth had swallowed thee.
    See'st thou not death within my wrathful looks?
    Go, villain, cast thee headlong from a rock,   120
    Or rip thy bowels and rend out thy heart
    T'appease my wrath; or else I'll torture thee,
    Searing thy hateful flesh with burning irons
    And drops of scalding lead, while all thy joints
    Be racked and beat asunder with the wheel;   125
    For if thou liv'st, not any element
    Shall shroud thee from the wrath of Tamburlaine.
Callapine. Well, in despite of thee, he shall be king.
    Come, Almeda, receive this crown of me.
    I here invest thee king of Ariadan,   130
    Bordering on Mare Roso, near to Mecca.
Orcanes. What! Take it, man.
Almeda. Good my lord, let me take it.
Callapine. Dost thou ask him leave? Here; take it.
Tamburlaine. Go to, sirrah, take your crown, and make up the   [135
    half dozen. So, sirrah, now you are a king you must give arms.
Orcanes. So he shall, and wear thy head in his scutcheon.
Tamburlaine. No; let him hang a bunch of keys on his standard, to
    put him in remembrance he was a jailor, that, when I take him, I may
    knock out his brains with them, and lock you in the stable,   [140
    when you shall come sweating from my chariot.
King of Trebizon. Away; let us to the field, that the villain may be
    slain.
Tamburlaine. Sirrah, prepare whips, and bring my chariot to my tent;

101 *for* to prevent   131 *Mare Roso* the Red Sea.

for, as soon as the battle is done, I'll ride in triumph through   [145
the camp.

Enter Theridamas, Techelles, and their train.

How now, ye petty kings? Lo, here are bugs
Will make the hair stand upright on your heads,
And cast your crowns in slavery at their feet.
Welcome, Theridamas and Techelles, both.   150
See ye this rout, and know ye this same king?

Theridamas.   Ay, my lord; he was Callapine's keeper.

Tamburlaine.   Well now you see he is a king. Look to him, Theridamas, when we are fighting, lest he hide his crown as the foolish king
of Persia did.   155

King of Soria.   No, Tamburlaine; he shall not be put to that exigent,
I warrant thee.

Tamburlaine.   You know not, sir.
But now, my followers and my loving friends,
Fight as you ever did, like conquerors;   160
The glory of this happy day is yours.
My stern aspect shall make fair Victory,
Hovering betwixt our armies, light on me,
Loaden with laurel wreaths to crown us all.

Techelles.   I smile to think how when this field is fought   165
And rich Natolia ours, our men shall sweat
With carrying pearl and treasure on their backs.

Tamburlaine.   You shall be princes all, immediately.
Come, fight, ye Turks, or yield us victory.

Orcanes.   No; we will meet thee, slavish Tamburlaine.   170

Exeunt.

IV,i.

*Alarm[s within]. Amyras and Celebinus issue from the tent
where Calyphas sits asleep.*

Amyras.   Now in their glories shine the golden crowns
Of these proud Turks, much like so many suns
That half dismay the majesty of heaven.
Now, brother, follow we our father's sword,
That flies with fury swifter than our thoughts   5
And cuts down armies with his conquering wings.

Celebinus.   Call forth our lazy brother from the tent,
For if my father miss him in the field,
Wrath, kindled in the furnace of his breast,
Will send a deadly lightning to his heart.   10

---

147 *bugs* bugbears.   164 *Loaden* laden.

Amyras.   Brother, ho! What, given so much to sleep,
    You cannot leave it when our enemies' drums
    And rattling cannons thunder in our ears
    Our proper ruin and our father's foil?
Calyphas.   Away, ye fools! My father needs not me,   15
    Nor you, in faith, but that you will be thought
    More childish-valorous than manly-wise.
    If half our camp should sit and sleep with me,
    My father were enough to scar the foe.
    You do dishonor to his majesty,   20
    To think our helps will do him any good.
Amyras.   What, dar'st thou then be absent from the fight,
    Knowing my father hates thy cowardice
    And oft hath warned thee to be still in field,
    When he himself amidst the thickest troops   25
    Beats down our foes to flesh our taintless swords?
Calyphas.   I know, sir, what it is to kill a man;
    It works remorse of conscience in me.
    I take no pleasure to be murderous,
    Nor care for blood when wine will quench my thirst.   30
Celebinus.   O cowardly boy! Fie, for shame, come forth!
    Thou dost dishonor manhood and thy house.
Calyphas.   Go, go, tall stripling, fight you for us both,
    And take my other toward brother here,
    For person like to prove a second Mars.   35
    'Twill please my mind as well to hear both you
    Have won a heap of honor in the field
    And left your slender carcasses behind,
    As if I lay with you for company.
Amyras.   You will not go, then?   40
Calyphas.   You say true.
Amyras.   Were all the lofty mounts of Zona Mundi
    That fill the midst of farthest Tartary
    Turned into pearl and proffered for my stay,
    I would not bide the fury of my father,   45
    When, made a victor in these haughty arms,
    He comes and finds his sons have had no shares
    In all the honors he proposed for us.
Calyphas.   Take you the honor, I will take my ease;
    My wisdom shall excuse my cowardice.   50
    I go into the field before I need?
        [*An*] *alarm* [*is sounded*] *and Amyras and Celebinus run in.*
    The bullets fly at random where they list;
    And should I go and kill a thousand men,

IV,i.
14 *proper* own. *foil* disgrace.   42 *Zona Mundi* a mountain range in
33 *tall* brave.   Tartary.

I were as soon rewarded with a shot,
And sooner far than he that never fights;   55
And should I go and do nor harm nor good,
I might have harm, which all the good I have,
Joined with my father's crown, would never cure.
I'll to cards. Perdicas!

[Enter Perdicas.]

Perdicas.   Here, my lord.   60
Calyphas.   Come, thou and I will go to cards to drive away the time.
Perdicas.   Content, my lord; but what shall we play for?
Calyphas.   Who shall kiss the fairest of the Turks' concubines first,
when my father hath conquered them.
Perdicas.   Agreed, i'faith.   *They play.* 65
Calyphas.   They say I am a coward, Perdicas, and I fear as little their
taratantaras, their swords, or their cannons as I do a naked lady in a
net of gold, and, for fear I should be afraid, would put it off and come
to bed with me.
Perdicas.   Such a fear, my lord, would never make ye retire.   70
Calyphas.   I would my father would let me be put in the front of such
a battle once, to try my valor. *Alarm[s within].* What a coil they keep!
I believe there will be some hurt done anon amongst them.

[Exeunt.]

IV,ii.

Enter Tamburlaine, Theridamas, Techelles, Usumcasane, Amy-
ras [and] Celebinus leading [in] the Turkish Kings; [and
Soldiers].

Tamburlaine.   See now, ye slaves, my children stoops your pride
And leads your glories sheep-like to the sword.
Bring them, my boys, and tell me if the wars
Be not a life that may illustrate gods,
And tickle not your spirits with desire   5
Still to be trained in arms and chivalry?
Amyras.   Shall we let go these kings again, my lord,
To gather greater numbers 'gainst our power,
That they may say it is not chance doth this,
But matchless strength and magnanimity?   10
Tamburlaine.   No, no, Amyras; tempt not Fortune so.
Cherish thy valor still with fresh supplies,
And glut it not with stale and daunted foes.
But where's this coward villain, not my son,

IV,ii.

67 *taratantaras* bugle calls.   1 *stoops* bends.
72 *coil* commotion.   4 *illustrate* adorn, render illustrious.

But traitor to my name and majesty?   15
     He goes in and brings Calyphas out.
Image of sloth, and picture of a slave,
The obloquy and scorn of my renown!
How may my heart, thus firèd with mine eyes,
Wounded with shame and killed with discontent,
Shroud any thought may hold my striving hands   20
From martial justice on thy wretched soul?
Theridamas. Yet pardon him, I pray your majesty.
Techelles and Usumcasane. Let all of us entreat your highness' pardon.
         [*They kneel.*]
Tamburlaine. Stand up, ye base, unworthy soldiers!
Know ye not yet the argument of arms?   25
Amyras. Good my lord, let him be forgiven for once,
And we will force him to the field hereafter.
        [*The Sons kneel.*]
Tamburlaine. Stand up, my boys, and I will teach ye arms,
And what the jealousy of wars must do.
O Samarcanda, where I breathèd first,   30
And joyed the fire of this martial flesh,
Blush, blush, fair city, at thine honor's foil,
And shame of nature, which Jaertis' stream,
Embracing thee with deepest of his love,
Can never wash from thy distainèd brows!   35
Here, Jove, receive his fainting soul again,
A form not meet to give that subject essence
Whose matter is the flesh of Tamburlaine,
Wherein an incorporeal spirit moves,
Made of the mould whereof thyself consists,   40
Which makes me valiant, proud, ambitious,
Ready to levy power against thy throne,
That I might move the turning spheres of heaven,
For earth and all this airy region
Cannot contain the state of Tamburlaine.   45
       [*He stabs Calyphas.*]
By Mahomet, thy mighty friend, I swear,
In sending to my issue such a soul,
Created of the massy dregs of earth,

25 *argument of arms* necessity of military life.
29 *jealousy of wars* military zeal.
30 *Samarcanda* Samarkand, Tamburlaine's birthplace.
32 *foil* disgrace.
33 *Jaertis' stream* the river Jarartes which flows east from Tartary to the Caspian Sea.
37–38 *A form . . . Tamburlaine* i.e.,
the spirit (form) of Calyphas is not worthy (meet) to serve as the immortal part (essence) of that mortal being (subject) which is Tamburlaine. The terms are derived from sixteenth century Aristotelian logic. He is saying, in effect, that Calyphas is unworthy to be his son and thereby carry on his spirit to posterity.
40 *thyself* i.e., Jove.

The scum and tartar of the elements,
Wherein was neither courage, strength, or wit,　　　　50
But folly, sloth, and damnèd idleness,
Thou hast procured a greater enemy
Than he that darted mountains at thy head,
Shaking the burden mighty Atlas bears,
Whereat thou trembling hidd'st thee in the air,　　　　55
Clothed with a pitchy cloud for being seen.
And now, ye cankered curs of Asia,
That will not see the strength of Tamburlaine,
Although it shine as brightly as the sun,
Now you shall feel the strength of Tamburlaine,　　　　60
And, by the state of his supremacy,
Approve the difference 'twixt himself and you.
Orcanes. Thou show'st the difference 'twixt ourselves and thee,
In this thy barbarous damnèd tyranny.
King of Jerusalem. Thy victories are grown so violent,　　　　65
That shortly heaven, filled with the meteors
Of blood and fire thy tyrannies have made,
Will pour down blood and fire on thy head,
Whose scalding drops will pierce thy seething brains,
And, with our bloods, revenge our bloods on thee.　　　　70
Tamburlaine. Villains, these terrors and these tyrannies—
If tyrannies war's justice ye repute—
I execute, enjoined me from above,
To scourge the pride of such as heaven abhors;
Nor am I made arch-monarch of the world,　　　　75
Crowned and invested by the hand of Jove,
For deeds of bounty or nobility;
But since I exercise a greater name,
The scourge of God and terror of the world,
I must apply myself to fit those terms,　　　　80
In war, in blood, in death, in cruelty,
And plague such peasants as resist in me
The power of heaven's eternal majesty.
Theridamas, Techelles, and Casane,
Ransack the tents and the pavilions　　　　85
Of these proud Turks, and take their concubines,
Making them bury this effeminate brat;
For not a common soldier shall defile
His manly fingers with so faint a boy.
Then bring those Turkish harlots to my tent,　　　　90
And I'll dispose them as it likes me best.
Meanwhile, take him in.

49 *tartar* dregs (as of a wine cask).
53 *he . . . head* the Titans who warred against Jove.
54 *burden . . . bears* i.e., heaven.
56 *for being seen* to avoid being seen.
89 *faint* faint-hearted, cowardly.

Soldiers.   We will, my lord.
> [*Exeunt Soldiers with the body of Calyphas.*]

King of Jerusalem.   O damnèd monster, nay, a fiend of hell,
   Whose cruelties are not so harsh as thine,   95
   Nor yet imposed with such a bitter hate!

Orcanes.   Revenge it, Rhadamanth and Æacus,
   And let your hates, extended in his pains,
   Excel the hate wherewith he pains our souls!

King of Trebizon.   May never day give virtue to his eyes,   100
   Whose sight, composed of fury and of fire,
   Doth send such stern affections to his heart!

King of Soria.   May never spirit, vein, or artier, feed
   The cursèd substance of that cruel heart;
   But, wanting moisture and remorseful blood,   105
   Dry up with anger, and consume with heat!

Tamburlaine.   Well, bark, ye dogs. I'll bridle all your tongues
   And bind them close with bits of burnished steel,
   Down to the channels of your hateful throats;
   And, with the pains my rigor shall inflict,   110
   I'll make ye roar, that earth may echo forth
   The far-resounding torments ye sustain;
   As when an herd of lusty Cimbrian bulls
   Run mourning round about the females' miss,
   And, stung with fury of their following,   115
   Fill all the air with troublous bellowing.
   I will, with engines never exercised,
   Conquer, sack, and utterly consume
   Your cities and your golden palaces,
   And with the flames that beat against the clouds,   120
   Incense the heavens and make the stars to melt,
   As if they were the tears of Mahomet,
   For hot consumption of his country's pride.
   And, till by vision or by speech I hear
   Immortal Jove say 'Cease, my Tamburlaine,'   125
   I will persist a terror to the world,
   Making the meteors, that like armèd men
   Are seen to march upon the towers of heaven,
   Run tilting round about the firmament
   And break their burning lances in the air,   130

---

97 *Rhadamanth and Æacus* with Minos, the judges of the Greek underworld.
102 *affections* emotions.
103 *artier* artery.
105 *remorseful* compassionate
113 *Cimbrian* possibly referring to the Cimbri, a celtic people who defeated several Roman armies in the second century B.C. but these people had no particular relation to bulls, and Marlowe's allusion defies explanation.
114 *females' miss* i.e., loss of their mates.

For honor of my wondrous victories.
Come, bring them in to our pavilion.

Exeunt.

     [*Enter*] *Olympia, alone.*   IV,iii.
Olympia. Distressed Olympia, whose weeping eyes
 Since thy arrival here beheld no sun,
 But, closed within the compass of a tent,
 Have stained thy cheeks and made thee look like death,
 Devise some means to rid thee of thy life,   5
 Rather than yield to his detested suit,
 Whose drift is only to dishonor thee;
 And since this earth, dewed with thy brinish tears,
 Affords no herbs whose taste may poison thee,
 Nor yet this air, beat often with thy sighs,   10
 Contagious smells and vapors to infect thee,
 Nor thy close cave a sword to murder thee,
 Let this invention be the instrument.
     Enter Theridamas.
Theridamas. Well met, Olympia. I sought thee in my tent,
 But when I saw the place obscure and dark,   15
 Which with thy beauty thou wast wont to light,
 Enraged, I ran about the fields for thee,
 Supposing amorous Jove had sent his son,
 The wingèd Hermes, to convey thee hence.
 But now I find thee, and that fear is past.   20
 Tell me, Olympia, wilt thou grant my suit?
Olympia. My lord and husband's death, with my sweet son's,
 With whom I buried all affections
 Save grief and sorrow, which torment my heart,
 Forbids my mind to entertain a thought   25
 That tends to love, but meditate on death,
 A fitter subject for a pensive soul.
Theridamas. Olympia, pity him in whom thy looks
 Have greater operation and more force
 Than Cynthia's in the watery wilderness,   30
 For with thy view my joys are at the full,
 And ebb again as thou depart'st from me.
Olympia. Ah, pity me, my lord, and draw your sword,

---

30 *Cynthia's . . . wilderness* i.e., the
power of the moon to govern the tides.

Making a passage for my troubled soul,
Which beats against this prison to get out   35
And meet my husband and my loving son.
Theridamas.   Nothing but still thy husband and thy son?
Leave this, my love, and listen more to me:
Thou shalt be stately queen of fair Argier,
And, clothed in costly cloth of massy gold,   40
Upon the marble turrets of my court
Sit like to Venus in her chair of state,
Commanding all thy princely eye desires;
And I will cast off arms and sit with thee,
Spending my life in sweet discourse of love.   45
Olympia.   No such discourse is pleasant in mine ears,
But that where every period ends with death,
And every line begins with death again.
I cannot love, to be an emperess.
Theridamas.   Nay lady, then, if nothing will prevail,   50
I'll use some other means to make you yield.
Such is the sudden fury of my love,
I must and will be pleased, and you shall yield.
Come to the tent again.
Olympia.   Stay, good my lord, and, will you save my honor,   55
I'll give your grace a present of such price
As all the world cannot afford the like.
Theridamas.   What is it?
Olympia.   An ointment which a cunning alchemist
Distillèd from the purest balsamum   60
And simplest extracts of all minerals,
In which the essential form of marble stone,
Tempered by science metaphysical,
And spells of magic from the mouths of spirits,
With which if you but 'noint your tender skin,   65
Nor pistol, sword, nor lance, can pierce your flesh.
Theridamas.   Why, madam, think ye to mock me thus palpably?
Olympia.   To prove it, I will 'noint my naked throat,
Which when you stab, look on your weapon's point,
And you shall see't rebated with the blow.   70
Theridamas.   Why gave you not your husband some of it,
If you loved him, and it so precious?
Olympia.   My purpose was, my lord, to spend it so,
But was prevented by his sudden end;
And for a present easy proof hereof,   75
That I dissemble not, try it on me.
Theridamas.   I will, Olympia, and will keep it for

---

61 *simplest extracts* in alchemy, the   62 *essential form* fundamental quality
elemental parts.   of a spirit.
                                                                            70 *rebated* blunted.

The richest present of this eastern world.

She anoints her throat.

Olympia.   Now stab, my lord, and mark your weapon's point,
That will be blunted if the blow be great.   80
Theridamas.   Here, then, Olympia.   [*He stabs her. She dies.*]
What, have I slain her? Villain, stab thyself!
Cut off this arm that murderèd my love,
In whom the learnèd rabbis of this age
Might find as many wondrous miracles   85
As in the theoria of the world.
Now hell is fairer than Elysium;
A greater lamp than that bright eye of heaven,
From whence the stars do borrow all their light,
Wanders about the black circumference;   90
And now the damnèd souls are free from pain,
For every Fury gazeth on her looks.
Infernal Dis is courting of my love,
Inventing masks and stately shows for her,
Opening the doors of his rich treasury
To entertain this queen of chastity,   95
Whose body shall be tombed with all the pomp
The treasure of my kingdom may afford.

Exit, taking her [body] away.

IV,iv.

[*Enter*] *Tamburlaine, drawn in his chariot by* [*the Kings of*]
Trebizon and Soria, with bits in their mouths, reins in his left
hand, and in his right hand a whip with which he scourgeth
them; Techelles, Theridamas, Usumcasane, Amyras, Celebinus;
[*Orcanes, King of*] *Natolia, and* [*the King of*] *Jerusalem, led*
by five or six common Soldiers.

Tamburlaine.   Holla, ye pampered jades of Asia!
What, can ye draw but twenty miles a day,
And have so proud a chariot at your heels,
And such a coachman as great Tamburlaine,
But from Asphaltis, where I conquered you,   5
To Byron here, where thus I honor you?
The horse that guide the golden eye of heaven

IV,iv.

84 *rabbis* learned men in general, and
not merely Jewish teachers.
93 *Dis* Pluto, god of the underworld.
94 *masks* lavish entertainments.

5 *Asphaltis* a bituminous lake near
Babylon.
6 *Byron* a city near Babylon.

And blow the morning from their nosterils,
Making their fiery gait above the clouds,
Are not so honored in their governor   10
As you, ye slaves, in mighty Tamburlaine.
The headstrong jades of Thrace Alcides tamed,
That King Ægeus fed with human flesh
And made so wanton that they knew their strengths,
Were not subdued with valor more divine   15
Than you by this unconquered arm of mine.
To make you fierce and fit my appetite,
You shall be fed with flesh as raw as blood
And drink in pails the strongest muscadel.
If you can live with it, then live, and draw   20
My chariot swifter than the racking clouds;
If not, then die like beasts, and fit for naught
But perches for the black and fatal ravens.
Thus am I right the scourge of highest Jove,
And see the figure of my dignity,   25
By which I hold my name and majesty!
Amyras.   Let me have coach, my lord, that I may ride,
And thus be drawn with these two idle kings.
Tamburlaine.   Thy youth forbids such ease, my kingly boy.
They shall to-morrow draw my chariot,   30
While these their fellow-kings may be refreshed.
Orcanes.   O thou that sway'st the region under earth
And art a king as absolute as Jove,
Come as thou didst in fruitful Sicily,
Surveying all the glories of the land,   35
And as thou took'st the fair Proserpina,
Joying the fruit of Ceres' garden-plot,
For love, for honor, and to make her queen,
So, for just hate, for shame, and to subdue
This proud contemner of thy dreadful power,   40
Come once in fury and survey his pride,
Haling him headlong to the lowest hell.
Theridamas.   Your majesty must get some bits for these,
To bridle their contemptuous cursing tongues,
That, like unruly never-broken jades,   45
Break through the hedges of their hateful mouths

---

8 *nosterils* nostrils. The 1590 spelling
is retained for the sake of the meter.

12–13 *headstrong . . . flesh* One of the
twelve labors of Hercules (Alcides) was
to capture the wild mares, fed with
human flesh, of Ægeus or Diomedes,
king of the Bistones in Thrace. Hercules
fed them the flesh of their master, after
which they became tame.

21 *racking* scudding before the wind.

32 *thou . . . earth* i.e., Pluto, god of
the underworld, who had carried off
Proserpina, daughter of Ceres, goddess
of the harvest, and made her his queen
in Hades.

40 *contemner* holder in contempt.

46 *hedges . . . mouths* i.e., teeth.

And pass their fixèd bounds exceedingly.
Techelles.   Nay, we will break the hedges of their mouths
   And pull their kicking colts out of their pastures.
Usumcasane.   Your majesty already hath devised   50
   A mean, as fit as may be, to restrain
   These coltish coach-horse tongues from blasphemy.
Celebinus.   How like you that, sir king? Why speak you not?
King of Jerusalem.   Ah, cruel brat, sprung from a tyrant's loins!
   How like his cursèd father he begins   55
   To practice taunts and bitter tyrannies!
Tamburlaine.   Ay, Turk, I tell thee, this same boy is he
   That must, advanced in higher pomp than this,
   Rifle the kingdoms I shall leave unsacked,
   If Jove, esteeming me too good for earth,   60
   Raise me to match the fair Aldeboran,
   Above the threefold astracism of heaven,
   Before I conquer all the triple world.
   Now fetch me out the Turkish concubines.
   I will prefer them for the funeral   65
   They have bestowed on my abortive son.
                          The Concubines are brought in.
   Where are my common soldiers now, that fought
   So lion-like upon Asphaltis' plains?
Soldiers.   Here, my lord.
Tamburlaine.   Hold ye, tall soldiers; take ye queens apiece—   70
   I mean such queens as were kings' concubines.
   Take them; divide them, and their jewels too,
   And let them equally serve all your turns.
Soldiers.   We thank your majesty.
Tamburlaine.   Brawl not, I warn you, for your lechery,   75
   For every man that so offends shall die.
Orcanes.   Injurious tyrant, wilt thou so defame
   The hateful fortunes of thy victory,
   To exercise upon such guiltless dames
   The violence of thy common soldiers' lust?   80
Tamburlaine.   Live continent, then, ye slaves, and meet not me
   With troops of harlots at your slothful heels.
Concubines.   O pity us, my lord, and save our honors.
Tamburlaine.   Are ye not gone, ye villains, with your spoils?
                          The Soldiers run away with the Ladies.
King of Jerusalem.   O, merciless, infernal cruelty!   85
Tamburlaine.   Save your honors! 'Twere but time indeed,
   Lost long before you knew what honor meant.
Theridamas.   It seems they meant to conquer us, my lord,

---

61 *Aldeboran* a star in the constellation   62 *astracism* constellation.
of Taurus, one of the fixed stars of   70 *tall* brave.
heaven.

And make us jesting pageants for their trulls.
Tamburlaine.   And now themselves shall make our pageant,   90
And common soldiers jest with all their trulls.
Let them take pleasure soundly in their spoils,
Till we prepare our march to Babylon,
Whither we next make expedition.
Techelles.   Let us not be idle then, my lord,   95
But presently be prest to conquer it.
Tamburlaine.   We will, Techelles. Forward, then, ye jades.
Now crouch, ye kings of greatest Asia,
And tremble when ye hear this scourge will come
That whips down cities and controlleth crowns,   100
Adding their wealth and treasure to my store.
The Euxine sea, north to Natolia,
The Terrene, west, the Caspian, north-north-east,
And on the south, Sinus Arabicus,
Shall all be loaden with the martial spoils   105
We will convey with us to Persia.
Then shall my native city Samarcanda,
And crystal waves of fresh Jaertis' stream,
The pride and beauty of her princely seat,
Be famous through the furthest continents;   110
For there my palace royal shall be placed,
Whose shining turrets shall dismay the heavens
And cast the fame of Ilion's tower to hell.
Thorough the streets, with troops of conquered kings,
I'll ride in golden armor like the sun,   115
And in my helm a triple plume shall spring,
Spanglèd with diamonds, dancing in the air,
To note me emperor of the three-fold world;
Like to an almond-tree y-mounted high
Upon the lofty and celestial mount   120
Of ever-green Selinus, quaintly decked
With blooms more white than Erycina's brows,
Whose tender blossoms tremble every one
At every little breath that thorough heaven is blown.
Then in my coach, like Saturn's royal son   125
Mounted his shining chariot gilt with fire,
And drawn with princely eagles through the path
Paved with bright crystal and enchased with stars,
When all the gods stand gazing at his pomp,
So will I ride through Samarcanda streets,   130

96 *prest* ready.
102 *Euxine* Black.
108 *Jaertis' stream* See note at IV,ii,
33.
118 *three-fold world* consisting of Europe, Asia, and Africa.

121 *Selinus* town in Sicily located on
a river of the same name.
122 *Erycina* Venus (who was worshipped at a temple on Mt. Eryx in
western Sicily).
125 *Saturn's royal son* i.e., Jove.

Until my soul, dissevered from this flesh,
Shall mount the milk-white way, and meet Him there.
To Babylon, my lords, to Babylon!

Exeunt.

V,i.

Enter the Governor of Babylon, upon the walls, with [Maximus and] others.

Governor.   What saith Maximus?
Maximus.   My lord, the breach the enemy hath made
Gives such assurance of our overthrow,
That little hope is left to save our lives
Or hold our city from the conqueror's hands.   5
Then hang out flags, my lord, of humble truce,
And satisfy the people's general prayers,
That Tamburlaine's intolerable wrath
May be suppressed by our submission.
Governor.   Villain, respects thou more thy slavish life   10
Than honor of thy country or thy name?
Is not my life and state as dear to me,
The city and my native country's weal,
As any thing of price with thy conceit?
Have we not hope, for all our battered walls,   15
To live secure and keep his forces out,
When this our famous lake of Limnasphaltis
Makes walls afresh with every thing that falls
Into the liquid substance of his stream,
More strong than are the gates of death or hell?   20
What faintness should dismay our courages,
When we are thus defensed against our foe,
And have no terror but his threatening looks?
         Enter another [Citizen], kneeling to the Governor.
Citizen.   My lord, if ever you did deed of ruth,
And now will work a refuge to our lives,   25
Offer submission, hang up flags of truce,
That Tamburlaine may pity our distress
And use us like a loving conqueror.
Though this be held his last day's dreadful siege,
Wherein he spareth neither man nor child,   30

V,i.

14 *As . . . conceit* as anything which may be of value in your thoughts.
  17 *Limnasphaltis* the bituminous lake of Babylon, of whose fabulous properties Marlowe may have read in Herodotus.

Yet are there Christians of Georgia here,
Whose state he ever pitied and relieved,
Will get his pardon, if your grace would send.
Governor. How is my soul environèd!
And this eternized city Babylon   35
Filled with a pack of faint-heart fugitives
That thus entreat their shame and servitude!
                    [*Enter, a Second Citizen.*]
Second Citizen. My lord, if ever you will win our hearts,
Yield up the town, save our wives and children;
For I will cast myself from off these walls   40
Or die some death of quickest violence,
Before I bide the wrath of Tamburlaine.
Governor. Villains, cowards, traitors to our state,
Fall to the earth, and pierce the pit of hell,
That legions of tormenting spirits may vex   45
Your slavish bosoms with continual pains!
I care not, nor the town will never yield
As long as any life is in my breast.
        Enter Theridamas and Techelles, with other Soldiers.
Theridamas. Thou desperate governor of Babylon,
To save thy life, and us a little labor,   50
Yield speedily the city to our hands,
Or else be sure thou shalt be forced with pains
More exquisite than ever traitor felt.
Governor. Tyrant, I turn the traitor in thy throat,
And will defend it in despite of thee.   55
Call up the soldiers to defend these walls.
Techelles. Yield, foolish governor; we offer more
Than ever yet we did to such proud slaves
As durst resist us till our third day's siege.
Thou seest us prest to give the last assault,   60
And that shall bide no more regard of parley.
Governor. Assault and spare not; we will never yield.
                    Alarm; and they scale the walls.

        Enter Tamburlaine [*drawn in his chariot by the Kings of Tre-
        bizon and Soria*]; *with Usumcasane, Amyras, and Celebinus;*
        [*Orcanes, the King of Natolia, and the King of Jerusalem, led
        by soldiers; and others*].
Tamburlaine. The stately buildings of fair Babylon,
Whose lofty pillars, higher than the clouds,
Were wont to guide the seaman in the deep,   65
Being carried thither by the cannon's force,
Now fill the mouth of Limnasphaltis' lake
And make a bridge unto the battered walls.

60 *prest* ready.

Where Belus, Ninus, and great Alexander
Have rode in triumph, triumphs Tamburlaine,   70
Whose chariot-wheels have burst th'Assyrians' bones,
Drawn with these kings on heaps of carcasses.
Now in the place where fair Semiramis,
Courted by kings and peers of Asia,
Hath trod the measures, do my soldiers march,   75
And in the streets where brave Assyrian dames
Have rid in pomp like rich Saturnia,
With furious words and frowning visages
My horsemen brandish their unruly blades.
        Enter Theridamas and Techelles, bringing [in] the Governor
                            of Babylon.
Who have ye there, my lords?   80
Theridamas.   The sturdy governor of Babylon,
    That made us all the labor for the town
    And used such slender reck'ning of your majesty.
Tamburlaine.   Go, bind the villain; he shall hang in chains
    Upon the ruins of this conquered town.   85
    Sirrah, the view of our vermilion tents
    Which threatened more than if the region
    Next underneath the element of fire
    Were full of comets and of blazing stars,
    Whose flaming trains should reach down to the earth,   90
    Could not affright you; no, nor I myself,
    The wrathful messenger of mighty Jove,
    That with his sword hath quailed all earthly kings,
    Could not persuade you to submission,
    But still the ports were shut. Villain, I say,   95
    Should I but touch the rusty gates of hell,
    The triple headed Cerberus would howl
    And make black Jove to crouch and kneel to me;
    But I have sent volleys of shot to you,
    Yet could not enter till the breach was made.   100
Governor.   Nor if my body could have stopped the breach,
    Shouldst thou have entered, cruel Tamburlaine.
    'Tis not thy bloody tents can make me yield,
    Nor yet thyself, the anger of the Highest,
    For though thy cannon shook the city walls,   105
    My heart did never quake or courage faint.
Tamburlaine.   Well, now I'll make it quake. Go, draw him up;

---

69 *Belus . . . Alexander* Belus, son
of Neptune, was the legendary founder
of Babylon; Ninus, the founder of
Nineveh, married Simiramis, who built
the walls of Babylon; Alexander the
Great of Macedon conquered Babylon
in 331 B.C.

71 *burst* broken.
77 *Saturnia* Juno, queen of the gods.
95 *ports* gates.
97 *Cerberus* the three-headed dog of
Hades.
98 *black Jove* Pluto.

Hang him up in chains upon the city walls,
And let my soldiers shoot the slave to death.
Governor.   Vile monster, born of some infernal hag   110
And sent from hell to tyrannize on earth,
Do all thy worst; nor death, nor Tamburlaine,
Torture, or pain, can daunt my dreadless mind.
Tamburlaine.   Up with him, then; his body shall be scarred.
Governor.   But, Tamburlaine, in Limnasphaltis' lake   115
There lies more gold than Babylon is worth,
Which, when the city was besieged, I hid.
Save but my life, and I will give it thee.
Tamburlaine.   Then, for all your valor, you would save your life?
Whereabout lies it?   120
Governor.   Under a hollow bank, right opposite
Against the western gate of Babylon.
Tamburlaine.   Go thither, some of you, and take his gold.
                          [*Exeunt some Attendants.*]
The rest forward with execution.
Away with him hence; let him speak no more.   125
I think I make your courage something quail.
              [*Exeunt Attendants with the Governor of Babylon.*]
When this is done, we'll march from Babylon
And make our greatest haste to Persia.
These jades are broken winded and half tired;
Unharness them, and let me have fresh horse.   130
          [*Attendants unharness the Kings of Trebizon and Soria.*]
So; now their best is done to honor me,
·Take them and hang them both up presently.
King of Trebizon.   Vild tyrant! Barbarous bloody Tamburlaine!
Tamburlaine.   Take them away, Theridamas; see them dispatched.
Theridamas.   I will, my lord.   135
          [*Exit Theridamas with the Kings of Trebizon and Soria.*]
Tamburlaine.   Come, Asian viceroys; to your tasks awhile,
And take such fortune as your fellows felt.
Orcanes.   First let thy Scythian horse tear both our limbs,
Rather than we should draw thy chariot,
And, like base slaves, abject our princely minds   140
To vile and ignominious servitude.
King of Jerusalem.   Rather lend me thy weapon, Tamburlaine.
That I may sheathe it in this breast of mine.
A thousand deaths could not torment our hearts
More than the thought of this doth vex our souls.   145
Amyras.   They will talk still, my lord, if you do not bridle them.
Tamburlaine.   Bridle them, and let me to my coach.
          [*Attendants bridle Orcanes King of Natolia, and the King of
          Jerusalem, and harness them to the chariot. The Governor of*

133 *Vild* vile.   140 *abject* abase.

Babylon appears hanging in chains on the walls. Enter Theri-
damas.]
Amyras.   See, now, my lord, how brave the captain hangs.
Tamburlaine.   'Tis brave indeed, my boy. Well done!
   Shoot first, my lord, and then the rest shall follow.   150
Theridamas.   Then have at him, to begin withal.
                                      Theridamas shoots.
Governor.   Yet save my life, and let this wound appease
   The mortal fury of great Tamburlaine.
Tamburlaine.   No, though Asphaltis' lake were liquid gold,
   And offered me as ransom for thy life,   155
   Yet shouldst thou die. Shoot at him all at once.
                                            They shoot.
   So, now he hangs like Bagdet's governor,
   Having as many bullets in his flesh
   As there be breaches in her battered wall.
   Go now, and bind the burghers hand and foot,   160
   And cast them headlong in the city's lake.
   Tartars and Persians shall inhabit there;
   And, to command the city, I will build
   A citadel, that all Africa,
   Which hath been subject to the Persian king,   165
   Shall pay me tribute for in Babylon.
Techelles.   What shall be done with their wives and children, my lord?
Tamburlaine.   Techelles, drown them all, man, woman, and child;
   Leave not a Babylonian in the town.
Techelles.   I will about it straight. Come, soldiers.   170
                      Exit [Techelles with Soldiers].
Tamburlaine.   Now, Casane, where's the Turkish Alcoran
   And all the heaps of superstitious books
   Found in the temples of that Mahomet
   Whom I have thought a god? They shall be burnt.
Usumcasane.   Here they are, my lord.   175
Tamburlaine.   Well said; let there be a fire presently.
                              [*They light a fire.*]
   In vain, I see, men worship Mahomet.
   My sword hath sent millions of Turks to hell,
   Slew all his priests, his kinsmen, and his friends,
   And yet I live untouched by Mahomet.   180
   There is a God, full of revenging wrath,
   From whom the thunder and the lightning breaks,
   Whose scourge I am, and Him will I obey.
   So, Casane; fling them in the fire.   [*They burn the books.*]
   Now, Mahomet, if thou have any power,   185
   Come down thyself and work a miracle.
   Thou are not worthy to be worshippèd

157 *Bagdet's* Bagdad's.

That suffers flames of fire to burn the writ
Wherein the sum of thy religion rests.
Why send'st thou not a furious whirlwind down   190
To blow thy Alcoran up to thy throne,
Where men report thou sitt'st by God himself?
Or vengeance on the head of Tamburlaine
That shakes his sword against thy majesty
And spurns the abstracts of thy foolish laws?   195
Well, soldiers, Mahomet remains in hell;
He cannot hear the voice of Tamburlaine.
Seek out another godhead to adore—
The God that sits in heaven, if any god,
For He is God alone, and none but He.   200
                    [*Enter Techelles.*]
Techelles.   I have fulfilled your highness' will, my lord.
Thousands of men, drowned in Asphaltis' lake,
Have made the water swell above the banks,
And fishes, fed by human carcasses,
Amazed, swim up and down upon the waves,   205
As when they swallow asafœtida,
Which makes them fleet aloft and gasp for air.
Tamburlaine.   Well, then, my friendly lords, what now remains,
But that we leave sufficient garrison
And presently depart to Persia,   210
To triumph after all our victories?
Theridamas.   Ay, good my lord, let us in haste to Persia;
And let this captain be removed the walls
To some high hill about the city here.
Tamburlaine.   Let it be so; about it, soldiers.   215
But stay; I feel myself distempered suddenly.
Techelles.   What is it dares distemper Tamburlaine?
Tamburlaine.   Something, Techelles, but I know not what.
But, forth, ye vassals! Whatsoe'er it be,
Sickness or death can never conquer me.   220
                              Exeunt.

✱

                                                            V,ii.
Enter Callapine, [King of] Amasia, [and train,] with drums
                    and trumpets.
Callapine.   King of Amasia, now our mighty host
Marcheth in Asia Major, where the streams
Of Euphrates and Tigris swiftly runs;

---

206 *asafœtida* a concreted resinous gum   207 *fleet* float.
with a strong odor, used in medicine
as an anti-spasmodic.

And here may we behold great Babylon,
Circlèd about with Limnasphaltis' lake,   5
Where Tamburlaine with all his army lies,
Which being faint and weary with the siege,
We may lie ready to encounter him
Before his host be full from Babylon,
And so revenge our latest grievous loss,   10
If God or Mahomet send any aid.
King of Amasia.   Doubt not, my lord, but we shall conquer him.
The monster that hath drunk a sea of blood
And yet gapes still for more to quench his thirst,
Our Turkish swords shall headlong send to hell;   15
And that vile carcass, drawn by warlike kings,
The fowls shall eat; for never sepulcher
Shall grace that base-born tyrant Tamburlaine.
Callapine.   When I record my parents' slavish life,
Their cruel death, mine own captivity,   20
My viceroys' bondage under Tamburlaine,
Methinks I could sustain a thousand deaths
To be revenged of all his villany.
Ah, sacred Mahomet, thou that hast seen
Millions of Turks perish by Tamburlaine,   25
Kingdoms made waste, brave cities sacked and burnt,
And but one host is left to honor thee,
Aid thy obedient servant Callapine,
And make him, after all these overthrows,
To triumph over cursèd Tamburlaine.   30
King of Amasia.   Fear not, my lord. I see great Mahomet,
Clothèd in purple clouds, and on his head
A chaplet brighter than Apollo's crown,
Marching about the air with armèd men,
To join with you against this Tamburlaine.   35
Renownèd general, mighty Callapine,
Though God himself and holy Mahomet
Should come in person to resist your power,
Yet might your mighty host encounter all,
And pull proud Tamburlaine upon his knees   40
To sue for mercy at your highness' feet.
Callapine.   Captain, the force of Tamburlaine is great,
His fortune greater, and the victories
Wherewith he hath so sore dismayed the world
Are greatest to discourage all our drifts;   45
Yet when the pride of Cynthia is at full,
She wanes again, and so shall his, I hope;

V,ii.
19 *record* call to mind.   45 *drifts* purposes.

For we have here the chief selected men
Of twenty several kingdoms at the least.
Nor ploughman, priest, nor merchant, stays at home;   50
All Turkey is in arms with Callapine;
And never will we sunder camps and arms
Before himself or his be conquerèd.
This is the time that must eternize me
For conquering the tyrant of the world.   55
Come, soldiers, let us lie in wait for him,
And if we find him absent from his camp,
Or that it be rejoined again at full,
Assail it and be sure of victory.

Exeunt.

[*Enter*] *Theridamas, Techelles, and Usumcasane.*   V,iii.
Theridamas.   Weep, heavens, and vanish into liquid tears!
Fall, stars that govern his nativity,
And summon all the shining lamps of heaven
To cast their bootless fires to the earth
And shed their feeble influence in the air.   5
Muffle your beauties with eternal clouds,
For Hell and Darkness pitch their pitchy tents,
And Death, with armies of Cimmerian spirits,
Gives battle 'gainst the heart of Tamburlaine.
Now in defiance of that wonted love   10
Your sacred virtues poured upon his throne,
And made his state an honor to the heavens,
These cowards invisibly assail his soul
And threaten conquest on our sovereign.
But if he die, your glories are disgraced,   15
Earth droops and says that hell in heaven is placed.
Techelles.   Oh, then, ye powers that sway eternal seats
And guide this massy substance of the earth,
If you retain desert of holiness,
As your supreme estates instruct our thoughts,   20
Be not inconstant, careless of your fame,
Bear not the burden of your enemies' joys,
Triumphing in his fall whom you advanced,
But as his birth, life, health, and majesty
Were strangely blessed and governèd by heaven,   25

V,iii.
4 *bootless* unavailing.   12 *state* throne.
8 *Cimmerian* black, coming from the
underworld.

So honor, heaven, till heaven dissolvèd be,
His birth, his life, his health, and majesty!
Usumcasane.   Blush, heaven, to lose the honor of thy name,
  To see thy footstool set upon thy head;
  And let no baseness in thy haughty breast   30
  Sustain a shame of such inexcellence,
  To see the devils mount in angels' thrones,
  And angels dive into the pools of hell.
  And though they think their painful date is out
  And that their power is puissant as Jove's,   35
  Which makes them manage arms against thy state,
  Yet make them feel the strength of Tamburlaine,
  Thy instrument and note of majesty,
  Is greater far than they can thus subdue;
  For, if he die, thy glory is disgraced,   40
  Earth droops and says that hell in heaven is placed.
    [*Enter Tamburlaine, drawn in his chariot by Orcanes King of
    Natolia, and the King of Jerusalem; Amyras, Celebinus, and
                        Physicans.*]
Tamburlaine.   What daring god torments my body thus
  And seeks to conquer mighty Tamburlaine?
  Shall sickness prove me now to be a man,
  That have been termed the terror of the world?   45
  Techelles and the rest, come, take your swords,
  And threaten him whose hand afflicts my soul.
  Come, let us march against the powers of heaven
  And set black streamers in the firmament
  To signify the slaughter of the gods.   50
  Ah, friends, what shall I do? I cannot stand.
  Come, carry me to war against the gods,
  That thus envy the health of Tamburlaine.
Theridamas.   Ah, good my lord, leave these impatient words
  Which add much danger to your malady.   55
Tamburlaine.   Why, shall I sit and languish in this pain?
  No, strike the drums, and, in revenge of this,
  Come, let us charge our spears and pierce his breast
  Whose shoulders bear the axis of the world,
  That if I perish, heaven and earth may fade.   60
  Theridamas, haste to the court of Jove;
  Will him to send Apollo hither straight
  To cure me, or I'll fetch him down myself.
Techelles.   Sit still, my gracious lord; this grief will cease
  And cannot last, it is so violent.   65
Tamburlaine.   Not last, Techelles? No, for I shall die.

---

38 *note* distinguishing mark.   to Greek legend, and not the axis of
59 *Whose . . . world* Atlas, who bears   the earth.
the heavens upon his shoulders according

See where my slave, the ugly monster Death,
Shaking and quivering, pale and wan for fear,
Stands aiming at me with his murdering dart,
Who flies away at every glance I give,   70
And when I look away, comes stealing on.
Villain, away, and hie thee to the field!
I and mine army come to load thy bark
With souls of thousand mangled carcasses.
Look, where he goes! But see, he comes again   75
Because I stay. Techelles, let us march
And weary Death with bearing souls to hell.
First Physician.   Pleaseth your majesty to drink this potion,
Which will abate the fury of your fit
And cause some milder spirits govern you.   80
Tamburlaine.   Tell me, what think you of my sickness now?
First Physician.   I viewed your urine, and the hypostasis,
Thick and obscure, doth make your danger great.
Your veins are full of accidental heat,
Whereby the moisture of your blood is dried.   85
The humidum and calor, which some hold
Is not a parcel of the elements,
But of a substance more divine and pure,
Is almost clean extinguishèd and spent,
Which, being the cause of life, imports your death.   90
Besides, my lord, this day is critical,
Dangerous to those whose crisis is as yours.
Your artiers, which alongst the veins convey
The lively spirits which the heart engenders,
Are parched and void of spirit, that the soul,   95
Wanting those organons by which it moves,
Cannot endure by argument of art.
Yet, if your majesty may escape this day,
No doubt but you shall soon recover all.
Tamburlaine.   Then will I comfort all my vital parts,   100
And live, in spite of death, above a day.

Alarm within.

[*Enter a Messenger.*]
Messenger.   My lord, young Callapine, that lately fled from your
majesty, hath now gathered a fresh army, and hearing your absence
in the field, offers to set upon us presently.

---

82 *hypostasis* accumulation of solids within a fluid.

84 *accidental* in excess of the proper amount.

86 *humidum and calor* moisture and heat, which in combination form the sanguine humor.

91 *day is critical* i.e., the stars are not in a proper conjunction for effecting a cure. Medicine and astrology were closely linked.

96 *organons* instruments.

Tamburlaine.   See, my physicians, now, how Jove hath sent   105
  A present medicine to recure my pain.
  My looks shall make them fly; and might I follow,
  There should not one of all the villain's power
  Live to give offer of another fight.
Usumcasane.   I joy, my lord, your highness is so strong,   110
  That can endure so well your royal presence,
  Which only will dismay the enemy.
Tamburlaine.   I know it will, Casane. Draw, you slaves!
  In spite of death, I will go show my face.
                  Alarm. Tamburlaine goes in, and comes out again
                                      with all the rest.
Tamburlaine.   Thus are the villains, cowards fled for fear,   115
  Like summer's vapors vanished by the sun;
  And could I but a while pursue the field,
  That Callapine should be my slave again.
  But I perceive my martial strength is spent.
  In vain I strive and rail against those powers   120
  That mean t'invest me in a higher throne,
  As much too high for this disdainful earth.
  Give me a map; then let me see how much
  Is left for me to conquer all the world,
  That these, my boys, may finish all my wants.   125
                                One brings a map.

  Here I began to march towards Persia,
  Along Armenia and the Caspian Sea,
  And thence unto Bithynia, where I took
  The Turk and his great empress prisoners.
  Then marched I into Egypt and Arabia;   130
  And here, not far from Alexandria,
  Whereas the Terrene and the Red Sea meet,
  Being distant less than full a hundred leagues,
  I meant to cut a channel to them both,
  That men might quickly sail to India.   135
  From thence to Nubia near Borno lake,
  And so along the Ethiopian sea,
  Cutting the tropic line of Capricorn,
  I conquered all as far as Zanzibar.
  Then, by the northern part of Africa,   140
  I came at last to Græcia, and from thence
  To Asia, where I stay against my will;
  Which is from Scythia, where I first began,
  Backward and forwards near five thousand leagues.

106 *recure* cure.
134 *cut a channel* build a canal. He
is, of course, indicating the site of the
present day Suez canal, a project which
several kings had attempted to execute
before Marlowe's time.

Look here, my boys; see what a world of ground   145
Lies westward from the midst of Cancer's line
Unto the rising of this earthly globe,
Whereas the sun, declining from our sight,
Begins the day with our Antipodes.
And shall I die, and this unconquerèd?   150
Lo, here, my sons, are all the golden mines,
Inestimable drugs and precious stones,
More worth than Asia and the world beside;
And from th'Antarctic Pole eastward behold
As much more land, which never was descried,   155
Wherein are rocks of pearl that shine as bright
As all the lamps that beautify the sky.
And shall I die, and this unconquerèd?
Here, lovely boys; what death forbids my life,
That let your lives command in spite of death.   160
Amyras.   Alas, my lord, how should our bleeding hearts,
Wounded and broken with your highness' grief,
Retain a thought of joy or spark of life?
Your soul gives essence to our wretched subjects,
Whose matter is incorporate in your flesh.   165
Celebinus.   Your pains do pierce our souls; no hope survives,
For by your life we entertain our lives.
Tamburlaine.   But, sons, this subject, not of force enough
To hold the fiery spirit it contains,
Must part, imparting his impressions   170
By equal portions into both your breasts.
My flesh, divided in your precious shapes,
Shall still retain my spirit, though I die,
And live in all your seeds immortally.
Then now remove me, that I may resign   175
My place and proper title to my son.
First, take my scourge and my imperial crown,
And mount my royal chariot of estate,
That I may see thee crowned before I die.
Help me, my lords, to make my last remove.   180
        [*They help Tamburlaine out of his chariot.*]
Theridamas.   A woeful change, my lord, that daunts our thoughts
More than the ruin of our proper souls.

---

149 *Antipodes* people who live in the
region of the setting sun. See note at
I,iii,52.

154–155 *And from . . . descried* Australia, of which rumors were current
in Marlowe's time, although the continent had not yet been discovered.

164–165 *Your soul . . . flesh* i.e., the
soul of Tamburlaine has bequeathed a
spirit (essence) to the bodies (subjects)
of his sons, since their bodies are parts
of his flesh.

168–171 *this subject . . . breasts* i.e.,
this body, unable longer to contain its
spirit, must divide that spirit equally
among its sons.

182 *proper* own.

Tamburlaine.　Sit up, my son; let me see how well
　　Thou wilt become thy father's majesty.

　　　　　　　　　　　　　　They crown Amyras.

Amyras.　With what a flinty bosom should I joy　　　185
　　The breath of life and burden of my soul,
　　If not resolved into resolvèd pains,
　　My body's mortifièd lineaments
　　Should exercise the motions of my heart,
　　Pierced with the joy of any dignity!　　　190
　　O father, if the unrelenting ears
　　Of death and hell be shut against my prayers,
　　And that the spiteful influence of heaven
　　Deny my soul fruition of her joy,
　　How should I step or stir my hateful feet　　　195
　　Against the inward powers of my heart,
　　Leading a life that only strives to die,
　　And plead in vain unpleasing sovereignty?

Tamburlaine.　Let not thy love exceed thine honor, son,
　　Nor bar thy mind that magnanimity　　　200
　　That nobly must admit necessity.
　　Sit up, my boy, and with these silken reins
　　Bridle the steelèd stomachs of those jades.

Theridamas.　My lord, you must obey his majesty,
　　Since fate commands and proud necessity.　　　205

Amyras.　Heavens witness me with what a broken heart

　　　　　　　　　　　　　　[Mounting the chariot.]

　　And damnèd spirit I ascend this seat,
　　And send my soul, before my father die,
　　His anguish and his burning agony!

Tamburlaine.　Now fetch the hearse of fair Zenocrate.　　　210
　　Let it be placed by this my fatal chair
　　And serve as parcel of my funeral.

Usumcasane.　Then feels your majesty no sovereign ease,
　　Nor may our hearts, all drowned in tears of blood,
　　Joy any hope of your recovery?　　　215

Tamburlaine.　Casane, no. The monarch of the earth,
　　And eyeless monster that torments my soul,
　　Cannot behold the tears ye shed for me,
　　And therefore still augments his cruelty.

Techelles.　Then let some god oppose his holy power　　　220
　　Against the wrath and tyranny of Death,
　　That his tear-thirsty and unquenchèd hate
　　May be upon himself reverberate!

　　　　　　　　　　　They bring in the hearse [of Zenocrate].

Tamburlaine.　Now, eyes, enjoy your latest benefit,

　　185 *joy* enjoy.

And when my soul hath virtue of your sight,   225
Pierce through the coffin and the sheet of gold,
And glut your longings with a heaven of joy.
So, reign, my son; scourge and control those slaves,
Guiding thy chariot with thy father's hand.
As precious is the charge thou undertak'st   230
As that which Clymene's brain-sick son did guide,
When wandering Phœbe's ivory cheeks were scorched,
And all the earth, like Ætna, breathing fire.
Be warned by him; then learn with awful eye
To sway a throne as dangerous as his;   235
For if thy body thrive not full of thoughts
As pure and fiery as Phyteus' beams,
The nature of these proud rebelling jades
Will take occasion by the slenderest hair
And draw thee piecemeal, like Hippolytus,   240
Through rocks more steep and sharp than Caspian cliffs.
The nature of thy chariot will not bear
A guide of baser temper than myself,
More than heaven's coach the pride of Phaëton.
Farewell, my boys! My dearest friends, farewell!   245
My body feels, my soul doth weep to see
Your sweet desires deprived my company,
For Tamburlaine, the scourge of God, must die.

                                                [*He dies.*]
Amyras.   Meet heaven and earth, and here let all things end,
For earth hath spent the pride of all her fruit,   250
And heaven consumed his choicest living fire.
Let earth and heaven his timeless death deplore,
For both their worths will equal him no more.

                                                [*Exeunt.*]

225 *when . . . sight* i.e., when, after
death, his spirit, freed from the body
and thus from the limitations of mortality, will be able to see the spirit of
Zenocrate with unclouded vision.
231 *Clymene's brain-sick son* See note
to *I Tamb.*, IV,ii,49.
232 *Phœbe* the moon.
237 *Phyteus'* Apollo's.
240 *Hippolytus* the son of Theseus by

Hippolyta. When Theseus remarried, his
new wife, Phaedra, fell in love with her
stepson and when he repulsed her advances, accused him of attempting to
dishonor her. Theseus caused his son to
be destroyed; his body was mutilated
as it was dragged along the ground by
the horses of his overturned carriage.
244 *Phaëton* the son of Apollo. See
note to *I Tamb.*, IV,ii,49.

Textual Notes

The two parts of *Tamburlaine* were printed for the first time in a single black letter octavo by Richard Jones in 1590. Two copies are today extant, the one in the Bodleian and the other in the Huntington Library. Jones issued another edition in 1593, the unique copy of which is in the British Museum, and another in 1597, of which the only extant copy is in the Huntington Library. Part I was printed separately for Edward White in 1605 and Part II in 1606. The present text follows closely the Huntington Library copy of the 1590 octavo, which clearly formed the basis for the later texts. It has been departed from only in the following instances:

TAMBURLAINE: PART ONE

I,i.

15 *their* (Dyce) his (1590)
19 *through* (1605) thorough (1590)
82 *Theridamas* Therid. (1590)
83 *stay'st* stayest (1590)
84 *press* prease (1590)
87 *greater [task]* (Eds.) greater (1590)
106, SD *remain* Manent (1590)
108 *threaten* thraten (1590)
135, SD *Ceneus* Conerus (1590)
182 *lords* (1605) Lord (1590)

I,ii.

SD *laden* loden (1590)
67 *they* (Eds.) thee (1590)
88 *Rhodope* (Dyce) Rhodolfe (1590)
146 *lance* (Dyce) lanch (1590)
178 *raze* rase (1590)
187 *renownèd* renowmed (1590)
206 *Boötes* Botees (1590)

224 *Ah* (Brooke) Are (1590)
238 *renownèd* renowmed (1590)
243 *statues* (1605) statutes (1590)

II,i.

11 *burden* burthen (1590)
27 *sinewy* (Dyce) snowy (1590)
42 *strait* (Dyce) straight (1590)

II,ii.

15 *pitched* (1593, 1605) pitch (1590)
49 *lance* lanch (1590)

II,iii.

7 *[of] heaven* (Eds.) heauen (1590)
26 *top* (Dyce) stop (1590)
30 *renownèd* renowmed (1590)
33 *and* (1605) not (1590)
47 *burden* burthen (1590)
55 *curtle-axe* cutle-axe (1590)

II,v.

6 *renownèd* renowmed (1590)
20 *embassage* ambassage (1590)
32 *aimed* (1605) and (1590)
49, SD *all except* Manent (1590)
72 *Casane* Casanes (1590)

II,vi.

30 *ingratitude* ingratude (1590)

II,vii.

50 *harpy* (1593) harpyr (1590)
52, SD *Tamburlaine* He (1590)

III,i.

16 *Renownèd* Renowmed (1590)

III,ii.

1 *Agydas* speech prefix omitted in 1590

III,iii.

SD *Bashaw* Basso (1590)
60, SD *Bashaws* Bassoes (1590)
66 *Morocco* Moroccus (1590)
96 *renowned* renowmed (1590)
158 *air* (Dyce) lure (1590)
188, SD and stay (1590)
196 *murdering* murthering (1590)
211, SD Baiazeth flies, and he pursues

him. The battell short, and they enter
(1590)
213 *foil* (Dyce) soil (1590)

IV,ii.

1, SD *Bajazeth* him (1590)
29 SD *Tamburlaine* He (1590)
45 *makes* (Dyce) make (1590)
49 *Clymene's* (Dyce) Clymeus (1590)

IV,iv.

SD *come* commeth (1590)
26–27 *My . . . yours* My . . . curses/
By . . . yours (1590)
41 SD *Bajazeth* He (1590). *the food* it
(1590)
54, SD *Bajazeth* him (1590)
114 *Morocco* Morocus (1590)

V,i.

SD *Damascus* Damasco (1590)

V,ii.

56 *Virgins* Omnes (1590)
132, SD *Attendant* An (1590)
183–184 *Hover . . . Elysium* one line
in 1590
340 *murdering* murthering (1590)
417 *Renownèd* Renowmed (1590)
453 *thee* the (1590)

TAMBURLAINE: PART TWO

Prologue.

8 *sad* (Eds.) said (1590)

I,i.

SD *Uribassa* Upibassa (1590) and at
line 20
13 *Gazellus* Byr. (1590) and throughout scene
22 *Slavonians* Sclavonians (1590). *Almains* Almans (1590)
23 *murdering* murthering (1590)
25 *Orcanes* (Dyce) omitted in 1590
64 *Illyrians* (1606) Illicians (1590)

I,ii.

37 *Gazellus* Byr. (1590)
45 *Orcanes* Nat. (1590) and at lines
54, 60, 80

I,iii.

7 *renownèd* renowmed (1590)
15 *Cairo* Cario (1590)
19 *Cairo* Cario (1590)

I,iv.

18 *precious* procions (1590)
79 *superficies* (Eds.) superfluities (1590)
93 *murdered* murthered (1590)

I,vi.

1 *Morocco* Moroccus (1590). *Fez* Fesse
(1590) and at lines 3, 13, 23
10 *Morocco* Morocus (1590)
17 *these* this (1590)
43 *Boötes'* Boetes (1590)
97 *orient* (Eds.) oriental (1590)

II,i.

2 *enflames* inflames (1590)
47 *consummate* (Dyce) consinuate (1590)

II,iv.

56 *author* (1606) anchor (1590)
123 *murdered* murthered (1590)
140 *statue* (1606) stature (1590)

III,i.

SD *Callapine* him (1590)

59 *Damascus* Damasco (1590)

III,ii.

39 *Those* (Dyce) Whose (1590)
82 *Murder* Murther (1590)

III,iii.

13 *friends* (Eds.) friend (1590)
33 *[any] issue* (Eds.) issue (1590)
56 *gabions* (Eds.) Galions (1590)

III,iv.

SD *Olympia* his wife (1590)
67-68 *And . . . Come* one line in 1590

III,v.

SD *with their train,* Almeda, with their traine (1590)
1 *Renownèd* Renowmed (1590)
126 *liv'st* liuest (1590)

IV,i.

6 *conquering* (Eds.) conquerings (1590)
29 *murderous* murtherous (1590)

IV,ii.

15, SD *Calyphas* him (1590)
54 *burden* burthen (1590)
82 *resist in* (Eds.) resisting (1590)
99 *Excel* (Dyce) Expel (1590)

IV,iii.

12 *murder* murther (1590)
71-72 *Why . . . precious* prose in 1590
83 *murderèd* murthered (1590)
87 *Elysium* Elisian (1590)

IV,iv.

SD *led by* led by with (1590)
81 *continent* (Eds.) content (1590)
83 *Concubines* Lad. (1590)
84, SD *The Soldiers* They (1590)

V,i.

24 *Citizen* omitted in 1590
38 *Second Citizen* Another (1590)
49 *Theridamas* omitted in 1590
62, SD *Orcanes . . . others* with others, the two spare kings (1590)
147, SD They bridle them (1590)

V,ii.

36 *Renownèd* Renowmed (1590)

V,iii.

1 *Theridamas* omitted in 1590
22 *burden* burthen (1590)
69 *murdering* murthering (1590)
82 *hypostasis* Hipostates (1590)
184, SD *Amyras* him (1590)
186 *burden* burthen (1590)
241 *cliffs* cliftes (1590)

The Major Critics

UNA M. ELLIS-FERMOR

TAMBURLAINE

I

They shall not grow old.

"Amidst the mortifying circumstances attendant upon growing old" not the least is this, that, in measure as we understand the rest of the world better, we understand Christopher Marlowe less. For to understand Marlowe demands eternal youth, and it is an all too frequent experience, as we re-read the early plays, to find lines becoming faint and distant that once held echoes of the harmony that "the morning stars sang together." This is, of course, peculiarly true of *Tamburlaine,* the first and most resplendent of the plays.

For Tamburlaine is no earthly or human growth, he is built out of no experience that life offers; rather he is built in proud defiance of all that the accumulated wisdom of the ages has declared to be the lot of man. He is the embodiment of a vision, framed of aspirations and of that glory of which

> . . . Youthful poets dream
> On summer eves by haunted stream.

He is passion's first challenge to a world which seems—as always to a lover—never to have assisted before at the spectacle of passion. Marlowe has a manner of taking that world by storm, or revealing to its astonished eyes—

From *Christopher Marlowe* (London: Methuen & Co., 1927), pp. 24–60. Reprinted by permission of the publisher.

The light that never was on sea or land

and the unique magic of the play derives from the fact that there is—in the first part, at least—no hint of the fading of that light. It is the drama of confidence stretching to such dazzling heights that we forget the wise saws and maxims of mediocrity, and are bewildered into believing with Marlowe that what has never been achieved is by no means therefore unachievable. "I throw my mind across the chasm," said the Indian hunter, "and my horse follows." That is Marlowe's spirit. The barriers between the possible and the impossible are down. There is but one absolute measure of all phenomena—the human will. And, curiously, in the crevices of our beings, there is something that still recognises this for essential truth and all other records of experience for accidents. Such is the response we make to the appeal of *Tamburlaine*.

For *Tamburlaine* must be in part to us what it primarily was to Marlowe, a poem of escape. It is a poem in which the thwarted instinct for beauty finds its outlet, not normally, perhaps even hysterically, but with a delirious rapture that raised it far above the lyric power of his contemporaries. All that is farthest from the calm, intellectual regularity of academic life he takes for his province. Barbaric and primitive war, barbaric and primitive love, bright oriental colour, and clamorous oriental music are the stuff of which *Tamburlaine* is made. The intoxication of wide spaces and swift movement, of the uncivilised splendour of the Scythian horses inspires its poetry. It is the poetry of imagination at last released and making its dream in defiance of fact. It is for this spontaneous love of beauty in its every form, for this catholicity of joy, that most of Marlowe's readers remember *Tamburlaine*.

It is difficult to separate the play from the great central figure that dominates it, nor is it necessary at first. For in Tamburlaine the passion, the exaltation, the poetry and the hyperbole are concentrated, and through him Marlowe speaks, though for the first time, with no uncertain voice. There is a line near the beginning of the play, when Menander is describing the Scythian shepherd, that goes to the heart of the matter and puts Marlowe's poetry and philosophy for us into some half-dozen unforgettable words:

Like his desire, lift upwards and divine . . .

The first impression that Tamburlaine makes is sudden, swift and amazing; he is compact of hyperbole, of passion, of exaltation. His audience is a little uncertain at first; interested and astonished, but withholding judgment. Then come the lines spoken to Theridamas:

> I hold the Fates bound fast in iron chains,
> And with my hand turn Fortune's wheel about,
> And sooner shall the sun fall from his sphere
> Then Tamburlaine be slain or overcome. [Pt. 1, I. ii. 173–76]

And the audience is lifted from the plane on which judgments are given or withheld, mastered by that eagerness which transcends criticism. It is boasting which has no parallel in the wise literature of gracious, civilised peoples. No Greek thinker ever touched such a passion except to rebuke and chastise its distant prototype, the ὕβρις of the drama. In the loose, fantastic and undisciplined poetry of Scandinavian scalds and Irish bards we may perhaps find something to put beside it, but, again, the boasts of Cuchulainn lack compactness and intensity beside Tamburlaine's. And at the same time there is something winning—almost childish—in his eagerness for the great battle with the Persian host. His thirst for sovereignty and love of arms are passions springing from no base source. And, in his crowning vision of the triumph in Persepolis, romance and fanatic fervour go hand in hand:

> And ride in triumph through Persepolis!
> Is it not brave to be a king, Techelles?
> Usumcasane and Theridamas,
> Is it not passing brave to be a king,
> And ride in triumph through Persepolis?
> [Pt. 1, II. v. 50–54]

On nearer view there is seen to be a peculiar quality attaching to these emotions, which lifts them clear of the contamination of the vulgar or the superficial. However fantastic it may be, Tamburlaine's hyperbole is seldom absurd, even when he describes in words which fail of their effect the mountain-tops melting at the sight of Zenocrate's beauty. There is an infectious magic about his boasting because, when we look closely at it we wonder whether, after all, the thing that it pursues is inconceivable. Lyly's hyperboles we set aside as trivial because we know that they were not for him the symbols or shadows of truth. And if Marlowe's extravagance had been like Lyly's, he, too, would have sacrificed the significance of character and of idea. But Tamburlaine is set upon the attainment of something that lies at the uttermost bounds of possibility, in unknown and uncharted country, so that the quest is followed with breathless anticipation and his desire finds an echo, faint or clear, in every mind. Thus, paradoxically, Tamburlaine is too near the essentials of life for ridicule. And when he declares his influence more potent than that of the gods, or prepares, against impossible odds, to win over Theridamas and his thousand horse, his tone recalls less the boasting of some Scandinavian thane than the fervour of religious fanaticism. He will scale the heavens, as Jove did, and become immortal: will and imagination will triumph over physical obstacles, over the conditions of man's life, over the apparent laws of man's nature. This is no other than the faith that moves mountains.

There must then be something of uncommon significance in Tamburlaine so to transmute these otherwise common elements, and the question of what this is brings us back to our first impression of the play as an expression of aspiration and of desire. This desire, which is in its nature vague, limitless and undefined, is more often than not betrayed and misinterpreted by Marlowe's effort to express it. This is perhaps the normal fate of any aspiration detached from the phenomena and terminology of everyday life, yet, even so, the clarity with which it is preserved in rare lines where its quality is unclouded, is startling. To define it, when Marlowe himself has almost failed, is ludicrous. It is an eternal concomitant of the spirit of man that transforms his effort into something endued with strange, far-reaching significance. For Tamburlaine embodies—

> Man's desire and valiance that range
> All circumstance, and come to port unspent

Having this, he has a quality which cannot be defined and yet cannot be mistaken.

But, from time to time throughout the play, Marlowe tries to define it. He looks for a concrete form with which to invest it, and for a time it almost seems that he is succeeding. The form he has chosen is a bold, unquestioning picture of the supreme glory of material power. Conquest and kingship are the bourne of Tamburlaine's aspiration; that, Marlowe tells us, is the form in which this instinct of man's spirit can most fitly express itself. And for a time we listen, overpersuaded by his urgency and wondering whether, after all, this may not be true. Perhaps the *'gloria mundi'* has never been more frankly worshipped or invested in colours more radiant than in those lines of Theridamas:

> A god is not so glorious as a king.
> I think the pleasure they enjoy in heaven
> Can not compare with kingly joys in earth.
>
> [Pt. 1, II. v. 57–59]

But even in the conclusion of this passage there is a decline as soon as Theridamas tries to put his vision into concrete terms of kingly power—a decline which fairly represents what happens throughout the play whenever this attempt is made.

For failure is inevitable; we realise it after the first two acts. The form Marlowe has chosen has no power to express the idea that inspired him, and the idea survives only in those moments in which it escapes and detaches itself. 'Nature,' Marlowe says, 'doth teach us all to have aspiring minds,' and there follows his idea of the soul, the restless, inspiring force of life, in perhaps the noblest lines he ever wrote. And then, at the end, comes the inevitable bathos. To what is all this aspiration and hunger directed? "To the ripest fruit of all," Marlowe tries to persuade us:

> The sweet fruition of an earthly crown.
>
> [Pt. 1, II. vii. 29]

We do not believe him. We go back to the lines about the "faculties" of the soul and take care never again to link them with what follows. For the fact is that Marlowe has suddenly—it may be all unconsciously—broken faith with his idea. The instinct is there, magically defined and passionate. The error, the inability to grasp in a weaker mood its full significance, occurs when Marlowe attempts to give it a specific direction. In a sense his mental biography is a history of successive attempts of this kind. The spirit of Tamburlaine eventually becomes subdued to what it works in and the aspiration of the early acts slips from him and is lost before we realise it. So it is with Marlowe himself, who began with writing *Tamburlaine* and ended with writing *Edward II*. Yet the fundamental idea, that man can, if he will, reach the sublime, that what has never been accomplished is not therefore impossible, remains unshaken to the end.

And so the first part of Tamburlaine becomes a study of the irresistible power of a mind concentrating upon an end which it pursues with unsleeping singleness of purpose. In the supreme moments of the early part of the play in which his career and his life alike hang in the balance, Tamburlaine is upheld, sustained and carried to triumph by nothing except this fixedness of purpose. He confronts Theridamas with the odds ninety-nine to the hundred against him. It is noticeable that Marlowe puts him physically at the mercy of the enemy:

> Keep all your standings, and not stir a foot;
> Myself will bide the danger of the brunt . . .
>
> . . . .
>
> Whom seek'st thou, Persian? I am Tamburlaine.
>
> [Pt. 1, I. ii. 150–51, 153]

He wins through on the hundredth chance, but—as is true of all his subsequent victories—it is a triumph of the mind. He rests everything upon the power to carry home his indomitable conviction:

> Forsake thy king and do but join with me,
> And we will triumph over all the world.
>
> [Pt. 1, I. ii. 171–72]

and it is the rest of this speech that, with its comparatively quiet, yet irresistible persuasion, turns the mind of Theridamas from his allegiance and fills him and the audience with that inexplicable faith upon which the development of the play depends.

Even when he has an army at his back, it is the mind of Tamburlaine that triumphs, not his cohorts. Marlowe does not always make this as clear as he might, but it is always there. It is the same sort of coercion that Tamburlaine exercises over the mind of Bajazet; it is revealed as soon as we try to penetrate the superficial crudeness of these scenes. For surely a king like Bajazet would have resisted Tamburlaine's insults and refused to give any response, if he had not been under a stronger compulsion than the fear of death. Tamburlaine at the highest moments of his power seldom employs physical force against his victims. He dominates

Bajazet's mind, and the power to resist goes out of the Turk. It is the way of a snake with a squirrel; it robs the victim of its sense of proportion by raising in its mind a mirage of inexplicable and unfounded terror. Marlowe does not make this quite clear, perhaps. An actor such as Alleyn would have done it for him with a look, a pause and a gesture, though for the reader of three hundred years later there is some delay before the intention is understood. But it is an integral part of the conception of the genius of Tamburlaine, and though Marlowe's hand falters sometimes, his idea never changes.

Tamburlaine, then, is a play in which the protagonists are ideas more or less adequately expressed through the minds and characters of men, and it follows that the most vital of these ideas are concerned with the nature of the mind, with its relations to the material universe and to that other, vaguer world which seems to envelop man, his motives, his actions and his surroundings, and which Marlowe at this stage still, for the most part, names God. There are other elements in *Tamburlaine,* of course, but they sink into insignificance beside those questions which occupied Marlowe's early years: 'What is the soul?' 'What is God?' And these bring inevitably with them a host of criticisms, explicit and implicit, of the existing efforts to explain the relationship between these two forces. The climax of this conflict is not reached until *Faustus,* but the beginnings are clear in *Tamburlaine.*

What does Marlowe at this period understand by 'the soul'? In general, it is, of course, the seat of thought and mental activity, the innermost part of man's being, the ultimate citadel of his personality; an imperishable essence. But, more than this, it is the source of the very power to think and of the restless desire for knowledge; the part which is mysteriously touched with beauty, the part to which God tunes his harmonies. All this is explicitly stated by Tamburlaine himself [Pt. 1, II. vii. 18–29; V. ii. 116], but we may go further and say that the soul is also the inspiration which sustains Tamburlaine, and in this sense the whole play becomes a study of the idea of the soul, which—

> Still climbing after knowledge infinite,
> And always moving as the restless spheres,
> Wills us to wear ourselves and never rest, . . .
>
> [Pt. 1, II. vii. 24–26]

What then (apart from the specific tendency with which Marlowe falsely seeks to invest this instinct in *Tamburlaine*) is the object of this striving? I do not think Marlowe succeeds in telling us this even implicitly, but I think he reveals enough of himself for conjecture to have a fairly firm basis.

To make this conjecture it is necessary to decide precisely what is here Marlowe's idea of God, and this is not an easy task because the allusions are confused. All creeds and forms of religious thought are mingled in the empire of Tamburlaine even as they were in the Asia Minor of the late middle ages—or, for the matter of that, in the mind of Christopher Marlowe in the late 16th century. 'Jove,' 'Jupiter,' 'the gods,' 'heaven,' appear alternately as mild euphemisms for the ideas the modern world conveys—equally evasively—under terms like 'Providence.' The word 'God' is used more distinctively (though sometimes 'Jove' has almost the same connotation). 'God' is generally used to express Marlowe's highest conceptions of the supreme power, and perhaps the noblest of these is found in the second part, where the idea of God as a spirit is clearly and unerringly expressed:

> ... He that sits on high and never sleeps,
> Nor in one place is circumscriptible,
> But everywhere fills every continent
> With strange infusion of His sacred vigor, ...
> [Pt. 2, II. ii. 49–52]

There is nothing vague or uncertain about this last line and we may safely take it as the supreme reach of Marlowe's imagination, touched once, though by no means maintained throughout the play. In interesting conjunction with it, stands Tamburlaine's claim that his spirit is itself part of the nature of God:

> ... the flesh of Tamburlaine,
> Wherein an incorporeal spirit moves,
> Made of the mould whereof thyself consists,
> Which makes me valiant, proud, ambitious,
> Ready to levy power against thy throne, ...
> [Pt. 2, IV. ii. 38–42]

To add to these two passages Tamburlaine's eulogy of the soul, is to come upon a rather interesting suggestion. For Marlowe appears to have been on the verge of formulating the idea that the spirit and 'desire' of man are neither more nor less than God in man. It is well to say only that he was upon the verge of this conclusion because I think that (any possibility of the influence of Plato being left out of the question for obvious reasons), had he effected the supreme conjunction between these ideas, there would have been no need for the writing of *Faustus*. But even in its incomplete state the conception, which is so obviously not derived from Plato, but is a tentative, imperfect, original idea, is startlingly modern, or at least startlingly independent of his contemporaries.

A man who had reached such an idea at twenty-three and who had, moreover, been through the mill of contemporary theological training might well have something interesting to say by way of comment upon those contemporaries. And much of the second part of *Tamburlaine* does, in point of fact, supply us with this comment in two complementary lines of thought.

In the second part of *Tamburlaine,* Mahometans and Christians are introduced with indiscriminate frequency. The direct references to the Christians are, for the most part, cautious and colourless, but a few are rich in significance. When he spoke of Mahometans, however, Marlowe had a freer hand and under this disguise the basis of his hostility to Christianity reveals itself. What he condemns in Mahometanism he condemns equally in Christianity (though for Christianity itself he reserves a contempt that he does not visit upon its rival). Mahomet appears at first as the prophet and friend of God, who is invoked promiscuously by Tamburlaine, by Turks and by Egyptians. Gradually the references begin to indicate his indifference to his worshippers and his helplessness, until finally Tamburlaine denounces him as a delusion, in the rather puzzling terms:

> In vain, I see, men worship Mahomet.
> My sword hath sent millions of Turks to hell, . . .
> And yet I live untouched by Mahomet.
> There is a God, full of revenging wrath, . . .
> Whose scourge I am, and Him will I obey. . . .
> Now, Mahomet, if thou have any power,
> Come down thyself and work a miracle.   [Pt. 2, V. i. 177–86]

> He cannot hear the voice of Tamburlaine.
> Seek out another godhead to adore—

> The God that sits in heaven, if any god,
> For He is God alone, and none but He.   [Pt. 2, V. i. 197–200]

What is revealed here is, I think, the refusal to accept the idea of a personal God who intervenes in the material concerns of men, and a denial of the validity of any religion which is based upon such a supposition. It is needless, of course, to remark that these incisive comments are the fruit of observation of Elizabethan Christians, not of fourteenth-century Mahometans.

In a few but daring comments upon Christianity, Marlowe's position is more clearly defined. The first clue is given by Bajazet's exclamation:

> Now will the Christian miscreants be glad,
> Ringing with joy their superstitious bells, . . .
>
> [Pt. 1, III. iii. 236–37]

Bajazet may be credited with a natural dislike of Christians, but when this dislike takes so specific a turn and reveals individual rancour against a definite quality, we must needs read into the epithet 'superstitious' the feelings of Marlowe and not of the Turk. The rest of the passage may be Bajazet's; the adjective is Marlowe's own comment and gives the key to his enmity. The evidence of this passage is not unsupported, for it is further explained by the parts given to Baldwin and the Christian leaders who, justifying themselves by casuistry, break the oaths that they have sworn by Christ. In this case the comment is bold and clear and Sigismund's lines:

> Our faiths are sound, and must be consummate,
> Religious, righteous, and inviolate.   [Pt. 2, II. i. 47–48]

are ironically denied by his own ultimate conduct.

Finally, Marlowe's hatred of the characteristic vices of the Christian character is proclaimed through the mouth of Orcanes in lines which ring with personal feeling:

> Can there be such deceit in Christians
> Or treason in the fleshly heart of man,
> Whose shape is figure of the highest God?
> Then if there be a Christ, as Christians say,
> But in their deeds deny him for their Christ, . . .
>
> [Pt. 2, II. ii. 36–40]

These lines have an inevitable stamp—a stamp which invariably characterises those utterances of Marlowe's that have a personal bearing or spring from intimate experience. Behind the conflict of ideas here there is keen pain. It would be impertinent to conjecture too closely as to the nature of this, but the tone of the passage leaves us actually in very little doubt as to the origins of Marlowe's disillusionment.

The references to Christ, as distinct from those to Christians, suggest (as indeed they do throughout his works) that Marlowe deliberately separated the two conceptions. It was the practice of Christianity that he hated, not its original inspiration or the personality of its founder. About these latter things, curiously enough, he troubled himself very little, or the history of his mental development might have been modified.

The conclusions that can be drawn from these passages leave us with the picture of a man whose hostility was directed not to religion itself but to religions; that is, to the forms with which his contemporaries desecrated the instinct which was for Marlowe

> The anchor of his purest thoughts . . . and soul
> Of all his moral being.

This manifests itself, not unnaturally, in the form of a hatred of the specific religion or 'superstition' which confronted him, so that Marlowe's utterances have sometimes almost the tone of Lucretius's and suggest a similarity in the experience and attitudes of the two men.

Such, then, are the ideas for the expression of which *Tamburlaine* exists, and it might perhaps be expected that, being primarily a vehicle for the expression of ideas, it should fail sometimes to fulfil the conditions of the art-form which these ideas have somewhat arbitrarily chosen. *Tamburlaine* appears to break down when we cease to regard it as a poetic expression of an idea and begin to consider its capacities as drama, and to offend most seriously in those two main functions which distinguish drama— that of revealing the interplay of characters of individual men and that of giving form to a selected part of the apparent incoherence of events. I think, however, that the breakdown is, in both cases, more apparent than real.

What preoccupies us with Tamburlaine is not his character.

For what, after all, is that character? If we gather together all the
suggestions in the first play we have not enough to give us a clear
picture.

Tamburlaine is for the most part endowed with the conventional attributes of a conqueror: when he is not expounding the
transcendant powers of the human will he demonstrates, rather
woodenly, the dignity, the pomp and the good-humoured arrogance of a man conscious of carrying all before him. As his triumph becomes more assured this arrogance loses its fascination
and becomes either the unbalanced recklessness which dares 'god
out of heaven,' or the extravagance that plays with the situation
like a child. The puerility of the scenes with Bajazet is part of
the conventional temperament of an oriental despot. The freakish, unrestrained moods of these later acts have little or nothing
to do with the glittering figure of the earlier scenes who spoke of
the destiny of man:

> To wear ourselves and never rest . . .
> Still climbing after knowledge infinite.

Yet in slight hints, scattered up and down the play, something
like a personality is indicated. There is that impetuous directness
of Tamburlaine's in a moment of crisis in which we seem to see
Marlowe falling back upon an individual mannerism of his own
to eke out his imperfect observation:

> Then shall we fight courageously with them,

Tamburlaine exclaims,

> Or look you I should play the orator?   [Pt. 1, I. ii. 129]

And, again, look at the cool rapidity with which he assesses Theridamas, the swiftness of his approval, decision and action: a direct method of going to work with another personality:

> With what a majesty he rears his looks!
> [Pt. 1, I. ii. 164]

and then, with the quickness of thought . . .

> Forsake thy king and do but join with me, . . .
> [Pt. 1, I. ii. 171]

Tamburlaine has some of the defects of this temperament, too.
He cannot retreat fighting and can offer only sullen obstinacy

against Zenocrate's plea for Damascus; he is as inarticulate in love as he is eloquent in war, and his attitude to Zenocrate at what is presumably the crisis of their relationship, has to be indicated by a clumsy piece of stage by-play, which is perhaps only less clumsy than the words that Tamburlaine—or Marlowe—would have found. Yet his very ruthlessness, when he rises to the crest of a momentous action, has a certain sublimity—

> Your fearful minds are thick and misty then,
> For there sits Death; there sits imperious Death, . . .
>
> [Pt. 1, V. ii. 47–48]

There is then a clear austerity about the character of Tamburlaine: he is not turned aside by any of the grosser temptations of his position; it is true to say that he is unaware of their existence. There are moments of deliberate relaxation when he sports with Bajazet, but he never lays aside his mastery of himself and of the situation, nor does any pleasure or subsidiary aim cloud his mind or come between him and the clear end of his ambition. He combines the force of Alexander with that steadfastness of vision that springs only from an inspiration, in its ultimate source religious. For all of this Marlowe had little or no suggestion except from his knowledge of his own heart:

> I will not spare these proud Egyptians,
> Nor change my martial observations
> For all the wealth of Gihon's golden waves,
> Or for the love of Venus, would she leave
> The angry god of arms and lie with me.   [Pt. 1, V. ii. 58–62]

After which it is not inconsistent that Tamburlaine should appear sometimes as a poet to whom the sources of poetry and of ambition seem cunningly intermingled in that force which men call Beauty—

> . . . mother to the Muses; . . .
> . . . With whose instinct the soul of man is toucht.

The Tamburlaine of the second part of the play is marked by a savageness, an ever-increasing extravagance, a lack at once of inspiration and of balance. The freakish, unrestrained moods of these later scenes have little or nothing to do with the glittering figure of the earlier part who spoke of the destiny of man:

> . . . To wear ourselves and never rest, . . .
> . . . Still climbing after knowledge infinite.

These later qualities are the logical outcome of the situation that
Marlowe created when he set out to write a 'second part' to the
study of a character who can, by the very nature of his being, only
have a first part. For Tamburlaine lives in the future and the
essence of his spirit is the forward reach and the aspiration which
must continue 'still climbing' if they are to live, and fail, even as
Marlowe's interpretation failed, when they reach 'the ripest fruit
of all.' There are certain instincts and desires at work in the mind
that are so wholly things of the spirit that to pursue them into
realisation and fulfilment is not within the power of human
thought, not even for Christopher Marlowe. But having committed himself, there was only one thing for Marlowe to do; to follow the decline and disintegration of that genius whose rise
had been his original theme. So the second part contains the
Nemesis whose very existence it was the triumph of the first part
to deny.

Tamburlaine's constant references to himself, in the second
part, as the minister of the vengeance of God, somehow detract
from his majesty and fall short of the sublime self-confidence of
his youth. More and more he appears to be a crazy fanatic, less
and less that strangely inspired interpreter of the needs of the
spirit. He is unbalanced now, rather than superhuman:

> And, till by vision or by speech I hear
> Immortal Jove say 'Cease, my Tamburlaine,'
> I will persist a terror to the world, . . .   [Pt. 2, IV. ii. 124–26]

Dignity and clearness of vision all go down before this increasing
insanity, and it is Tamburlaine himself who alters, not the situa-
tions. The chariot drawn by the tributary kings is not essentially
more extravagant than Bajazet in his cage; it is the bearing of
Tamburlaine that has lost its mastery and become frenzied. Chivalry has no place in such a character, and his treatment of the
Governor of Babylon loses severely by comparison with the corresponding slaughter of the Damascan virgins in the first part. (To
the end, though, Marlowe shows no clear appreciation of the finer
shades of relationship between a man and his fellows and Tamburlaine's defect here is but the result of the absence of this grace.)

The Tamburlaine of the second part has sunk down to an oriental despot, savage, extravagant, half insane; a type of which history furnishes enough records and for the creating of which none of the high instincts are needed that produced the original idea of the play. Yet to the end some flashes of the old quality recur, and one of Tamburlaine's last phrases speaks of 'Thoughts, as pure and fiery as Phyteus' beams.'

When we look at the other characters of the double play we find that a few of them repay close examination. The two best have a startling and almost disproportionate interest, they are sympathetic studies which isolate two of the background figures —Mycetes in the first part and Calyphas in the second.

Mycetes may be an imbecile but he, like Calyphas, says some remarkably good things, and both say them in a tone which detaches itself from the rest of the performance and stands out in a different key. Marlowe manipulated Theridamas, Techelles 'and the rest' as he expressively calls them, because they had to fill in certain portions of the play; for some reason he knew what was passing in the minds of Mycetes and Calyphas and let them talk, even irrelevantly, not because he wanted them to fill out the play, but because they had some kind of passport to his sympathy.

Part of Mycetes we meet again in *Edward II,* and certain of his phrases and turns of thought have the very note of Shakespeare's *Richard II.* He is addicted to exuberant and irrelevant imagery, some of it, such as the picture of the bloodstained ankles of his white horses, singularly beautiful, even if slightly perverted. He is also gifted with flashes of significant thought, which have no counterpart in the moods of the other persons or in the theme of the play. There is a faint, tremulous melancholy about him, such as invades the minds of low-spirited men, and it is a relief to find Marlowe—who shows himself, in *Tamburlaine,* unconscious of much that did not bear upon his high adventure—capable of entering wholly into this state of mind:

> Return with speed, . . .

[The speech would sit well upon Richard the Second, but is curiously out of place in this Persia.]

> . . . time passeth swift away.
> Our life is frail, and we may die to day.   [Pt. 1, I. i. 67–68]

Even more delicately does Marlowe touch the hysterical collapse of the Persian king upon the battlefield:

> Accursed be he that first invented war!
> They knew not—ah, they knew not, simple men—
> How those were hit by pelting cannon shot
> Stand staggering like a quivering aspen leaf. . . .
>
> [Pt. 1, II. iv. 1–4]

Such touches as these constitute a rare counterpoint to the great predominant theme of Marlowe's writing, and a clue to his mind's development may be found in watching these subordinate tones gradually increase in number and significance until, in *Edward II,* the pale cast of thought subdues the whole play.

Calyphas is a bolder study, but he also contributes elements that have nothing to do with the tone or conduct of the play, and the two episodes in which he figures seem to be included mainly that he may speak his mind. And his criticism is worth hearing, though perhaps it is dangerous in such a drama to let the light of so frank and sane a judgment play upon the situation. For Calyphas comes very near persuading us that he is the only sane man in a group of madmen, or that Marlowe had had a sudden movement of impatience with the absurdity of his conception and had joined the audience in laughing at his chief characters. However it comes about, Calyphas seems to have been born a humorist. (We are prepared to find him the only member of his family in which any trace of this quality appears.) It is small wonder, then, that he did not always see eye to eye with them, or they with him. He offers to cleave the skull of the Turkish deputy, provided someone will hold him in the meantime—an offer which there was unfortunately no one to appreciate in the Persian court, least of all Tamburlaine himself. His dealing with his brothers is masterly, and again, coming from Marlowe, unexpected. But there is no denying the sure, if momentary, control of the sources of irony:

> Go, go, tall stripling, fight you for us both,
> And take my other toward brother here,
> For person like to prove a second Mars.
> 'Twill please my mind as well to hear both you
> Have won a heap of honor in the field
> And left your slender carcasses behind,
> As if I lay with you for company.   [Pt. 2, IV. i. 33–39]

Zenocrate, on the other hand, presents a more elusive surface than do any of the chief characters. She is talked about, but she very seldom talks—or very seldom to the point. She tells Agydas that she loves Tamburlaine, yet little personality is revealed by her colourless phrases. At Tamburlaine's orders she embarks upon a 'flyting' match with Zabina and continues to obscure her identity with equal skill. Twice only does she seem to speak as Zenocrate and not as the mouthpiece of some other agent: while waiting for the fall of Damascus and on her deathbed. In the first she is full of terrors for Tamburlaine, terrors that are themselves significant of Marlowe's imagination and that help to give perspective to the scene:

> Ah, Tamburlaine my love, sweet Tamburlaine,
> That fights for scepters and for slippery crowns, . . .
> Ah, mighty Jove and holy Mahomet,
> Pardon my love! Oh, pardon his contempt
> Of earthly fortune and respect of pity, . . .
>
> [Pt. 1, V. ii. 292–93, 300–302]

There is a certain gentle, conventional piety about her attitude which shows understanding on Marlowe's part, and the whole speech is a fine ode on the theme *"Sic transit gloria mundi."*

And the deathbed speeches bear this out: she takes leave of her husband, of her sons and of the surrounding friends; she ends with pious advice to her children to follow in their father's footsteps, and leaves life with the hope "to meet your highnesse in the heavens." As far as Zenocrate is anything at all she is a virtuous, god-fearing Elizabethan matron, and may well bear some resemblance to Catherine Marlowe, the shoemaker's wife of Canterbury, who must, at this stage of Marlowe's life, have been the only woman with whom he had been brought into close and daily contact.

The figures that move to and fro behind these main characters, filling out the needs of the story with colour, rhetoric and slender characterisation, are harder to differentiate. The slight conception of his minor figures with which Marlowe began his plays was not always enough to carry him through five acts, and instead of developing fresh suggestions as he handled it, it seems to have worn thinner. Theridamas in this way gives a faint promise of personality in his earliest scenes, but the promise is never fulfilled. The rest, distinguished only by their names, combine to form a harmonious and shadowy background like the figures of a bas-relief or the design on a Greek vase. The scenes with Bajazet show to an extraordinary degree this emptiness of personality. Bajazet, surrounded by his court, has an irresistible likeness to the king in a Christmas pantomime, and withal is as delightfully explicit and prone to instructive descriptions of his rank, power, virtues and intentions. There are passages when he is talking to the Kings of Fez and Morocco—both alone and in the presence of Tamburlaine—that read like a parody, though we may be assured no purpose was further from Marlowe's mind. Nor does his adversity become him better. He has no better weapon at command than vituperation which is of a piece with his former boasting, while Theridamas, Usumcasane and Techelles fill out the rôles of children drawing the attention of their schoolmaster to fresh signs of wickedness on the part of the one that is already in disgrace. At the end Marlowe attempts to invest this grotesque figure with some dignity, and forces his imagination into action, but even so the participation in Bajazet's emotions is the outcome of a deliberate effort, which brings together the elements proper to such a passion but does not necessarily subject the poet to it. Bajazet's death speech, for all its panoply of tempests and clouds, is not spontaneous and has more than a hint of labour.

In a medley such as this it is hard to trace any underlying structure. *Tamburlaine,* so far from interpreting life by indicating its form, appears as formless and incoherent as life itself. The first part, in this, errs less than the second, but even the first has no progress, crisis or solution. The final triumph and marriage of Tamburlaine is perhaps a climax, but it is too long deferred to have a direct connection with the original impulse, and the idea has been anticipated and handled so often that it has lost its freshness. Tamburlaine's rise to power cannot fill five acts of a play without complications, and a complication would be a denial of the very nature of Tamburlaine's genius, which triumphs, not after a struggle, but without it. Thus, before his play was begun, Marlowe had committed himself to a theme that was in its essence undramatic. It is a foregone conclusion, then, that there will be no dramatic form. In the second part of the play where the original impulse is gone, the difficulty of giving any appearance of structural unity increases enormously. Not only is this part episodic and filled with wholly irrelevant matter, such as the story of Olympia and Tamburlaine's speech on fortification, or with events that are only partly relevant such as the career of Calyphas, but the very theme itself is structurally incapable of sustaining interest. It is obvious that, of all the emotions that may be roused in an audience by the action of a play, almost the only one possible to the plot of *Tamburlaine* is surprise, an emotion that can only be evoked to a limited degree. The audience is in a state of suspense during the earliest acts of the double play, and suspense gives way to amazement as triumph follows triumph. As soon as the point is reached at which there is no longer any un-certainty in the mind of the audience—that is, as soon as repeti-tion of the triumph has made the situation familiar and caused it to be expected, there is no more suspense. There are, in point of fact, about two more acts, but they have to be helped out with Bajazet and the Virgins of Damascus—episodes which are irrele-vant to the too simple original theme.

Now the second part suffers a little all through from this dis-ability. Tamburlaine's career of conquest continues without the suspense or the zest that accompanied it in the first three acts. There is much talk of the magnitude of the armies that come against him, but there is no reaction when the triumph follows, because there is no surprise. Surprise is created in such an action as this not by the nature of the events themselves which are all too similar, or by the fact that each one is a little more impressive than the one before, but by each one advancing upon the one be-fore to a degree that outruns the anticipations of the audience. This works clearly enough when Tamburlaine, from being com-mander of a handful of shepherds, leaps to the head of Therida-mas's thousand horse. This is unexpected, and surprise, interest and anticipation are created. From this Tamburlaine becomes the victorious field-marshal of the Persian forces: again, an advance relatively greater than the former and outrunning that degree of expectation which had been created by the first. The difficulty with the second part—before Marlowe ever began to write it— was that this standard of advances could not be maintained, and anything that fell short of it was doomed to forfeit interest and to force the poet upon meretricious—and not always successful—devices for holding the attention. Marlowe's error is really a very simple mathematical one; the rise of Tamburlaine's career throughout the second part could be practically formulated as an arithmetical progression, whereas that of the first part has the more rapid rise of a geometrical progression, and it is this last formula alone which can be relied upon to outrun the anticipations of an audience and create surprise and interest. Looking at Tamburlaine's position at the beginning of the second part in the light of this, it is obvious that nothing short of that war against the gods which he himself speaks of would have been a fit climax to a sequence so begun. . . . It is just possible that Marlowe himself perceived this and that the madness that destroyed Tamburlaine is the vengeance of the heavens that he attacked.

But other expressions of the idea of form are possible though not proper to drama, and it is for signs of these that we must look; for Marlowe had, from the beginning, a fine instinct for the formal quality of an idea.

In the details of form in *Tamburlaine,* this is clear enough, for Marlowe tends always to shape his speeches as lyrics or as odes, by the use of a reiterated line or by deliberate repetition and development of theme. This is revealed at its best in Tamburlaine's speech by the deathbed of Zenocrate (a speech in which, moreover, the formal value of the colour images subordinates the human emotion to the decorative design). But this is not the only case, and Zenocrate, Orcanes, Theridamas, Techelles and Usumcasane all use this device with rhetorical or with lyric effect. In this way, work distantly suggestive of that of the Greek chorus is done by some of the minor characters. Marlowe can, again, mould a speech exquisitely upon a rhetorical description, an argument or the expression of a single passion. There is, thus, fineness of line about isolated details of this design. But, more than this, Marlowe has an instinctive understanding of the severe austerity of decorative art and something of its quality is always present in the background of his play, in the grouping of his figures and in the apportioning of his speeches. This is finely illustrated in the scene in which Theridamas, Usumcasane and Techelles lament over the approaching death of Tamburlaine. The scene contributes little that is of value at such a stage in a play, and is, therefore, perhaps undramatic. But the whole passage with its reiterated lines and interwoven themes, its words that are half song and that seem inevitable to reproduce themselves in pose and movement, admits of exquisite staging in a conventional form modelled on the groupings of an Etruscan frieze or a Greek vase. It becomes more and more clear that in most of the grouped scenes of *Tamburlaine,* Marlowe saw neither a realistic picture of the historical figures (which would have been impossible) nor the final result of the setting upon the Elizabethan stage. I think his intense power of vision provided him with a picture which often had nothing to do with either of these and that this vision had a tendency to conform to the structural demands of the plastic arts rather than to those of drama. *Tamburlaine,* viewed as one might view a strip of design from a Greek vase, appears to be ordered with a certain intermittent harmoniousness of form, giving unity to that background before which moves the dominant figure of Tamburlaine.

II

It happens sooner or later to every reader of *Tamburlaine* to feel, for a time at least, that the play is little more than a series of images, all relevant to the dominant emotions (though by no means always to their immediate setting), all startling and arresting at the first glance, and yet leaving the reader in the end with a feeling of vague dissatisfaction, to look elsewhere for the secret of Marlowe's poetry.

One group of these images forms a kind of accompaniment to the personality of Tamburlaine; it is full of barbaric wealth and metallic splendour, clamorous with the noise of arms and trumpets, and vivid with blood. Above all it is brilliant, with the hard, blatant lustre of gold and jewels, whose names and colours seem to echo the clang and fanfare of military music. Marlowe uses their resources to bring before us the objects and the themes upon which Tamburlaine's mind dwelt:

> Their plumèd helms are wrought with beaten gold,
> Their swords enamelled, and about their necks
> Hangs massy chains of gold. . . .   [Pt. 1, I. ii. 124–26]

> And with our sun-bright armor, as we march
> We'll chase the stars from heaven and dim their eyes
> That stand and muse. . . .   [Pt. 1, II. iii. 22–24]

There is a like instinctive propriety, too, in those gloomy images, redolent of Senecan horror, that begin to accompany Tamburlaine's progress through the later acts of the double drama. As the darkness of his temper grows deeper the "furies of the black Cocytus lake" wait upon him with their attendant train of ghosts and Stygian snakes and pitchy clouds. Like the imagery of Seneca, and yet true to Marlowe's dominant theme, it is sublime in its highest reaches, where Tamburlaine gives orders to—

> . . . set black streamers in the firmament
> To signify the slaughter of the gods.   [Pt. 2, V. iii. 49–50]

It is a relief to turn from this to another group of images through which he reveals his idea of Zenocrate, who brings with her the radiance of the "lamps of heaven," the gleam of silver or crystal and the milk-white of ivory. She is like—

> . . . Flora in her morning's pride,
> Shaking her silver tresses in the air, . . .
>
>   [Pt. 1, V. ii. 77–78]

And this radiance, welcome among the heavy colours of this barbaric play, is also an integral part of Tamburlaine's mind; it is the reflection of his vision of Zenocrate, as are the others of his thirst "for sovereignty and love of arms."

Much has been made of Marlowe's love of colour and, for simple, strong tones, his instinct cannot be questioned. But it is only the simple and the strong tones that he dwells upon; his is not a subtle colour-sense. In all the range of both parts of *Tamburlaine* he speaks only of blood-red, black, gold, crystal, silver and milk-white. So startling and decorative are the effects that he achieves with these, that we forget at first there is no mention in the whole ten acts of the green of grass, of the blue of the sky, or the browns, greys and violets of the English landscape. Except for a dubious reference to sapphires (by which I suspect him to mean diamonds) there is nothing to indicate that Marlowe was not colour-blind to the whole range of the spectrum beyond red and yellow. Too much allowance can hardly be made for the deliberate choice of tones that suited his decorative scheme and for his valuing colour rather as a contribution to the form of his poem than for its intrinsic subtlety and beauty. But the fact remains that colour is not the fittest medium for the expression of Marlowe's thought and, though its fascination is not lost upon him, there is no sign of such response to the delicate interplay of tones as is revealed in any fifty lines of *Comus*. Beside Milton's vast range of colour epithets Marlowe's take on a medieval simplicity. His finest *tours-de-force*, the 'white,' 'silver,' 'snow,' 'blood,' 'scarlet,' 'jet,' of Tamburlaine's tents, seem crude beside Milton's complicated tones: 'azure,' 'violet,' 'dusky,' 'silver,' 'saffron,' 'rose,' 'grey,' 'sooty,' 'yellow,' 'amber,' 'russet,' 'tawny,' 'Turkis blue' and 'emerald.'

This happens partly because Marlowe's images are often mainly decorative and ornamental. A few, even so, have rare beauty; though the best of them are not untinged with the artificiality of youth. Mycetes' horses with their milk-white legs fantastically splashed with crimson blood are a decorative detail. The same formal beauty is felt in the suddenly inserted line: "Brave horses bred on the white Tartarian hills." And when Tamburlaine says that he will—

> Batter the shining palace of the sun,
> And shiver all the starry firmament, . . .
>
> [Pt. 2, II. iv. 105–6]

we have reached the highest splendour of purely decorative imagery. But from that level Marlowe too often declines in *Tamburlaine*, and there is much that is not even effective rhetoric. In this case his images have little or no harmony with the emotions that form the background of the passage and serve rather to illustrate them than to echo their associations. We miss the spontaneous harmony between the individual image and its setting that we feel when Fortinbras cries, at the sight of the dead and dying Danish court:

> O, proud death,
> What feast is toward in thine eternal cell . . . ?

or when Banquo, on the night of Duncan's murder, feels that—

> . . . There's husbandry in Heaven,
> Their candles are all out. . . .

Yet such imagery as that of Tamburlaine is not devoid of power, though it is most effective when it is cumulative, when one rhetorical picture leads on to another and the final impression is achieved by the weight of the whole rather than by the incisiveness of any one. Tamburlaine's description of his triumph in the last act of *Part I* is just such an effective, cumulative series of little pictures no one of which can be picked out as having the quality of poetry. Jove, the Furies, and Death are all there; there are showers of blood, and meteors in Africa; dead kings lie at Tamburlaine's feet, while on the banks of Styx are souls clamouring to be carried over to the land of shades. It is all there, but it has a tendency to find its way to the imagination through the reason —which is not the way of poetic imagery.

Worse still, from this point of view, are those unassimilated allusions, astronomical, geographical, historical, mythological, in which Marlowe's knowledge is hardly subdued at all to the purposes of poetry. His imagination has been overpowered by the material it worked in, and no transmutation has been achieved; not even that partial conversion which gives the rhetorical imagery of the long 'set' speeches. Through both parts of the play, but more painfully in the second, we are stopped by inventories of persons and places and other irrelevant technicalities that stir no emotion in us and cannot ever have held magic associations even for Marlowe. The number of these proves, on careful view, astonishingly great. It will be enough to look at one case, and that of the 'name catalogue' is perhaps most suggestive because, in the first place, Marlowe is obviously doing his duty by a tradition that he inherited from Virgil, and because, in the second, he unfortunately challenges comparison with Shakespeare and with Milton who discovered, in this matter, a more excellent way.

It is immaterial which catalogue we take. There is a good one at the beginning of the third act, where Bajazet enumerates his own titles (surely unnecessarily?) to the emissary he is about to send to Persia. They are fine titles—at least as high-sounding as the 'Warwick and Talbot,' or the 'Morocco and Trebizond' of more lasting fame.

> Hie thee, my basso, fast to Persia.
> Tell him thy lord, the Turkish emperor,
> Dread lord of Afric, Europe, and Asia,
> Great king and conqueror of Græcia,
> The ocean, Terrene, and the coal-black sea,
> The high and highest monarch of the world, . . .
>
> [Pt. 1, III. i. 21–26]

Why is it that there is no magic or emotional appeal here? The names may have been full of associations for Marlowe, but, if so, it is curious that they communicate nothing. For the magic that clings to proper names has nothing to do with associations in the mind of the reader and derives its power, in some mysterious way, only from the poignancy of its appeal to the mind of the poet. Most of us go down to our graves knowing nothing about Vallombrosa beyond the two lines which give us all our denotation of the name—and which we shall carry with us as long and as surely as we shall our indifference to all other associations of the word. And curiously enough, on the one occasion upon which Marlowe stumbled upon the secret, the name he immortalised had less previous significance even than Vallombrosa. Who but an antiquary could have found pathos or passion in the name Persepolis till Marlowe wrote the five lines that will live as long as any passage in his plays?

But for the most part I suspect that Marlowe was inclined to introduce names in the raw, straight from his note-books into the speech. They sound laboured, as if he were trying to carry conviction to himself and his readers. If he were a modern writer we should say that he was trying to convey an impression of local colour but that he had not yet learnt the alphabet of that branch of technique. His mood seems logical and scientific rather than imaginative or poetic, and names, which roll through Milton's mind as phrases in the symphony of human history, refused to yield their secret to Marlowe. And this is part of the strict justice of art, for what did Marlowe care for—

> ... What resounds
> Of fable or romance of Uther's son,
> Begirt with British or Armoric knights,
> And all who since, baptiz'd or infidel,
> Jousted in Aspramont or Montalban,
> Damasco or Morocco or Trebizond,
> Or whom Biserta sent from Afric shore
> When Charlemain with all his peerage fell
> By Fontarabbia ...

This incidental imagery, beautiful as it is at its best, only gives us the measure of part of Marlowe's poetry, for, as I have said, *Tamburlaine* is scattered with long passages of majestic description which, though they never rise to the first rank of poetry, have a power and impressiveness that is the highest reach of rhetoric and trembles continually upon the verge of poetry itself.

The first of these is the picture which Tamburlaine unfolds to Zenocrate of her life as his empress. It is deliberate; a kind of inventory of the elements which ought to make up a striking picture: the swift steeds, the Median silk, the jewels, the ivory sledge and the frozen mountain-tops that dissolve at the sight of Zenocrate. Some of these "set" descriptions—such as that of the tents [Pt. 1, IV. i. 48–64]—Marlowe moulds better than others. But always we feel the poet rousing himself and rallying his resources; he is never swept away by the sudden uprush of emotion. It is the same with the description of Tamburlaine himself [Pt. 1, II. i. 7–30]. We abandon the description as soon as we have read it, relying for our impression of Tamburlaine upon his own speeches, the direct expression of his mind. Perhaps we remember something of his "stature tall and straightly fashioned," of his "pale complexion" and the "knot of amber hair." But there is only one line that is indelibly written upon our memories, and it has nothing to do with what Tamburlaine looked like, nor is it in any sense an image. It is simply an idea—the idea of a mind "lift upward and divine."

The same might be said of other passages. Callapine's description of the kingly state in the first act of the Second Part [Pt. 1, I. iii. 28–53], one of the most picturesque passages in the play; or the pompous gloom of the destruction of Larissa with its holocaust of flaming turrets, meteors, dragons, lightning and other natural phenomena leading inevitably to the Furies, Lethe and Styx. There is even a fine apocalyptic quality about this, a quality that Marlowe's heavier work is already beginning to show. In Theridamas's description of Tamburlaine [Pt. 2, III. iv. 44–67] much that has already been said is again borne out. We can feel the machine getting to work; that it is a powerful machine and works splendidly does not alter the fact that the result is a product, not a growth. Moreover, the crude material horrors which he tries to use here were never, for Marlowe, the gateway to terror or pity as they were for Seneca and Kyd; it was not from the picture of blood and slaughter that he was to evoke either emotion. And when all is said, this apparently remarkable speech contains little more than the unused materials that were discarded when, with truer inspiration, Marlowe wrote: "I hold the Fates fast bound in iron chains."

And this brings us to the conclusion to which a study of the imagery of *Tamburlaine* inevitably leads, that the highest inspiration lies elsewhere and that the great poetry of these early plays is not poetry of imagery at all, but poetry of ideas. We forget the rhetoric and the fantastic decorative colouring when Tamburlaine speaks the language that came instinctively to Marlowe—the language of thought, not of the senses:

> Our souls, whose faculties can comprehend
> The wondrous architecture of the world
> And measure every wandering planet's course,
> Still climbing after knowledge infinite,
> And always moving as the restless spheres,
> Wills us to wear ourselves and never rest, . . .
>
> [Pt. 1, II. vii. 21–26]

Here is the poetry of Marlowe's early years, not in the descriptions of the tents nor even in the apotheosis of Zenocrate.

For it is lines such as these that we come upon a rare quality: that of emotion which is the outcome not of the experience of the senses, but of thought. Spenser, Shakespeare, Milton, Shelley—whether they eventually outgrow it or not—begin by deriving their experience through the senses; in their early years the sensuous is the dominant element in their poetry, and they are dependent upon their senses for their belief in beauty and in poetry itself. In Milton's early poetry there is perhaps a clearer revelation of fully-developed senses than in the poetry of any one other man. Milton sees; he sees colour, form, movement, and he sees them all more clearly, with subtler differentiations than, apparently, Shakespeare himself. He hears, and he has left such a revelation of the appeal of music to the senses as cannot readily be paralleled in our literature:

> . . . Such as the meeting soul may pierce
> In notes, with many a winding bout
> Of linkèd sweetness long drawn out,
> With wanton heed and giddy cunning,
> The melting voice through mazes running

Untwisting all the chains that tie
The hidden soul of harmony. . . .

Moreover, the early poems are full of the scents of balm and cassia and nard, of "rich distilled perfumes" and the "odorous breath of morn." He feels as if he had touched it, the quality of the 'spongy air' into which Comus flings his spells. He tastes nectar and ambrosia and distinguishes the rough rinds of fruits.

But Marlowe reveals in the whole range of *Tamburlaine,* only one of these faculties, that of vision, and of vision limited chiefly to colours of the simplest kind. It is true, there is an indefinite reference to "cassia, ambergris and myrrh" as there is to "speech more pleasant than sweet harmony." But the "heavenly quintessence" that the poets "still from their immortal flowers of poesy" is not a physical thing, and the cherubim that "sing and play before the King of Kings" yield a curiously vague harmony. "The God that tunes this music to our souls" is a noble line, and we may be tolerably certain that Marlowe heard the music of the spheres. But there are no indications to suggest that he had ears for any other.

With such limitation as this, then, what is the nature of Marlowe's poetry? Simply this. There is nothing vague about his thought or imagination, but he does not catch the high light of physical beauty upon the world he reveals. He sees it as clear in line and form as Milton, but where Milton pauses to caress the vision for its exquisiteness, as in the Vallombrosa passage, where he adds lingering image to image, Marlowe gives only a passing comment to that aspect and, before we realise it, has carried us on to the idea of which he finds physical beauty only a symbol. He begins to speak of Zenocrate like "Flora in her morning pride"; there is some dalliance with "silver tresses" and "resolvèd pearl" and then, swift as thought, the inevitable lift

What is beauty? saith my sufferings then.

There follows in the next thirty lines one of the most penetrating pieces of meditation upon this evasive theme that has ever been attempted by a poet. It is this quality in Marlowe's mind which, already in *Tamburlaine,* gives a curious chill, an austere effect, to a poetry which is, paradoxically, instinct with passion. Again and again we feel nearer to the reticence and simplicity of sculpture than to the expression of any other form of art.

In the early poetry of Milton, then, we have the 'yellow-skirted fays,' the spells of Comus and music that

> Dissolves him into ecstasies
> And brings all Heaven before his eyes. . . .

And Shakespeare, too, hears a harmony that is very close to this:

> . . . As sweet and musical
> As bright Apollo's lute, strung with his hair.

so that

> . . . When love speaks, the voice of
>   all the Gods
> Makes Heaven drowsy with the harmony.

Even Wordsworth is preoccupied with the torrent that haunted him "like a passion"; and Shelley himself gives more than half his rapture to the silver moonlight and the whirling spheres through which glides the "pearly and pellucid car" of Mab.

But these things have not much meaning for Marlowe; he is absorbed with the thought of

> Our souls, whose faculties can comprehend
> The wondrous Architecture of the world. . . .

And it is the same with him all through. When rapture touches him he is, as to the language of the senses, speechless, except for an image or two. He cannot give direct utterance to an emotion or an impression made upon his senses, because that is not the habit of his thought. He may perhaps succeed in touching upon accompanying emotions or images, but it is in the world of the ideas that lie behind these outward forms that he moves famil-iarly, and in the almost mystic utterance of the spirit itself that his wealth lies. He is most himself when he strikes out a line such as "Like his desire, lift upwards and divine" but there is nothing concrete there, and it hardly borrows anything from the physical world. Even when in *Faustus,* he tries to describe Helen, he can-not tell us what she looks like; he can speak only of the thousand Greek ships and the topless towers of Ilium; of the evening air

and the stars. . . . What does this tell us of Helen? Nothing—as
Spenser or as Milton would have told us. Marlowe can only speak
as we imagine Homer himself, or Æschylus, would have done,
giving no picture but only an undying record of that experience
which is the eternal contemporary of mankind. This, as is the
nature of that which is born of the spirit, can only be imperfectly
recorded in a language framed to meet the needs of men who
dwell chiefly among concrete objects and sensuous experience.
And so, whether it be with Æschylus or with Marlowe, this experience will find difficulty in expressing itself in concrete language,
and will at best give us a few indirect phrases that are, to one
man, meaningless, to another, the key to the profundities of the
poet's mind. This, from the time of his earliest play, is Marlowe's
use of language, for this was the rare and individual quality of
his thought.

The quality, then, which emerges most clearly from these two
dramas is a rare simplicity. Marlowe's mind is single, direct, un-
confused. Given his evaluation of the world's phenomena, his
sense of proportion is unerring and his restraint severe. The idea
of his play is so simple and self-contained that he is involved in
continual danger in trying to make a drama out of it at all. His
tendency in treating his people is to take from them precisely
what he needs for the expression of his idea and to leave the rest
of the personality colourless and undefined. There is no irrelevant interplay. He seems to have seen his play less as a drama than
as a pageant or a fresco, a fresco which has more than a hint of
the limpidity of, say, Puvis de Chavannes. In image and phrasing,
for all their force, the same strictness may be found. Though
there is more that is lyrical and rhetorical than dramatic in *Tamburlaine,* it is not true to say that his imagery is irrelevant or exuberant. To do this is to regard it in its relation to the conduct of
the play, which was never Marlowe's main interest. In its relation
to the central idea, to which all else is subsidiary, the imagery of
Tamburlaine is, like the characterisation and in less degree the
form, an interpretation of, or a contrasting background to, the
genius of the central figure which it was Marlowe's sole purpose
to reveal.

ETHEL SEATON

Marlowe's Map

'Give me a Map.' These words, put into the mouth of the dying Tamburlaine, bring Christopher Marlowe into line with all those 'aspiring minds' to whom a map can be a satisfaction of curiosity and a source of delight. They are a great and varied company, from Charlemagne studying his 'fair silver tables,' to the school-boy Hakluyt having his first lesson in map-reading in the Middle Temple, even to Mr. Conrad in our own day, if one may venture to identify him with his mouthpiece, yet another Marlow. Before him, no one has expressed in prose the stay-at-home's pleasure in such a study more fully than Burton; he 'never travelled but in map or card,' and could not but think 'that it would please any man to look upon a geographical map, . . . to behold, as it were, all the remote provinces, towns, cities of the world, and never to go forth of the limits of his study. . . . What greater pleasure can there now be, than to view those elaborate maps of Ortelius, Mercator, Hondius, &c.?'

Burton is the inheritor of the Elizabethan interest in maps, fostered in all readers of early voyages, and satisfied in students by the fine productions of the cartographers of Venice and Antwerp. That Marlowe shared this educated taste is suggested by the demand of his hero for a map in which to tread again the 'interminable roads' of a life's conquests, to lament over 'the little done, the much to do.' That his interest had some thoroughness seems

First published in *Essays and Studies* X (Oxford, 1924):13–35. Reprinted by permission of The English Association (London).

to be attested by the frequency with which, in locating countries, he refers to the Tropic Circles, and by an actual reference to the science of map-making. When Tamburlaine is encamped before Damascus (Part 1, IV. iv), he boasts that with his sword for pen, he will anew reduce the countries to a map, of which the meridian-line will pass through that city:

> Here at Damascus will I make the point
> That shall begin the perpendicular.   [Pt. 1, IV. iv. 79–80]

Marlowe knew that the cartographer of his time had a wide choice for his initial meridian of longitude, his perpendicular, though already the island of Ferro in the Canaries was becoming standardized. He knew also that it was a sign of territorial conquest; for a quarter of a century controversy on spheres of influence had raged between Spaniards and Portuguese round the meridian, the Line of Demarcation, or Repartition.

These seem unmistakable signs that Marlowe used a map with pleasure and intelligence. Yet his geographical knowledge is one of the points on which his editors have been most severe. 'Marlowe's notions of geography are as vague as Æschylus's,' said Bullen despairingly, when he caught his author letting the Danube flow into the Mediterranean; and when it came to Zanzibar being on the west coast of Africa, he accepted the emendation to east without even a note. In guessing at the whereabouts of some of Marlowe's towns commentators evidently felt that the one thing safely to be assumed was an indifference to exactitude. German scholars seem to stand almost alone in suggesting that it would be fairer to Marlowe to seek his sources, and find whether his knowledge and his ignorance are those of the man or the period.

All the names in the Jacobean Burton's list of 'elaborate maps' might have been known to the Elizabethan Marlowe. Mercator's fame has best withstood the tooth of time, but in his own day it was no greater than that of his friend and fellow-worker, Abraham Ortelius. The vast monument of Ortelius's industry, the *Theatrum Orbis Terrarum*, published in 1570 at Antwerp, was constantly re-issued, revised, translated, in the attempt to keep pace with discovery and to supply the demand for geographical knowledge. Both the man and his atlas were well known in England, and by the ordinary inquirer of the time the work was accepted as authoritative, however some seamen might question its accuracy in the minutiæ of coast-lines. Sir Humfrey Gilbert and his friend Gascoigne the poet consulted it for the North-west passage; Daniel Rogers, diplomatist, antiquarian, and kinsman of the compiler, wrote dedicatory poems for it; Humfrey Lluyd sent from his deathbed his description of Anglesey and map of Wales for insertion in it; Mulcaster asked Ortelius for advice on the teaching of elementary drawing; Camden had the substantial honour of a presentation copy; Hakluyt reproduced its map of the world, as the best available, in his *Principal Navigations,* and later wrote to Ortelius begging him to make a panoramic map, such as might be contained in small compass, rolled on rollers in a wooden frame; this would be of great service to politicians, citizens, and students of Oxford and Cambridge!

Ortelius received many a compliment, including one from Dr. Dee, on the beauty of his maps, and they are indeed a triumph of clearness and elegance, and comparatively modern in general outline. The orientation sometimes differs from that familiar to us, since there was no necessity to identify the North with the top of the page. It is disconcerting to our prejudices to find, for instance, the coastline of Palestine displayed horizontally instead of perpendicularly; or Asia Minor hanging like a great pendant instead of jutting out squarely above Cyprus. The coloured copies, painted in Ortelius's own workshop, vary in preciseness and beauty, but all, whether plain or coloured, show the legibility that was one of his chief aims. Another aim, accuracy of nomenclature, is less well attained, but the difficulties were well-nigh insuperable, especially in half-known lands, or in countries like those of the Levantine seaboard, where conquest upon conquest has blurred a clear map into an ill-rubbed palimpsest. This conscientiousness fortunately did not make Ortelius despise the pictorial flourishes that turn the medieval map into an ideal playground. In his seas, mermaids, dolphins, and flying-fish rise above the surface, the whale waits open-mouthed to swallow Jonah,

---

OVERLEAF: Map of Africa from Ortelius,
Theatrum Orbis Terrarum, 1570

DVL:

Laflitem

Garton

Angella

Barbada

Cana

Cofur

Satra

Rabon

RID.

Elcama

Guademez

Berdoha

Calbis

Ser

Alguechet

Ziffa

Bug:

Afuan

Macada

Afua

Mecha, hic
Mahometis sepulchrū
visitur

Araban

Lasuf

Nagora

ESERTA

Sar die tā

Ghcogan

Gaoga

Dacrur

BELLO

Tiruti

Suachen

Canca

Nagora

REGIO.   NVBIA

Regnum olim Chri
stiana religione im:
butum; hac tem:
pestate vix
ullam reli
gionҭ
magnҭ
cunt.

Garnoga

Anda Mara

Canfila

DAFILA

Cano

Casc:
na.

Guangara

Dangala

Nubia

Hymi

Goram

Dofili

BARNA
GASSO.

Dobaron

Canna

Finacan

Eferr

Cantca

Gialch. Lucat.

Marua

Abaracl

Delacria

Amazen

Borno
lacus

Borno

Saraho
sfun

Coquere

Carna

S. Michel

Della
uisione.

Zegzeg

Zanfa
rā

Chileur

Baro

Tomi.

Coiberia

Zumera

Deouan Dangol

ZANFARA

Hic Niger flu: per 60 mill:
fi sub terram condit.

Ermita

Bacinete

Agaba

Cassumo

Dolas

NIN.

Beniu.

BIAFAR   AMAZEN.

Arnasen

Abiami

Baza

Ceme:
nia,

Afuga

Gazzelli

Bellet

Corcora

Babehuclec

Yagnc

de Insane

Biafra

Syr

Ambian
cantina

Soua

Betmaria

Angote

Angotina

FATIGAR

MEDRA

Medrã

Mairagazi

Ambadarr

Machi:
Ha.

Belegua
ze.

Bugana

S. Croce

Olabi

OLABI.

Bored

Aiuodo

Guden

Vangue

Hic longe lateҭ imperitaҭ
magnus princeps Presbiter
Iohās totius Africҭ potentiss:
Rex

Amanҭ m:

ZE
Fungi

Aquat:

Barrena

Corisbo.

Dangra fl.

Lac:
Niger

Chedasaflan

BELLEGVAN

Macciva

Damut

VAN
GVE

Cotla

COTLA

Azu
ga

La semita

FVN
GI.

Iyguo

MELIN
DE.

Melin

Bucuapa

Gabam fl.

Vasc: fl.

DAMVT

GOYAME.

Nilus fl.

Bilibrana

Cemen

Bucuapa

C. de S. Catarma

Serra cōpida

Vamba

AMBI
AN.

Ambian

Zaflan

Mombaza

niero

Fremo

Bancare

Vamba fl.

Giara

Goraua

Fungi

Gorage

C. da Iuan
da mom

C. Almada

Praia Formosa

Bibi fl.

AGAG.

Agag

Noua

Camu

Zen
zibar

Angila

Manicōgo

Tacui

QVARA

FVNGI.

Gafar

S. Rafel

QVI
LOA.

MANI
CON
GO.

Coyla

Zaire

CAFA
TES.

Quara

Casable.

Tirut

Quiloa

Magale

PI(VS

C. de cam
Ioan

C. de loui

Zebit mons

Cazates

Amazonum
regio.

Betzum
m:

S. Lazoro

Drie fl.

Iac.

M. zet

MOZAM
BIQVE

S. Michel

Deserta

Baga
midri.

Zem:
bere

Armeta

Camur

AGAG.

Mozam
biq fl.

Farran

S. Antonio

DAGAS

C. de Area

Arcas mons

Calhuras.

Mai
tachasi

AGAG

Agag

Basā fl.

CA

Manafara

C. Negro

ZANZI
BAR hҭc pars
Africҭ meridionalis
quҭ veteribus in:
cognita fuit, a Persis
Arabibusҭ, scrip:
toribus voҭcantur.

Quiricui

CEFALA.

Maruzo

Baicos
de pra
tel

R. Matan

Fotanan

C. de las bal
sas.

Zimbro.

R- Ruema

Cefala

Ilheos de S.
Vincent Manuila

C. de cocrira

Simbaoe

Buro.

Baxos de
la India

Cuara

TROPICVS

Plaia de lagunas

Dele

Terra do
baffi

rta.

Belugaras

Manice mons

C. dos
corrientes

C. d S. Rodto

G. de S. Antonio

C. della volta

Gal.

R. de lago

C. di S. Maria

Cortada

Punta de S. Maria

de Iua
de Lisboa

P. grad

Terra di
nadal

167

caravels and galliasses scud before the wind, slaves ply the oar in 'pilling brigandines,' and galleons grapple, with bursts of smoke and flame. In his eastern countries, strange animals roam about and 'fill the gaps,' as Swift complains, and in China beyond the Great Wall, as Milton remembered,

> . . . across the barren plains
> Of Sericana, the Chineses drive
> With sails and wind, their cany waggons light.

All this, though geographically reprehensible, must have been of untold value in stimulating the fancy and imagination of the student.

It is difficult to compute how many copies of the *Theatrum* found their way into England; that Englishmen did buy it, we know from the letters of Ortelius himself.[1] Some college libraries would acquire it, and the collections of diplomatists and antiquarians could hardly afford to be without it. The close relations existing between noblemen, adventurers, scholars, and poets of the period make it probable that the latter had little difficulty in consulting such a book. Lord Lumley's library, to which Hakluyt had access, and of which Humfrey Lluyd was librarian, would almost certainly have a copy. Sir Walter Raleigh, who, according to Aubrey, always took a box full of books on his voyages, was not the man to be deterred from possessing one by its high cost.

There is then every possibility that Marlowe could see and even consult the *Theatrum,* although the library of Corpus Christi College has now no copy;[2] the query, can it be proved that he did so, is more searching. The proof seems to lie in one of his very 'mistakes.' In the map of Africa, Zanzibar the island is duly marked on the east coast as Zenzibar, but a far more imposing Zanzibar, a province, appears in large type as the 'Westerne part of Affrike,' precisely where Marlowe places it. A closer survey of the map shows that Techelles, in the account of his triumphal march (II *Tamburlaine,* I. vi), is merely transcribing into verse some of the salient names of the map. His first march passes

---

[1] One copy was bought by a certain Mr. Garth, surely that Mr. Richard Garthe, 'one of the Clearkes of the Pettie Bags', in whose cabinets Hakluyt delightedly beheld 'strange curiosities'.

[2] For this information I am indebted to the courtesy of the Librarian of the College.

... along the river Nile
To Machda, where the mighty Christian priest,
Called John the Great, sits in a milk-white robe, ...

[Pt. 2, I. vi. 59–61]

The eye is drawn to Machda, an Abyssinian town on a tributary of the Nile, by the neighbouring note: *Hic longe lateq; imperitat magnus princeps Presbiter Iões totius Afrĩcę potentiss: Rex.* Techelles continues:

From thence unto Cazates did I march,
Where Amazonians met me in the field, ...   [64–65]

Where the Nile rises in a great unnamed lake, the district Cafates has for its chief town Cazates, and is called *Amazonum regio.* Then comes the crux:

And with my power did march to Zanzibar,
The western part of Afric, where I viewed
The Ethiopian sea, rivers and lakes,
But neither man nor child in all the land.   [67–70]

Beside Cape Negro appears in large print the province-name ZANZIBAR, with the note: *hęc pars Afric̨ meridionalis quę veteribus incognita fuit, a Persis Arabibusq; scriptoribus vocatur.* Between this western part and South America the sea is named *Oceanus Æthiopicus* in flourished letters; in the province small rivers abound, and to north and south of the name Zanzibar is that word so useful to the cartographer in difficulties, *Deserta.* Marlowe, it must be observed, is therefore vindicated when he speaks of Zanzibar as not *on* the western coast, but as itself the western part. He is equally explicit later, when Tamburlaine examines his map and accepts his general's conquests as his own; reversing the actual order of march, he passes

... along the Ethiopian sea,
Cutting the tropic line of Capricorn,
I conquered all as far as Zanzibar. ...

[Pt. 2, V. iii. 137–39]

Actually the name Zanzibar is to the north of the Tropic, but the coloured maps make it clear that the province includes the whole southern portion of the continent, from Cape Negro to the Cape of Good Hope and so round to Mozambique. In this location of the province Zanzibar, or more commonly Zanguebar, on the western coast, Ortelius is at variance with many contemporary authorities, and the map of Africa by Gastaldo (1564), which otherwise he followed very closely, does not include it at all. Later cosmographers, such as Livio Sanuto, make its eastern position quite clear. The transference is possibly due to a confused understanding of Marmol, who, with Barros, is referred to in the introductory notes to the map. In any case, the responsibility for that oft-emended *western* rests with Ortelius, not with our Marlowe.

Techelles has reached his southernmost point; turning northwards, he passes successively through Manico, by the coast of Byather, and so 'to Cubar, where the negroes dwell.' On the map, Manico, curtailed by Marlowe for his metre, appears in full style as the province Manicongo, Byather the province in its more correct and modern form of Biafar, while above the province and town of Guber is printed in bold type *Nigritarum Regio.* Then comes the last stage of the journey:

> . . . [I] made haste to Nubia.
> There, having sacked Borno, the kingly seat,
> I took the king and led him bound in chains
> Unto Damascus, . . .   [Pt. 2, I. vi. 75–78]

In the map, Borno, the chief town of Nubia, lies near the shore of *Borno lacus,* that 'Borno Lake' which Tamburlaine himself mentions later. So ends a passage in which one can almost follow Marlowe's finger travelling down the page as he plans the campaign; it is difficult to know whether his memory or the printer is responsible for the slight differences of spelling.

Almost beyond doubt, then, Marlowe knew Ortelius's map of Africa, for he could not have obtained all this detail from the representation of Africa in the much-reproduced map of the world, from which many of his chosen names are omitted, notably Zanzibar itself. It does not, however, follow that he knew the whole atlas, for separate maps were commonly reproduced in cosmographies. Tamburlaine is sown almost as thick with place-names as the sky with stars; can it be shown that any of these, outside Africa, are derived from Ortelius?

A close examination of the geographical names in *Tamburlaine* leads to an interesting conclusion. In Part 1, Marlowe works on a large scale, without much detail; his armies move through continents and countries, and the provinces mentioned are such as were familiar to men of any education: Media, Armenia, Syria, Tartary. Not more than ten towns are named, and most of these were commonplaces to an Elizabethan: Constantinople, Argier, Damascus, Venice, Morocco. Many of the names and epithets, such as Græcia, Parthia, the Euxine, the ever-raging Caspian Lake, would be familiar to any student of the classics, and Persepolis plays the part later taken by Samarkand, Tamburlaine's own town, which is not so much as named here. The setting is almost completely bounded by medieval geography; only twice does the Elizabethan, with his knowledge of a new hemisphere, break away beyond 'Alcides' posts,' as when, with a side-glance at Drake's exploit, and a lordly disregard of chronology, he makes Tamburlaine's ambition reach

> to th' Antarctic pole,

and again

> Even from Persepolis to Mexico,
> And thence unto the Straits of Jubalter, . . .
>
> [Pt. 1, III. iii. 255–56]

In Part 2, however, provinces of more recent interest are called by their contemporary names, such as Natolia, Amasia, Caramania. The Euxine becomes also the *Mare Magiore,* the Red Sea is also named *Mare Roso.* Some thirty towns are mentioned, many of which are written off a modern map, and some are so little known that commentators have either passed them over in silence, or else have arbitrarily identified them by mere resemblance of sound, with slight regard for the importance of their site in the action. Did Ortelius furnish Marlowe with any of these? A glance at the titles of his maps shows that many could well be useful: *Tartaria, Persiæ Regnum, Terra Sancta, Egyptia, Natolia, Turcicum Imperium.*[3] Within these bounds the characters of Part 2 have their being, as a brief survey of the action will recall.

Two lines of movement can be followed, that of the Turkish

---

[3] The early date, and the frequency of editions and translations of the *Theatrum* with its *Parergon,* make it difficult to draw conclusions for the date of either Part of *Tamburlaine.* I have cited here a coloured copy of 1584 (British Museum, Maps, C. 2. d. 1) as being near in time to the assumed date of the play.

army and that of Tamburlaine's forces. The play opens with the
Turks at their outposts on the Danube. Under fear of Tamburlaine's pressure on their eastern frontiers, they make a truce with
the Christians, withdraw their troops into Asia Minor, are
checked by news of treacherous pursuit, and, halting, give battle
at a place not precisely named, but apparently in the neighbour-
hood of Mount Orminius. Meanwhile Tamburlaine, who at the
close of Part 1 was in Egypt, 'at truce with all the world,' is after
many years again on the march, and we hear of him at Alexandria, Larissa, and Aleppo. The gradual approach of the two armies draws to a meeting, and a battle is fought, again unnamed,
but seemingly near the confines of Natolia, not far from Aleppo.
Then Tamburlaine, with his train of captive kings, turns to
subdue Babylon, to conquer the rallying Turks, his last victory,
and to oppose 'the wrath and tyranny of death,' his only defeat.

Such is the main outline of the action; whether Marlowe shows
reasonable exactitude in his plan and in the details, is a question
that Ortelius may help to resolve. It would be well first to recall
the rather different nomenclature of the sixteenth century. Natolia is much more than the modern Anatolia; it is the whole
promontory of Asia Minor, with a boundary running approximately from the modern Bay of Iskenderûn eastward towards
Aleppo, and then north to Batum on the Black Sea. Of this region
Marlowe only twice uses the names Asia Minor or Asia the Less,
while Asia and Asia Major denote either the whole continent, or
the part of Asia beyond this boundary. Orcanes, king of Natolia,
exactly describes its importance when he says:

> My realm, the center of our empery,
> Once lost, all Turkey would be overthrown; . . .
>
> [Pt. 2, I. i. 55–56]

In Part 1, however, there are signs that Marlowe follows medieval
authority in using Africa to denote the Turkish empire, and making Memphis its centre. Soria, the name regularly used by Italian
writers and by Ortelius, represents Syria, or more narrowly Syria
north of Palestine; it replaces in Part 2 the form Siria of Part 1.
Egyptia in Part 1 includes Siria, for Damascus is Egyptian; in
Part 2, Egypt is distinct from Soria, and its capital is Cairo,
named for the first time.

Commentators, crediting Marlowe with neglectful vagueness, have themselves neglected the indications that he has been careful to give. There seem to be two chief causes of confusion. The belief that the Turco-Hungarian battle was fought in Europe has led to the search for Natolian towns in Bulgaria, and for Mount Orminius in Transylvania. Similarly, the apparent failure to identify Larissa, and more pardonably Balsera, has led to utter misunderstanding of Tamburlaine's movements.

The first of the two muddles is the easier to deal with. As I have elsewhere shown,[4] Marlowe boldly 'lifted' all the circumstances of this apparently imaginary campaign from the famous battle of Varna in 1444, a date actually some forty years later than Tamburlaine's death. From the chroniclers of Varna are drawn the truce and its terms, the Christians' treachery and the excuses for it, the Turkish wrath, disillusionment, and triumph. Marlowe does not, however, commit himself to the site of Varna for this anachronistic battle, but seems purposely to transport it into Asia Minor, and to prefer indication to precise location. The Turkish troops were in fact withdrawn into Asia Minor, and it was a lightning-move by the Sultan that hurled them back into Europe to meet the truce-breakers at Varna; Marlowe seems content to leave them in Natolia. When the treachery is hatched, Frederick reports that Orcanes has dismissed

> ... the greatest part
> Of all his army pitched against our power
> Betwixt Cutheia and Orminius' mount,
> And sent them marching up to Belgasar,
> Acantha, Antioch, and Cæsarea,
> To aid the kings of Soria and Jerusalem.
>
> [Pt. 2, II. i. 16–21]

That, as Ortelius reveals, precisely describes the movement of the Turkish army through Asia Minor. Cutheia is the modern Kutayeh, the classical Cotyaeum, and appears in the map of Natolia as Chiutaie, both district and town. As the capital of Natolia, it was an important place; Leunclavius, in his notes to the *Annales Turcici* (1588), gives the many forms of its name current. Mount Horminius is shown only in the map of *Græcia* in the *Parergon,*

---

[4] *Times Lit. Suppl.*, 16 June, 1921 (correspondence).

situated in Bithynia east and slightly south of the modern Scutari. For the single use of these two names, however, Marlowe had probably yet another source. Belgasar and Acantha appear in the map of Asia as Beglasar and Acanta, in a line leading roughly south-east through Asia Minor, while the former is to be found again as Begbasar in *Natolia,* and as Begasar in *Turcicum Imperium.* When in the next scene, Orcanes with the rear-guard ('the [little] power I haue left behind') hears of the Hungarians' treacherous advance, he is on the point of marching 'from proud Orminius' mount To fair Natolia.' Here Marlowe seems, in disaccord with Ortelius, to speak as if there were also a town Natolia, an invention that he repeats later, or else to consider the mountain as only on the outskirts of Natolia proper. The battle seems to take place near here, for after it Orcanes still has to haste and meet his army.

Meanwhile Tamburlaine is also on the move. In the first scene, the Turk Gazellus says of him that he

> . . . now in Asia,
> Near Guyron's head, doth set his conquering feet
> And means to fire Turkey as he goes.   [Pt. 2, I. i. 16–18]

But he must be referring to Tamburlaine's outposts, for almost immediately he gives other news of him:

> . . . Tamburlaine hath mustered all his men,
> Marching from Cairon northward with his camp,
> To Alexandria and the frontier towns, . . .   [Pt. 2, I. i. 46–48]

Guyron is not an invention of Marlowe's, but occurs twice in the *Theatrum,* as Giuron in the map of Asia, and as Guiron in *Turcicum Imperium;* it is a town near the upper Euphrates, north-east of Aleppo, in the latter map not far from the confines of Natolia, and therefore a possible outpost. The report of Tamburlaine proves correct; having travelled from Cairo *via* Alexandria, he is encamping at Larissa, as his first speech in Act I, scene 4, tells us:

> Now rest thee here on fair Larissa plains,
> Where Egypt and the Turkish empire parts,
> Between thy sons that shall be emperors, . . .
>   [Pt. 2, I. iv. 5–7]

Broughton was very 'hot' when he quoted Milton to illustrate this: 'The scene here seems to lie

> 'Twixt old Euphrates and the brook that parts
> Egypt from Syrian ground.'

It is in fact by the brook itself, but Marlowe's exact description of the site has been obscured by the frequent omission of the comma after *parts,* that in the Octavo of 1590 completes the needed isolation of the line. It gives the exact position in which we find Larissa in the map of the Turkish Empire, a sea-coast town, south of Gaza; in the map of Africa already cited, it lies a little to the north of the dotted boundary line. It is on the biblical Brook of Egypt, and is the Rhinocolura of the classical period, the 'most ancient city Larissa' of the Crusades, the El Arîsh of the modern map. By more perhaps than mere coincidence, Marlowe chooses for the scene of Zenocrate's death the town where the soldiers wept for the death of Baldwin of Jerusalem. It is fitting that the pillar placed in memory of her should be inscribed in 'Arabian, Hebrew, Greek,' for, Greek being the speech of Egypt to an Elizabethan classical student, these are the languages of the three lands which almost meet in 'fair Larissa plains.'

As a boundary town, Larissa is suitable also for the meeting-place of Tamburlaine with his generals, and for the starting-point of their concerted operations against the Turks. Delayed there by his grief and vengeance, Tamburlaine sends on ahead a flying column; when the last scene at Larissa closes, he sets out

> ... Towards Techelles and Theridamas,
> That we have sent before to fire the towns,
> The towers and the cities of these hateful Turks, ...
> [Pt. 2, III. ii. 146–48]

These words prepare us definitely for the next scene, of which equally definitely the opening lines tell us the situation, the speaker being Theridamas:

> Thus have we marched northward from Tamburlaine,
> Unto the frontier point of Soria,
> And this is Balsera, their chiefest hold,
> Wherein is all the treasure of the land.   [Pt. 2, III. iii. 1–4]

Here is a difficulty at first sight, for Balsera or Balsara (which Mil-

ton scans as Balsára) is undoubtedly the common Elizabethan
form of the modern Basra; yet Basra is certainly not 'northward
from Tamburlaine,' nor can it by any stretch of geographical
imagination be called a 'frontier point of Soria.' It is significant
that the name of this besieged fortress is given only this once, and
with no unfamiliar name is a printer so likely to err as with one
that ignorance immediately assumes to be well-known; 'security
is mortals' chiefest enemy.' It is an obvious absurdity that Tamburlaine, advancing from Egypt against Asia Minor, should send
a skirmishing party right off his line of march, across the dreaded
Arabian Desert, to the very country that he is reserving for his
next campaign. We have seen once already that Marlowe can be
trusted in his points of the compass; if, before emending to southward, we take him on trust here, we must assume that the unknown town is on the northern or Natolian frontier of Soria, for
the column has started from Larissa on the southern frontier.
Ortelius can help us out with a suggestion. In the map of Natolia,
especially noticeable in the coloured copies as a frontier point, is
the town Passera, with the first 's' long. This may well be Marlowe's Balsera. The objection occurs that the arbitrary choice of
an insignificant town is not probable, but, as will be shown, Marlowe often makes just such a choice. Moreover, this particular
episode is a patchwork of borrowed scraps, and it seems to be his
practice to situate his invented episodes in places unimpeachable
by their very obscurity.

When the hold has been seized, Theridamas prepares to meet
Tamburlaine,

> Who by this time is at Natolia,
> Ready to charge the army of the Turk.

Again the scenes are strictly linked; the next (III. v. 86–87) brings
us to the Turkish camp, where a messenger breaks in and is the
first speaker:

> Here at Aleppo, with an host of men,
> Lies Tamburlaine, this king of Persia . . .
> Who means to girt Natolia's walls with siege,
> Fire the town, and over-run the land.
>
> [Pt. 2, III. v. 3–4, 8–9]

That 'Here' is a splendid southward gesture, telling whence the messenger has come hotfoot, for the enemy is at his heels, and enters upon this very scene. The Turks themselves are 'in Natolia,' and on its eastern confines, for the snake-like trail of their army covers the land

> ... from the bounds of Phrygia to the sea
> Which washeth Cyprus with his brinish waves, ...
>
> [Pt. 2, III. v. 11–12]

Now comes a difficulty. Again Marlowe uses caution and refrains from committing himself to a definite site for his invented battle. The only indication of place comes later, when Tamburlaine reminds his pampered jades of 'Asphaltis, where I conquered you,' and rewards with queens apiece his common soldiers that fought 'So Lion-like upon Asphaltis plains.' The name that springs unbidden to the mind is *Lacus Asphaltites,* but a moment's reflection shows its unsuitability. Tamburlaine is last heard of at Aleppo, the Turks are in Natolia, and the battle must take place in that direction. The only reference in the Marlovian canon to the Dead Sea is in *Edward II,* where the English name is used with a play upon its Latin equivalent. When Marlowe speaks later in *Tamburlaine* of Limnasphaltis, and of Asphaltis lake, he is referring to the bituminous waters of the Euphrates near Babylon. For the first time Ortelius affords no help; Marlowe seems, like a mischievous 'hare,' to have succeeded in putting us off the scent. He has done two things to confuse: he speaks of Natolia as if it were a town; then he introduces for the site of his battle Asphaltis, a place apparently not known to classical or modern geography.

Yet there is a clue left. Twice, and with some emphasis, does the Sultan Callapine refer boastfully to the coming conflict as 'the Perseins' sepulchre.' To any classical student poring over this cockpit of the world, remembrance would inevitably come of other campaigns, other conquerors, and of these the greatest is that 'Chief spectacle of the world's preeminence,' Alexander the Great, the most familiar of all ancient worthies to the Elizabethan. Issus and Arbela, Alexander's two great defeats inflicted on the Persians, lie roughly to west and to east of that area north of Aleppo whither Marlowe has led his Tamburlaine. Each of these battlefields could suggest the phrase, 'the Perseins' sepul-

chre.' Again, Abraham Hartwell, the Elizabethan translator of
the chronicler Minadoi, uses the very word when he describes the
defeat, in Marlowe's lifetime, of the Persians by the Turks, as
'the perpetual sepulcher of a couragious and warlike people.'
But, even granted that Alexander's victories may be in Marlowe's
mind, why Asphaltis? The bituminous nature of the Euphrates
basin is a commonplace of cosmography and of the history of
Alexander's campaign. Plutarch's life of the conqueror describes
his naïve surprise and still more naïve experiment, when, after
leaving Arbela, he first saw what Tennyson has called 'the Mem-
mian naphtha-pits.' Marlowe, like Hakluyt, might have heard the
contemporary testimony of the merchant, John Eldred, who journeyed from Babylon to Aleppo in 1583, and heard the many
'springs of tar' blowing and puffing like a smith's forge.

After this break, which leaves us with the area between Aleppo
and the Tigris on which to exercise conjecture, the thread can be
picked up again with the help of Ortelius. Tamburlaine, on his
expedition to Babylon, halts with his harnessed captives at Byron
(IV, iii). It is the last stage of his journey, for in the maps of Asia
and *Turcicum Imperium*, Biron is only a few miles up-stream
from Babylon or Bagdet itself; it is the town of which Gazellus,
who so strangely drops out of the play after Act II, is viceroy.
Finally Tamburlaine reaches the eternized city of Babylon:

> Where Belus, Ninus, and great Alexander
> Have rode in triumph, triumphs Tamburlaine, . . .
>   [Pt. 2, V. i. 69–70]

Hither to 'Asia Major, where the streams / Of Euphrates and
Tigris swiftly runs,' Callapine pursues with a fresh army, and
halts so near that he can 'behold great Babylon, Circléd about
with Limnasphaltis Lake'; Ortelius portrays the lake, but does
not name it. Callapine falls upon the Persians, trusting to their
being 'faint and weary with the siege,' but his army flees 'Like
summer's vapors, vanished by the sun,' and Callapine owes his
escape only to his great and unseen ally who 'Gives battle 'gainst
the heart of Tamburlaine.'

The conqueror's legacy to his sons is the extent of the world yet
left for conquest. On the map he traces the five thousand leagues

of his journeys, arrogating to himself the campaigns of his under-
kings through Africa and beyond Græcia. Regretfully he sees
worlds yet to conquer:

> . . . see what a world of ground
> Lies westward from the midst of Cancer's line . . .
> And from th'Antarctic Pole eastward behold
> As much more land, which never was descried, . . .

> [Pt. 2, V. iii. 145–55 *passim*]

The gold mines, spices, and jewels of the New World, the glittering ice-wall of the Antarctic, lure him still: 'And shal I die, and
this vnconquered?' It is the cry of Alexander, reversed in accor-
dance with those new world-conditions that nothing brings home
to the mind so forcibly as a map. The play ends on the note of the
aspiring motto adopted by Charles V, *Plus ultra,* There *is* more
beyond.

With the aid of Ortelius, we can thus make our own plan of
the campaigns of Tamburlaine in Part 2; only twice are we left
in comparative uncertainty, and each time it is for an invented
battle. Marlowe's caution in battle-sites had begun even in Part 1,
for where the defeat of Bajazeth was located by one at least of his
authorities as Mount Stella near Ancyra, he is never more explicit
than 'in Bithynia.'

Encouraged, we turn to Ortelius for help in identifying names
that have no place on the lines of march, but are scattered lavishly
through the play, and we find that, without a single exception,
every non-classical name appears in the *Theatrum.* Marlowe must
have turned the atlas to and fro, and picked out a name here and
there, attracted partly, but not entirely, by its sonority.

When Callapine plans his escape from Egypt (I. iii), a Turkish
galley lies waiting for him in 'Darotes' streams' that run 'By
Cairo . . . to Alexandria bay.' In Africa and *Turcicum Imperium,*
Darote or Derote is a town at the bend of the westernmost arm of
the Nile delta, that is, on the river-way from Cairo to Alexandria.[5]
Callapine has to buy over his jailer with the bribe of kingship,
and later he keeps his promise by investing him

---

[5] In the half-page map, *Ægypti Recentior Descriptio,* Deruti is on an arm of the
river branching eastwards to Rosetta.

> . . . king of Ariadan,
> Bordering on Mare Roso, near to Mecca.
>
> [Pt. 2, III. v. 130–31]

This exactly describes the position in the map of Africa of this unimportant town that Marlowe arbitrarily selected; it appears again in *Turcicum Imperium,* but much less conspicuous, and the sea there is not called *Mar Rosso.* Again another example: Tamburlaine's son Amyras, reproaching his brother for cowardice, vows that he would not so incur his father's fury for

> . . . all the lofty mounts of Zona Mundi
> That fill the midst of farthest Tartary. . . .
>
> [Pt. 2, IV. i. 42–43]

In Europe and Russia, the range of *Zona mundi montes,* or *Orbis Zona montes,* runs southwards through northernmost Tartary from the coast near Waygatz and Petsora, in the coloured maps most obviously 'farthest Tartary.'

The journeys of Tamburlaine's three generals (I. vi) were evidently planned by Marlowe with the *Theatrum* before him. The southward march through Africa of Techelles has already been traced. In the same map Marlowe would find the towns conquered by Techelles and Usumcasane in the north of Africa: Azamor, Fes, Tesella (south of Oran), the province Gualata, and *Canarię Insulę.* Just as he shortened Manicongo into Manico for his metre, so here he shortens Biledulgerid into Biledull, with the excuse that the name of this province is so divided here in two layers. *Estrecho de Gibraltar* here, and in Europe and Spain, gives him 'the narrow straight of Gibraltar,' so that it is not necessary even for the metre to replace this new form by that of *Tamburlaine,* Part I, *Jubaltér.*

For the last series of exploits Marlowe seeks variety, and forsakes Africa for Europe; Theridamas tells how by the river Tyros he subdued

> Stoka, Padalia, and Codemia;
> Then crossed the sea and came to Oblia
> And Nigra Silva, where the devils dance,
> Which, in despite of them, I set on fire.
> From thence I crossed the gulf called by the name
> Mare Majore of th' inhabitants.   [Pt. 2, I. vi. 83–88]

With some variations of spelling that make one wonder whether Marlowe's o's and a's were almost indistinguishable, all these names cluster round the north-west shore of the Black Sea, the Mare Majore. The River Tyros (the Dniester) acts as the southern border of the province Podolia; Stoko is on it, and Codemia lies to the north-east on another stream. Partly separating Codemia from Olbia, and thus perhaps suggesting an otherwise unneces-sary sea-journey, is the thick, green, hollow square of Nigra Silva, but even in this picture atlas, there is never a devil dancing there. It is disconcerting to find the Black Forest cropping up thus near Odessa, but a quotation given by Mercator in his later atlas ex-plains both the position and the ill repute: 'La Forest Hercynie va iusques . . . a ce qu'elle aye atteint les derniers Tartares, ou elle se nomme la Forest noire ou obscure, sans bornes, sans chemins, ny sentiers fraiez: et tant pour la cruauté des bestes farouches, que pour *les monstrueuses terreurs des Faunes espouventables,* du tout inaccessible aux humains.'[6]

With the map of Europe still open, Marlowe plays the same game on a smaller scale with the petty kings of the Turkish army, gathering their levies from their subject-towns (III. i). The king of Jerusalem naturally raises his from 'Judæa, Gaza, and Sca-lonians' bounds'; that the town of Ascalon appears in the map as Scalona effectively disposes of the 1605 Quarto's absurd change to Sclauonians, apparently a confused reminiscence of the earlier enumeration of Sigismond's composite army of 'Slavonians, Al-mains, Rutters, Muffs, and Danes.'

For the king of Trebizond, Marlowe's finger traces from west to east the northern seaboard of Asia Minor: Chio, Famastro, Amasia (here the province only), Trebisonda, Riso, Sancina. For the king of Soria, he passes from Aleppo south-westward to the sea-coast near Cyprus, and chooses Soldino and Tripoli, and so inland again to Damasco; and in passing it may be said that this form Damasco, which is that of four out of five of the modern maps in the *Theatrum,* replaces in Part 2, except for a single

---

[6] French text of 1619, p. 227: ["The Hercynian forest goes until . . . it reaches the last Tartars, where it is called the Black or Shadowy forest, without bounds, without roads, or even foot-paths: (and you can say as much of) the cruelty of the ferocious beasts as you can about *the monstrous terrors of the dreadful animals;* all of which is inhospitable to men."] Cf. A. H. Gilbert, *A Geographical Dictionary of Milton, s.v.* Hercynian Wilderness.

genitive use, the form Damascus regular in Part 1. When the king of Soria is enumerating later his further reinforcements (III. v), he adds Halla; this might well be thought to be one of the many variants of Aleppo (Alepo, Halep, Aleb), but it appears in the map of the world as a separate town to the south-east of Aleppo.

With the same geographical justice does Marlowe treat his Christian leaders; Frederick complains of the cruel Turkish massacres done

> Betwixt the city Zula and Danubius;
> How through the midst of Varna and Bulgaria,
> And almost to the very walls of Rome, . . .　[Pt. 2, II. i. 7–9]

Zula, which has vanished from the average modern map, appears in the *Europe* of Ortelius to the north of the Danube, in the province of Rascia; the same map offers a possible explanation of that puzzling *Rome,* which cannot mean Rome though it may mean Constantinople: the word may have been suggested by ROMA in large type just north of Constantinople, violently and ludicrously separated from its NIA.

The last of all these scattered names carries us farther afield; the passage must be quoted in full, for a very pretty problem of punctuation is involved:

> He brings a world of people to the field:
> From Scythia to the oriental plage
> Of India, where raging Lantchidol
> Beats on the regions with his boisterous blows,
> That never seaman yet discoverèd,
> All Asia is in arms with Tamburlaine.
> Even from the midst of fiery Cancer's tropic
> To Amazonia under Capricorn,
> And thence as far as Archipelago,
> All Afric is in arms with Tamburlaine; . . .　[Pt. 2, I. i. 67–76]

Broughton's note, 'Lantchidol was the name of the part of the Indian Ocean lying between Java and New Holland,' was possibly due to the reproduction of the *Typus Orbis Terrarum* in Hakluyt, or to the mention of the sea in Willes's translation of Pigafetta's voyage in his *History of Travayle* (1577, f. 446 *verso*). Marlowe could read of it there or could, before Hakluyt, find it in the original map, where *Lantchidol Mare* borders a promontory of yet unexplored land, in outline suggesting the north-west of Australia, but here merely designated *Beach*. The name, apparently a native one, may have recalled to Marlowe's mind, through its English synonym, the phrase that he knew from other sources, 'Oriental plage.' But with that map of the world before him, and with the map of Africa in his head, Marlowe did not make the mistake that almost every editor has made for him by altering the punctuation of the Octavo of 1592. He did not think that Asia, or even its farthest isles, extended 'under Capricorn'; yet that is how almost every editor punctuates the lines. No, the sense-division is at 'Tamburlaine'; from Scythia to the farthest East Indies, all Asia is in arms with Tamburlaine; from the Canaries (the juncture of Cancer and the Meridian) southward to *Amazonum Regio* and the land under Capricorn, and thence northward again to the islands of the Mediterranean, all Africa is in arms with Tamburlaine. The second part is a summary of the generals' campaigns in Africa, to be expanded and detailed later. . . .

Emboldened by this evidence of knowledge and reasonableness on Marlowe's part, we can attack at last that apparently insuperable difficulty of the Danube flowing into the Mediterranean. Knowing as we do that Marlowe had studied the shores of the Black Sea, north, south, east, and west, we cannot believe that he made such a blunder. Yet there it is. Orcanes, when actually 'on Danubius banks,' utters himself thus:

> Our Turkey blades shall glide through all their throats,
> And make this champion mead a bloody fen.
> Danubius' stream, that runs to Trebizon,
> Shall carry, wrapped within his scarlet waves,
> As martial presents to our friends at home,
> The slaughtered bodies of these Christians.
> The Terrene main, wherein Danubius falls,
> Shall by this battle be the bloody sea.
> The wandering sailors of proud Italy
> Shall meet those Christians, fleeting with the tide,
> Beating in heaps against their argosies, . . . [Pt. 2, I. i. 31–41]

As an act of faith, inspired by the trustworthiness of Marlowe on other points, we may assume that he intends some meaning. Here are two statements, mutually contradictory, and equally absurd: first the Danube flows to Trebizond, then it falls into the Mediterranean. Yet Shakespeare says almost the same thing, and no modern editor cries out on his ignorance:

> . . . Like to the Pontick Sea,
> Whose icy current and compulsive course
> Ne'er feels retiring ebb, but keeps due on
> To the Propontick and the Hellespont,
> Even so my bloody thoughts, with violent pace,
> Shall ne'er look back, ne'er ebb to humble love.
>
> [*Othello* III. iii.]

Annotators quote from Philemon Holland's version of Pliny, but an even clearer description of the violent flow of the Bosporus from north to south is given by the sixteenth-century traveller, Petrus Gyllius, who sums up quaintly thus: 'The Mæotis is the mother of the Pontus, and the Pontus the father of the Bosporus, the Propontis, and the Hellespont. . . . So great is the rapidity of the Bosporus that the current is visible as it is forced out into the Propontis.' This last is precisely Marlowe's idea. He sees the waters of the Danube sweeping from the river-mouths in two strong currents, the one racing across the Black Sea to Trebizond, the other swirling southwards to the Bosporus, and so onward to the Hellespont and the Ægean. Both currents bear the slaughtered bodies of Christian soldiers, the one to bring proof of victory to the great Turkish town, the other to strike terror to the Italian merchants cruising round the Isles of Greece. Nicholas Nicholay, one of Marlowe's recognized authorities, definitely connects the 'compulsive course' with the flow of rivers: 'But for so much as many great rivers . . . from Europe doe fall into the Blacke and Euxine Sea, it commeth to pass that beyng full, she gusheth out through the mouth of her wyth great vyolence intoo the Sea Pontique (i.e., Propontic) and from thence through the streit of Hellesponthus . . . into the Sea of Egee.' Perondinus, another source, in speaking of Bajazeth's defeat by Tamburlaine, uses an expression that may have given the idea to Marlowe: *Eufrates . . . maiore sanguinis et aquarum vi ad mare Rubrum volveretur;* here, like Marlowe, he considers the main sea into which the inland sea opens to be the outlet of the river, for *Mare Rubrum* can include the modern Arabian Sea, as it does in the *Turcicum Imperium* of Ortelius.

The whole question of the Mediterranean was much debated

in the sixteenth century, cosmographers being divided in opinion
on the westerly or the north-easterly source of its waters. Gyllius,
sent to Constantinople to collect information for the French king,
thinks the subject worth some chapters. The matter was so much
a commonplace of educated knowledge that Marlowe takes its
familiarity for granted, and goes a step beyond. Shakespeare describes the process, and characteristically uses it as a metaphor for
the feelings of an individual. Marlowe assumes the process, sees
with poetic clairvoyance what might actually be the grim result,
and paints the picture, partly for its own sake, and partly for its
effect. It is an example of what Mr. Lewis Einstein has said: 'Marlowe regarded eloquence as the instrument by which the imagination should be freed.'

As we follow these tracks through the *Theatrum*, the conviction grows that Marlowe used this source at least with the accuracy of a scholar and the common-sense of a merchant-venturer,
as well as with the imagination of a poet. The assurance is all the
more welcome as it supports the growing belief, expressed by such
a critic as Swinburne, and by such an authority on Marlowe as
Professor Tucker Brooke, that he was something more than a
dramatist of swashbuckling violence and chaotic inconsequence—
a *Miles Gloriosus* of English drama. Here we find order for chaos,
something of the delicate precision of the draughtsman for the
crude formlessness of the impressionist. Panoramic though his
treatment still may be, there is method in his seven-league-booted
strides. We wrong Marlowe if, in our eagerness to praise his high
moments of poetic inspiration, we mistakenly depreciate his qualities of intellect, of mental curiosity, and logical construction.
We do him wrong, being so majestical, to see in him only this
show of violence. Here are a careful setting of the stage, and a
linking of scene with scene by place-indications as capable,
though not as beautiful, as those of Shakespeare.

This precise handling of a source need not be thought a sign
of pedantry in Marlowe; scholarly he was, but not pedantic, not
the type to

> ... love a cell
> And—like a badger—with attentive looks
> In the dark hole sit rooting up of books.

The proof of this seems to lie in the fact that, after the Second

Part of Tamburlaine, he did not thus use the *Theatrum* again, although the map of the Mediterranean was clear in his mind when he wrote *The Jew of Malta*. The book had served his purpose, and with the royal 'forward view' of genius, he passed on. De Quincey's words are illustrated: 'All action in any direction is best expounded, measured, and made apprehensible by reaction': the completeness of Marlowe's reaction is the measure of his growth. The impulse came rather, as has been suggested to me, from an interest in strategy. He was playing a great game of chess, with kings and conquerors for pieces, and for chess-board the *Theatrum Orbis Terrarum: a Kriegspiel,* such as many recently have played with the aid of flags on pins; but his game, being imaginary, without our bitter urgency, was excellent sport. It has been said that the Second Part is a mercenary afterthought, that the parade of geographical terms covers a weakening of poetic impulse. Yet at the least it was a final effervescence of boyishness, of satisfaction in youthful cleverness, in 'pulling the thing off,' pardonable in a young graduate of twenty-four. At most, it was something more. Even in this his poetic power found outlet. Even here, from the bare outlines of maps, and perhaps from the dry statements of cosmographers, he 'bodied forth the forms of things unknown.' He saw the Polar cliffs as 'rocks of shining pearl'; he heard the boisterous waves of raging Lantchidol beat on an uncharted coast. He pored over this great atlas until the countries 'came alive,' and the creatures of his brain went through such adventures as fell to the lot of many an Englishman of his time. His Techelles, halting on the western coast of Africa, '*viewed* the Ethiopian Sea'; the word is significant. It is the same experience of poetic apprehension as Keats more strongly felt, and more felicitously expressed, when he saw the rapt wonder of his Cortes, 'Silent upon a peak in Darien.'

ROY W. BATTENHOUSE

Tamburlaine, the "Scourge of God"

The title-page of Marlowe's *Tamburlaine* (1590) presents "two Tragicall Discourses" concerning a mighty monarch who "(for his tyranny, and terrour in Warre) was tearmed, THE SCOURGE OF GOD." A dozen times in the play[1] Tamburlaine gives himself this appellation, and the last syllables of his dying breath reassert it. Quite evidently, "Scourge of God" is more than a phrase that happened to catch the playwright's fancy. It designated in Elizabethan interpretation, as scholarship can discover, a type of presumptuous obedience which God providentially allows but also eventually confounds to the dismay of the Scourge.

In Renaissance writings of many kinds we find the general theory that God punishes in two ways: internally, by sending maladies of the mind and perturbations of the passions; and externally, by permitting the ravages of tyrants, who are made to serve God as His scourges. In using the second of these two means of punishment, God permits evil agents to rage for a time, that He may use them in punishing the wickedness of other men, while also letting each scourge bring on his own destruction through

---

Reprinted by permission of the Modern Language Association of America from *PMLA* LVI (1941):337–48. This essay has been revised by the author for inclusion in the present collection. Its point of view has not been changed. Battenhouse has explored the play's background in fuller detail in his *Marlowe's "Tamburlaine": A Study in Renaissance Moral Philosophy* (Nashville, Tenn., 1941, 1964).

[1] [See Part 1, III. iii. 44–45, IV. ii. 31–32; Part 2, I. iv. 60–64, II. iv. 80, IV. ii. 71–83 and 124–26, IV. iv. 24 and 99, V. i. 92 and 181–83, V. iii. 45 and 248.] The term is used also by the Prologue, by the Souldan of Egypt [Part 1, IV. iii. 9], by Orcanes [Part 2, III. v. 21–22], and by Usumcasane [Part 2, V. iii. 37–38].

his unruly passions, whether or not he dies at the hands of some human adversary.

The whole concept is an ancient one, but invoked in Marlowe's day by Protestant moralists especially, in order to emphasize that retributive justice is not confined to an after-world. An important classical source for this doctrine was Plutarch, who had taught that God abandons the wicked to tyrants, whom He uses as rods for punishing sin.[2] Another source was Plotinus, who explained that bad men hold sway because of the feebleness, folly, and sloth of their victims; that Providence permits great wrong-doers to inflict punishment on the less wicked; that nevertheless the great wrong-doers receive ultimately an appropriate punishment.[3] Plutarch and Plotinus were often cited in Elizabethan treatises. But a more basic text for expounding the "Scourge of God" concept was Isaiah x: 5–16, where Assyria is described as the rod of God's anger.

Calvin, in his commentary on this passage in Isaiah[4] makes much of the point that the Assyrian, though at heart ambitious and avaricious, is nevertheless made to serve God's purpose. The Assyrian, furious and proud, treads his enemies under foot,

> which is the vttermost of all rage, for what can men do more than with shame and contempt to stamp them *vnder feete* whom they haue vanquished?

Then this scourge recites his conquests, boasts of the ease of his victories, and finally vaunts himself against God. But the Assyrian's boastings, says Calvin, are "so many bellowes (as it were) to kindle the wrath of God." God's flame will utterly consume the Assyrian's glory. And the burning will be a light to God's faithful, exhibiting to them God's revenge. Calvin at one point applies Isaiah's doctrine to the interpretation of Renaissance history. He remarks:

---

[2] Bernard Latzarus, *Les Idées Religieuses de Plutarque* (Parish, 1920), p. 69.

[3] *Enneads*, III. ii. 8.

[4] *A Commentary Vpon the Prophecie of Isaiah* (1609), pp. 115–22, which I quote from the Huntington Library copy. The commentary appeared in Latin in 1551, in French in 1552, both editions dedicated to Edward VI. Later Latin editions appeared in 1559, 1570, and 1583; and a 1572 French translation of the 1570 Latin edition was the basis of C. Cotton's English translation, entered to Harrison and Bishop as early as 21 Jan. 1577, then on 26 Jan. 1608 to Kingston, and printed by him in 1609.

So at this day there are diuers diseases in the Church which the Lord will purge and heale . . . Wherefore wee must not maruell if he lets loose the bridle to tyrants, and suffreth them still to exercise their crueltie against his Church: for the consolation is readie, to wit, *hauing vsed them as his vassals to correct his people, he will visit their pride and arrogancie.*   (pp. 119–20; italics mine)

Alongside Calvin's commentary we may wish to recall a passage from a book which many scholars consider Marlowe's principal source for the story of Tamburlaine, Thomas Fortescue's *The Forest* (1571). Its chapter 15 of Part I is entitled "How for the most parte, cruel kings and bloody tirants are the Ministers of God, and how notwithstanding they continually end in state most wretched and extreme misery." The chapter begins by saying that certain wicked idolaters are called "Ministers of God" because, in accord with the prophecy of Isaiah, they "enter at the gates of Babylon" as "executors of Gods iust wil for the punishment of *Babilon.*" In illustration, Cyrus, Darius, Totila—and Tamburlaine—are named. Then, after quoting Tamburlaine's boast to be the "Ire of God," Fortescue remarks:

whence we haue in fine to conclude, that all such cruel and incarnate deuils are instruments wherewith God chastiseth sin, as also with the same approueth and tryeth the iust, and yet they notwithstanding are not hence held for iust, ne shall they escape the heuy iudgement of God. For necessary it is that example of it happen, but woe be vnto him by whom it happeneth.

(fol. 35r, second edition, 1576)

This interpretation of Tamburlaine is likely also to have been Marlowe's. Yet an editor of the play such as Miss Ellis-Fermor, when reprinting Fortescue's full story of Tamburlaine in *The Forest,* Part II, Chapter 14, has omitted giving us the earlier chapter in which Fortescue interpreted the story's meaning.

We can consolidate this meaning by taking time to consult other Elizabethans, besides Fortescue and Calvin, who used the "Scourge of God" concept in interpreting history. Philip Mornay, a Huguenot whose *De la Verité de la Religion Chrestienne* (1581) was translated by Sidney and Golding, took care to explain in his book how various heroes of history have been, in ways beyond their understanding, instruments of divine providence. One ex-

ample, briefly cited, is that of Cyrus, who was led by ambition
("and ambition, as ye know, cannot be welliked of God") to make
war upon the Assyrians; but God adapted Cyrus' design to His
own historical purpose.[5] Titus, similarly, was led by his own passion to attack Jerusalem; but God thus made Titus an executor
of justice against the Jews who crucified Christ. Mornay's prime
example, however, is Attila, whose career has a pattern much like
that of Isaiah's typical scourge:

> Ye must thinke that when this great Robber cast lots in his Countrie
> of Scythia, whether he should leade the third part of that land, he
> had another meaning than to reforme the world. Yet not withstand-
> ing, all men acknowledge him to be a necessary scurge of GOD, and
> to haue come in due season. Yea, and he himselfe considering that
> he had conquered much more of the Countrie, than euer he hoped
> at the first to haue seene, insomuch that he had ouercome euen
> those which were counted the strength of the World: as barbarous
> as he was, he fell to thinke of himself, that he was the Scurge
> whereby God chastised the World. Not that God is not able to chas-
> tise vs himselfe whensoeuer he listeth . . . but that as a Maister of a
> howshold holdeth skorne to whippe his Slaues himselfe . . . but
> causeth (peradventure) the groome of his stable to doe it, to the in-
> tent to show them the iustenesse of his displeasure: Euen so doth
> God punish the wicked one by another. . . .   [p. 209]

Could not this whole passage of commentary be applied equally
to Marlowe's Tamburlaine? Its motif of *whipping* we find quite
literally staged in Part 2 of *Tamburlaine*.

Often Elizabethan authors speak of war itself as "a scourge of
the wrath of God."[6] Fulke Greville, for instance, condemns war
as "the perfect type of Hell," but also justifies war as, by Heaven's
overruling power, "The sword of Justice, and of Sinne the ter-

---

[5] *The Trewnesse of the Christian Religion* (1587), p. 208. Regarding the providential punishment visited in turn on Cyrus, see Bodenham's *Belvedere* (1600), the section "Of Tyrants."

[6] Thus says Nicholas Breton in *Characters Upon Essays Moral and Divine* (1615).
Note further in *The Good and the Bad* (1616) Breton's character of "An Unworthy
King": he is "the scourge of sin . . . he knows no God, but makes an idol of nature . . ." (Cf. *Tamburlaine* Pt. 1, II. vii. 18). See also Gascoigne's "Dulce Bellum In-
expertis," stanzas 12 ff. (ed. Cunliffe, *Works of Gascoigne*, I, 143 ff.); and Greville's
"A Treatie of Warres" (ed. Grosart, *Works of Greville*, II, 103 ff.), esp. stanza 6. Burton is summarizing a well-established view when he says that war is "the scourge of
God, cause, effect, fruit and punishment of sin." (ed. Shilleto, *Anatomy of Melancholy*, I. 61).

ror."[7] He explains that war is a form of tyranny grounded in man's sin, arising when man gives rein to the rebellion that lives in his nature.[8] When man strives to become God, he becomes merely the Scourge of God:

> Men would be tyrants, tyrants would be gods,
> Thus they become our scourges, we their rods.

Greville points to Nimrod and to the Turkish empire as two notable examples of a prosperous tyranny founded on war. He explains that Mahomet's religion is, essentially, a Religion-of-War: it refines men for hazard only; it considers virtues of peace effeminate; its discipline is not how to use but how to get; its Church is "mere collusion and deceit." So Mahomet's followers, boldly "climbing vp vnited staires" of diligent wickedness, have prevailed over the Christians, because the Christians are split between a doctrine of peace and a pope who stirs them up to war.[9]

Nimrod, whom Greville has cited as type-example of a Scourge, was known to Renaissance readers through Du Bartas. His career as there sketched has a pattern much like Tamburlaine's. At an early age Nimrod tyrannized over shepherds. And because whoever aims

> At fancied bliss of Empire's awful lustre
> In valiant acts must passe the Vulgar sort,
> Or Mask (at least) in lovely Vertue's Port

he ambitiously avoided ease, hardened himself, and won fame as a hunter. Then, "snatching Fortune by the tresses," he "hunteth men to trap." Through winning some men by promises, others by presents, and still others by "rougher threats," Nimrod usurped the World's "maiden Monarchy." When next he went on to build the tower of Babel, God says:

> . . . I meant to be their Master,
> My self alone, their Law, their Prince, and Pastor;
> And they, for Lord a Tyrant fell have ta'en them;
> Who (to their cost) will roughly curb & rein-them

---

[7] "A Treatie of Warres," stanzas 29, 50.

[8] Stanzas 17, 64. Cf. *Caelica*, LXII.

[9] Stanzas 18, 65 ff. Cf. Du Bartas' "The Miracle of Peace," sonnet 36 (ed. Grosart, *Works of Sylvester*, II, 42).

> Who scorns mine arm, & with these braving Towrs
> Attemps to scale this Crystall Throne of Ours.

Punishment consisted of confounding the people's language, and the commentator Senlisien remarks on the internal nature of this intervention:

> God . . . sendeth not lightning, winde, nor tempest against the tower; but contenteth himself to strike the proud and puffed vp braines of the builders. . . . Who would have thought that God had had so readie such kinde of rods to punish mankinde withall? . . . God . . . treading as it were with woolen feete, and stealing on softly, is able with an arme of Iron to surprise and seize upon these builders, and turne by diuers means their vaine purposes and weake endeauours to naught.[10]

There is commonly in all such stories an ultimate punishment for the Scourge. The tyrant Caesar, so Philip Mornay said, was slain miserably

> To shewe vnto Tyrannes that the highest step of their greatnesse is tyed to a halter, and that they be but Gods scourges which he will cast into the fyre when he hath done with them. . . .[11]

And La Primaudaye affirmed that for tyrants God has His own secret but sure stroke of revenge—"God will returne into their bosom the euill which they haue done."[12] This faith sustained the important Elizabethan doctrine that men should not for private reasons take God's revenge into their own hands.

The concept of the "Scourge of God" has, therefore, two complementary aspects: it serves to explain historical calamities by showing that they are chastisements of sin permitted by God; and it assures tyrants that God is not helpless before their power but that He will, when He has used them, destroy them utterly, creeping up on them (in Senlisien's simile) "as it were with woolen feete."

There is good reason, certainly, for supposing that Marlowe was not ignorant of the meaning of this concept. If his six years at Cambridge were spent in reading for Holy Orders, as is clearly

---

[10] *Babilon* (1596), pp. 21–22.

[11] [Mornay, *On the Truth of the Christian Religion,*] p. 196. Cf. George Whetstone, *A Mirror of True Honnour and Christian Nobilitie* (1585), pp. 8–9; and Greville, *Caelica,* XXXIV.

[12] The Second Part of *The French Academie* (1594), p. 326.

implied by his holding the Archbishop Parker scholarship, then surely he had read Isaiah, and probably the commentary of Calvin, and very likely Mornay and Du Bartas, whom we know to have had an early popularity in Protestant England. From almost any one of the histories of Tamburlaine Marlowe could have got the fact that Tamburlaine proclaimed himself the Scourge of God, and in reading the history provided in Giovius' *Elogia Virorum bellica virtute illustrium*[13] he probably took good note of the fury, cruelty, and ambition which Giovius makes characteristic both of Tamburlaine and of that other famed scourge, Attila.[14] But unless Marlowe had been well read in religious and moral philosophy, the hints from the histories would never have prompted him to invent a whole series of extra-historical incidents by which, in the drama, Tamburlaine spectacularly proclaims his nature and fulfils its type-destiny.

The Scythian Tamburlaine is, like the Scythian Attila and like typical Turks and Titans, a Scourge of God. In terms of Isaiah's philosophy of history, his rise can be thought to have providential purpose because of the wickedness of the Persians, the Turks, and the Babylonians. He is a rod for their chastisement. The scourging which he administers is, except in the case of the virgins of Damascus, more or less deserved: Mycetes is a vain and foolish king; Cosroe is a usurper; Bajazet is proud and cruel. Tamburlaine is perhaps more wicked than they; but God uses the wicked to punish the wicked. The destruction and slaughter which Tamburlaine undertakes in his lust for glory are a scandal permitted under God's providential justice.

The conqueror's religion is a Religion of War. Marlowe provides appropriate ceremonial rites to accompany this false Religion. The invented banquet scene (Part 1, IV. iv) is surely not only a Senecan Thyestean banquet but also, by Marlowe's implication, a travesty of The Lord's Supper. First come "Full bowls of wine unto the god of war"; then "a second course of crowns" (i. e. pastries in the shape of crowns). As the tyrant-master hands

---

[13] According to John Bakeless, *Christopher Marlowe* (New York, 1937), the works of Paulus Giovius were in the libraries of both Corpus Christi College and the University while Marlowe was at Cambridge.

[14] The *Elogia* (ed. of Basle, 1575) contains the stories of Attila (pp. 14–17), of Tamburlaine (pp. 102–7), and of Bajazet (pp. 107–11). In each case the moral monstrosity of the hero is emphasized.

this worldly-bread to his lieutenant-disciples he invests them with titles promissory of the rewards they are to have for service in his kingdom; and he exhorts them to pagan versions of "valour" and "magnanimity." Then, invoking "holy Fates," he goes forth to triumph by the sword. The travesty is Marlowe's contrivance for giving us spectacular evidence of the moral significance of Tamburlaine's career.

Further, let us note the circumstances within which Marlowe has set his hero's claim to be a Scourge of God. We hear this title first announced in a mere two lines at the very center of Part 1's action (III. iii), just after Tamburlaine has become Asia's emperor and is planning to attack the Turkish emperor Bajazet. Next we hear it used as a text for elaborate sermon (in IV. ii), once he has conquered Bajazet and is engaging in holiday rites during a siege of Damascus. Against a background of "milk-white" tents, which (by Marlowe's irony) are said to be "gentle flags of amitie," Tamburlaine summons Bajazet as a footstool, and mounting to his throne on Bajazet's back, bids "heaven behold / Their scourge and terror tread on emperors." Identifying himself as "chiefest lamp of all the earth," he goes on to promise (after a reference to "Clymene's brain-sick son," which Marlowe surely has tucked in for irony) to

> Fill all the air with fiery meteors.
> Then, when the sky shall wax as red as blood,
> It shall be said I made it red myself,
> To make me think of nought but blood and war.
>
> [Pt. 1, IV. ii. 52–55]

(If we compare this promise of meteor-blood in the skies with the promise offered Faustus through Christ's blood in the firmament, it seems likely that Marlowe is emblematizing in Tamburlaine a perverse gospel, in effect that of an antichrist.)

There follows, on the day of red tents, the hellish banquet I have already described. Then, on the day of black tents, we see Tamburlaine offer the supplicating Damascus virgins his sword point and the fate of being trampled under foot by charging horsemen. The symbolism of such behavior accords with Calvin's emphasis (noted earlier in my essay) on the Scourge's proclivity for treading *under foot* his victims. A treading on Bajazet's back had been reported in the histories of Tamburlaine, but Marlowe as divinity student may have known that the archetypal source for this motif is an account in Lactantius[15] of how Sapores, King of the Persians, used for his footstool Valerian, a Roman emperor whom Lactantius regards as providentially thus punished for having persecuted Christians (as in Marlowe's drama Bajazet had been doing). Tamburlaine's biographers had placed his boast of being a "Scourge of God" *after* his slaughter of the virgins, and as an answer to a Genoan merchant who protested this action. But Marlowe has omitted this episode, having already used its boast for the earlier enthronement ceremony on Bajazet's back. This alteration of the source biographies tells us much regarding Marlowe's pondering of the "Scourge of God" claim and his consequent decision to ritualize it and thus make it central to *his* story's implicit meaning.

Throughout the play Tamburlaine lives up to the kind of action appropriate to his assumed role as Scourge of God. Until such time as Heaven decides to cast its Scourge into the fire, he is permitted to continue on his way of rising pride and mounting conquest. The story in Du Bartas of a shepherd-Nimrod who will "roughly curb & rein" the people and attempt to "scale this Crystall throne" of Heaven finds spectacular parallel in Tamburlaine's harnessing of the captive kings and in his mad proposals to storm heaven. A preliminary instance of this heaven-storming is dramatised earlier, at Zenocrate's death, in the hero's threatening to "break the frame of heaven"; and here the added touch of having him attempt to manufacture a "star" by burning Larissa strikes me as a Marlowe-designed contrast to the Wise Men of the gospel story—just as, also, I sense in the "pillar" Tamburlaine erects a contrast (by Marlowe's intention, not the hero's) to the pillar erected by holy Jacob for commemorating a quite different ladder-to-heaven than "divine" Zenocrate's spirit. We need to bear in mind, in this Part II of the drama, that Marlowe had no source-material available from the histories of Tamburlaine. He had to invent episodes, and did so I think out of his Divinity School knowledge of the kind of behavior likely for a Scourge of God.

[15] *On the Manner in Which the Persecutors Died,* ch. V, tr. *Ante-Nicene Fathers* (New York, 1899), VII, 302.

Finally, we have the catastrophic spectacle of Tamburlaine's blasphemy and death. In Isaiah's description of the Scourge of God we found the prediction that the wicked Assyrian after having been used by God to punish wicked nations would proudly say of his conquests:

> By the strength of my hand I have done it, and by my wisdom; for I am so prudent; and I have removed the bounds of the people, and have robbed their treasures, and I have put down the inhabitants like a valiant man;

and that then God Himself would "punish the stout heart of the king of Assyria and the glory of his high looks." This is the ultimate fate which Marlowe has invented for Tamburlaine, signalizing it with an emblematically pagan kind of "Triumphal Entry"—into Babylon. Riding in a chariot drawn by slave-kings, Tamburlaine likens himself to Belus, the son of Nimrod,[16] to Ninus, legendary Assyrian conqueror,[17] and to Alexander.[18] For Elizabethan readers these ancient kings were all stock examples of pride, ambition and impiety.

Moreover, Babylon has a symbolic importance as being in Christian tradition a type—opposite of Jerusalem the Holy City. The dramatic moment therefore is highly significant. Tamburlaine, calling himself God's Scourge, has, like the Assyrian of Isaiah's prophecy, punished the world's wickedness epitomized by Babylon. His usefulness as Scourge may now be regarded as at an end, and we may expect him, like the Assyrian, to boast himself against God.

---

[16] For this identification of Belus, see Bodenham, *Belvedere* (Spenser Society Reprint, 1875), p. 62. The building of the tower of Babel was popularly assigned sometimes to Belus, sometimes to Nimrod, sometimes to Ninus.

[17] Nearly all writers of history, says Orosius, "definitely state that Kingdoms and wars began with Ninus," who "for fifty years . . . maintained a reign of bloodshed throughout Asia." See *Against the Pagans*, ed. Raymond (New York, 1936), pp. 32, 42. The wickedness of both Ninus and Nimrod is commented on in Bale's *God's Promises*, Act III, 13–17. Thomas Heywood in *An Apology for Actors* (1612) says that Ninus is presented on the stage as a warning against ambition. See Shaks. Soc. Rep. (1841), p. 53.

[18] In *F. Q.* I. v. 48 Spenser lists Alexander, Nimrod, and Ninus as men whom Pride has caused to fall. He attributes to Alexander the fault of boasting himself the son of Jove. (This had been stressed in Lydgate's story of the "tirant" Alexander; see *Fall of Princes*, IV, 1107 ff., ed. Bergen, II, 504 ff.) A list of companions-in-hell given by Caesar's ghost in the anonymous *Caesar's Revenge* (II. i) includes, among others, Belus, Ninus, Cyrus and Alexander ("the conquering youth that sought to fetch his pedigree from Heauen").

He fulfils our expectation—first of all by announcing (like the
Tower of Babel builders) that here in Babylon he will establish
his empire by building a "citadel." Then we hear him order by
way of celebration both a drowning and a burning—the drowning of every captured man, woman, and child, and the burning of
the books of "Mahomet, / Whom I have thought a God." None
of the biographies of Tamburlaine provided Marlowe any basis
for this; on the contrary, Perondinus (and a few others) describe
Tamburlaine as having respect for Mahometan shrines and esteeming the priests of Mahomet.[19] But Marlowe is concerned to
show a Tamburlaine now so self-confident of his own power that
he is ready to disown Mahomet and propose himself as a substitute for Mahomet:

> In vain, I see, men worship Mahomet.
> My sword hath sent millions of Turks to hell,
> Slew all his priests, his kinsmen, and his friends,
> And yet I live untouched by Mahomet.
> There is a God, full of revenging wrath,
> From whom the thunder and the lightning breaks,
> Whose scourge I am, and Him will I obey.   [Pt. 2, V. i. 177–83]

The God he here claims to obey is little other than his own wrathful imagination, since he has no notion of a Lord God, who may
visit wrath on *him*. In his daring to burn the Koran he may be
compared to the character Infidelitas in John Bale's *Three Laws,*
who dared to burn Lex Christi—and thereupon was visited with
fire from Deus Pater. That ironic outcome awaits the blindly
tragic Tamburlaine, although first we must listen to his mockery
of all worship and sacred law:

> Now, Mahomet, if thou have any power,
> Come down thyself and work a miracle.
> Thou art not worthy to be worshippèd
> That suffers flames of fire to burn the writ
> Wherein the sum of thy religion rests.
> Why send'st thou not a furious whirlwind down
> To blow thy Alcaron up to thy throne,
> Where men report thou sitt'st by God himself?
> Or vengeance on the head of Tamburlaine

[19] See U. M. Ellis-Fermor's edition of *Tamburlaine* (1930), p. 266 n.

> That shakes his sword against thy majesty
> And spurns the abstracts of thy foolish laws?
> Well, soldiers, Mahomet remains in hell;
> He cannot hear the voice of Tamburlaine.
> Seek out another godhead to adore—
> The God that sits in heaven, if any God,
> For He is God alone, and none but He.   [Pt. 2, V. i. 185–200]

If the last three lines are somewhat puzzling, we should compare the scepticism of the mockers of Christ at Calvary. Their
blasphemy, let it be recalled, showed itself not in any outright
denial of the existence of God, but in challenging His providence
by taunting an alleged prophet of His to save himself by miracle.
To an Elizabethan audience Tamburlaine's behavior must have
seemed analogous to that. For even though Mahomet is for Christians a false prophet, yet Tamburlaine is guilty of a basic impiety
in rejecting his own Asian world's holiest law-giver, one whom he
himself had formerly "thought" to be a God. Calvin had said that
if idolaters lift themselves up against their own forged gods they
thereby show themselves contemners of *all* divine power.[20] And
Raleigh in his *History of the World* (III. 6. 4) tells a story of how
Xerxes, a believer in Apollo who behaved impiously in sacking
Apollo's temple, was justly punished for this by a death providentially arranged by God. God was chastizing impiety, even
though this impiety was toward a false God, Apollo. This background of Protestant thinking, we may suppose, guided Marlowe
in designing his dramatization of Tamburlaine. Though he permits Tamburlaine to declare a tentative belief in "The God
that sits in heaven," such belief is no doubt meant by Marlowe to
contrast with that of pious Orcanes (in Act II, Part II), who believed in a God of "outstretched arm," one who "sits on high and
never sleeps," whose sacred vigor is not confined to heaven, and
who proves himself a "perfect God" by visiting revenge on flout-
ers of moral law. This belief of Orcanes accords with that of Sylvester's Du Bartas, that the Almighty is not

> . . . an idle God
> That lusks in Heav'n and never looks abroad,
> That crowns not Vertue, and corrects not Vice;

---

[20] *Commentary on Isaiah,* ed. cit., p. 118, italics mine.

rather, God is "the soule, the life, the strength, the sinew, / That quickens, moves, and makes this Frame continue."[21] Tamburlaine's disbelief in any such God is what dooms him.

Only sixteen lines after his challenge to Mahomet, Tamburlaine cries: "But stay, I feel myself distempered suddenly." He has got his answer, speedily. His illness, although from one point of view simply a natural event, takes on by another perspective the cast of a supernatural intervention. A physician reports that Tamburlaine's veins are "full of accidental heat" which is drying up his blood. But the play's auditors, while understanding this medically as a case of choler turning into choler adust, were also no doubt expected to interpret such a fate as due to sin and to God's providential way of punishing sin. We may recall La Primaudaye's dictum, quoted earlier in our essay: "it is often said of the wicked in the Scripture, that GOD will return into their bosom the euill they haue done." Tamburlaine's own raging passions have become the fire into which God is casting his Scourge. Blasphemy, according to Calvin, is the greatest of sins, and God is not powerless to punish it. Marlowe's timing of the punishment, at the climax of a madness which has been increasing throughout Part 2 and precipitates into overt blasphemy, is in accord with Calvin's view that no sudden disaster happens by chance.

Even Tamburlaine suspects that some "daring God" is tormenting his body and seeking to conquer him. He responds by calling for a war against the Gods:

> Come, let us march against the powers of heaven
> And set black streamers in the firmament
> To signify the slaughter of the Gods.   [Pt. 2, V. iii. 48–50]

But gradually he realizes that his striving and railing is in vain, "For Tamburlaine the scourge of God must die." His is not a repentant death, like that of Sigismund in Act II. Sigismund had recognized, at *his* moment of overthrow, the justice of God's punishing him. Sigismund had prayed that his deathbed penance might "Conceive a second life in endless mercy!" [Pt. 2, II. iii. 9] Tamburlaine merely oscillates between rebellious fury and an occasional fancy of a higher throne in heaven, before resigning

---

[21] *The First Week,* Seventh Day, 114–19 and 160–61, ed. Grosart, I, 84.

himself finally to the "eyeless Monster," death. Tamburlaine's end is that of a blind worldling. Marlowe, I think, expected his audience to assess it by comparing it to the more hopeful outlook which Sigismund and Orcanes attained amid crisis.

More basically, he expected his audience to understand Tamburlaine's tragedy as an instance of the unwitting self-destruction God assigns his presumptuous Scourges. A pagan Scourge can aspire to setting "black streamers in the firmament" but cannot, like Faustus, envision "Christ's blood streaming" in the firmament. Tamburlaine therefore dies not in despair of a salvation he has been offered and has neglected, but instead in a desperate illusion of gaining an immortality through his sons. His resort to this substitute hope as a comfort to compensate for his own dashed ambitions is Marlowe's measure of the hell of vanity into which this Scourge has been cast. A burning body, and a faith as futile as it is fitful, is Tamburlaine's punishment.

If my reading of the play is valid, it raises for students of Marlowe a larger problem. Was Marlowe, actually, the "atheist" he is so often reputed to be? If *Tamburlaine* really has the patterned dramatic design which I am contending that it has, can we still believe that Marlowe was "a rationalist intelligence blasting its destructive way through all that was held in reverential awe by its contemporaries and ruthlessly desecrating the Holy of Holies"?[22] It is altogether possible that we are not justified in taking our notions of Marlowe from the libels of Kyd and Baines, but that we ought, instead, to be guided by what we can learn of Marlowe by studying the patterns of sin and tragedy exhibited in his plays.

[22] F. S. Boas, *Marlowe and His Circle*, 2nd ed. (1931), p. 77. The view of Boas has been continued by romantic interpreters such as Kocher and Levin. I have offered a reasoned reply to it in "Marlowe Reconsidered: Some Reflections on Levin's *Overreacher*," *JEGP* LII (1953), 531–42.

HELEN L. GARDNER

The Second Part of
TAMBURLAINE THE GREAT

Criticism has been harsh to the second of Marlowe's plays on the career of Tamburlaine. It is usually regarded as an inferior sequel to the first part, repeating its theme with a different ending. Some critics have seen in it a study of degeneration, a picture of the great adventurer of the first part growing more bloodthirsty, cruel and boastful, until, at the height of his triumphs, he is cut off. Miss Ellis-Fermor, in her edition of both parts, feels that the second is very different from the first and ascribes this difference to a change in Marlowe's feeling towards his hero; but she feels that the result of this change is boredom with his theme and imaginative poverty in handling it. "Of the events and episodes available to Marlowe when he wrote the first part of *Tamburlaine*," she writes, "very few had been omitted. There was, consequently, little left of the original legend when a second part was to be written. He had, beyond doubt, a clear conception of the development the chief character should suffer, and this differed so far from the conception of the first part as to endanger the effectiveness of a play written on similar lines. . . . In this situation, then, with his sources for the life already drained and his sympathies no longer strongly enough engaged to stimulate his imagination to constructive plotting, he seems to have been driven to eke out his

First published in the *Modern Language Review* XXXVII (1942):18–24 and here reprinted by permission of the Modern Humanities Research Association and of the editors.

material by introducing irrelevant episodes, some of which he weaves in skilfully, others of which are, and look like, padding. . . . The first part alone reveals Marlowe's mind at work on a characteristic structure; much of the second, though flashes of power and passages of thought as clear as anything in the earlier part occur at intervals throughout, is, by comparison, journeyman work. The form of the whole is no longer an inevitable expression of an underlying idea" (pp. 41 and 46).

It is the argument of this article that the second part of *Tamburlaine* has been misjudged and that while it is true that Marlowe's sympathies have changed since he wrote the first part, it is not true that this makes his play ineffective, since the change of sympathies has meant a change of theme, and the change of theme has, in turn, necessitated a change of structure. The second part of *Tamburlaine* is not a mere continuation of the first; it is different in intention and plan. The subsidiary episodes, which seem irrelevant padding if we regard the play as a rewriting of the first part with a different ending, are relevant when we recognize the theme and the play's structure. It cannot be claimed that the second part of *Tamburlaine* is a great play, but it can be claimed that it is better than it is commonly supposed to be, and that it shows in some degree the Shakespearian method of plotting, in which episodes and sub-plots are linked to the main plot by idea, rather than the primitive structure of *Tamburlaine, Part I,* or *Dr. Faustus.* In its conception, it looks forward to *Dr. Faustus,* rather than backwards to *Part I,* though it makes, of course, continual reference to the first part and shows indeed many ironic contrasts with it.

The theme of the first part of *Tamburlaine* is the power and splendour of the human will, which bears down all opposition and by its own native force achieves its desires. Tamburlaine is shown to us in the double rôle of warrior and lover. In both he is irresistible and the play reaches its climax in his conquest of Zenocrate's father, the Soldan, and the crowning of Zenocrate as Queen and Empress of the kingdoms he has conquered. The structure of the play is extremely simple and could be plotted as a single rising line on a graph; there are no setbacks. The world into which Tamburlaine, the unknown Scythian shepherd, bursts like a kind of portent is decadent, divided and torn by petty strife. Little dignity or grandeur is given to his opponents and, as Miss Ellis-Fermor justly remarks, the tragic pity, voiced by Zenocrate, for 'the Turk and his great emperess' is allowed only slight scope. Opposition appears to melt away at Tamburlaine's mere appearance. Theridamas, sent with an army against him, is won over by his presence and comes over to his side without a battle; Cosroe, who dethrones his brother and plans to use Tamburlaine for his own purposes, is easily overthrown. In love the path is equally straight. Zenocrate, betrothed to the Prince of Arabia, when captured by Tamburlaine, makes no defiance. We are not even shown a wooing; at their second meeting, she is already in love with him and yields without a show of resistance, seeming to range herself on his side, as the others do, by instinct.

The theme of the second part is very different. Man's desires and aspirations may be limitless, but their fulfilment is limited by forces outside the control of the will. There are certain facts, of which death is the most obvious, which no aspiration and no force of soul can conquer. There is a sort of stubbornness in the stuff of experience which frustrates and resists the human will. The world is not the plaything of the ambitious mind. There are even hints in the play that there is an order in the world, of which men's minds are a part, and that man acts against this order at his peril. This theme of the clash between man's desires and his experience demands a more complex structure for its expression than was demanded by the theme of the triumphant human will in the first part. If the first part can be plotted as a steadily rising line, the second can be thought of as two lines, the line of Tamburlaine and that of his enemies. Neither rises or falls steadily, but on the whole it can be said that the forces opposing Tamburlaine grow in strength during the first half of the play and reach their zenith in the third act, and that after this we see the power of Tamburlaine reasserting itself, until, at the moment of his greatest triumph, he is struck down by death. But a graph of two lines does not really express the play's structure, since it leaves unrepresented the force that in the end destroys the hero. This force (it can be called Necessity or God, according to one's interpretation of Marlowe's religious thought) appears from time to time in the body of the play and in the end reduces the contest between Tamburlaine and his foes to an episode in the world's pattern; it provides a kind of ground swell to the whole play. The truth of this analysis can only be brought out by a detailed examination of the plot.

The second part, like the first, does not open with the hero, but with his opponents; but, whereas in the first part they are shown as despicable, in the second they are dignified and worthy of respect. At the beginning of the first part we saw the kingdom of Persia fallen into the hands of a fool, whose brother was plotting with the aid of a faction at the court to dethrone him. In the second part we find the Turkish kings deciding upon a truce with the Christians, in order to secure their rear against attack while they fight with Tamburlaine. That is to say, the first part showed us a world of disunity and strife, which fell an easy prey to Tamburlaine's ambition, while the second shows us a world aware of the menace of Tamburlaine and organizing itself to oppose him. By the second scene of the first act the truce has been made and Orcanes with his allies is prepared for Tamburlaine's attack. In the third scene we meet Callapine, the captive son of Bajazeth, who, by promises and bribes, wins over his gaoler, Almeda, to betray his trust and assist in an escape. This scene, in which a servant of Tamburlaine's is won over from him by the lure of money and glory, would be inconceivable in the first part. There all the attraction and the lures are on Tamburlaine's side; he is a kind of magnet, attracting the ambitious towards him. The treachery of his servant at the opening of the second part suggests that we have no longer to do with the conquering demi-god of the first part; the Tamburlaine spell is not working. In the next scene Tamburlaine himself appears and the same feeling is just hinted at. For all his power of will, he is unable to mould his sons as he pleases. He is distressed by their unwarlike appearance, satisfied by the bloodthirsty remarks of two of them, but baffled by the unabashed cowardice of Calyphas. Miss Ellis-Fermor's notes to this scene speak of "that hint of frustration and anxiety which grows more definite as this part of the play progresses." But both the scene of Callapine's escape and that of Calyphas's unnatural pacificism give only hints and the old Tamburlaine soon reasserts himself. His companions, Theridamas, Techelles and Usumcasane, enter with news of conquering campaigns and of great armies come to fight on his side. The first act ends with Tamburlaine apparently all-powerful, banqueting in triumph among his subject kings.

The second act opens with a setback for the enemies of Tamburlaine. The Christian kings decide to break their truce with the Turks, on the ground that faith need not be kept with infidels. When the news of this treachery is brought to Orcanes, he, an unbeliever, makes the famous appeal to the Christ whom the Christians worship, to show his Godhead by punishing the perjury of his servants. Marlowe could not resist the opportunity of underlining the contrast between the faith of Christians and their works, but the real meaning of the episode lies in the lines in which Marlowe, through the mouth of Orcanes, expresses his belief that the God who "everywhere fills every continent with strange infusion of his sacred vigour" is a God of purity as well as of power, and that he punishes the sins of men. Orcanes's appeal to Christ is answered; the Christians flee in discomfiture, acknowledging their fate is just. The opponents of Tamburlaine, weakened at the beginning of the act, end in a stronger position through having surmounted the trial, and the whole moral feeling of the episode tells against the arrogance of Tamburlaine. The action passes at once and without warning to the deathbed of Zenocrate and here the moral is too clear to need any pointing; it is given with sad brevity by the watching Theridamas:

> Ah, good my lord, be patient. She is dead,
> And all this raging cannot make her live.
>
> [Pt. 2, II. iv. 119–20]

The third act opens with a scene which is obviously intended to parallel Act 1, scene 6. There, Tamburlaine, having summoned his subject kings, assessed his forces for the coming campaign: here, Callapine, having been crowned with his father's crown Emperor of Turkey, is told by his tributary kings what strength they can bring for the coming struggle with Tamburlaine. This scene shows Callapine at the peak of his power; the confederation against Tamburlaine is at its height. By contrast, Tamburlaine in the next scene is at his most dejected, celebrating the death of Zenocrate by the futile and savage burning of a town. Having lost his wife, he turns to his sons for consolation, only to find himself baffled by the weakness of Calyphas. His attention is distracted by the other two, who show a dutiful indifference to pain, but a hint is given here of another of those forces which hamper us in the execution of our ambitions, the resistance of other wills, which refuse to accept the parts we assign to them.

This theme is developed in a subsidiary episode, which has usually been regarded as mere padding, that of Theridamas and Olympia, the Captain's wife. In reading this episode, one recalls the parallel situation of the first part, when Zenocrate, captured as a prize of war, also charms her conqueror by her beauty. There the conqueror was as successful in love as in war and his captive responded to his passion before he spoke of it. Theridamas, the hero of this episode, is associated in our minds with Tamburlaine, as his closest friend and most loyal follower; his fortunes have followed those of his master. The rebuff he suffers here at the hands of Olympia, who prefers death to his love, and eludes him finally, when he seems to have absolute power over her, by a clever ruse, seems to reflect back on Tamburlaine himself.

The death of Olympia follows immediately upon the murder of Calyphas, which is itself an example of failure coming on the heels of success. Act 3 ends with a scolding match between Tamburlaine and the Turkish kings and in Act 4, scene 1 Tamburlaine wins his first great victory over Orcanes and his allies; but the moment of triumph is spoilt by the cowardice of Calyphas and he celebrates his victory by the murder of his son, whom he can kill, but cannot force to obey him. It is possible that Marlowe had some sympathy with the effeminate Calyphas (he certainly provides him with some good ironic comment on his father); but one must be careful not to read a modern criticism of the value of military exploits into what may have seemed to the Elizabethans obvious wrong-headedness, nor must one overestimate the value of the silence with which he dies. Nevertheless, it is worth noting that though the bystanders plead for his life, Calyphas himself says nothing. This may be a deliberate touch, the last defiance of the weakling, or it may be that Marlowe forgot the victim in his interest in the executioner; or, perhaps, his father's reference to his "fainting soul" is to be taken literally. But the whole treatment of Calyphas suggests something more subtle than the traditional coward; his distaste for war and his refusal to find his father impressive are positive rather than negative attitudes, and his silent death may be due partly to his realization of his father's implacability and partly to his desire to infuriate him by not cowering. In the general development of the play, the two episodes of Olympia and Calyphas taken together prepare us for the dénouement; they both show the limitations of human power, here thwarted by other human wills. Occurring as they do, at the moment of Tamburlaine's first military success in this play, they hint at the hollowness of such triumphs; and, in this context, the mad bombast of Tamburlaine, which, in the last scene of the fourth act, culminates in the yoking of the conquered kings to his chariot, is seen for what it is: an impious assertion of human pride, ludicrous in its excess, and by its exaggeration revealing the palpable falseness of his claim to absolute power.

Throughout the fifth act the power of Tamburlaine grows and that of his foes declines. The Governor of Babylon makes a show of resistance, but yields to pressure: the conquered kings have a moment of revolt, but are soon "bridled." Tamburlaine, defying Mahomet, and with him conventional religious observances, claims that he is the great servant and instrument of the only true God.

> There is a God, full of revenging wrath,
> From whom the thunder and the lightning breaks,
> Whose scourge I am, and Him will I obey.   [Pt. 2, V. i. 181–83]

It is at the height of his power that Tamburlaine is struck down. Even when dying he can, by his mere presence, put the army of Callapine to flight; but his last and greatest victory is only the prelude to death. Through the last half of the play, as his power has grown, so have the warnings of fate, mere hints in the first act, grown louder. Now sickness proves him a man who "was termed the terror of the world." In words gentler and graver than one would expect, and which are often overlooked, Tamburlaine, in his dying admonition to his heir, himself moralizes his end:

> Nor bar thy mind that magnanimity
> That nobly must admit necessity.   [Pt. 2, V. iii. 200–201]

It is by necessity that "Tamburlaine the scourge of God must die."

It cannot be claimed that the execution of *Tamburlaine, Part II* is equal to the conception, but the play contains less irrelevance than is usually imagined, and it is an interesting early attempt at a more complicated tragic pattern than the first part or *Dr. Faustus* can show. Its tragic pattern is not unlike that of *Sejanus,* where we are shown the fortunes of Sejanus and the group opposed to him, and Tiberius at Capreae operating as a kind of Fate. In *Sejanus* also the catastrophe comes with great suddenness, after an apparent triumph, and there is the same wavering movement in the fortunes of Sejanus and his enemies as in those of Tamburlaine and Callapine. The basis of the pattern in *Tamburlaine, Part II* is the struggle of Tamburlaine and Callapine; but into this conflict of military and political power is woven the theme of necessity, a necessity which Marlowe tries to moralize. It is moralized early in the play by the answer which the prayer of the good heathen Orcanes receives, and, in the later half, by the mad pride of Tamburlaine, which gives his death the quality of a punishment. The first part of *Tamburlaine* glorifies the human will: the second displays its inevitable limits. It is a first handling of the theme of *Dr. Faustus*—a weaker handling, because Tamburlaine's ambitions are cruder than those of Faustus, and because there is little feeling in *Tamburlaine, Part II* for the paradoxes that make up the tragedy of the later play. Faustus, aiming at being more than man, becomes less, for he cuts himself off from the common mercies of God; desiring all knowledge, he finds the great secret barred from him, for he may learn nothing "that is against our kingdom"; desiring all power, he finds himself the slave of Mephistopheles, who, he had thought, was to be his servant. *Dr. Faustus,* in spite of its mutilated state, expresses clearly the great tragic idea of the essential vanity of desires which refuse to take into account the limitations of humanity. The theme of *Tamburlaine, Part II* is less profoundly tragic than this, and Marlowe shows little sense that the goods which Tamburlaine pursues are in the end themselves unsatisfying. The play proclaims only the idea of necessity, which the magnanimous mind must 'nobly admit,' and its moral is the simple medieval one of the inevitability of death. But the arrival of that final check to Tamburlaine's fantasies of omnipotence is more carefully prepared for than is usually admitted and the earlier episodes of the play, sometimes judged to be mere padding, are mainly anticipations of the final catastrophe and variations on the underlying theme.

G. I. DUTHIE

The Dramatic Structure of Marlowe's *TAMBURLAINE THE GREAT* Parts 1 and 2

According to the Prologue to Part 2 of *Tamburlaine,* Marlowe wrote Part 2 as a result of the popularity of Part 1. Part 1 is, then, a complete play in itself, and in the following study I propose in the first place to speak of Part 1 *per se.*

I

What are the essentials of the plot-material out of which *1 Tamburlaine* is made? The following answer might perhaps be given. A Scythian shepherd, endowed with a mind of astonishing power and with a uniquely compelling personality, and inspired by a soaring ambition, embarks on a career of ruthless conquest with the aim of becoming a pre-eminent ruler. He achieves success after success, and, to round off the play, finally "takes truce with all the world" and marries the lady whom he loves: he had taken her prisoner at the beginning of his career, and, some time after her capture, she had come to love him. The main content of the play, according to this view, consists of the amazing series of triumphs which Tamburlaine enjoys, these being presented as a result, on the one hand, of the operation of Fate, and, on the other, of the tremendous strength of Tamburlaine's ambition, his overwhelming confidence in his own destiny (which he communicates

First published in *English Studies* (London, 1948), pp. 101–26. Édited by F. P. Wilson. Reprinted by permission of The English Association (London).

to others too), and the extraordinary energy and mental vitality which he brings to his war-making.

If this is a fair summary of the essential stuff of *1 Tamburlaine,* it must, I think, be granted that Marlowe has set himself to make a play out of dramatically unpromising material. Unchecked development along a straight, even although upward-slanting, line can hardly be called truly dramatic development. The aspiring mind hardly furnishes promising psychological material for drama if there is no conflict in that mind, no interplay of opposing motives. And it has been claimed that the content of *1 Tamburlaine* is in fact undramatic. In her very interesting book on Marlowe, Professor U. M. Ellis-Fermor writes as follows:[1]

> *Tamburlaine,* so far from interpreting life by indicating its form, appears as formless and incoherent as life itself. The first part, in this, errs less than the second, but even the first has no progress, crisis or solution. The final triumph and marriage of Tamburlaine is perhaps a climax, but it is too long deferred to have a direct connection with the original impulse, and the idea has been anticipated and handled so often that it has lost its freshness. Tamburlaine's rise to power cannot fill five acts of a play without complications, and a complication would be a denial of the very nature of Tamburlaine's genius, which triumphs, not after a struggle, but without it. Thus, before his play was begun, Marlowe had committed himself to a theme that was in its essence undramatic. It is a foregone conclusion, then, that there will be no dramatic form. . . . It is obvious that, of all the emotions that may be roused in an audience by the action of a play, almost the only one possible to the plot of *Tamburlaine* is surprise, an emotion that can only be evoked to a limited degree. The audience is in a state of suspense during the earliest acts of the double play, and suspense gives way to amazement as triumph follows triumph. As soon as the point is reached at which there is no longer any uncertainty in the mind of the audience—that is, as soon as repetition of the triumph has made the situation familiar and caused it to be expected, there is no more suspense. There are, in point of fact, about two more acts, but they have to be helped out with Bajazeth and the Virgins of Damascus —episodes which are irrelevant to the too simple original theme.

For myself, I cannot help disagreeing with this estimate of *1 Tamburlaine.* I cannot agree that the play has "no progress,

[1] *Christopher Marlowe* (1927), pp. 44–45.

crisis or solution," nor that the final triumph and marriage of Tamburlaine has no "direct connection with the original impulse," nor that "a complication would be a denial of the very nature of Tamburlaine's genius, which triumphs, not after a struggle, but without it," nor that the episodes of Bajazeth and the Virgins of Damascus are "irrelevant to the too simple original theme," nor that the play has "no dramatic form."

It is clear that at one crucial point there is a very real conflict in the hero's mind. This is at V. ii. 72–127, a soliloquy by Tamburlaine in which we find him caught between two possible courses of action. Is he to continue in his former ways as a ruthless conqueror? He would like to. But he cannot help being affected by Zenocrate's grief for her country and her father. Is he to allow this to deflect him from his habitual inexorability? The struggle in his mind is severe; in her tear-filled eyes

> . . . angels in their crystal armors fight
> A doubtful battle with my tempted thoughts
> For Egypt's freedom and the Soldan's life,
> His life that so consumes Zenocrate, . . .   [Pt. 1, V. ii. 88–91]

The words "tempted" and "doubtful" are significant—we have mental conflict in the hero and we have genuine dramatic suspense. Zenocrate's anxiety for her father is a most powerful inducement to Tamburlaine to change his ways. The irresistible conqueror has never stood in such danger of defeat as he now stands—Zenocrate's sorrow is more likely to turn him from his ruthless course than any enemy he has previously encountered: her sorrows, he says,

> . . . lay more siege unto my soul
> Than all my army to Damascus' walls;
> And neither Persians' sovereign nor the Turk
> Troubled my senses with conceit of foil
> So much by much as doth Zenocrate.   [Pt. 1, V. ii. 92–96]

Is he going to allow her to deflect him, or is he going to resist her?

This conflict in Tamburlaine's mind is resolved, and its resolution conditions the nature of the conclusion of the play. Tamburlaine not only spares the Soldan's life but also declares to him that he will

> . . . render all into your hands,
> And add more strength to your dominions
> Than ever yet confirmed th'Egyptian crown.
>
> [Pt. 1, V. ii. 384–86]

His own words make it clear that the course he is taking is the result of Zenocrate's influence—

> Come, happy father of Zenocrate,
> A title higher than thy Soldan's name.
> Though my right hand have thus enthrallèd thee,
> Thy princely daughter here shall set thee free,
> She that hath calmed the fury of my sword,
> Which had ere this been bathed in streams of blood
> As vast and deep as Euphrates or Nile.   [Pt. 1, V. ii. 370–76]

Had it not been for the influence of Zenocrate, Tamburlaine
would have behaved otherwise towards the conquered Soldan.
But what Marlowe presents us with is not a simple matter of
Tamburlaine abrogating his old principles and substituting new
ones for them. Having declared that he is going to "render all"
into the Soldan's hands, he goes on—

> The god of war resigns his room to me,
> Meaning to make me general of the world.
> Jove, viewing me in arms, looks pale and wan,
> Fearing my power should pull him from his throne.
> Where'er I come the Fatal Sisters sweat,
> And grisly Death, by running to and fro
> To do their ceaseless homage to my sword.   [Pt. 1, V. ii. 387–93]

He still claims that his "honor" consists

> . . . in shedding blood
> When men presume to manage arms with him.
>
> [Pt. 1, V. ii. 414–15]

This is the sort of thing that he has been saying from the beginning of the play. The resolution of the mental struggle of V. ii.
72ff. consists of a determination by Tamburlaine not to give up
his old principles, but to maintain them though allowing them
to be modified to some extent by the influence of Zenocrate.

Zenocrate signifies Beauty. Beauty sits in her face (V. ii. 80–81).
Now in the crucial soliloquy at V. ii. 72ff. Tamburlaine declares
that a warrior must admit Beauty as an influence upon him—

And every warrior that is rapt with love
Of fame, of valor, and of victory,
Must needs have beauty beat on his conceits.

[Pt. 1, V. ii. 117–19]

But the influence of Beauty must not be excessive—

But how unseemly it is for my sex,
My discipline of arms and chivalry,
My nature, and the terror of my name,
To harbor thoughts effeminate and faint!
Save only that in beauty's just applause,
With whose instinct the soul of man is touched;
And every warrior. . . .   [Pt. 1, V. ii. 111–17]

And he declares that he, Tamburlaine, will both "conceive" and "subdue" Beauty (V. ii. 120)—he will both admit and resist its influence. Beauty can influence a warrior in two directions. First, it can encourage him in his warlike career. Zenocrate has encouraged Tamburlaine unhesitatingly up to the point where Damascus is besieged and the Soldan is threatened, and at the end Tamburlaine can still think of her as "adding more courage to [his] conquering mind" (V. ii. 453). But secondly, Beauty can also urge a warrior towards clemency: it can try to arouse compassion in him, to exert a softening influence upon him. And Tamburlaine believes that it is possible to give way too much to this softening influence, so that one is degraded from the status of great warrior. That, he insists, he himself must avoid.

On the face of it, the upshot of this soliloquy is that Tamburlaine determines to allow Beauty to affect him as far as its encouraging influence goes, but that he determines to resist its softening influence. On the face of it, that is what he means when he says that he will both "conceive" and "subdue" Beauty. If that is the entire result of the soliloquy, however, we must surely be prepared at the end to find him refusing to be lenient to the Soldan. But that is just what we do not find. We find him sparing the Soldan and declaring that it is Zenocrate who has calmed the fury of his sword. Moreover it is very shortly after the soliloquy that he first avows his intention to spare the Soldan, and in making this avowal he indicates that the decision has been made for the sake of Zenocrate:

> *Theridamas.*   We know the victory is ours, my lord,
> 　　But let us save the reverend Soldan's life
> 　　For fair Zenocrate that so laments his state.
> *Tamburlaine.*   That we will chiefly see unto, Theridamas,
> 　　For sweet Zenocrate, whose worthiness
> 　　Deserves a conquest over every heart.　　　　[Pt. 1, V. ii. 140–45]

The word "conquest" here points back to "battle" in V. ii. 89.
Now I do not think it could be seriously suggested that in the
soliloquy Tamburlaine resolves to resist the influence of Zenocrate's grief, and then, almost immediately, decides briskly, after
Theridamas's short plea on her behalf, to give in after all. I believe that by the end of the soliloquy he has decided to be merciful to the Soldan. When he declares that he will both "conceive"
and "subdue" Beauty, I believe that by "conceiving" it he means
more than admitting its influence as an encouragement in his
martial exploits. He means that, doubtless: but I think he also
means that he will admit its moderating influence as far as the
sparing of the Soldan is concerned. He will admit its moderating
influence—but not beyond the point where that ceases to be consistent with his honour as a warrior. Should Beauty ever tempt
him to be weak, spineless, effeminate, he would refuse to give in
to it: but he may spare the Soldan without pusillanimity. I believe that this solution of his problem is implied in the soliloquy
itself: it is at any rate certainly the solution at which he has arrived by the end of the play when, at V. ii. 370, he enters leading
the captive Soldan.

The modifying effect of Beauty on Tamburlaine in the end is
to create in him a disposition to show pity in a greater degree
than he has been willing to do before. We may say that what is
opposed to Beauty during the conflict in his mind is Honour as
he has up to now conceived it—that is, a conception of Honour
which excludes Pity after a certain point. Before the psychological crisis it has been his custom on the first day of an engagement
to pitch white tents in his camp, indicating to his enemies that
if they surrender now all their lives will be spared. It is not until
the third day, when his tents are black, that his wrath demands
the blood of all "without respect of Sex, degree or age" (IV. i. 63).
Under certain circumstances, then, he is already prepared to be
merciful. But it seems clear that what is required of him at the

critical moment in V. ii is that he shall be merciful beyond the limits to which he has previously been willing to go. When he announces that he is going to spare the Soldan he says, as we have seen, that had not Zenocrate calmed the fury of his sword it

> . . . had ere this been bathed in streams of blood
> As vast and deep as Euphrates or Nile.   [V. ii. 375–76]

Tamburlaine modifies his old ideal of Honour. But he does not jettison it. The old ideal had been imperfect: it had not allowed sufficient scope to Pity. Now, revised, adjusted, it can still stand. And, inasmuch as Beauty has not only a softening but also an encouraging influence on a warrior, Zenocrate remains an inspiration which adds more courage to Tamburlaine's conquering mind (V. ii. 452).

It is to be noticed that after the soliloquy Tamburlaine immediately asks "Hath Bajazeth been fed to day?" (V. ii. 129). And when, shortly afterwards, he asserts that Zenocrate "Deserves a conquest over every heart," he goes on immediately to speak insultingly to Bajazeth (V. ii. 146). There is not much evidence here of any change in Tamburlaine in the direction of lenity! But we must remember that though he has accepted the idea of the moderating effect of Beauty he has also insisted that it shall not be allowed to derogate from his honour as a warrior, and we may suggest that in making him persist in his former attitude to Bajazeth Marlowe is simply emphasizing the fact that Tamburlaine is not giving up his role of conqueror—he is not by any means altogether revoking his former values. In the same way, we may be somewhat disconcerted to find at the end of the play that no sooner has Tamburlaine shown his leniency to the Soldan in deference to Zenocrate than he goes on to rant about the god of war resigning his room to him—his old bombast rings out again unaltered. But what the audience or reader has to do here (V. ii. 371–416) is, I think, to imagine a combination of the two attitudes which are indicated side by side—the willingness of the hero to be merciful beyond his former wont, and his insistence on the fact that he will not allow himself to be reduced to anything less than a great warrior. I believe that at the end we are meant to see a Tamburlaine who is ready to admit in due proportion the moderating and encouraging influences of Beauty—a Tamburlaine animated by a single new ideal consisting of a modification of his original conception of Honour. But apparently all that Marlowe can do to convey this is to make him speak now in terms indicating a resolve to be merciful and generous as not before, and now in terms exactly like those he was in the habit of using before.

At V. ii. 72ff., then, we have a psychological crisis in the hero, and its resolution conditions the nature of the conclusion of the play. Now the direct preparation for this crisis begins at the end of IV. ii, where Zenocrate first begs Tamburlaine to be merciful to Damascus—

> Yet would you have some pity for my sake,
> Because it is my country's and my father's.   [123–24]

But Tamburlaine's reply is uncompromising—

> Not for the world, Zenocrate, if I have sworn.   [125]

He will not be merciful contrary to his oath—his honour demands that he shall keep his oath. The oath consists of the declaration that if the city is surrendered while Tamburlaine's tents are white all inside will be spared—if it is surrendered while the tents are red those inside who are armed will be slain—and if it holds out until the tents are black not one of the inhabitants shall escape. Tamburlaine will not, even for Zenocrate's sake, be compassionate beyond the bounds of his established practice—and it is clear that that is what she is asking him to be, for her "Yet would you have some pity" comes immediately after his threats as to what will happen "when they see me march in black array."

Then in IV. iv. Zenocrate appears sad. Tamburlaine asks her why, and she replies—

> My lord, to see my father's town besieged,
> The country wasted, where myself was born,
> How can it but afflict my very soul?
> If any love remain in you, my lord,
> Or if my love unto your majesty
> May merit favor at your Highness' hands,
> Then raise your siege from fair Damascus' walls,
> And with my father take a friendly truce.
>
> [Pt. 1, IV. iv. 63–70]

But again Tamburlaine is firm—

> Zenocrate, were Egypt Jove's own land,
> Yet would I with my sword make Jove to stoop.
>
> [Pt. 1, IV. iv. 71–72]

He will not give up the aim and the methods that have brought him to the point where he now is. He will not buy Zenocrate's father's love with the sacrifice of his ambition. Zenocrate is submissive, and yet at the same time she pleads again, this time for her father himself—

> Honor still wait on happy Tamburlaine;
> Yet give me leave to plead for him, my lord.
>
> [Pt. 1, IV. iv. 83–84]

And now Tamburlaine makes a concession to her—

> Content thyself; his person shall be safe,
> And all the friends of fair Zenocrate,
> If with their lives they will be pleased to yield,
> Or may be forced to make me emperor;
> For Egypt and Arabia must be mine.   [Pt. 1, IV. iv. 85–89]

But it is a grudging concession—witness that "If" and the ring of the last line.

Then in V. i and ii we have the episode of the Virgins of Damascus. Here we see the idea of genuine pity arising in Tamburlaine's mind for the first time: but it arises only to be rejected, unhesitatingly if regretfully. He is sincerely sorry for the Virgins—

> What, are the turtles frayed out of their nests?
> Alas, poor fools, must you be first shall feel
> The sworn destruction of Damascus?
> They know my custom; could they not as well
> Have sent ye out when first my milk-white flags,
> Through which sweet Mercy threw her gentle beams,
> Reflexing them on your disdainful eyes,
> As now when fury and incensèd hate
> Flings slaughtering terror from my coal-black tents,
> And tells for truth submissions comes too late?
>
> [Pt. 1, V. ii. 1–10]

There is real compassion here. But he cannot and will not break his oath: he must give full scope to his idea of Honour—

> Virgins, in vain ye labor to prevent
> That which mine honor swears shall be performed.
> Behold my sword, . . .   [Pt. 1, V. ii. 43–45]

And after he has ordered their deaths he reiterates his old principle emphatically—

> I will not spare these proud Egyptians,
> Nor change my martial observations
> For all the wealth of Gihon's golden waves,
> Or for the love of Venus, would she leave
> The angry god of arms and lie with me.
> They have refused the offer of their lives;
> And know my customs are as peremptory
> As wrathful planets, death or destiny.   [Pt. 1, V. ii. 58–65]

He has felt pity. (And we may ask ourselves whether the idea of pity would have occurred to him had it not been for Zenocrate's previous pleading.) He has felt pity: but he is still unprepared to allow himself to be merciful beyond the bounds laid down in his former practice. We see his old imperfect conception of Honour being assailed by the idea of Pity, but it is still not seriously threatened by that idea, and it stands firm. Then comes the soliloquy at V. ii. 72ff., showing that now there is a conflict in Tamburlaine's mind. This conflict is led up to from the end of IV. ii, from which point onwards the principal interest is, in my opinion, the clash between the idea of Pity, suggested by Zenocrate, and Tamburlaine's old idea of Honour according to which pity cannot be exercised contrary to the warrior's previous oath. Tamburlaine has no difficulty in resisting the idea of Pity up to the soliloquy: but in connection with the Virgins of Damascus he for the first time feels a certain inclination towards Pity. Thus the episode of the Virgins of Damascus is definitely relevant to the dramatic development. So also is the episode of Bajazeth, who is Tamburlaine's last and most conspicuous victim before the question of Honour versus Pity arises.

I am claiming that Acts IV and V are thoroughly dramatic. There is a working up to a psychological crisis—the crisis involves suspense—there is a solution of the crisis—and so the play comes to a dramatically satisfying conclusion. But it may be suggested that the play *as a whole* does not have satisfactory dramatic shape. It may be suggested that Marlowe set out to produce a play from material essentially undramatic (simply the successive victories of a conqueror endowed with an aspiring mind), that by the end of Act III he found that he had done all that could be done with that material, and that in Acts IV and V he proceeded to a new theme which he could and did treat in truly dramatic fashion. This is essentially the view taken by Miss Leslie Spence.[2]

"As early as the end of Act II," she says,[3] "the audience is convinced that no one can defeat him,

> Whose smiling stars give him assurèd hope
> Of martial triumph, ere he meet his foes.
>
> [Pt. 1, III. iii. 42–43]

His early insistence on the invincibility of Tamburlaine left Marlowe under the dramatic necessity of furnishing for the remaining three fifths of his drama elements of conflict other than military struggle, even though military success was the only ambition of the historic conqueror. Act III, in which Marlowe tried to subordinate concern for the outcome of the battle to humorous debate and farcical treatment, lacked intensity and was dramatically unsuccessful. It was clear that the dramatist must create another interest. Searching the universe for something which had a chance of conquering his invincible, heaven-guarded hero, Marlowe seems to have made the choice determined on by Seneca's desperate Juno, when she sought to overcome Hercules, whom nothing on sea, on earth, or under the earth could conquer:

> sed vicit omnes, quaeris Alcidae parem?
> nemo est nisi ipse. bella iam secum gerat
>
> [Hercules Furens, 84–85]

The dramatist decided that only Tamburlaine could conquer Tamburlaine. From the elements of character furnished by history— military invincibility, ambition, and wrath—no momentous inner struggle could be evolved. Accordingly, Marlowe added love and some pity to oppose the fiercer propensities of the great Scythian. Against a background of military rigor, which the display of ensigns, the torture of Bajazeth, the slaying of the maidens, and the destruction of Damascus all accentuate, the emotions of Tamburlaine fight, till, in the conflict of his passions, he admits the sorrows of Zenocrate

[2] See *Modern Philology* XXIV (1926–27):181 ff., and *Publications of the Modern Language Association of America*, XLII (1927):604 ff.
[3] PMLA XLII:620.

> . . . lay more siege unto my soul
> Than all my army to Damascus' walls.
>
> [Pt. 1, V. ii. 92–93]

Shall he adhere to his military rules in dealing with Zenocrate's father? Not until the very end of the play is this question settled. On the struggle of Tamburlaine with himself was built the dramatic conflict of the last two acts. . . . By the end of Act II Marlowe had made Tamburlaine so gloriously invincible that the center of interest could no longer be physical strife. Hence the inner struggle and the love story.

In my opinion Miss Spence does excellently to point out how Marlowe endows Tamburlaine with emotional complexity. But I am not happy about the suggestion that Marlowe found himself at the end of Act II in an apparent impasse, that he tried in Act III to get out of it by one way and failed, and that he tried in Acts IV and V to get out of it by another way and this time succeeded. I believe that the entire play was conceived from the start as a single coherent dramatic structure.

I am sure that when Marlowe composed the soliloquy at V. ii. 72ff. he himself had the beginning of the play in mind. The soliloquy ends as follows:

> I thus conceiving and subduing both,
> That which hath stopped the tempest of the gods,
> Even from the fiery-spangled veil of heaven,
> To feel the lovely warmth of the shepherds' flames
> And march in cottages of strowèd weeds,
> Shall give the world to note, for all my birth,
> That virtue solely is the sum of glory,
> And fashions men with true nobility.   [Pt. 1, V. ii. 120–27]

Now there appears to be some textual corruption here. It does not make very good sense to say that something has "stopped the tempest of the gods to feel the lovely warmth of shepherds' flames." Various emendations have been proposed, and the best thing to do in my opinion is to emend "stopped" to "stoopped" (Dyce) and "tempest" to "topmost" (Deighton). Both of these emendations postulate scribal or compositorial errors of a likely enough kind. "Stopped" may be a case of the accidental omission of a single letter: "tempest" may show a double misreading of a manuscript "o" as "e" (quite likely in Elizabethan script) and also a metathesis—

a scribe or compositor, thinking that his copy read "tepmest," might very well emend to "tempest." It seems to me that these two emendations are suggested by the passage as it stands. It may be that the line "And march in cottages of strowèd weeds" also requires emendation: but it does make sense—in the note in her edition Miss Ellis-Fermor suggests the interpretation "and move in spheres no higher than weed-strown cottages."

Now the second to the fifth lines of this passage, with the two emendations we have accepted, at once remind us of a passage near the beginning of the play in which Tamburlaine says

> Jove sometimes maskèd in a shepherd's weed,
> And by those steps he hath scaled the heavens,
> May we become immortal like the gods. [Pt. 1, I. ii. 198–200]

The reference is probably to Jove's love for Mnemosyne: in Ovid's *Metamorphoses,* vi. 114, we are told that Jove tricked Mnemosyne in the guise of a shepherd. At I. ii. 198–200 Tamburlaine is still at the beginning of his career: it is only a short while since he has taken off his shepherd's clothing: and he is determined to raise himself from the humble position to which he was born. At I. ii. 198–200 he declares that he[4] may ultimately become godlike, for, after all, Jove himself at one time appeared outwardly as a shepherd. Tamburlaine has appeared outwardly as a shepherd—has actually been a shepherd—and he may end up as an immortal like Jove. Always conscious of his humble birth, Tamburlaine takes comfort from the principle that, in the career of a conquering warrior (i.e. as regards Honour), what counts is not birth but a man's qualities—his manliness, bravery, energy, strength, his abilities: in a word, "virtue."[5] To his chief supporters he says at Pt. 1, IV. iv. 122–26:

> Deserve these titles I endow you with
> By valor and by magnanimity.
> Your births shall be no blemish to your fame,
> For virtue is the fount whence honor springs,
> And they are worthy she investeth kings.

This idea inspires him from the start. At I. ii. 198–200 he takes

---

[4] And Theridamas, whom he is at this point trying to persuade to join him. But of course the "shepherds weed" is not relevant to Theridamas.

[5] See *N.E.D.,* virtue, 5, †6, and 7.

comfort from the fact that Jove "sometimes masked in a shepherd's weed." But by V. ii. 72ff. he has risen to a position of eminence and he is now afraid that he may lose it and fall back into the humble position he was born to. And in this soliloquy he again refers to Jove's disguising himself as a shepherd. But this time he does not take comfort from that, but a warning. What induced Jove to disguise himself as a shepherd was his love for Mnemosyne—his love of her beauty. Jove was influenced by Beauty to degrade himself. Tamburlaine must not let that happen to him. And so he must (on the one hand) "subdue" Beauty. Beauty sits in Zenocrate's tearful face—Beauty, "mother to the Muses" (V. ii. 81): and in Greek mythology the mother of the Muses was Mnemosyne. Beauty "stooped the topmost of the gods . . . to feel the lovely warmth of shepherds' flames." That must not happen to Tamburlaine. And so, while he has by V. ii. 120 already resolved that he will admit the softening influence of Beauty as far as the sparing of the Soldan is concerned, he finishes the soliloquy with a passage which clearly indicates that he will not allow that influence to prevail to the extent of destroying his "virtue"—he will not allow it to degrade him from the status of great warrior to the humble status from which he started out. He declares that in spite of his lowly birth he will by his deeds show the world that "Virtue solely is the sum of glory." He will still allow his own "virtue" scope.

There can be no doubt, I think, that when he wrote V. ii. 72ff. Marlowe had I. ii. 198–200 in his mind. And I think that the spectator or reader is meant to recall that earlier passage. But furthermore, if we consider that when in I. ii he wrote the line "Jove sometimes masked in a shepherd's weed" Marlowe was thinking of Jove's love for Mnemosyne and of how it caused Jove to humble himself, and if we consider that already before that he has shown us that Tamburlaine has fallen in love with Zenocrate, can we not say that as early as I. ii Marlowe has at any rate at the back of his mind the situation that will arise in Acts IV and V?

It seems to me significant that in I. ii, the first scene in which Tamburlaine appears, we see him in the company of Zenocrate. In his speech at I. ii. 34ff. he indicates his military ambitions— to conquer Asia, to be a terror to the world, to rise far above his humble origin: and it is, I think, significant that he does this in a speech in which he avows his intention of marrying Zenocrate and sharing with her the exalted position at which he is aiming. He had obviously conceived his military aspirations before he captured her; but, by showing him at his first appearance declaring his love for her and his intention of making her his consort when he shall have risen to eminence, Marlowe contrives to give the audience the impression that she is from the start a source of inspiration to him in his pursuit of military glory. He takes off his shepherd's clothing and puts on complete armour as befits a man with his ambition: and I think that Marlowe knew what he was doing when he placed the passage in which Tamburlaine does this in between two passages in which he declares his determination to wed Zenocrate:

> I am a lord, for so my deeds shall prove,
> And yet a shepherd by my parentage.
> But, lady, this fair face and heavenly hue
> Must grace his bed that conquers Asia
> And means to be a terror to the world,
> Measuring the limits of his empery
> By east and west, as Phoebus doth his course.
> Lie here, ye weeds that I disdain to wear!
> This complete armor and this curtle-axe
> Are adjuncts more beseeming Tamburlaine.
> And madam, whatsoever you esteem
> Of this success and loss unvaluèd,
> Both may invest you empress of the East.
> And these, that seem but silly country swains,
> May have the leading of so great an host
> As with their weight shall make the mountains quake,
> Even as when windy exhalations,
> Fighting for passage, tilt within the earth.   [Pt. 1, I. ii. 34–51]

We are here given the impression that Beauty encourages Tamburlaine to raise himself. At the crisis in V. ii the question arises whether it will cause him to lower himself again. Here in I. ii the inspiration of Zenocrate is suggested in connection with Tamburlaine's doffing of his shepherd's weeds: and this points forward to V. ii. 120–27.

At the outset, then, our attention is directed to the relationship of Tamburlaine and Zenocrate. At the end of IV. ii Marlowe begins to prepare for the crisis in V. ii which also, of course, has to do with their relationship. What happens between I. ii and IV. ii? We see Tamburlaine's succession of triumphs, presented as the work partly of Fate and partly of his own "virtue." It cannot, of course, be denied that Marlowe is intensely interested in the aspiring mind whose ambitions are directed to "the sweet fruition of an earthly crown"—that he is intensely interested in that in itself. It would be remarkable if Zenocrate did not drop into the background to some extent during the hero's rise to power. But the audience is, I think, meant to recall her significance from I. ii; and in any case she does step into the foreground from time to time between I. ii and IV. ii. In III. ii she avows her love for Tamburlaine. And after this she approves of his military ambitions and of his methods of warfare. When he is about to fight against Bajazeth she hopes for victory for him—

> And may my love, the king of Persia,
> Return with victory and free from wound!
>
> [Pt. 1, III. iii. 132–33]

She speaks scornfully to Zabina, as Tamburlaine would have her do. She prays that he may be strengthened against Bajazeth—

> And let his foes, like flocks of fearful roes
> Pursued by hunters, fly his angry looks,
> That I may see him issue conqueror. [Pt. 1, III. iii. 192–94]

She has the same sort of blind confidence in his success as he himself has—

> If Mahomet should come from heaven and swear
> My royal lord is slain or conquerèd,
> Yet should he not persuade me otherwise
> But that he lives and will be conqueror. [Pt. 1, III. iii. 208–11]

One part of the influence of Beauty upon a warrior is to encourage him in his warlike exploits, and Zenocrate does this up to the point where her own country and her own father are affected. It is only after Tamburlaine has laid siege to Damascus that she seeks to have him modify his ideals, and even as she does so she shows by her words that she does not want him to give them up—

> Honor still wait on happy Tamburlaine;
> Yet give me leave to plead for him, my lord.
>
> [Pt. 1, IV. iv. 83–84]

The second aspect of the influence of Beauty has begun to emerge.
After the fall of Damascus Zenocrate's own feelings of pity rise to
a climax at V. ii. 257ff., and she repents of Tamburlaine's and her
own treatment of Bajazeth and Zabina—

> Ah, mighty Jove and holy Mahomet,
> Pardon my love! Oh, pardon his contempt
> Of earthly fortune and respect of pity, . . .
> And pardon me that was not moved with ruth
> To see them live so long in misery! [Pt. 1, V. ii. 300–302, 306–7]

Even here she has no thought of swerving from her loyalty to
Tamburlaine: in this speech (V. ii. 284–308) she is very much concerned for his welfare. But she has undergone a change of heart;
and shortly afterwards we find her speaking compassionately to
the dying Arabia (V. ii. 349–53). She has undergone a change of
heart: she has come to realize that a conqueror should be merciful. In the earlier portion of the play, in his presentation of Zenocrate, Marlowe emphasizes exclusively the power and desire of
Beauty to encourage the warrior. Then in the later portion of
the play, where we have this change of heart in Zenocrate, Marlowe conveys the idea that Beauty is essentially compassionate,
and emphasizes its desire to induce clemency in the warrior—
though at the same time it also remains an encouraging influence.
The change of heart in Zenocrate ultimately results in a change
in Tamburlaine; and their marriage symbolizes the establishment of the ideal relationship between Beauty and the warrior.

At the end we have a Tamburlaine changed by the influence of
Zenocrate who has herself changed. The play is throughout concerned with the relationship between these two characters. I think
it is true to say that we are never intended to forget Zenocrate
during Tamburlaine's rise to power. In the note on III. ii. 9–10
in her edition Miss Ellis-Fermor comments: "The figure of Zenocrate is substantially an addition of Marlowe's and the story of
her relations with Tamburlaine is skilfully interwoven with that
of his rising career, serving both to indicate the passage of time
and to give variety." But it does much more than that. I agree as
to the skilful interweaving; but that is part of the very theme of
the play. Again, in her book on Marlowe (p. 43) Miss Ellis-Fermor
says that "as far as Zenocrate is anything at all she is a virtuous,
god-fearing Elizabethan matron": but she is much more than

that—she is Beauty incarnate. Miss Ellis-Fermor states[6] that in
Part 1 Zenocrate "only speaks effectively once . . . when, in the
absence of Tamburlaine, she chants the moving lament over the
Turkish monarchs and the prayer against Tamburlaine's worship
of the glory of the world."[7] It must be agreed that she becomes a
much more living character after the conflict of loyalties, to Tamburlaine on the one hand and to Damascus and the Soldan on the
other, has arisen in her mind: she becomes psychologically much
more interesting then. This is only to be expected. Before conflict
arises in Tamburlaine's mind he is made interesting by virtue of
his aspiring mind and his astonishing series of victories: there is
no way of making Zenocrate interesting to anything like the same
extent in the first half of the play. But that does not alter the fact
that all through she is of fundamental importance as regards the
main theme.

If we took the Prologue as indicating the theme of *1 Tamburlaine* we should have to say that the theme was simply the successive conquests of its hero:

> From jigging veins of rhyming mother wits,
> And such conceits as clownage keeps in pay,
> We'll lead you to the stately tent of war,
> Where you shall hear the Scythian Tamburlaine
> Threat'ning the world with high astounding terms
> And scourging kingdoms with his conquering sword.
> View but his picture in this tragic glass,
> And then applaud his fortunes as you please.

But I believe that in this Prologue Marlowe refers to only a portion of the plot-material. He refers to that portion which would
doubtless be the most popular.[8] I suggest that the complete plot-
design he conceived from the outset was, briefly, as follows. Tamburlaine, a Scythian shepherd, endowed with an aspiring mind,
determines to become a world potentate by military conquest; at
the beginning of his career he comes under the spell of Zenocrate,
whose beauty inspires him further in his original ambition; he

[6] Edition of *Tamburlaine*, p. 54.

[7] V. ii. 284–308.

[8] Cf. the 1590 title-page: "Tamburlaine / the Great. / Who, from a Scythian
Shephearde, / by his rare and woonderfull Conquests, / became a most puissant and
migh- / tye Monarque. / And (for his tyranny, and terrour in / Warre) was
tearmed, / The Scourge of God. / Deuided into two Tragicall Dis- / courses, . . ."

proceeds to raise himself by triumph after triumph; meanwhile Zenocrate falls in love with him, they become betrothed, and she supports him in his aspirations and approves of his methods; but then these aspirations and methods threaten her own country and kindred, and, without being disloyal to Tamburlaine, she tries to persuade him to be merciful; she regrets his and her own previous want of pity; at first Tamburlaine resists her pleas; but then a conflict arises in his mind; he resolves it in a way of which she can approve; and the play concludes with their marriage. On the symbolic level the theme of the play is the nature of the influence that Beauty should have on the conception of Honour held by a man whose aspiration is directed towards the achievement of empire by conquest. It is, of course, an essential part of a drama embodying the above plot-design that the successive victories of the hero should be actually shown. It may be that there is a danger right from the start that this will overshadow the rest in its appeal to the audience's imagination. If it actually does, then Marlowe has failed. I can only say that in my opinion it does not. The play seems to me to be from beginning to end a coherent dramatic structure.

II

We may say that at the crisis of *1 Tamburlaine* Marlowe shows us the hero assailed by Beauty and the outcome is that the hero suffers a defeat at its hands and at the same time wins a victory over it. (We are entitled to use this metaphor because Tamburlaine speaks in military terms at V. ii. 88–96.) He suffers a defeat inasmuch as he allows the influence of Beauty to persuade him to change his ways. But he wins a victory inasmuch as he is still prepared to "subdue" Beauty whenever that shall appear to him to be necessary. Of course, as we have seen, Zenocrate has had no desire to persuade him to *abandon* his ideal of Honour: but if she should ever do so he would firmly withstand her, and he has won a victory inasmuch as he has come to this decision.

What now about the plot-material of *2 Tamburlaine?* The popularity of Part 1 induced Marlowe to write Part 2. But what a task he set himself when he embarked on this sequel! How was he to treat Tamburlaine dramatically this time? Does he in fact do so? I think he does. And it is by imitating to some extent the

design of Part 1. In Part 1 the most dangerous foe that Tamburlaine had to face was Zenocrate (see V. ii. 88–96). In Part 2 Marlowe confronts him with an even more dangerous foe—Death
himself.

The description of the dramatic culmination given in the Prologue to Part 2 is misleading. We are there told that in this Part

> . . . death cuts off the progress of his pomp
> And murderous Fates throws all his triumphs down.

This implies that the play is to have a "falls of princes" theme—
that Tamburlaine's death is to be a defeat and nothing else. But
that is not the impression we are left with at the end of the play.

The first occurrence of his distemper is at V. i. 216. From this
point on we are concerned with Tamburlaine's attitude to his
inexorably approaching death. His attitude to Death changes between the onset of his sickness and his death itself. He feels himself distempered at V. i. 216. His first reaction is "Sickness or
death can never conquer me" (V. i. 220). When next we see him
(in V. iii) he is determined to resist Death—to oppose him by
force and win this fight as he has before won so many:

> What daring god torments my body thus
> And seeks to conquer mighty Tamburlaine?
> Shall sickness prove me now to be a man,
> That have been termed the terror of the world?
> Techelles and the rest, come, take your swords,
> And threaten him whose hand afflicts my soul.
> Come, let us march against the powers of heaven
> And set black streamers in the firmament
> To signify the slaughter of the gods.   [Pt. 2, V. iii. 42–50]

We have had Tamburlaine threatening the gods before; but now
there is a pathetic twist to it:

> Ah, friends, what shall I do? I cannot stand.
> Come, carry me to war against the gods,
> That thus envy the health of Tamburlaine.
>
> [Pt. 2, V. iii. 51–53]

Tamburlaine goes on speaking of his intention to combat Death,
though in the midst of it he seems to be convinced that Death will
win after all. Techelles says that Tamburlaine's "grief" cannot

last, it is so violent; and with grim humour Tamburlaine replies

> Not last, Techelles? No, for I shall die.   [Pt. 2, V. iii. 66]

But shortly after this his physician gives him some hope and he is momentarily comforted: he will

> . . . live, in spite of death, above a day.
> [Pt. 2, V. iii. 101]

Up to this point we might well suppose that Marlowe was preparing us to regard Tamburlaine's death as a total defeat. Tamburlaine seems so to regard it as it approaches; and we remember the words of the Prologue.

But now Tamburlaine's attitude to death changes. He accepts the fact that it is inevitable, but now he regards it as a translation to higher spheres:

> But I perceive my martial strength is spent.
> In vain I strive and rail against those powers
> That mean t'invest me in a higher throne,
> As much too high for this disdainful earth.
> [Pt. 2, V. iii. 119–22]

And he speaks of his spirit as being too fiery for his body to contain (V. iii. 168–69). He now regards death as a gateway to a higher life. But what of his plans for earthly conquest? There are parts of the world which he has still not conquered:

> And shall I die, and this unconquerèd?
> [Pt. 2, V. iii. 150, 158]

Allowing that for him death is not a defeat inasmuch as it is an entrance to a nobler life, is it not still the case that it is a defeat inasmuch as he has not yet fulfilled all his earthly ambitions? Not altogether: for he is convinced that, though he himself is to die, his spirit will live on in the world in the breasts of his two surviving sons:

> But, sons, this subject, not of force enough
> To hold the fiery spirit it contains,
> Must part, imparting his impressions
> By equal portions into both your breasts.
> My flesh, divided in your precious shapes,
> Shall still retain my spirit, though I die,
> And live in all your seeds immortally.   [Pt. 2, V. iii. 168–74]

In his belief it is not even true to say that his flesh is about to perish, for his sons are his flesh. His spirit will survive on earth in his flesh—his sons will continue his career of conquest—and he himself will pass to a higher existence. Thus, essentially, Death has not defeated him: he has defeated death: he has shown that he is immortal on earth.

Tamburlaine triumphs in death. But at the same time it is, of course, true that Death *has* won a victory of a sort. For Tamburlaine did not will his own death: it was forced upon him: he was in this respect passive, a victim. And, having proclaimed his own triumph, Tamburlaine admits that nothing can prevent his actual departure: his last words emphasize the defeat aspect—

> For Tamburlaine, the scourge of God, must die. [V. iii. 248]

In Part 1 he was assailed by Beauty and the result was that he partially submitted to and partially triumphed over it. In Part 2 he is assailed by Death and the result is similar—he is in one sense defeated by it and in another sense triumphs over it. In the act of giving in to it he proclaims his immunity to it: in the act of proclaiming his immunity to it he has to submit to it.

But what of Part 2 as a whole? From the point where Tamburlaine first feels distempered it has a coherent dramatic shape. Does the play as a whole have a coherent dramatic shape?

In dealing with Part 1 we saw that the conclusion concerns Tamburlaine's attitude to Zenocrate and that at his first appearance in the play he enters along with her. In a similar way in Part 2 Marlowe at the outset prepares us for the main theme. In Part 2 we first encounter Tamburlaine in I. iv. In his very first speech he refers to his and Zenocrate's sons and their hoped-for future—they "shall be Emperors" (I. iv. 7). In his next speech he expresses his love for them (lines 18–19) but fears that their looks are not "martial as the sons of Tamburlaine" (line 22). Zenocrate declares that "when they list, [they have] their conquering father's heart" (line 36). Tamburlaine goes on to speak of his youngest son's future, and at lines 59–60 he says

> When I am old and cannot manage arms,
> Be thou the scourge and terror of the world.

Already in the first scene the attention of the audience is drawn to the idea of Tamburlaine's sons as his successors, continuing after him to pursue his aims by his methods—Calyphas will not

have a foot of land from his father unless he bears a "mind courageous and invincible" (line 73); and he that would place himself in Tamburlaine's chair must "armed wade up to the chin in
blood" (line 84). All this is in I. iv. Tamburlaine's illness first
attacks him at the end of V. i. And in between Marlowe gives
much attention to Tamburlaine's sons, their education in his
methods of waging war, his concern to imbue them with his own
ambitions in their role of successors to him. Zenocrate dies in II.
iv. Almost her last words are to her sons—a plea to them to resemble in their lives their father's excellence (line 76). Then in
III. ii. Tamburlaine lectures his sons on the technique of waging
war (lines 53ff.). His ambition is to make them soldiers

> And worthy sons of Tamburlaine the Great.   [92]

He wants to teach them not only the art of war but also

> . . . to bear courageous minds,
> Fit for the followers of great Tamburlaine.   [143–44]

("Followers" presumably means "successors.") Then in IV. ii, to
the defeated Turkish kings, he says

> See now, ye slaves, my children stoops your pride
> And leads your glories sheep-like to the sword.   [1–2]

And he continues—

> Bring them my boys, and tell me if the wars
> Be not a life that may illustrate gods,
> And tickle not your spirits with desire
> Still to be trained in arms and chivalry?   [3–6]

When Tamburlaine is riding in his chariot drawn by the captive
kings, his son Amyras wants to be similarly drawn (IV. iv. 27–28.)
And a little later Tamburlaine speaks of his son Celebinus to the
captive King of Jerusalem—

> Ay, Turk, I tell thee, this same boy is he
> That must, advanced in higher pomp than this,
> Rifle the kingdoms I shall leave unsacked,
> If Jove, esteeming me too good for earth,
> Raise me to match the fair Aldeboran,
> Above the threefold astracism of heaven,
> Before I conquer all the triple world.   [Pt. 2, IV. iv. 57–63]

The idea of Tamburlaine's sons as his successors, imbued with the same spirit as he is, pursuing, after him, the same aims by the same methods, runs right through the play, and cannot anywhere be very far from the audience's mind as it watches Tamburlaine's own further career of conquest as unfolded in this second drama. The material concerning Calyphas is, of course, extremely relevant to this theme and is not introduced simply to give variety. Calyphas refuses to be another Tamburlaine, and rejects his father's values. I do not think that Marlowe can be said to be altogether unsympathetic to Calyphas: he sees that there are different possible points of view: but, as regards his dramatic design as a whole, he intends his audience to accept Tamburlaine's point of view and not that of Calyphas. As far as the total plan of the play is concerned it is Tamburlaine's and not Calyphas's values which emerge triumphant. Calyphas is the unworthy son: unfit to succeed his father, he is killed ignominiously.

Before we can state in full the dramatic design of Part 2 we must say something about the Tamburlaine-Zenocrate relationship, which forms part of it.

The Zenocrate of Part 2 is essentially the same character as the Zenocrate of Part 1. She at the same time commends Tamburlaine's values and seeks to mitigate extravagance and immoderation in him. Considering the nature of the conclusion of Part 1 we might perhaps have expected that in Part 2 there would be no contrariety of attitude whatever between Tamburlaine and Zenocrate, no pull at all between them in opposite directions. But this is not so. The nature of the conclusion of Part 1 made it possible for Marlowe in Part 2 to show the two characters again in partial opposition and partial agreement. Tamburlaine had decided both to "conceive" and to "subdue" Beauty. At the end of Part 1 he succeeded in balancing the conceiving and subduing of it. But he is resolved that in the future he must be careful not to "conceive" it too much. He must always be on guard in case he (still the aspiring conqueror) should ever be influenced by Zenocrate to go too far in the direction of gentleness. And so, while still admitting her double influence, he is always prepared to resist its moderating element if necessary. As for her: we may imagine her deciding that she must still keep urging Tamburlaine to moderation, there being always a danger that he may return to courses of utter ruthlessness. And so, while still supporting him in his role as conqueror, she must always be prepared to restrain him if necessary. These are in fact the attitudes we find in them in Part 2. In Part 2 Zenocrate's first speech (I. iv. 9–11) is an implied plea to Tamburlaine to give up his war-making because of the perils involved—

> Sweet Tamburlaine, when wilt thou leave these arms
> And save thy sacred person free from scathe
> And dangerous chances of the wrathful war?

And Tamburlaine in circumlocutory fashion declares that he never will. Shortly afterwards, Tamburlaine having delivered a bloodthirsty speech, Zenocrate protests—

> My lord, such speeches to our princely sons
> Dismays their minds before they come to prove
> The wounding troubles angry war affords. [Pt. 2, I. iv. 85–87]

She still wants to restrain him. But at the same time she still admires and encourages him as a conqueror. On her deathbed she speaks her hopes that he will continue to live in his resplendent glory—

> Live still, my lord! Oh, let my sovereign live!
> And sooner let the fiery element
> Dissolve and make your kingdom in the sky,
> Than this base earth should shroud your majesty; . . .
>   [Pt. 2, II. iv. 57–60]

And she bids her sons in their lives resemble their father's "excellency" (II. iv. 76). In Part 2 she still exerts herself when necessary to restrain immoderation in Tamburlaine, but she still encourages him in his martial career.

When she dies, Tamburlaine feels lost. He needs her: he is not self-sufficient. In Part 1 he had declared at the end that she added "more courage to [his] conquering mind" (V. ii. 452). As a conqueror he needed the help of her encouragement (cf. Part 1, V. ii. 117–19). Now that she has been removed by Death he has been deprived of an essential part of his inspiration as a warrior. He tries to keep this inspiration alive by carrying her body with him as he proceeds further in his conquests; and, apostrophizing her picture, he says

> At every town and castle I besiege,
> Thou shalt be set upon my royal tent;
> And when I meet an army in the field,
> Whose[9] looks will shed such influence in my camp,
> As if Bellona, goddess of the war,
> Threw naked swords and sulphur balls of fire
> Upon the heads of all our enemies.   [Pt. 2, III. ii. 36–42]

But this attempt to defeat Death (for that is what it is) fails miserably: what happens is that Tamburlaine becomes filled with a fury greater than any he has shown heretofore. The moderating influence of Zenocrate is removed. And though Tamburlaine wants her encouraging influence to persist, and tries to make it persist, it does not—he now shows not courage so much as blind rage. Zenocrate is dead: both elements of her influence are gone: Death has attacked Tamburlaine in the first instance through Zenocrate, and Death has won the day. Death will attack him a second time later on, and its second victory will be counterbalanced by a triumph on the part of Tamburlaine.

The Tamburlaine of Part 2 is certainly a less impressive figure than the Tamburlaine of Part 1. Miss Ellis-Fermor rightly speaks of the Tamburlaine of Part 2 as "marked by a savageness, an ever-increasing extravagance, a lack at once of inspiration and of balance." "The freakish, unrestrained moods of these later scenes," she says,[10] "have little or nothing to do with the glittering figure of the earlier part. . . ." Her view is that in Part 2 Marlowe had embarked on an undertaking which by its very nature entailed a debasing of the character of Tamburlaine even against the playwright's will. His savagery and frenzy, she says,[11] "are the logical outcome of the situation that Marlowe created when he set out to write a 'second part' to the study of a character who can, by the very nature of his being, only have a first part. For Tamburlaine lives in the future and the essence of his spirit is the forward reach and the aspiration which must continue 'still climbing' if they are to live, and fail, even as Marlowe's interpretation failed, when they reach 'the ripest fruit of all'." But I think that Marlowe knew what he was doing, and that Tamburlaine's later

---

[9] Dyce emended to "Those."
[10] *Christopher Marlowe*, p. 39.
[11] Ibid., p. 39.

frenzy, related to his loss of Zenocrate, is relevant to the dramatic design of Part 2. It is part of Death's initial victory in a drama the main theme of which is Tamburlaine versus Death.

The figure of Zenocrate, then, is relevant to the dramatic design of Part 2 because she is the first object of Death's attack on Tamburlaine. She is also relevant to it because his sons are her sons too. As she dies she urges them to resemble their father's excellence. We may be sure that she would not have approved of Calyphas's conduct after her death. At I. iv. 65–66 Calyphas says

> But while my brothers follow arms, my lord,
> Let me accompany my gracious mother.

This suggests that his mother represents complete opposition to the following of arms; but, as we have seen, she does not. Calyphas is presented not only as an unworthy son of Tamburlaine but also as an unworthy son of Zenocrate. The other two sons, Tamburlaine's successors, do try to resemble their father, and do thus try to obey their mother's final request.

Miss Ellis-Fermor, holding that Part 1 has "no progress, crisis or solution,"[12] believes that Part 2 is to an even greater extent lacking in dramatic structure. "In the second part of the play," she says,[13] "where the original impulse is gone, the difficulty of giving any appearance of structural unity increases enormously." "Marlowe's error," she maintains,[14] "is really a very simple mathematical one; the rise of Tamburlaine's career throughout the second part could be practically formulated as an arithmetical progression, whereas that of the first part has the more rapid rise of a geometrical progression, and it is this last formula alone which can be relied upon to outrun the anticipations of an audience and create surprise and interest." This would be a perfectly sound condemnation of Part 2 if the theme were simply the continued military triumphs of a world conqueror. But I believe that this is only a portion of the theme and that Part 2, like Part 1, has a coherent dramatic pattern.

I should summarize the essentials of the plot of Part 2 as follows. Tamburlaine continues his career of conquest, still loving

---

[12] *Christopher Marlowe,* p. 45.
[13] Ibid., p. 45.
[14] Ibid., p. 46.

and inspired by Zenocrate, but still resolved to resist any attempt by her to influence him excessively, as he sees it, in the direction of gentleness. Early in the play he shows that he is conscious that he will grow old and that he will die: and so he concerns himself to prepare his sons to be worthy successors to him (i.e. he prepares to win a victory over Death). He encourages and trains them. One is unworthy (both as a son of Tamburlaine and as a son of Zenocrate): the other two he finds satisfactory. Meanwhile Death attacks Tamburlaine in the first instance through Zenocrate, and she dies. Her restraining influence is now removed. Tamburlaine tries to keep her encouraging influence alive by carrying her body and her picture with him on his martial journeys; but it is gone too, and Tamburlaine becomes, instead of a type of inspired courage and mental fire, a type of fury and savage rage. Death has won this initial bout. Then Death attacks Tamburlaine directly. At first Tamburlaine attempts resistance (foolishly, of course), but then he acquiesces, and his death, a defeat in one sense, is a triumph in another, since his two surviving sons, his own flesh containing his own spirit, will continue his work on earth while he himself steps on to a higher plane of being. All this is surely a well-conceived dramatic design.

In so far as Death is a more terrible adversary than Zenocrate (or Beauty) was, the conclusion of Part 2 cannot be said to leave us with an impression of bathos. Nevertheless it is certainly true that Marlowe's imagination is much more powerfully at work in Part 1 than in Part 2. Part 2 is a much inferior play to Part 1. I have in this essay been concerned with one point only. There is much more which I believe should be said about these plays. But I have been concerned only to argue that both have coherent dramatic structure. However much they may offend us by their rant and bombast and by their bloodthirstiness and violence, they are at any rate dramas in the true sense of that word.

EUGENE M. WAITH

Tamburlaine, the Herculean Hero

His looks do menace heaven and dare the gods,
His fiery eyes are fixed upon the earth
As if he now devised some stratagem,
Or meant to pierce Avernus' darksome vaults
To pull the triple headed dog from hell.

The brilliance of the heroic image Marlowe created in *Tamburlaine* has proved to be both attractive and blinding. The glittering verse, the sound of trumpets, the movement of armies across the stage, seem to have concealed more than they have revealed of one essential part of the play's meaning, the author's attitude towards his hero. The question of whether this extravagantly unconventional protagonist is presented with approval or disapproval has received answers so various and contradictory that a reader of the criticism might easily conclude that the play contains no sure indications of attitude—that Tamburlaine is whatever his audience makes of him. However, one point on which all critics agree is that Marlowe had a well-defined attitude towards his hero. It is worth seeking again even at the cost of another reconsideration of a play which has been much discussed.

The spectacular circumstances of Marlowe's life have figured in the interpretation of his plays from his own times down to ours, for if he was an atheist, a homosexual, a spy, a scoffer and

From *The Herculean Hero in Marlowe, Chapman, Shakespeare and Dryden* (London: Chatto & Windus Ltd.), pp. 60–87. Reprinted by permission of the author and publisher.

a quarreller, it seems more than a coincidence that he chose for principal characters an atheistical warrior, a scholar who sold his soul to the devil, a homosexual king, a Machiavellian schemer. An older group of critics emphasized what might be called the brighter side of Marlowe's unconventionality by interpreting Tamburlaine's boundless ambition as a joyous assertion of Marlowe's Renaissance paganism—a celebration of human worth in general and of his own aspirations in particular.[1] To more recent critics this sort of interpretation has seemed to rest upon a romanticized view of the Renaissance. Hence a somewhat grimmer picture has been drawn of a Tamburlaine who is the mirror image of a resolute defier of convention, remarkably "advanced" in his freedom of thought, but pathologically attracted by cruelty, and characterized, as one critic has put it, by "abnormal nervous energy" and "uncoordinated personality factors."[2]

The difficulties which attend upon such identifications of Marlowe and Tamburlaine may be illustrated from the most impressive of these studies, Paul H. Kocher's *Christopher Marlowe*. Looking at the play for the light it may throw on the mind and character of Marlowe, Kocher finds that Part 1 is dominated by two religious conceptions: one, that the law of nature commands Tamburlaine and others to seek regal power; the other, that in his conquest Tamburlaine is acting as the scourge of God. Though the first conception is thoroughly anti-Christian, the second is, of course, perfectly compatible with Christianity, so that Kocher is faced with a conflict in Marlowe's thought as he understands it. He asks whether these ideas may not be harmonized "by simply amputating the Christian appendages" but concludes that even then some inconsistency remains.[3] In considering the character of Calyphas, Tamburlaine's cowardly son in Part 2, Kocher

---

[1] The criticism has often been reviewed in recent years, as by Roy W. Battenhouse in some detail in *Marlowe's Tamburlaine* (Nashville, Tenn.: Vanderbilt University Press, 1941 [pp. 1–17]).

[2] T. M. Pearce, "Christopher Marlowe, Figure of the Renaissance," *University of New Mexico Bulletin, English Language and Literature Series* I, no. 1 (1934):31, 36. See also Paul H. Kocher, *Christopher Marlowe* (Chapel Hill, N.C., University of North Carolina Press, 1946, and London, Oxford University Press); Mario Praz, "Christopher Marlowe," *English Studies* XIII (1931):209–23; William Empson, "Two Proper Crimes," *The Nation* 163 (1946):444–45; Willard Thorp, "The Ethical Problem in Marlowe's *Tamburlaine*," *Journal of English and Germanic Philology* 29 (1930): 385–89; Michel Poirier, *Christopher Marlowe* (London, Chatto & Windus, 1951).

[3] Kocher, pp. 70–81.

finds that in certain scenes the boy is made ridiculous but that in the first scene of Act IV his mockery of the warrior code of conduct is "a personal outburst by the dramatist." Kocher speculates that Marlowe was "thoroughly satiated and weary with excess" by this time but that Calyphas' mockery "cannot have been any part of Marlowe's plan for the drama."[4] The dangers of this method of interpretation are obvious. Although it would be naive to expect perfect consistency of an Elizabethan play, it is an act of ethical desperation to discount or "amputate" whatever does not fit with a predetermined picture of Marlowe's opinions, or to explain all discordant elements as lapses and unpremeditated changes in the artist's plans. Such an interpretation takes the opinions of Marlowe as reported by his contemporaries, Thomas Kyd, Richard Baines, and others, as fixed points of reference and, rather than explain any contradictory ideas which appear in the play, explains them away. Whether or not Marlowe held the opinions ascribed to him (a matter which has never been established beyond doubt), the attitudes expressed in *Tamburlaine* should be determined by a careful weighing of all the evidence given in the play. The knowledge of Marlowe's reputation hinders almost as much as it helps such a process.

Unfortunately, the refusal to identify Marlowe with his hero by no means solves the problem of interpretation. The crucial problem remains: is Tamburlaine presented with approval or disapproval? As J. C. Maxwell says, "No one can ever have doubted that Marlowe displays in a high degree the imaginative sympathy with his hero which is required for successful dramatic presentation,"[5] but sympathy does not mean approval, and even the critics who agree on Marlowe's objectivity in creating Tamburlaine differ as to the attitude the play presents. It has been said that Marlowe makes his hero both physically and morally more admirable than he appears in the sources,[6] but it has also been suggested that Part 2, where the sources provide much less of the action, shows a progressive disenchantment with the hero.[7]

---

[4] Ibid., pp. 275–76.

[5] "The Plays of Christopher Marlowe," *The Age of Shakespeare*. ed. Boris Ford (London, Penguin Books, 1955 [p. 162]).

[6] Leslie Spence, "Tamburlaine and Marlowe," *Publications of the Modern Language Association* 42 (1927):604–22.

[7] Helen L. Gardner, "The Second Part of 'Tamburlaine the Great'," *Modern Language Review* 37 (1942):18–24.

The two parts of the play together have been read as a chronicle of the Renaissance discovery that human nature cut off from its divine source is not emancipated but impoverished,[8] or even as an indictment of Tamburlaine from a conservative Renaissance point of view, and hence "one of the most grandly moral spectacles in the whole realm of English drama."[9] Roy Battenhouse, from whose study these last words are quoted, sees Tamburlaine's death as the divine punishment such as a "scourge of God" was inevitably given, once his mission had been accomplished.

There could scarcely be greater diversity of opinion, yet through it all runs a discernible pattern. The critics who believe that Marlowe approves of Tamburlaine either try to show that he passes over his hero's disagreeable qualities to emphasize others (such as the aspiration for knowledge and beauty) or believe that Marlowe, as a rebel against the morality of his time, approves of Tamburlaine's cruelty, pride, atheism and ruthless exercise of power. Those who believe that Marlowe disapproves of Tamburlaine assume that such behaviour must be recognized as bad, and that Marlowe's frank portrayal of it indicates his moral condemnation. Neither group of critics suggests the possibility that Tamburlaine's faults might be an integral part of a kind of heroic nature familiar to Marlowe and his audience and unlikely to offend anyone but "precise" churchmen or the poet's enemies. It is possible, of course, that Marlowe's attitude toward his hero shifts from scene to scene, or from Part 1 to Part 2, but it seems to me more likely that his concept of heroic character is sufficiently complex to include what appear to be contradictory elements and that his attitude, going beyond simple approval or disapproval, remains constant.

Hercules, as he appears in Sophocles, Euripides, and above all Seneca, is revitalized in Tamburlaine. No one of the older plays was used as a model, but Hercules was often in Marlowe's mind as he wrote.[10] Several allusions in the play make this fact indis-

---

[8] M. M. Mahood, *Poetry and Humanism* (London: Jonathan Cape, 1950 [pp. 54–56]).

[9] Battenhouse, *Marlowe's Tamburlaine*, p. 258.

[10] I have referred in Chapter 2 (pp. 52–53) to the fact that Hercules was well known on the English stage at this time. The lines of "Ercles' vein" which Shakespeare gives to Bottom in *A Midsummer Night's Dream* (c. 1595) seem to glance at Jasper Heywood's translation (1561) of Seneca's *Hercules Furens* (see *New Cambridge Shakespeare*, 1924 [p. 109]), though it is unlikely that it was ever publicly acted (see H. B. Charlton, *The Senecan Tradition in Renaissance Tragedy* [Manchester University

putable, and, as Mario Praz pointed out many years ago, there are striking resemblances between Tamburlaine and Hercules Oetaeus.[11] However, it is finally less important to decide whether Marlowe was deliberately fashioning a Herculean hero than to remember that the traditional depictions of Hercules, especially those from Rome and Renaissance Italy, were thoroughly familiar to him. It is not surprising that Tamburlaine, who had already been used by Louis Le Roy and others as a symbol of the physical and intellectual vigour of the Renaissance,[12] should suggest the Greek hero to him. I believe that his attitude towards Tamburlaine, as expressed in the play, is very similar to the attitudes found in some of the portrayals of Hercules discussed in the previous two chapters. The images created by Seneca and Pollaiuolo can be of great assistance to the spectator of the twentieth century, partially cut off from the traditions in which Marlowe wrote; for they prepare the eye to discern the outlines of Marlowe's heroic figure.

The figure is vast. The very structure of the play conveys this impression, for the succession of scenes—some of them might almost be called tableaux—stretching over great expanses of time and space, presents the man in terms of the places he makes his

---

Press, 1946], pp. cliv–clv). To give the joke point there must have been some more popular stage version of Hercules such as the *1 and 2 Hercules* referred to by Henslowe as being staged in 1595 (Chambers, II, 143–44). It has not been determined whether Thomas Heywood's *Silver Age* and *Brazen Age* were written early enough to be the plays Henslowe refers to; they were certainly too late to have been known to Greene in 1592 when he was writing his *Groatsworth of Wit* and, *a fortiori*, to Marlowe in 1587–88. It is impossible to be sure when Hercules achieved such notoriety, but it seems likely that he was already familiar at the time that Marlowe was writing *Tamburlaine*. From Greene's and Shakespeare's allusions it is obvious that this Hercules was a speaker of extravagant tirades, and this characteristic may have strengthened the association in Marlowe's mind with the hero he was creating. Heywood's plays do not provide any valuable points of comparison with the plays I am treating because, although they give us the only extant major treatment of Hercules on the Elizabethan stage, they are spectacles rather than coherent dramatizations of heroic character, and they have no great literary merit.

[11] Mario Praz, "Machiavelli and the Elizabethans," *Proceedings of the British Academy* XIV (1928):71ff. See also Battenhouse, pp. 196ff., where the parallel to Seneca's Hercules is used to show that Marlowe depicts Tamburlaine as the type of insatiable conqueror who falls victim to his own covetousness. Since my interpretation of Seneca is totally different from Battenhouse's, the parallel does not seem to me to show anything of the sort.

[12] See Hallet Smith, "Tamburlaine and the Renaissance," *Elizabethan Studies, University of Colorado Studies*, Series B, II, 4 (Boulder, Colorado, 1945); Erich Voegelin, "Das Timurbild der Humanisten," *Zeitschrift für öffentliches Recht* XVII (1937): 545–82.

and the time which at the last he fails to conquer. It is no accident that we always remember the effect of Marlowe's resounding geography, for earthly kingdoms are the emblems of Tamburlaine's aspirations. At the end of his life he calls for a map, on which he traces with infinite nostalgia his entire career and points to all the remaining riches which death will keep him from:

> And shall I die, and this unconquered?
>
> [Pt. 2, V. iii. 150][13]

To be a world-conqueror in the various senses which the play gives to the term is the essence of Tamburlaine's character. That this insight is conveyed in part by the sprawling structure of the play is an important advantage to weigh against some of the obvious disadvantages of such a structure in the theatre. Although complication and even conflict in its fullest sense are almost missing, each successive episode contributes something to the dominant idea—the definition of a hero. There is a forward movement of the play in unfolding not only the narrative but the full picture of the hero. When the play is well acted and directed, it has ample theatrical life, no matter how much the form is indebted to epic.

The first view we have of Tamburlaine is a kind of transformation scene. It is preceded by the brief, and basically snobbish descriptions given at the court of Mycetes, the ludicrously incompetent king of Persia, to whom Tamburlaine is a marauding fox,[14] a "sturdy Scythian thief," and the leader of a "Tartarian rout" (I. i. 31, 36, 71). The Tamburlaine who walks on the stage dressed as a shepherd and leading Zenocrate captive has some of the outward appearance suggested by these descriptions, and the earlier impression of social inferiority is conveyed in the words of Zenocrate, who at first takes him for the shepherd he seems to be (I. ii. 7). However, his words and actions reveal a strikingly dif-

---

[13] In the performance of Tamburlaine directed by Tyrone Guthrie in New York in 1956 a very large map was spread on the floor of the stage, making possible an extraordinarily effective theatrical image. Tamburlaine walked on the map as he pointed to his conquests, and at the end fell down on it, almost covering the world with his prone body.

[14] Battenhouse has pointed to the Machiavellian combination of the fox image in this scene with that of the lion in the following scene (p. 209). See also Harry Levin, *The Overreacher* (Cambridge, Mass.: Harvard University Press, 1952 [pp. 37–38], and London: Faber & Faber [p. 56]).

ferent man: he boasts like a genuine hero if not a gentleman, and exchanges his shepherd's weeds for complete armour and curtle-axe. Before our eyes he assumes the outward appearance which matches his warrior's spirit.

Tamburlaine is a proud and noble king at heart, yet his Scyth-ian-shepherd origins give a clue to the absolute difference between him and the world's other kings. His is the intrinsic kingliness of the hero, associated with the ideal of freedom, whereas other kings are presented as oppressors, the products of a corrupt system. The garb of the Scythian shepherd, even though he discards it, relates Tamburlaine to the simpler world of an earlier, mythical time. The king he becomes carries with him into a decadent world something of this primitive simplicity. Like his successors, Chap-man's Bussy and Dryden's Almanzor, he is an early edition of the "noble savage."

Thus far Tamburlaine appears as a hero in the classic mode, but when he tells Zenocrate that her person "is more worth to Tamburlaine / Than the possession of the Persian crown" (I. ii. 90–91), the influence of the romance tradition is apparent. In fact, for the moment it seems that the "concupiscible power" of his soul dominates the "irascible power," though the subsequent ac-tion shows that this is not true. Tamburlaine's love, expressed in the poetry of the famous speech beginning "Disdains Zenocrate to live with me?" (I. ii. 82–105), further distinguishes him from his rival warriors. Their pride and their ambition are not accompa-nied by the imagination which informs his promises to Zenocrate:

> With milk-white harts upon an ivory sled,
> Thou shalt be drawn amidst the frozen pools,
> And scale the icy mountains' lofty tops,
> Which with thy beauty will be soon resolved.
>
> [Pt. 1, I. ii. 98–101]

The cold fire of this speech is the first testimony of Tamburlaine's imaginative scope and of the paradoxes of his nature; the icy mountain tops are the first memorable image of his aspiration.

The arrival of Theridamas with the Persian forces provides for another surprising revelation of the hero. We have just seen him in the guise of a lover; we now see him as an orator, overcoming Theridamas with words. Marlowe insists on the unexpectedness of these aspects of the hero. "What now? in love?" says Techelles

(I. ii. 106), and, when Tamburlaine asks whether he should "play the orator," replies disdainfully that "cowards and faint-hearted runaways / Look for orations" (I. ii. 130–31). In defiance of this advice, Tamburlaine delivers his brilliantly successful oration, winning from Theridamas the tribute that even Hermes could not use "persuasions more pathetical" (I. ii. 210). Yet, surprising as this eloquence is to Tamburlaine's followers, it is not alien to the Renaissance concept of the Herculean hero. Cartari specifically reminds his readers that Hercules, like Mercury, whom he has just discussed, has been called a patron of eloquence. It is, so to speak, perfectly proper to present a Herculean hero as orator.

Tamburlaine begins his oration with a complimentary picture of Theridamas, but soon turns to himself with the famous boast, "I hold the Fates bound fast in iron chains," and the comparisons of himself to Jove. The effect of the speech is double, for though it displays the hero as orator, it also presents, by means of eloquence, his self-portrait as conqueror of the world and even as demigod. Such self-praise might be taken as Marlowe's way of portraying a man who will say anything to get ahead or of pointing to the ironical contrast between a man's pride and his accomplishment, but one of the puzzling features of *Tamburlaine* is that the hero's actions also show him in the guise of a demigod, and only his death proves that he does not control the fates. Even death is not presented unequivocally as defeat. Tamburlaine's extravagant boasts, like those of Hercules, are largely made good, so that he and his followers become the amazement of the world. In Usumcasane's words, "These are the men that all the world admires."

Before Tamburlaine unleashes his persuasive forces Theridamas comments on his appearance in words which emphasize the importance of visual impressions in this play:

> Tamburlaine! A Scythian shepherd so embellishèd
> With nature's pride and richest furniture!
> His looks do menace heaven and dare the gods.
> His fiery eyes are fixed upon the earth
> As if he now devised some stratagem,
> Or meant to pierce Avernus' darksome vaults
> To pull the triple-headed dog from hell.   [Pt. 1, I. ii. 154–60]

Again we have the transformation of the Scythian shepherd into a noble warrior, but here even the armour appears as part of nature's endowment of the hero. The eyes fixed on the earth are the symbolic equivalent of one of Tamburlaine's best-known speeches, in which he makes an earthly crown the ultimate felicity, but this fixation on the earth is accompanied by looks which menace heaven and also suggest a Herculean conquest of hell. The description is perfect, though to use it when the character described stands before the audience is to risk a ludicrous incongruity.[15] Marlowe depends on unhesitating acceptance of the verbal picture.

Marlowe's heavy dependence on description is again illustrated in the next scene, when Menaphon gives Cosroe an even fuller account of Tamburlaine's looks than we have had from Theridamas. In this speech the hero's body is made symbolic of his character. He is tall like his desire; his shoulders might bear up the sky like Atlas; his complexion reveals his thirst for sovereignty; he has curls like Achilles; and his arms and hands betoken "valor and excess of strength" (II. i. 7–30).

One of Tamburlaine's most important traits, his infinite aspiration, receives its first major treatment in a much discussed speech in the second act about the "thirst of reign and sweetness of a crown" (II. vii. 12–29). Menaphon's encomium of Tamburlaine's physical beauty provides a clue to the understanding of this passage. Just as his body seems beautiful not simply in itself but in that it expresses his character, so Tamburlaine extols the "sweet fruition of an earthly crown" not because anything the earth has to offer has final value for him, but because domination of the earth represents the fulfilment of his mission—the fulfilment of himself. The speech is about the infinite aspiration taught us by nature and the never-ending activity to which the soul goads us. "The sweet fruition of an earthly crown" is indeed bathos, as it has often been called, unless the earthly crown means something rather special in this play.

---

[15] Passages describing action supposedly taking place onstage in Seneca's plays have been used to support the contention that the plays were never intended for the stage. It is interesting to see a technique so nearly approaching Seneca's here and later in Dryden. This obviously proves nothing about Seneca, but it shows that such an effect was accepted by certain audiences and conceivably might have been by Seneca's audience.

There is a good deal of evidence that it does. In an earlier scene Usumcasane says, "To be a king, is half to be a god," and Theridamas replies, "A god is not so glorious as a king" (II. v. 56–57). Tamburlaine never puts it quite thus, for it is clear that like Hercules he already considers himself partly divine, yet kingship is obviously glorious to him. The "course of crowns" which he and his followers eat in Act IV, Scene iv, is the visual equivalent of the constant references to sovereignty. The earth itself is despicable—inert—the negation of heroic energy, as appears in the speech of Theridamas immediately following the lines about the earthly crown:

> For he is gross and like the massy earth
> That moves not upwards, nor by princely deeds
> Doth mean to soar above the highest sort.
>
> [Pt. 1, II. vii. 31–33]

but ruling the earth is not an end in itself. It is a manifestation of the will to "soar above the highest sort." When Tamburlaine seizes his first crown, the crown of Persia, he makes the act symbolic of his will:

> Though Mars himself, the angry god of arms,
> And all the earthly potentates conspire
> To dispossess me of this diadem,
> Yet will I wear it in despite of them, . . .   [Pt. 1, II. vii. 58–61]

His contempt for earthly potentates and the assertion of his will combine in his conception of himself as the scourge of God, a conception which he shares with Hercules (III. iii. 41–54).[16] He is the avenger, nemesis to the mighty of the world, contemptuous demonstrator of the absurdity of their claims, liberator of captives. He is not so much the instrument as the embodiment of a divine purpose. His serene confidence that his will is seconded by destiny gives him the magnificence of the hero who transcends the merely human. The activities of such a hero are always confined to the earth, though always pointing, in some sense, to a goal beyond. Thus Seneca's Hercules Oetaeus, while rejoicing in his earthly deeds, never forgets that he is destined to become a star. Toward the end of Part 2 Tamburlaine begins to speak of an

---

[16] On the importance of this idea in *Tamburlaine*, see Battenhouse, pp. 99–113.

otherworldly goal,[17] but even before this time the thrones and crowns of the world stand for something which though *in* the earth is yet not *of* it. Their importance to Tamburlaine lies in taking them away from tyrants like Bajazeth, for whom they have intrinsic value. Tamburlaine's last instructions to his son are to sway the throne in such a way as to curb the haughty spirits of the captive kings (Part 2, V. iii. 234–41). An earthly crown represents the sweet fruition of his purpose in being.

Tamburlaine's moving description of the aspiration for sovereignty has the utmost value in the play in presenting his double attitude towards the earth. And as he both seeks and despises earthly glory, he both claims and defies the power of the gods. "Jove himself" will protect him (Pt. 1, I. ii. 179); not even Mars will force him to give up the crown of Persia (Pt. 1, II. vii. 58–61). He does not belong entirely to either earth or heaven. Though he has distinctly human characteristics, both good and bad, he has something of the magnificence and the incomprehensibility of a deity.

Tamburlaine speaks of Mars as "the angry god of war," and the words might serve as self-description, for when he is angry the awe that his looks inspire is almost that of a mortal for a god. Agydas, when Tamburlaine has passed, "looking wrathfully" at him, expresses a typical reaction:

> Betrayed by fortune and suspicious love,
> Threat'nèd with frowning wrath and jealousy,
> Surprised with fear of hideous revenge,
> I stand aghast; but most astonièd
> To see his choler shut in secret thoughts,
> And wrapt in silence of his angry soul.
> Upon his brows was portrayed ugly death,
> And in his eyes the fury of his heart,
> That shine as comets, menacing revenge,
> And casts a pale complexion on his cheeks.
>
> [Pt. 1, III. ii. 66–75]

Later a messenger speaks of "The frowning looks of fiery Tamburlaine, / That with his terror and imperious eyes / Commands

---

[17] Early in Part 1 he promises Theridamas friendship "Until our bodies turn to elements, / And both our souls aspire celestial thrones" (I. ii. 235–36), but here the reference seems more conventional.

the hearts of his associates" (IV. i. 13–15), and the Governor of Damascus calls him "this man, or rather god of war" (V. i. 1). Anger is the passion most frequently displayed in his looks, his words, and the red or black colours of his tents.

Not only is he a man of wrath, as the Herculean hero characteristically is; he is also fiercely cruel. This trait of character receives a continually increasing emphasis; it is strikingly demonstrated in Tamburlaine's treatment of Bajazeth. In Scene ii of Act IV the defeated emperor is brought on in his cage, from which he is removed to serve as Tamburlaine's footstool. But Scene iv is even more spectacular. Tamburlaine, dressed in scarlet to signify his wrath towards the besieged city of Damascus, banquets with his followers while the starving Bajazeth in his cage is insulted and given scraps of food on the point of his conqueror's sword. In the midst of these proceedings Tamburlaine refuses Zenocrate's plea that he raise the siege and make a truce with her father, the Soldan of Egypt. In the last act of Part 1 we see Tamburlaine order the death of the virgins of Damascus, who have been sent to beg for mercy after the black colours have already indicated Tamburlaine's decision to destroy the obstinate city. With inhuman logic he points out that it is now too late and that they "know my customs are as peremptory / As wrathful planets, death or destiny" (V. ii. 64–65). At the end he says that his honour—that personal honour which is the basis of the hero's *areté* —"consists in shedding blood / When men presume to manage arms with him" (V. ii. 414–15). Tamburlaine's is a cosmic extension of the cruelty Achilles shows to Hector or Hercules to the innocent Lichas. Though it is a repellent trait, it is entirely consistent with the rest of the character. Instead of passing over it, Marlowe insists on it. One need not assume, however, that Marlowe himself loved cruelty nor, on the other hand, that he is depicting here a tragic flaw. It is an important part of the picture, a manifestation of Tamburlaine's "ireful Virtue," to use Tasso's phrase, and one of the chief occasions for wonder. One may disapprove and yet, in that special sense, admire.

Marlowe's method of constructing his dramatic portrait is essentially dialectical. Not only is love balanced against hate, cruelty against honour, but these and other traits are constantly brought out against a background of parallels or contrasts. Tamburlaine is contrasted with other monarchs and with Zenocrate. In the last act an entire city is his antagonist. Throughout the play his followers are like variations on the Tamburlaine theme, imitating his ferocity and zest for conquest, but incapable of his grandeur. The first three monarchs with whom the hero is contrasted are the foolish Mycetes, his brother, Cosroe, and the emperor Bajazeth. Mycetes is a grossly comic foil in his inability to act or speak well, to control others or himself. In the opening speech of the play he deplores his own insufficiency to express his rage, "For it requires a great and thundering speech" (I. i. 1–3), a thing Tamburlaine can always provide.

In a low-comedy scene in the first act, he comes alone on to the battlefield, the picture of cowardice, looking for a place to hide his crown. This action in itself takes on great significance when we come, three scenes later, to Tamburlaine's praise of crowns. Mycetes curses the inventor of war and congratulates himself on the wisdom that permits him to escape its ill effects by hiding the crown which makes him a target. To put the censure of war and the praise of scheming wisdom in the mouth of such a character inclines the audience to see virtue in the hero's pursuit of war and in a kind of wisdom more closely allied to action.

The contrast with Cosroe is another matter. Patently superior to his brother Mycetes, Cosroe appears to be an ordinarily competent warrior and ruler. In fact, his one crippling deficiency is his inability to recognize the extraordinary when he sees it in the person of Tamburlaine. His attempt to pat Tamburlaine on the head, and reward him for a job well done by giving him an important post in the kingdom, as any normal king might do, is as inept, given the nature of Tamburlaine, as the feckless gesturing of Mycetes. Cosroe is perfectly familiar with the rules of the game as it is generally played in the world, where the betrayal of a Mycetes is venial and competence has at least its modest reward. His cry of pain when Tamburlaine turns against him, "Barbarous and bloody Tamburlaine" (II. vii. 1), expresses the outrage of one who finds that the rules he has learned do not apply. Tamburlaine's strategy is so much more daring and his treachery so much more preposterous that they are beyond the imagination of Cosroe.

Bajazeth, Tamburlaine's third antagonist, is no mere moderately successful king. A proud and cruel tyrant, he rejoices in the sway of a vast empire. With his first words a new perspective opens up: "Great kings of Barbary, and my portly bassos" (III. i. 1). Here is a ruler served by kings. "We hear the Tartars and the eastern thieves, / Under the conduct of one Tamburlaine, / Presume a bickering with your emperor." The tone is superb. One notes the condescension of "one Tamburlaine" and the hauteur of "presume a bickering." He is assured ("You know our army is invincible"); he is used to command ("Hie thee, my basso . . . Tell him thy lord . . . Wills and commands, for say not I entreat"); and he is obeyed by thousands ("As many circumcisèd Turks we have, / And warlike bands of Christians renièd, / As hath the ocean or the Terrene sea / Small drops of water . . .").

If Cosroe is a little more like Tamburlaine than is his foolish brother, Bajazeth is decidedly more so. He speaks of "the fury of my wrath" (III. i. 30), and shows his cruelty by threatening to castrate Tamburlaine and confine him to the seraglio while his captains are made to draw the chariot of the empress. The famous (and to a modern reader ludicrous) exchange of insults between Zabina and Zenocrate reinforces the parallel. Yet Marlowe emphasizes the ease with which this mighty potentate is toppled from his throne. The stage directions tell the story: *"Enter Bajazeth, pursued by Tamburlaine. They fight briefly and Bajazeth is overcome."* (III. iii. 211 ff.). This contrast brings out what was suggested by the contrast with Cosroe, the truly extraordinary nature of Tamburlaine. For Bajazeth is what Mycetes would like to be but cannot be for lack of natural aptitude. He is what Cosroe might become in time with a little luck. As a sort of final term in a mathematical progression, he presents the ultimate in monarchs, and in himself sums up the others. That even he should fall so easily defines the limitations of the species and sets Tamburlaine in a world apart. He is not merely more angry, more cruel, more proud, more powerful. Though sharing certain characteristics with his victims, he embodies a force of a different order.

Zenocrate, by representing a scale of values far removed from those of the warrior or the monarch, provides further insights into Tamburlaine's character. Something has already been said of his courtship of her in the first act, when, to the surprise of

Techelles, he shows that he is moved by love. The inclusion in his nature of the capacity to love is a characteristic Renaissance addition to the classical model of the Herculean hero. One recalls that Tasso's Rinaldo, though chiefly representing the "ireful virtue," is susceptible to the charms of Armida. Yet Zenocrate is not an enchantress like Armida nor is Tamburlaine's love for her presented as a weakness.[18] Love, as opposed to pure concupiscence, is a more important part of Tamburlaine than of Rinaldo. As G. I. Duthie has pointed out, it modifies considerably his warrior ideal,[19] leading him to spare the life of the Soldan and "take truce with all the world" (V. ii. 466).

Marlowe leaves no doubt that the commitment to Zenocrate is basic and lasting, but it is not allowed to dominate. Tamburlaine refuses Zenocrate's plea for Damascus, and when he also refuses the Virgins of Damascus he says:

> I will not spare these proud Egyptians,
> Nor change my martial observations
> For all the wealth of Gihon's golden waves,
> Or for the love of Venus, would she leave
> The angry god of arms and lie with me.   [Pt. 1, V. ii. 58–62]

This clear evaluation of the claims of Venus as opposed to those of Mars precedes by only a few lines the long soliloquy in which he extols the beauty of Zenocrate. Here he admits that he is tempted to give in to Zenocrate, who has more power to move him than any of his enemies. By implication it is clear that this power is due to her beauty, which is so great that if the greatest poets attempted to capture it,

> Yet should there hover in their restless heads
> One thought, one grace, one wonder, at the least,
> Which into words no virtue can digest.   [Pt. 1, V. ii. 108–10]

---

[18] I cannot agree with Battenhouse (pp. 165 ff.), who believes that the comparison of her to Helen of Troy in Tamburlaine's lament for her death shows her to be a "pattern of pagan, earthly beauty" and "devoid of religion or conscience." Her attitude towards her father and towards the deaths of Bajazeth and Zabina leads to an opposite conclusion.

[19] "The Dramatic Structure of Marlowe's 'Tamburlaine the Great,' Parts I and II," *English Studies* (*Essays and Studies,* New Series) I (1948):101–26. I do not wholly agree as to the extent of the modification Duthie sees. I am not so sure as he is that the marriage of Tamburlaine and Zenocrate symbolizes the establishment of an ideal relationship between beauty and the warrior.

But on the verge, as it might seem, of capitulating to this softer side of his nature, he first reproves himself for these "thoughts effeminate and faint," and then presents beauty as the handmaid of valour. This passage is a textual crux,[20] and its syntax is so treacherous that a close analysis of the meaning is nearly impossible, but I think it is fair to say that Tamburlaine's convictions about the role of beauty are given in the lines:

> And every warrior that is rapt with love
> Of fame, of valor, and of victory,
> Must needs have beauty beat on his conceits.
>
> [Pt. 1, V. ii. 117–19]

The conclusion of the speech looks forward to what beauty may inspire Tamburlaine to do, and it is as important a part of his mission as the scourging of tyrants. This is to show the world "for all my birth, / That virtue solely is the sum of glory, / And fashions men with true nobility" (V. ii. 125–27); that is, that the hero's goal is to be attained by an innate power which has nothing to do with the accidents of birth. To Theridamas, Techelles and Usumcasane he has said much the same thing, assuring them that they deserve their titles

> By valor and by magnanimity.
> Your births shall be no blemish to your fame,
> For virtue is the fount whence honor springs, . . .
>
> [Pt. 1, IV. iv. 123–25]

In several ways the power of love and beauty is subordinated to Tamburlaine's primary concerns. The encomium of Zenocrate leads to the statement of beauty's function in the warrior's life and then to Tamburlaine's intention of demonstrating true nobility. Furthermore, the entire soliloquy is carefully framed. Before it begins, Tamburlaine orders a slaughter, and after his lines about true nobility he calls in a servant to ask whether Bajazeth has been fed. Tamburlaine's love for Zenocrate, extravagant as it is, is part of a rather delicately adjusted balance of forces.

Zenocrate is a pale character beside the best heroines of Shakespeare and Webster, but her attitude towards Tamburlaine is an

---

[20] See Ellis-Fermor's note, V. 2. 114–27.

important part of the meaning of the play. After her initial mistake—not wholly a mistake—of thinking he is just the Scythian shepherd he seems to be, her feelings towards him change rapidly. When she next appears she defends him to her companion, Agydas, who still sees Tamburlaine as a rough soldier. He asks:

> How can you fancy one that looks so fierce,
> Only disposed to martial stratagems? [Pt. 1, III. ii. 40–41]

Zenocrate replies by comparing his looks to the sun and his conversation to the Muses' song. When Tamburlaine enters he rewards each of them with behavior suited to their conception of him: *"Tamburlaine goes to her, and takes her away lovingly by the hand, looking wrathfully on Agydas, and says nothing."* [III. ii. 65 ff.].

Zenocrate enters enthusiastically into the exchange of insults with Bajazeth and Zabina, but it is her speeches after the sack of Damascus and the suicides of Bajazeth and Zabina which truly reveal her attitude towards Tamburlaine. Sorrowing for the cruel deaths of the Virgins of Damascus, she asks:

> Ah, Tamburlaine, wert thou the cause of this,
> That term'st Zenocrate thy dearest love?
> Whose lives were dearer to Zenocrate
> Than her own life, or aught save thine own love?
> [Pt. 1, V. ii. 272–75]

His cruelty is recognized for what it is without its impairing her love. Similarly, when she laments over the bodies of the emperor and empress, she acknowledges Tamburlaine's pride, but prays Jove and Mahomet to pardon him. This lament is a highly effective set-piece, whose formality gives it a special emphasis. Its theme, the vanity of earthly power, is resoundingly stated in the refrain, "Behold the Turk and his great emperess!" which occurs four times, varied the last time to "In this great Turk and hapless emperess!" (V. ii. 291, 294, 299, 305). But within the statement of theme there is a movement of thought as Zenocrate turns from the most general aspect of the fall of the mighty to what concerns her more nearly, its bearing on Tamburlaine. The orthodoxy of the moral she draws from this spectacle of death is conspicuous, and nowhere more so than in the central section:

> Ah, Tamburlaine my love, sweet Tamburlaine,
> That fights for scepters and for slippery crowns,
> Behold the Turk and his great emperess!
> Thou, that in conduct of thy happy stars,
> Sleep'st every night with conquest on thy brows,
> And yet wouldst shun the wavering turns of war,
> In fear and feeling of the like distress,
> Behold the Turk and his great emperess!   [Pt. 1, V. ii. 292–99]

The culmination of the speech is its prayer that Tamburlaine may be spared the consequences of "his contempt / Of earthly fortune and respect of pity (V. ii. 301–2).

When Tamburlaine's enemies inveigh against his pride and presumption, their protests have a hollow ring, and Marlowe may seem to be laughing at the point of view they express. He is certainly not doing so when he puts criticism of the same faults in the mouth of Zenocrate. Through her an awareness of the standard judgment of Tamburlaine's "overreaching" is made without irony and made forcefully. Through her it is also made clear that such an awareness may be included in an unwavering devotion, just as Deianira's devotion can digest even the grave personal slight she suffers from Hercules. Zenocrate both presents the conventional view of hubris more convincingly than any other character, and shows the inadequacy of this view in judging Tamburlaine.

A contrast on a larger scale forms the final episode of Part 1: Tamburlaine is pitted against the great city of Damascus. Since Zenocrate pleads for the city, this is an extension of the contrast between the hero and heroine. Since the city is ruled by Tamburlaine's enemies, it is the climax in the series of contrasts between him and the representatives of corrupt worldly power. His first three enemies are individuals of increasing stature, but the Governor of Damascus and his allies, the Soldan and Arabia, are none of them imposing figures. Instead, the city of Damascus becomes the collective antagonist, to which Tamburlaine opposes his personal will. Much more than the individual monarchs of the first acts, the city seems to represent the point of view of society, which Zenocrate also adopts when she becomes the spokesman for conventional morality. When the delegation of virgins asks the conqueror for mercy, the appeal is in the name of the whole community:

Pity our plights! O, pity poor Damascus!
Pity old age . . .
Pity the marriage bed . . .
O, then, for these and such as we ourselves,
For us, for infants, and for all our bloods,
That never nourished thought against thy rule,
Pity, O pity, sacred emperor,
The prostrate service of this wretched town; . . .

[Pt. 1, V. ii. 17–37 *passim*]

Tamburlaine's refusal is based on the absolute primacy of his will—of the execution of whatever he has vowed. He is as self-absorbed as Hercules, whose devotion to his areté obliterates any consideration for Deianira or Hyllus, in *The Women of Trachis*. Homer portrays the hero's uncompromising adherence to his own standard of conduct in the refusal of Achilles to fight. In Book IX of the *Iliad*, when he is waited on by the delegation of warriors, including his old tutor, Phoenix, heroic integrity directly opposes obligation to others—to friends and allies in war. The "conflict between personal integrity and social obligation" was inherent in the story of the Wrath of Achilles, according to Cedric Whitman, but Homer gave it special importance, seeing it "as an insolubly tragic situation, the tragic situation *par excellence*."[21] In the Renaissance it is not surprising to find "social obligation" represented by the city, but in this case it is an enemy city. Instead of being urged to fight for friends Tamburlaine is urged to spare citizens whose only fault is the acceptance of the rule of their foolish, and finally weak, Governor. Hence the social obligation denied by Tamburlaine is not that of supporting his friends' cause but of conforming to an ideal of behaviour which places mercy above justice. The code of Tamburlaine is a more primitive affair. His word once given is as inflexible as destiny, and the imposition of his will upon Damascus is also the carrying out of a cosmic plan. To the demands of a segment of society he opposes a larger obligation to free the world from tyrants. Marlowe's setting him against Damascus reaffirms both his colossal individuality and his god-like superiority. The siege of this city is used to present the core of the problem of *virtus heroica*.

---

[21] *Homer and the Heroic Tradition* (Cambridge, Mass.: Harvard University Press, 1958 [p. 182], and London: Oxford University Press [p. 182]). See also C. M. Bowra, *The Greek Experience* (London: Weidenfeld & Nicolson, 1957 [Chap. II], and New York: World Publishing Co. [Chap. II]).

Marlowe puts far less emphasis upon the benefactions of his hero's career than was put upon the benefactions of Hercules; the punishment of the wicked is what Tamburlaine himself constantly reiterates. Nevertheless, the punishment of Damascus is balanced by the hero's generosity in sparing the Soldan. This is not a matter of just deserts. It is Tamburlaine's god-like caprice to spare Zenocrate's father. Because he does so the end of Part 1 suggests a positive achievement. Zenocrate's greeting of her "conquering love" is a mixture of wonder and gratitude, and even the vanquished Soldan joins in the general thanksgiving.

Whether Part 2 was planned from the first, as some have thought, or written in response to the "general welcomes Tamburlaine receiv'd," as the Prologue says, its general conception is strikingly similar to that of Part 1. Its structure is again episodic, though the episodes are somewhat more tightly knit. The pattern is again a series of encounters between Tamburlaine and his enemies, leading at last to the one unsuccessful encounter—with death. To Mycetes, Cosroe and Bajazeth correspond the vaster alliance of Bajazeth's son Callapine and his allies. To the conflict between the factions in Persia corresponds the fight between Orcanes and Sigismund after a truce has been concluded. Here again, but even more circumstantially, we have the jealous struggles, the hypocrisies and the betrayals of conventional kings. Sigismund is a despicable figure, Orcanes a rather sympathetic one—even more so than his structural counterpart, Cosroe. He is portrayed as a religious man, is given some fine lines on the deity, ". . . He that sits on high and never sleeps, / Nor in one place is circumscriptible" (II. ii. 49–50), and, though born a pagan, acknowledges the power of Christ. That religion spares him none of the humiliations accorded to the enemies of Tamburlaine suggests that his religion, like his statecraft, is conventional. He is far from being the worst of men or the worst of rulers, yet, like the kings in Part 1, he is given to boasting of his power and position and making snobbish remarks about Tamburlaine's lowly origin. It may be significant that he offers his partial allegiance to Christ as a means of obtaining the victory over Sigismund, who is a perjured Christian. This bargaining religion is the foil to Tamburlaine's impious self-confidence.

Other elements of the pattern of Part 1 are also imitated here.

The siege of Damascus is matched by the siege of Babylon; Bajazeth in his cage is matched by the conquered kings in harness, to whom Tamburlaine shouts the famous "Holla, ye pampered jades of Asia!" (IV. iv. 1), so often parodied. Tamburlaine in his chariot, actually whipping the half-naked kings who draw him, is a powerful theatrical image. Preposterous as the scene may be, it is satisfyingly right as a visual symbol of one of the principal themes of the play. Part 2 develops the theme more fully than Part 1, giving it a prominent place in the dying hero's instructions to his eldest son:

> So, reign, my son; scourge and control these slaves,
> Guiding thy chariot with thy father's hand.
>
> . . . .
>
> For if thy body thrive not full of thoughts
> As pure and fiery as Phyteus' beams,
> The nature of these proud rebelling jades
> Will take occasion by the slenderest hair
> And draw thee piecemeal, like Hippolytus . . .
>
> [Pt. 2, V. iii. 228–29, 236–40]

Another theme developed in Part 2 is the cruelty of Tamburlaine. It is so prominent here that it may seem to mark a loss of sympathy for the hero. Certainly the brutality to the conquered kings and to the Governor of Babylon, and above all Tamburlaine's murder of his son, constitute more vivid and more shocking examples than even the treatment of Bajazeth. Yet one need not conclude that Marlowe has changed his mind about his hero. All of these scenes may be understood as part of a rhetorical amplification of a theme which is, after all, unmistakable in Part 1. Furthermore these scenes serve to emphasize other aspects of Tamburlaine's character indicated in Part 1. The portrait is not changed: its lines are more deeply incised.

The scenes presenting Calyphas, the cowardly son, are perhaps the most shocking of all, and may be used as examples of the amplified theme of cruelty in Part 2. In the first of them (I. iv) Celebinus and Amyras, the two brave sons, win paternal approval by vying with each other in promises to scourge the world, while Calyphas is furiously rebuked for asking permission to stay with his mother while the rest are out conquering. As in all the scenes with the three sons, the patterning is obvious to the point of being crude, and the humour in the depiction of the girlish little boy not much to our taste. Nevertheless, the scene does more than show how hard-hearted Tamburlaine can be. For members of the audience who have not seen Part 1 it presents Tamburlaine's relationship to Zenocrate, and for the rest it restates that relationship in different terms. The scene opens with a loving speech to Zenocrate, who replies by asking Tamburlaine when he will give up war and live safe. It is this question which the scene answers by asserting the primacy of the irascible powers in Tamburlaine's nature. In spite of his love he identifies himself with "wrathful war," and as he looks at her, surrounded by their sons, suddenly thinks that his boys appear more "amorous" than "martial," and hence unworthy of him. Zenocrate defends them as having "their mother's looks" but "their conquering father's heart" (I. iv. 35–36), and it is then that they proclaim their intentions. Tamburlaine's rebuke to Calyphas is a statement of his creed, glorifying the "mind courageous and invincible" (I. iv. 73), and drawing a portrait of himself comparable to several in Part 1:

> For he shall wear the crown of Persia
> Whose head hath deepest scars, whose breast most wounds,
> Which being wroth sends lightning from his eyes,
> And in the furrows of his frowning brows
> Harbors revenge, war, death and cruelty; . . .   [Pt. 2, I. iv. 74–78]

The furrowed brows belong to the angry demigod of Part 1, and if the picture is somewhat grimmer, it is partly because of the hint that the demigod must suffer in the accomplishment of his mission.

The next scene with Calyphas (III. ii) takes place after the death of Zenocrate, and like the former one, makes its contribution to the development of Tamburlaine's character. As the earlier scene began with the praise of Zenocrate, so this one begins with her funeral against the background of a conflagration betokening Tamburlaine's wrath. Again Calyphas is responsible for an unexpected note of levity when he makes an inane comment on the dangerousness of war just after his father has concluded stern instructions to his sons how to be "soldiers / And worthy sons of Tamburlaine the Great" (III. ii. 91–92). The consequence is not only a rebuke but a demonstration. Never having been wounded in all his wars, Tamburlaine cuts his own arm to show his sons how "to bear courageous minds" (III. ii. 143). Here his cruelty and anger are turned against himself, as perhaps they always are in some sense in the scenes with Calyphas.

The last of these scenes (IV. i) is the most terrible and by far the most important, for Calyphas here prompts Tamburlaine to reveal himself more completely than ever before. In the first part of the scene the boy has played cards with an attendant while his brothers fought with their father to overcome the Turkish kings. He has scoffed at honour and, like Mycetes, praised the wisdom which keeps him safe (IV. i. 49–50). When the victors return, Tamburlaine drags Calyphas out of the tent and, ignoring the pleas of his followers and of Amyras, stabs him to death. It is almost a ritual killing—the extirpation of an unworthy part of himself, as the accompanying speech makes clear:

> Here, Jove, receive his fainting soul again,
> A form not meet to give that subject essence
> Whose matter is the flesh of Tamburlaine,
> Wherein an incorporeal spirit moves,
> Made of the mould whereof thyself consists,
> Which makes me valiant, proud, ambitious,
> Ready to levy power against thy throne,
> That I might move the turning spheres of heaven,
> For earth and all this airy region
> Cannot contain the state of Tamburlaine.   [Pt. 2, IV. ii. 36–45]

To interpret this murder as merely one further example of barbarous cruelty is to accept the judgment of Tamburlaine's enemies. The cruelty is balanced against one of the most powerful statements of the spirituality of Tamburlaine. It is the "incorporeal spirit" which makes him what he is, a hero akin to the gods, and which, because it cannot bear to be other than itself, pushes him to the execution of his cowardly son. As the great aspiring speech of Part 1 obliges us to see an earthly crown as the goal to which Tamburlaine's nature forces him, so this speech and its accompanying action oblige us to accept cruelty along with valour, pride and ambition as part of the spirit which makes this man great. The soul of Calyphas, by contrast, is associated with the "massy dregs of earth" (IV. ii. 48), lacking both courage and wit, just as Theridamas described the unaspiring mind as "gross and like the massy earth" (Part 1, II. vii. 31).

So far does Tamburlaine go in asserting his affinity to heaven and contempt for earth, that for the first time he hints that sovereignty of the earth may not be enough for him. It is an idea which has an increasing appeal for him in the remainder of the play. He makes another extreme statement in this scene when his enemies protest the barbarity of his deed. "These terrors and these tyrannies," he says, are part of his divine mission,

> Nor am I made arch-monarch of the world,
> Crowned and invested by the hand of Jove,
> For deeds of bounty or nobility; . . .   [Pt. 2, IV. ii. 75–77]

To be the terror of the world is his exclusive concern.

The emphasis on terror is consistent with the entire depiction of his character. The denial of nobility is not. It is an extreme statement which the emotions of the moment and dialectical necessity push him to. Allowing for an element of exaggeration in this speech, however, the scene as a whole, like the other scenes with Calyphas, presents a Tamburlaine essentially like the Tamburlaine of Part 1, and not seen from any very different point of view. As he grows older, as he encounters a little more resistance, his character sets a little more firmly in its mould. It remains what it has always been.

The death of Zenocrate is, as every critic has recognized, the first real setback to Tamburlaine. In view of her association with the city in Part 1 it is appropriate that Tamburlaine makes a city suffer for her death by setting fire to it. His devotion to her and to the beauty she represents appears in the speech he makes at her deathbed (II. iv. 1–37), in his raging at her death, in the placing of her picture on his tent to inspire valour (III. ii. 25–33), and in his dying address to her coffin (V. iii. 224–27). As G. I. Duthie says, death is the great enemy in Part 2, and his conquest of Zenocrate is in effect his first victory over Tamburlaine.[22] As he had to make some concessions to Zenocrate in Part 1, so in Part 2 he has to come to terms with the necessity of death. The process begins with the death of Zenocrate, to which his first reac-

---

[22] "The Dramatic Structure of Marlowe's 'Tamburlaine the Great'," pp. 118, 124.

tion is the desire for revenge. Not only does he burn the town where she died; he also orders Techelles to draw his sword and wound the earth (II. iv. 96–97). This prepares us somewhat for his later order, when death has laid siege to him, to "set black streamers in the firmament, / To signify the slaughter of the gods" (V. iii. 49–50). By keeping always with him the hearse containing her dead body he refuses wholly to accept her death as he now defies his own.

Only in the last scene of Act V does cosmic defiance give way to acceptance, and when this happens, Tamburlaine's defeat by death is partially transformed into a desired fulfilment. I have already mentioned his hint that the earth cannot contain him. It is followed by a suggestion that Jove, esteeming him "too good for earth" (IV. iv. 60), might make a star of him. Now he says:

> In vain I strive and rail against those powers
> That mean t'invest me in a higher throne,
> As much too high for this disdainful earth.
>
> [Pt. 2, V. iii. 120–22]

and finally:

> But, sons, this subject, not of force enough
> To hold the fiery spirit it contains,
> Must part, . . .   [Pt. 2, V. iii. 168–70]

Like Hercules Oetaeus, he feels that his immortal part, that "incorporeal spirit" of which he spoke earlier, is now going to a realm more worthy of him, though imparting something of its power to the spirits of his two remaining sons, in whom he will continue to live. In these final moments we have what may be hinted at earlier in his self-wounding—a collaboration with death and fate in the destruction of his physical being. For the psychologist the drive towards self-destruction is latent in all heroic risks; it is the other side of the coin of self-assertion. Though Marlowe could never have put it this way, his insight may be essentially similar.

From the quotations already given it will be apparent that Tamburlaine's attitude toward the gods changes continually. He boasts of their favour or defies them to take away his conquests; likens himself to them, executes their will, waits for them to receive him into their domain, or threatens to conquer it. Tambur-

laine's religious pronouncements, especially his blasphemies, have
attracted a great deal of critical comment from his day to ours.
Since Marlowe himself was accused of atheism, the key question
has been whether or not Tamburlaine is a mouthpiece for his
author. Some critics emphasize Tamburlaine's defiance of Mahomet and the burning of the Koran, but these episodes are
surely no more significant than his "wounding" of the earth. As
Kocher has pointed out (p. 89), his line, "The God that sits in
heaven, if any god" (V. i. 199) contains in its parenthetical comment more blasphemy for a Christian than does the whole incident of the Koran. Yet even this questioning of God's existence
is only one of the changes of attitude just cited. To try to deduce
Marlowe's religious position from these speeches is a hopeless undertaking, and to try to decide on the basis of the biographical
evidence which of them Marlowe might endorse is risky and
finally inconclusive. Somehow the relationship of these opinions
to the rest of the play must be worked out. Either their inconsistency is due to carelessness (in this case carelessness of heroic
proportions) or it has some bearing on the heroic character. Seneca's Hercules displays a similar variety of attitudes. In the earlier
play he thanks the gods for their aid in his victory over the tyrant,
Lycus, and offers to kill any further tyrants or monsters the earth
may bring forth. Moments later, as his madness comes upon him,
he says:

> To the lofty regions of the universe on high let me make my way,
> let me seek the skies; the stars are my father's promise. And what if
> he should not keep his word? Earth has not room for Hercules, and
> at length restores him unto heaven. See, the whole company of the
> gods of their own will summons me, and opens wide the door of
> heaven, with one alone forbidding. And wilt thou unbar the sky
> and take me in? Or shall I carry off the doors of stubborn heaven?
> Dost even doubt my power?   [*Hercules Furens,* ll. 958–65]

In the first lines of *Hercules Oetaeus* he again boasts of his activities as a scourge of tyrants and complains that Jove still denies
him access to the heavens, hinting that the god may be afraid of
him. Later (ll. 1302–3) he almost condescends to Jove, remarking
that he might have stormed the heavens, but refrained because
Jove, after all, was his father. Greene could quite properly have
inveighed against "daring God out of heaven with that atheist

Hercules." At the end of *Hercules Oetaeus* the hero accepts his fate with calm fortitude and even helps to destroy himself amidst the flames. These changes in attitude are perhaps more easy to understand in Hercules, since his relationship to the gods was in effect a family affair. Tamburlaine is not the son of a god, but his facile references to the gods, sometimes friendly, sometimes hostile, may be interpreted as part of the heroic character of which Hercules is the prototype. He has the assurance of a demigod rather than the piety of a good man.

Such assurance, rather than repentance, breathes in the lines in which Tamburlaine advises his son Amyras:

> Let not thy love exceed thine honor, son,
> Nor bar thy mind that magnanimity
> That nobly must admit necessity.
> Sit up, my boy, and with these silken reins
> Bridle the steelèd stomachs of those jades.
>
> [Pt. 2, V. iii. 199–203]

The advice to admit necessity[23] may reflect Tamburlaine's own acceptance of his death, but in context it refers primarily to the necessity for Amyras to take over Tamburlaine's throne. The whole speech shows Tamburlaine's conviction of the rightness of what he has done. The place of love is again made subordinate to honour, the hero's chief concern. Magnanimity is stressed as it is in Tamburlaine's advice to his followers to deserve their crowns "by valour and magnanimity" (Part 1, IV. iv. 123). Even the bowing to fate is to be done nobly, as Tamburlaine himself is now doing. Finally, the heroic enterprise of controlling tyrants is to be continued. There is no retraction here, no change in the basic character. He has come to terms with death, but this is more a recovery than a reversal. He has spoken earlier in the play of his old age and death, but, very humanly, has rebelled when death struck at Zenocrate and then at himself. Now he has regained calm with self-mastery.

Though the suffering of Tamburlaine is so prominent from

---

[23] Helen L. Gardner has written about the importance of the theme of necessity in Part 2 in an excellent essay, "The Second Part of 'Tamburlaine the Great'," *Modern Language Review* 37 (1942):18–24. I cannot agree with her that Marlowe's sympathies are much changed, however, nor that the moral of Part 2 is "the simple medieval one of the inevitability of death."

the death of Zenocrate to the end, retribution is not what is
stressed. The last scene of the play presents a glorification of the
hero approaching apotheosis. It opens with a formally patterned
lament, spoken by Theridamas, Techelles and Usumcasane, the
last section of which expresses the theme of the scene, Tamburlaine as benefactor:

> Blush, heaven, to lose the honor of thy name,
> To see thy footstool set upon thy head;
> And let no baseness in thy haughty breast
> Sustain a shame of such inexcellence,
> To see the devils mount in angels' thrones,
> And angels dive into the pools of hell.
> And though they think their painful date is out
> And that their power is puissant as Jove's,
> Which makes them manage arms against thy state,
> Yet make them feel the strength of Tamburlaine,
> Thy instrument and note of majesty,
> Is greater far than they can thus subdue;
> For, if he die, thy glory is disgraced,
> Earth droops and says that hell in heaven is placed.
>
> [Pt. 2, V. iii. 28–41]

His sons live only in his life, and it is with the greatest reluctance
that Amyras mounts the throne at Tamburlaine's command.
When he speaks in doing so of his father's "anguish and his burning agony" (V. iii. 209), he seems to imply that Tamburlaine's
sufferings are the inevitable concomitants of his greatness and his
service to humanity. It is he who pronounces the final words:

> Meet heaven and earth, and here let all things end,
> For earth hath spent the pride of all her fruit,
> And heaven consumed his choicest living fire.
> Let earth and heaven his timeless death deplore,
> For both their worths will equal him no more.
>
> [Pt. 2, V. iii. 249–53]

Full of Herculean echoes, the lines form a perfect epitaph for the
hero, the product of earth and heaven.

Three times in this scene Tamburlaine adjures his son to control the captive kings and thus maintain order. He compares the
task with Phaëton's:

> So, reign, my son; scourge and control those slaves,
> Guiding thy chariot with thy father's hand.

As precious is the charge thou undertak'st
As that which Clymene's brain-sick son did guide,
When wandering Phoebe's ivory cheeks were scorched,
And all the earth, like Aetna, breathing fire.
Be warned by him; then learn with awful eye
To sway a throne as dangerous as his; . . .   [Pt. 2, V. iii. 228–35]

Despite his ambition and pride, Tamburlaine is no Macbeth to seek power "though the treasure / Of nature's germens tumble all together, / Even till destruction sicken. . . ."[24] Rather, he identifies himself with universal order, as does Seneca's Hercules. The very chariot which is a symbol of his cruel scourging is also the symbol of control and hence of order. Compared to the chariot of the sun, it is also the bringer of light.

In the depiction of the Herculean hero there is no relaxation of the tensions between his egotism and altruism, his cruelties and benefactions, his human limitations and his divine potentialities. Marlowe never lets his audience forget these antitheses. In the first scene of Act V this great benefactor orders the Governor of Babylon to be hung in chains on the wall of the town. He rises from his deathbed to go out and conquer one more army. It is Marlowe's triumph that, after revealing with such clarity his hero's pride and cruelty, he can give infinite pathos to the line, "For Tamburlaine, the scourge of God, must die" (V. iii. 248).

In obtaining a favourable reception for his hero among the more thoughtful members of his audience Marlowe could no doubt count on not only some familiarity with the heroic tradition in which he was working, but also on the often-voiced regard for the active life. Gabriel Harvey, it will be recalled, asks who would not rather be one of the nine worthies than one of the seven wise masters. He also expresses another attitude on which Marlowe could count, the Stoic regard for integrity—truth to oneself. Harvey prefers Caesar to Pompey because Pompey deserts himself, while Caesar remains true to himself. He notes that it was Aretine's glory to be himself.[25]

The last moments of the play appeal to the spectator's pity by insisting on the tragic limitation of Tamburlaine as a human being. "For Tamburlaine, the scourge of God, must die" is compa-

[24] *The Complete Works of Shakespeare*, ed. G. L. Kittredge (Boston: Ginn & Co., 1936 [IV. 1. 58–60]).
[25] *Gabriel Harvey's Marginalia*, pp. 134, 156.

rable to Achilles' lines: "For not even the strength of Herakles
fled away from destruction, / although he was dearest of all to
lord Zeus . . ." But the play's dominant appeal is to the wonder
aroused by vast heroic potential. The very paradoxes of Tamburlaine's nature excite wonder, and this was supposed in Marlowe's
time to be the effect of paradox. Puttenham, in his familiar *Arte
of English Poesie,* calls paradox "the wonderer." Tamburlaine's
"high astounding terms," for which the Prologue prepares us,
clearly aim at the same effect. Many years later, Sir William Alexander, the author of several Senecan tragedies, wrote that the
three stylistic devices which pleased him most were: "A grave
sentence, by which the Judgment may be bettered; a witty Conceit, which doth harmoniously delight the Spirits; and a generous
Rapture expressing Magnanimity, whereby the Mind may be inflamed for great Things." The last of these three he found in
Lucan, in whose "Heroical Conceptions" he saw an "innate Generosity"; he remarked the power of "the unmatchable Height of
his Ravishing Conceits to provoke Magnanimity."[26] Marlowe was
undoubtedly influenced by the style of the *Pharsalia,* the first
book of which he had translated, and in any case Alexander's
words might justly be applied to *Tamburlaine.* The epic grandeur of the style,[27] with its resounding catalogues of exotic names,
its hyperboles, and its heroic boasts and tirades, "expresses magnanimity," that largeness of spirit so consistently ascribed to the
great hero. Alexander testifies that such a style may inflame the
mind "for great things," and general as this description is, it
serves well for the feeling aroused by the play. Another name for
it was admiration.

[26] *Anacrisis* (1634?), in *Critical Essays of the Seventeenth Century,* ed. J. E. Spingarn
(Bloomington: Indiana University Press, 1957 [I, 182, 183], and London: Oxford University Press [I, 182, 183]).
[27] Harry Levin has written brilliantly of this style in *The Overreacher* (Cambridge,
Mass.: Harvard University Press [especially pp. 10 ff.], and London: Faber & Faber
[pp. 30 ff.]), where he comments on the superb appropriateness of the term of Puttenham's for hyperbole. As he says, "It could not have been more happily inspired to
throw its illumination upon Marlowe—upon his style, which is so emphatically himself, and on his protagonists, overreachers all" (p. 23). See also M. P. McDiarmid,
"The Influence of Robert Garnier on some Elizabethan Tragedies," *Etudes Anglaises*
XI (1958):289–302; and Donald Peet, "The Rhetoric of Tamburlaine," *ELH* 26
(1959):137–55. Commenting on Marlowe's use of amplification, Peet remarks that
"there can be little doubt that Marlowe wants us to *marvel* at Tamburlaine," whether
or not he seeks approval (p. 151).

CLIFFORD LEECH

The Structure of TAMBURLAINE

When *Tamburlaine* was first published in 1590, it was described
on its title page as "Deuided into two Tragicall Discourses"—a
curious reminiscence of George Whetstone's *Promos and Cassan-
dra,* which in 1578 was similarly described as "Deuided into two
Comicall Discourses"—and each part of *Tamburlaine* was divided into five acts. The publication of 1590, however, does not
command our full confidence, for Richard Jones, the printer, admitted in his prefatory address "To the Gentlemen Readers" that
he had excised passages that he found "far unmeet for the matter"
which the play as a whole presented. Even so, there is a *prima
facie* case for accepting the division into two parts, each with its
characteristic Marlowe prologue, and into five acts for each part,
as having authorial warrant. Indeed, few Elizabethan plays have
a more evident five-act structure than *1 Tamburlaine,* though—
as so often with Shakespeare too—we do not find a simple following of the Terentian formula for such a division.

   In the simplest terms, we can put it like this: in Act I Tamburlaine, seen against the background of quarreling between the
brothers in the Persian court, captures Zenocrate and wins over
Theridamas by the force of eloquence, in Act II, as Cosroe's ally
he defeats Mycetes, and then overcomes Cosroe and becomes King
of Persia; in Act III he conquers Bajazeth the Turk; in Act IV

First published in *Tulane Drama Review (TDR)* 8, no. 4 (Summer 1964):32–46.
© 1964 by *Tulane Drama Review;* © 1967 by *The Drama Review.* Reprinted by permission. All rights reserved.

there is a recession as the Soldan of Egypt marches against him; in Act V he conquers Damascus, part of the Soldan's dominions, and then defeats the Soldan himself. Each act, apart from Act IV, corresponds to a step in his march of conquest, and the exceptional function of Act IV is evidently to make an effective pause, preparing for the climactic encounter which will lead to Tamburlaine's "truce with all the world" and his crowning of Zenocrate as his queen. Within each of these acts, moreover, Marlowe has achieved effects of extreme contrast.

In Act I, there is fun at the expense of the King of Persia, Mycetes, and it is easy, in remembering the play as a whole, to forget how very thoroughly comic the opening scene is. Here we find the King straining after a feeble pun:

> But I refer me to my noblemen
> That know my wit and can be witnesses.
>
> [Pt. 1, I. i. 21–22]

and his imagery, in a way that Longinus talks of,[1] falls into the puerile and frigid:

> Then hear thy charge, valiant Theridamas,
> The chiefest captain of Mycetes' host,
> The hope of Persia, and the very legs
> Whereon our state doth lean, as on a staff
> That holds us up and foils our neighbor foes.   [57–61]

He gives us *sententiae* that in no way vary the trite:

> Return with speed; time passeth swift away.
> Our life is frail, and we may die today.   [67–68]

And he can expose himself by a simple misuse of a word, as with "dainty" here:

> And from their knees even to their hoofs below
> Besmeared with blood; that makes a dainty show.   [79–80]

In his exchange with Cosroe, his ambitious brother, a school-boy's pun may be used against him and made cruder by Mycetes' disregard of the interruption:

---

[1] *Peri Hupsous*, Chap. III.

Mycetes.   Well, here I swear by this my royal seat—
Cosroe.   You may do well to kiss it then. [*Aside*]
Mycetes.   —Embossed with silk as best beseems my state, . . .

[97–99]

Marlowe, in fact, promising in his prologue "high astounding terms," boldly begins with the reverse—with a puerile imitation of regal language. The contrast between this in the first scene and the manner of Tamburlaine in the second is an extreme one. And here Tamburlaine does not fight. He has captured Zenocrate before the scene begins; he wins over Theridamas during its course, by the mere strength of his utterance. It is, of course, grandiloquence that he gives us, but it is grandiloquence that never puts a word wrong. Marlowe could not have achieved so complete a contrast between the present and future Kings of Persia except by relying on their different manners of speech.

Act II depends at first on the same contrast. Mycetes is still at sea with his words, and his feebleness can be communicated through the very halting of his prosody:

> He tells you true, my masters; so he does.
> Drums, why sound ye not when Meander speaks?
>
> [Pt. 1, II. ii. 74–75]

—where the jejune "so he does" is followed by the stumbling line with which Mycetes concludes the first scene in which he appears in this act. However, Marlowe makes the contrast evident in action when Mycetes and Tamburlaine meet in scene four, Mycetes trying to hide his crown, anxious to preserve the symbol of his royalty, and Tamburlaine first taking it by force and then giving it back to him until he has won it by conquering a whole army. It is true that here, for the first time and in an important way, the symbol of Tamburlaine's ambition becomes absurd in being exposed as a mere and arbitrary symbol; but the immediate impact of the encounter is to drive home the contrast between the two men. For the rest of the act, Cosroe is Tamburlaine's adversary: Cosroe the man of modest ambition is crushed by Tamburlaine the man with a boundless dream. There is not absurdity in Cosroe, but merely ordinariness; and thus Act II is finally built on a double antithesis.

The main subject of Act III, as we have seen, is the conquering of Bajazeth, but we also meet Zenocrate again for the first time since I, ii. To the dismay of her attendant lord Agydas, she declares her love for the conqueror and her fear that he will turn from her "unworthiness." Tamburlaine enters unseen as the two of them speak, and listens to them in silence for forty lines. Then still he does not speak, and this stage-direction follows: *"Tamburlaine goes to her, and takes her away lovingly by the hand, looking wrathfully on Agydas, and says nothing."* After leaving the stage with her, still without a word spoken, he sends Agydas a dagger to dispatch himself with. This is the only silent entry that Tamburlaine ever makes, and it comes immediately after III. i. in which Bajazeth with his subsidiary kings enters *"in great pomp"* and declares at length the might of his army. Tamburlaine dominated in words in Act I, thus winning Theridamas to his side, and his eloquence continued in Act II. His majestic silence here becomes an instrument to make him more impressive than Bajazeth, and incidentally of course disposes of Agydas. At the same time Techelles and Usumcasane decide to "crave . . . triple worthy burial" for the "wise and honourable" Agydas, whose suicide was "manly done." It is the first time we have seen the death of one of Tamburlaine's enemies away from the battlefield, the first hint that the price of Tamburlaine's assertion may be high. Thus in the juxtaposition of the first two scenes of Act III there is a new and startling mode of contrasting Tamburlaine with the next monarch he is to overthrow, and in the juxtaposition of the winning of Zenocrate with the killing of Agydas the first note of dubiety.

The third scene is climactic. The forces of Bajazeth and Tamburlaine confront each other and hurl defiance. They go off-stage to fight, leaving Zabena and Zenocrate enthroned, each with an attendant, and the women fall to an interchange of abuse and threat: the formality of the staging counterpoints the relaxed vulgarity of the language. And then for a moment the scene becomes wholly formal. The battle is halted, the queen and the betrothed consort invoke their gods, each speaking six lines in turn:

> *Zenocrate.*   Ye gods and powers that govern Persia,
>   And made my lordly love her worthy king,
>   Now strengthen him against the Turkish Bajazeth,
>   And let his foes, like flocks of fearful roes

> Pursued by hunters, fly his angry looks,
> That I may see him issue conqueror.
> *Zabena.*   Now, Mahomet, solicit God himself,
> And make him rain down murdering shot from heaven
> To dash the Scythians' brains, and strike them dead
> That dare to manage arms with him
> That offered jewels to thy sacred shrine
> When first he warred against the Christians.
>
> [Pt. 1, III. iii. 189–200]

Then the formality is fully dissolved with the defeat and capture of Bajazeth. The Turkish crown is seized from Zabena; Bajazeth laments; Tamburlaine glories; as the Turk and his empress are put in bonds, they cry out against the prophet who has not saved them:

> *Bajazeth.*   Ah, villains, dare ye touch my sacred arms?
> O Mahomet! O sleepy Mahomet!
> *Zabina.*   O cursèd Mahomet, that mak'st us thus
> The slaves to Scythians rude and barbarous!
>
> [Pt. 1, III. iii. 268–71]

Here the contrast between formality and disorder depends on a subtle interplay within the scene; but this complexity of scene three is contrasted with the firm parallelism instituted by the wholly formal (yet themselves contrasted) scenes one and two.

The new adversary introduced in Act IV, Zenocrate's father the Soldan, is also presented in a way that points a contrast with Tamburlaine. In scenes one and three we see the Soldan marshalling his troops and, joined by the King of Arabia in scene three, on the march to the battlefield. There is indignation here: "The slave usurps the glorious name of war" (IV. i. 68), says the Soldan when he learns of Tamburlaine's procedure with the white, red, and black tents—here mentioned for the first time. They talk of Bajazeth's "slavery" and their "sorrow" for it. There is no boasting here, as with Bajazeth, no homespun ambition, as with Cosroe, no feeble bluster, as with Mycetes. Tamburlaine's new enemies are presented formally, generically, as good men wronged and resolute.

In the second and fourth scenes Tamburlaine seems only incidentally concerned with the march towards Damascus and the encounter with the Soldan. The baiting of Bajazeth here and the distributing of crowns as a course at a banquet work equally to bring Tamburlaine's glory into question. We are still much more concerned with him than with his adversaries: he holds the stage even as he indulges in a relaxed brutality and depreciates the crowns' worth (once his "sole felicity"). Zenocrate joins in the baiting of Bajazeth, but begs Tamburlaine to spare her father; he refuses.

In the final act there is an extraordinary series of variations in the directing of our sympathy. Tamburlaine condemns to death the Virgins of Damascus, but shows a kind of contemptuous pity—

> What, are the turtles frayed out of their nests?
> Alas, poor fools, . . .   [Pt. 1, V. ii. 1–2]

—and is never more eloquent than when he tells the girls of the death that sits on his sword's point. He reiterates his resolve not to "spare these proud Egyptians," and then speaks his famous soliloquy on Zenocrate and beauty and its power. Bajazeth and Zabena despair and die, and Zenocrate pities them, feeling fear that Tamburlaine may have to pay for his cruelty or may be subject himself to the turn of Fortune's wheel. The King of Arabia dies, expressing his love for Zenocrate. Tamburlaine spares the defeated Soldan, crowns Zenocrate, and "takes truce with all the world": in the background of his triumph lie the bodies of Bajazeth, Zabena, and Arabia.

Professor G. I. Duthie has argued that dramatic shape is given to *1 Tamburlaine* through the conflict that arises in the hero's mind between his passion for conquest and his passion for Zenocrate, which leads him to feel an impulse to tenderness and finally to spare Zenocrate's father.[2] Certainly we have seen him changing his mind about the Soldan, and have noticed a new touch of pity in his words to the Virgins of Damascus. Moreover, when he is wooing Zenocrate in I. ii. and promising her great splendor and the gift of himself, there is a hint of embarrassment when Techelles shows surprise:

> *Techelles.* What now? in love?
> *Tamburlaine.* Techelles, women must be flatterèd.
> But this is she with whom I am in love.   [106–8]

2 "The Dramatic Structure of Marlowe's *Tamburlaine the Great, Parts I and II*," *English Studies 1948* (London: 1948), pp. 101–26.

The contrast between Tamburlaine's two lines here shows a momentary shame before a firm resolve is re-established. But it is, I think, difficult to follow Professor Duthie in seeing this strand in the play as dominant. There is, along with it, the awakening first of love and then of pity in Zenocrate herself. There is the crown-motif, where we have seen the symbol debased in Mycetes' pathetic attempt to keep his own circlet safe, in the appearance of the crowns at the banquet, in Tamburlaine's refusal to crown Zenocrate after the defeat of Bajazeth (for as yet he has no crown worthy of her), in Zenocrate's realizing that crowns are "slippery" as she sees the dead Bajazeth and Zabena. There is the growing savagery of Tamburlaine's acts: not much is made of the defeat of Mycetes and Cosroe; the death of Agydas comes home more directly; the treatment of Bajazeth and Zabena has a harsh dark comedy not far from desperation; the slaughter of the Virgins shows Tamburlaine in the trap of his own commitment; the device of the colored tents, announced in Act IV, has a similar effect of automatism. In fact, the sparing of the Soldan, like the glimpse of pity when Tamburlaine sees the Virgins, like the final truce-making with the world, appears a nugatory gesture which runs counter to the general direction which Tamburlaine must now follow. We have seen, moreover, that the adversaries of Tamburlaine are differently presented from one another: increasingly he is opposed to men with a better cause.

There is good reason to accept the statement in the prologue to Part 2 that the sequel resulted from the popularity of Part 1: Marlowe had exhausted his historical sources in that part, and seems to have had to look hard for fresh matter. He found the Sigismund episode in the events that led to the battle of Varna in 1444; he conflated stories from *Orlando Furioso* and Belleforest's *Cosmographia* to produce the story of Olympia.[3] For the deaths of Zenocrate and Calyphas he used his own invention. Moreover, there is one prominent feature of Part 2 which is characteristic of sequels—the free use of incidents which parallel incidents in the original play. Professor M. A. Shaaber has drawn attention to a similar phenomenon in his study of the relations of the two parts of *Henry IV*.[4] In the present instance it will be useful to list

[3] Introduction to Ellis-Fermor, op. cit., pp. 41–45.
[4] "The Unity of *Henry IV*," *Joseph Quincy Adams Memorial Studies* (Washington, 1948), pp. 217–27.

the most evident parallelisms—noting, however, a recurrent distinction that is made in Part 2:

1. Each Part begins with characters and conflicts not directly involving Tamburlaine. In Part 1 we see the clash between Mycetes and Cosroe, in Part 2 the warfare between the Turks and the Christians of eastern Europe. But Tamburlaine is farther away in the second case, and the matter of Sigismund's breach of faith has a fullness of reverberation quite unlike anything in Part 1: it not only entertains, without fully affirming, the idea of retribution, but it invites thought about the conditions under which men can live together. Moreover, in this section of the play we have a major battle in which Tamburlaine is not concerned.

2. The silent rebuke of Agydas in Part 1, followed by his receiving the dagger, has an affiliation with the killing of Calyphas, who is not allowed to speak when his father returns for the execution. There is inversion here, not merely in the matter of the silence (of Tamburlaine in Part 1, of his victim in Part 2) but in the fact that Calyphas has damaged Tamburlaine's glory with a touch of absurd comment. The disposal of Agydas, though pathetic in relation to the victim, is triumphant for Tamburlaine.

3. Bajazeth's cage is paralleled by the chariot drawn by kings. Both are demonstrations of Tamburlaine's power that the hero needs, but the chariot, an even crueller device than the cage, is also ludicrous: a brace of kings provides an inefficient means of haulage. Not surprisingly, and surely in accord with Marlowe's intention, "Holla, ye pampered jades of Asia" became a play-scrap sure of a laugh.

4. The slaughter of the Virgins of Damascus has an echo in the wanton treatment of the Turkish concubines in Part 2, IV. iii. At Damascus, as we have seen, Tamburlaine spoke with eloquence and a grim regret: he was tied in the matter. But there is a squalid spitefulness in the way he tells his soldiers to use the Turkish women as they please. The women ask for pity, and the captive kings protest; but this is how the matter is unheroically conducted:

> *Orcanes.*   Injurious tyrant, wilt thou so defame
> The hateful fortunes of thy victory,
> To exercise upon such guiltless dames

The violence of thy common soldiers' lust?

Tamburlaine.   Live continent, then, ye slaves, and meet not me
With troops of harlots at your slothful heels.

Concubines.   O pity us, my Lord, and save our honors.

Tamburlaine.   Are ye not gone, ye villains, with your spoils?

[*The soldiers run away with the ladies.*]

King of Jerusalem.   O merciless, infernal cruelty!

Tamburlaine.   Save your honors! 'Twere but time indeed,
Lost long before you knew what honor meant.

[Pt. 2, IV. iv. 77–87]

This is Tamburlaine's revenge for the funeral rites which the concubines have given to Calyphas.

5. The siege of Damascus and the siege of Babylon both come at the beginning of a final act, both end in total slaughter. But the taking of Damascus was part of Tamburlaine's campaign against the Soldan; the taking of Babylon is an isolated incident in what appears to be indiscriminate conquest.

6. In Part 2 Callapine occupies a position roughly corresponding to his father Bajazeth's in Part 1. But Callapine, though twice defeated, is free at the end of the play and can be regarded as a continuing threat to the empire that Tamburlaine wished to leave behind him.

7. The suicide of Olympia after her husband's death corresponds to Zabena's suicide following Bajazeth's. But Tamburlaine is not involved in the incident in Part 2, and Theridamas' love for Olympia contrasts with the general indifference to Zabena while she lived.

It will be apparent that the parallels are in each case incomplete, and that the general effect of the difference is to make Tamburlaine's stature shrink even as he tries to magnify it. This is reinforced in several other ways in Part 2. Theridamas, Callapine and even Almeda can echo the aspirations after kingship and sensual splendor that are associated only with Tamburlaine in Part 1; in Act I, v–vi, Tamburlaine receives reports of conquest from his generals Theridamas, Techelles, and Usumcasane though they wage war in his name, the glory and activity in this part are not wholly his; indeed, it is remarkable how often in Part 2 the scenes in which Tamburlaine appears are wholly static, as he receives his generals' reports in I. v–vi, mourns for Zenocrate in II. iv. educates his sons in I. iv and III. ii. and demonstrates his chariot in IV. iv—all this in contrast to the ceaseless activity of the Turks who struggle against him. It is easy, moreover, to observe the direct demonstration of his power's limits. He tries to compensate for Zenocrate's death by embalming her body, by burning the town in which she died and forbidding the world to build it up again, by talking of leading his army against the Jove who has taken her away. He can kill Calyphas, but cannot silence our memory of the boy's ridicule; he can educate his sons in the theory of warfare, but even the two survivors give no impression of strength; Callapine can bribe Almeda to let him escape (no one escaped from Tamburlaine in Part 1, no one was disloyal to him); and Tamburlaine himself cannot survive the sickness that comes on him in Act V.

Professor Duthie would make Part 2 an affair of Tamburlaine's reconciliation with death: he comes to realize he must die, but is victorious over death in transmitting his empire to his sons.[5] But this seems not only to disregard the manifest insufficiency of Amyras and Celebinus but to go against the whole drive of the play. It would indeed be wrong to think that *II Tamburlaine* has become an *Anti-Tamburlaine:* the hero is still the center of interest; it is what happens to him—and only incidentally what happens to Sigismund or Zenocrate or Calyphas or Olympia— that poses for us a question about the human condition. The prologue to Part 2 makes it clear that we have a "fall" to contemplate. There is a double force in the pronoun "his" in the brief description:

> . . . his Second Part,
> Where death cuts off the progress of his pomp
> And murderous Fates throws all his triumphs down.

We are to watch the man's (and not merely the play's) "second part"—i.e., his decline. Despite all its complications, Part 1 showed us a rise, and we are here concerned with the unwinding of the spring, as we are in *Faustus* from the moment when the bond is signed. Tamburlaine has made a pact with himself, in disregard

---

[5] Loc. cit.

of other human beings (even, ultimately, of Zenocrate) and of cosmic processes. Part 2, in fact, is a tragedy. Part 1 by itself is much more difficult to classify: we might call it tragedy *in posse,* for the fall of Part 2 can be seen as implicit in the mesh that Tamburlaine is caught in by the time he has conquered Bajazeth.

Tamburlaine's part is slightly longer in Part 2 than in Part 1: in both cases he speaks approximately one-third of the total number of lines in the play. And he is on stage in both parts for more than half the play's total length. In Part 1 he appears, however, in ten of the seventeen scenes; in Part 2 in ten out of twenty-one. Moreover, we have noted the strong static element in the Tamburlaine scenes of Part 2, in contrast with the activity of the Turks. And in Part 2 the hero seems to be placed in a geographical context far wider than his immediate situation. In Part 1 we follow his fortunes all the time, in Persia, in Turkey, in the Soldan's dominions. In Part 2 the action begins somewhere in the west of Turkey or in Thrace; we listen to reports of conquest by Tamburlaine's generals through the length and breadth of Africa; we follow Theridamas in his adventure at Balsera. For the most part we are not even sure where Tamburlaine is. For these reasons, despite the approximate equality of his shares in the two parts, our general impression from reading is that he is less prominent in Part 2 than in Part 1. In fact, he says as much but does far less.

A moment ago I referred to Tamburlaine's indifference to cosmic processes, which becomes at times defiance of the gods—as when he threatens war in revenge for Zenocrate's death or for his own sickness, or when he burns the Koran. It might seem that Marlowe is suggesting the direct interposition of a divine power when the fatal sickness comes upon Tamburlaine sixteen lines after he has defied Mahomet, or when Sigismund is destroyed, against the odds, after breaking the oath which he swore by Christ. But no character in the final scenes comes near hinting that Tamburlaine has been stricken through blasphemy (though in Part 1 Zenocrate feared that he would pay for his treatment of Bajazeth and Zabena). And although Orcanes is convinced that in Sigismund's defeat Christ has spoken, Gazellus is ready to see only the chance of war in operation:

> 'Tis but the fortune of the wars, my lord,
> Whose power is often proved a miracle.
>
> [Pt. 2, II. iii. 31–32]

And even if the divine powers are to be seen as exacting retribution, they are singularly deaf to prayer. In V. ii. Callapine thinks the Turks may come upon Tamburlaine, weary from the siege of Babylon,

> And so revenge our latest grievous loss,
> If God or Mahomet send any aid.   [Pt. 2, V. ii. 10–11]

A moment later he formally prays to Mahomet for help:

> Ah, sacred Mahomet, thou that hast seen
> Millions of Turks perish by Tamburlaine,
> Kingdoms made waste, brave cities sacked and burnt,
> And but one host is left to honor thee,
> Aid thy obedient servant Callapine,
> And make him, after all these overthrows,
> To triumph over cursèd Tamburlaine.   [Pt. 2, V. ii. 24–30]

Neither God nor Mahomet gives the help the Turks depend on, and indeed the captive kings and Olympia and the total population of Babylon die without guilt. Certain processes seem to be implied, but not a personal care felt by a divine power. The gods, in fact, seem more remote here than in Part 1, or perhaps we should say that their indifference to human welfare has here been demonstrated as extreme. The ultimate outrage—Sigismund's breaking of his most solemn oath (an outrage against the thing sworn by, and against the men sworn to), the supreme defiance of his people's collective wisdom in Tamburlaine's affront to Islam —appears merely and automatically to institute a compensating process.

The play indeed is humanist, but not Christian humanist. And this impression is strengthened by the fact that Tamburlaine has now become the technician. In Part 1 his eloquence, his appearance, his strong arm, the sense of invincibility he gave to his men —these were enough, it seemed, to ensure victory. But here in III. ii. he tells his sons about scaling walls, undermining towns, choosing the "quinque-angle form" for fortification. Then he proceeds to a full description of how a fort should be built and defended. In the following scene he is echoed by Theridamas, giving orders for the reduction of Balsera. With the magnitude of the conquest, these men have had to become scientifically competent, and we are bound to feel that the earlier *brio* has gone.

Indeed a tiredness seems manifestly displayed at the siege of Babylon. But here we should note a textual puzzle. In Part 1, whenever the different-colored tents are mentioned, the order is white-red-black (signifying mercy to all, mercy only to the unarmed, no mercy for any). Yet in V. i. of Part 2 we are told that the city has lasted out until Tamburlaine's "last day's dreadful siege" (29), and yet we are twice told that the tents are red ("vermilion," 86; "bloody," 103). This could be Marlowe's forgetfulness of his own symbolism; it could be a sign of incipient disorder in Tamburlaine's arrangements. In any event, it is surprising that Theridamas and Techelles come to the Governor with an offer of mercy:

> To save thy life, and us a little labor,
> Yield speedily the city to our hands, . . .   [50–51]

When the Governor refuses, Techelles draws attention to the breaking of custom:

> Yield, foolish governor; we offer more
> Than ever yet we did to such proud slaves
> As durst resist us till our third day's siege.   [57–59]

The Governor still resists; the assault is successfully made; the Governor is spectacularly killed and the people are drowned. It makes a grim show, but there is less refinement in the cruelty than there was in Bajazeth's cage or the chariot drawn by the kings. Babylon gave some trouble in the taking: the first result was an unexpected offer of mercy, the second a slapdash slaughter without glee. Some readers may wonder if it was Marlowe who was growing tired, hard put to it for fresh device. But the tendency of the play may incline us to the view that he was dramatizing a tiredness which was psychologically accurate. Afterwards it seems as if the imminence of death gives Tamburlaine renewed energy, with which he can defeat Callapine once more and trace on the map his great march of conquest.

At the beginning of this essay, I was able to point to the neatness of Part 1, where we follow Tamburlaine's fortunes in five clearly marked stages. Each act, moreover, seemed to be given a special character, built up on contrasts peculiar to it. Part 2, though nominally divided into acts, has nothing of this neatness. The Sigismund episode occupies the opening scenes of Act I and the opening scenes of Act II. Callapine escapes from Tamburlaine's prison in I. iii. meets the other Turks in III. i, confronts Tamburlaine in III. v. The Olympia episode occupies two scenes in Act III and (after an interval of two major scenes) one scene in Act IV. The siege of Babylon, as we have seen, plays no necessary part in the struggle between Tamburlaine and Callapine. The act division may be Marlowe's, as that of Part 1 was surely his; but he does not seem to have paid it much attention, does not seem to have worked with a sense of five-unit composition. In fact, that would probably have stood in the way of Part 2's special effect. Tamburlaine, as we first saw him, was a man who imposed his own pattern on the world: we may draw back from the dispatching of Agydas, the tormenting of Bajazeth, the slaughter of the Virgins, but these people suffer what Tamburlaine has imposed on them; it is true that Bajazeth's and Zabena's escape through suicide suggests a limit to his power, but it is not a limit that exists within the frame of a lifetime; and, though at the end there is a conflict between the claims of conquest and beauty, it does not diminish Tamburlaine's avowed self-confidence or his power to do what his resolved will chooses. Because a human will thus decrees the shape of events, the pattern imposed is neat and readily discernible. But it has become evident, I think, that in Part 2 the world is not one which Tamburlaine has at his command. It is a world where other men win victories, though not against him, where his jailer is corruptible and his most important prisoner escapes to fight again, where Zenocrate cannot be saved, where his education of Calyphas goes wrong, where his follower Theridamas loses his love through a simple trick, where something becomes oddly disordered at the siege of Babylon. Outside the immediate world of men there are, as we have seen, cosmic processes at work. Within the world of men there is an appearance of the haphazard. Of course, the hero is still a major force, compelling devotion from his main followers, inflicting anguish on those who oppose him. But he is no longer in full control: he cannot be properly in control in this newly chaotic arena. And so Marlowe seems to have let the play give an impression of the haphazard, bringing in an element of surprise foreign to Part 1. The death of Zenocrate is unprepared for; so too is the whole Olympia episode; the Babylon affair is a work of supererogation, as so many of men's concernments are. The very stroke of death for Tamburlaine could be chance, or could be the result of a particularly rash moment of self-aggrandizement.

Even so, there were guiding lines. As the prologue tells us, we see the deaths of the hero and his wife. It was necessary, too, that we should see Tamburlaine's attempts to provide against death by training his sons, and that we should see the failure of that—in Calyphas' cowardice and irreverence (for there are both strains in him) and in the sedulous second-rateness of Amyras and Celebinus. We had to see the continuing existence of an opposition to Tamburlaine's empire, an opposition finally enduring in Callapine's escape after defeat in Act V. And, of course, having recognized the need for the Tamburlaine scenes to be frequently static (as the hero lets others work for him, or tries to prepare for his empire's future, or hurls defiance at the heavens who will not join battle with him), Marlowe saw to it that scenes of movement and of inactivity alternated. Yet as a whole it was a deliberately casual structure that he employed, the only structure possible for the full development of the effect central to Part 2.

That *II Tamburlaine* was written because of *I Tamburlaine's* success seems indubitable, but I hope I may have been able to suggest that, in the range of its effects and in the depth of its implication, the sequel has some right to be considered the greater play. In any event, the differences between these closely linked plays are extreme. Part 2 may echo its predecessor, but never was there an echo more self-creative than this.

ROBERT KIMBROUGH

1 TAMBURLAINE
A Speaking Picture in a Tragic Glass

That Christopher Marlowe was not an impetuous young free-thinker who wrote over the head of his audience, but was a dedicated dramatic artist who knew well the ideas of his age, considered popular drama a serious art-form, and demonstrated a consummate skill in exercising his audience's potential aesthetic strength while he satisfied its basic desire to be entertained would amount to a series of commonplaces were not the few established facts of Marlowe's life so loaded with provocative connotations. A just fascination with the man and thinker has led to a neglect of the artist, his works being read as biographical documents and philosophical treatises—for, indeed, Marlowe left *only* his plays, a few poems, and some translations; no Shavian prologues, Keatsian letters, or Miltonic commonplace book in which may be found his ideas plainly stated. But to hear Marlowe speaking for himself through, say, Tamburlaine, we must throw out the basic assumption of dramatic criticism: that Shakespeare is not Macbeth, that Miller is not Willy Loman. Although Una Ellis-Fermor was the leading advocate of the theory that Marlowe consciously and subconsciously created his characters and themes only as expressions of his inner conflicts and radical ideas, even she could not show why in Marlowe's case we should cease thinking of drama as one of the more impersonal art forms; she could say only

First published in *Renaissance Drama* VII (1964):20–34. Reprinted by permission of the author and Northwestern University Press.

that "Marlowe's successful incursion into drama is one of the notable paradoxes of the history of that art."[1]

Roy Battenhouse, in reaction to the romanticizing of Miss Ellis-Fermor and others, tried to show in 1941 that Marlowe was a traditionally straightforward, typically moral Elizabethan, a position recently endorsed, in part, by the late Leo Kirschbaum and, more strongly, by Douglas Cole.[2] But the reaction is as illogical as the original assertion; biography and criticism are separate arts. They can be mutually reinforcing and enlightening only when each is complete in its own right. For example, we should try to understand the relative importance of the Baines document *and* the M.A. in theological and moral philosophy in Marlowe's biography before we bring either (preferably both) into criticism of *Doctor Faustus*. Furthermore, by following too closely the matter of Marlowe's possible atheism, or free-thinking, we pass by what might be an important approach to the more important matter of the relevance of his achievement for the study of Shakespeare. Both were successful dramatists writing for the same audience, but to Marlowe fell the task of stopping the "jigging veins of rhyming mother wits" and starting new dramatic conventions.

If, then, we are to distinguish between Marlowe's own ideas and those which are part of objective dramatic method, if we are to use his plays as valid supplementary biographical evidence, and if we are to delve a little further into the poetics of drama from 1587 to 1611, a close analysis of Marlowe's achievement as a dramatist and a total evaluation of his contribution to Elizabethan drama are needed. Irving Ribner last year in this publication pointed out that such a reconsideration is desirable, that signs of it are in the air, and that the task will be the work of more than one person. But Marlowe's anniversary year is a fitting time to define further the nature of his achievement and to suggest what was his contribution. I should like then to focus in this essay on *1 Tamburlaine* not just because it was Marlowe's first play and because it has been considered more often than others as a vehicle for the expression of personal thought, but mainly because even

---

[1] "Paul Kocher, *Christopher Marlowe*" (a rev.) *RES* XXIV (1948):248.

[2] Battenhouse, *Marlowe's "Tamburlaine"* (Nashville, 1941); Kirschbaum, "Introduction," *The Plays of Christopher Marlowe,* Meridian Books (Cleveland and New York, 1962); and Cole, *Suffering and Evil in the Plays of Christopher Marlowe* (Princeton, 1962).

the most recent criticism still does not recognize Marlowe's dramatic innovation and technical control in the play.

David Bevington, in his interesting structural analysis (unfortunately weakened because of his belief that "the homogeneous structure of the two [*Tamburlaine*] plays . . . inevitably suggests an entity of ten acts"), states that Marlowe's use of a traditional moral structure came into conflict with his subject; the ambiguous final effect left by the play is, then, simply an "ironic result."[3] Moody Prior also believed that the ambiguity of the play was the result of an artistic lapse on Marlowe's part.[4] To him the lack of control leads to failure, whereas to Bevington it provides an accidental Empsonian richness. Although Douglas Cole recognizes two separate plays, he needs the second to illustrate his thesis concerning Marlowe's use of irony and can only conclude that *1 Tamburlaine* presents "a paradox which is more of a problem than a resolution."[5] The main strength of Cole's analysis of the play is his demonstration of Marlowe's ability to dramatize acute suffering and grief, but it is just such an ability which J. B. Steane denies the playwright. In fact with Steane, whose study was issued during the past spring, we tend to come full circle, returning on Una Ellis-Fermor: "the mind of the author, as we see it in his play, is divided. A particular combination of evils is justified and even gloried in, though opposed fitfully by the misgivings, revulsions or positive assertions of normal moral judgment."[6] My own opinion is far otherwise: *1 Tamburlaine* is a carefully constructed play that successfully, but rudely, presented playgoers and playwrights with a conception of drama that integrated pageantry, blank verse, and ethical study—a study that, unlike plays stemming from the English Morality tradition, deliberately eschewed open preachment of the moral.[7]

I

This threefold purpose is forcefully indicated in the prologue, which has often and rightly been called Marlowe's "manifesto":

[3] *From "Mankind" to Marlowe* (Cambridge, Mass., 1962), pp. 199–217.

[4] *The Language of Tragedy* (New York, 1947), pp. 44–46.

[5] *Suffering and Evil*, pp. 86–103.

[6] *Marlowe: A Critical Study* (Cambridge, 1964), pp. 111–12.

[7] Because of the scope and nature of the present essay I cannot go into matters of structure and style, but see Bevington, pp. 199–211, and Donald Peet, "The Rhetoric of *Tamburlaine*," *ELH* XXVI (1959):137–55.

From jigging veins of rhyming mother wits,
And such conceits as clownage keeps in pay,
We'll lead you to the stately tent of war,
Where you shall hear the Scythian Tamburlaine
Threat'ning the world with high astounding terms
And scourging kingdoms with his conquering sword.
View but his picture in this tragic glass,
And then applaud his fortunes as you please.

Subtly in manner but boldly in method, Marlowe announced that the audience would "hear" a manner of expression which would be shocking and amazing, full of surprise and wonder, and that the audience should watch Tamburlaine's majestic actions in order to decide for itself whether or not it wished to applaud or hiss. The last line should not be taken as a typical Elizabethan plea for applause. Because it comes at the beginning of the play and because of the way in which the play develops, it is meant to suggest that within pageantry and through amazing rhetoric, the play will present a study of a grand figure in action, judgment of whom is left to the viewers. Although Marlowe's calling his play a "tragic glass" would certainly have indicated that the action should be entertained with the same attitude that would be assumed in reading a work like *A Mirror for Magistrates, The Steel Glass,* or *The English Mirror,* I cannot agree with Battenhouse that Marlowe's purpose was openly, forcefully didactic; rather, the marked innovation in the play is that it presents a picture of individual conduct which, like the high astounding terms, is shocking, and which by its very nature must have evoked an ethical evaluation from at least the more learned spectators.

The materials for the picture have been discussed so often, and so many works have been suggested in which Marlowe might have found them, that in 1945 Hallett Smith could well say, "the known sources are already so many that the term *source* is ceasing to have a meaning in this context."[8] In spite of the many possibilities that have been advanced, all scholars agree in the main with the thesis of C. H. Herford and A. Wagner, presented in 1883, that the primary sources are Pedro Mexia's *Silva de varia lección,* 1542, and Petrus Perondinus' *Vita magni Tamerlanis,* 1553.[9] From these

---

[8] "Tamburlaine and the Renaissance," *Elizabethan Studies and Other Essays in Honor of George F. Reynolds* (Boulder, 1945), p. 129.

[9] *The Academy* XXIV (1883):265–66.

works Marlowe could have derived the basic outline of Tamburlaine's character and the plot for his play. Both authors painted Tamburlaine as ambitious, proud, and cruel, but intelligent and fair in dealings with his own forces. Both emphasized that Tamburlaine rose from obscurity, that he was ruthless yet victorious in all his campaigns, and that he retired to a peaceful existence in which he died a quiet, natural death. Here was the stuff of drama, but why an ethical study?

Although the sources say Tamburlaine retired undefeated, the rest of the information that they present certainly affords material for a play in the traditional morality pattern. Marlowe must have realized, however, that to change the Tamburlaine story would have meant failure at the box office, for, as W. D. Briggs, Alfred Harbage, and Miss M. C. Bradbrook have reminded us, the Elizabethan audience had a sharp and lively interest in seeing historical material acted out, and the history of Tamburlaine was available not only to scholars such as Marlowe, but to the reading public. In 1571, Thomas Fortescue translated the Mexia version in his popular *Forest,* as did George Whetstone in *The English Mirror,* of 1586. Pierre de la Primaudaye used Perondinus when he told the story of the Scythian conqueror in his *French Academy,* written in 1577 and translated into English in 1586. Thus the history of Tamburlaine was probably as well known in 1587 as any that appeared in popular Elizabethan works. How extensive the Elizabethan reading audience was we still do not know, but it is a reasonable assumption that Tamburlaine was a familiar figure to many of the playgoers. Regardless of whether Marlowe might have wanted to do so or not, he could not have adapted his sources to show a fall from high estate. But the problem of a ruthlessly ambitious, amoral hero who never suffered defeat could be treated ethically with no changes in the basic characterization and story of Tamburlaine.

II

In *1 Tamburlaine* the inner quality which Marlowe chose to study was man's natural ambition, or urge to aspire, a quality which could lead either to virtù or to Christian virtue because each state could be attained only by actively following the will. Yet when Tamburlaine says "That virtue solely is the sum of

glory" he only mouths traditional terms. For him the sum of glory
is an earthly crown; what he calls virtue, the world called ambition. Tamburlaine's motivation and the theme of ambition are
made explicit at the end of Act II, scene vii, in the famous "thirst
of reign" speech. The first six lines are objective statement, and
the rest reveal the way in which Tamburlaine has rationalized his
actions. When reading the speech, one should keep in mind Marlowe's "bombastic" method: the padding, or inflating, of basic
syntactic units with verbal material for special effect. I have put
the essential elements in italics; but the bombast is itself important, for it helps to confirm what the earlier action has implied: Tamburlaine is self-conscious, sensuous, imaginative, intelligent, and dynamic:

> *The thirst of reign and sweetness of a crown,*
> That caused the eldest son of heavenly Ops
> To thrust his doting father from his chair,
> And place himself in the imperial heaven,
> *Moved me to manage arms against thy [Cosroe's] state.*
> What better precedent than mighty Jove?
> *Nature,* that framed us of four elements
> Warring within our breasts for regiment,
> *Doth teach us all to have aspiring minds.*
> *Our souls,* whose faculties can comprehend
> The wondrous architecture of the world
> And measure every wandering planet's course,
> Still climbing after knowledge infinite,
> And always moving as the restless spheres,
> *Wills us to wear ourselves and never rest,*
> *Until we reach the ripest fruit of all,*
> That perfect bliss and sole felicity,
> *The sweet fruition of an earthly crown.*   [Pt. 1, II. vii. 12–29]

That man's natural appetite became inordinate after Adam's fall,
making man's four elements war "within our breasts for regiment," was traditional. But God gave man the gift of reason to
discipline his microcosmic elements, and Tamburlaine indicates
that he knows the function of reason in the five lines that follow
"Our souls." By his conclusion, however, it is clear that he considers reason to be subordinate to natural appetite. Whether or
not we agree with the romantic critics from Ingram through Boas
that this is "bathos" is beside the point; the conclusion was prob-

ably shocking bathos to many in Marlowe's audience, for Tamburlaine has not agreed to the *a priori* assumptions that God ruled nature, that God-given reason could rule natural passions, and that man should use his reason to come into harmony with God's macrocosm by ordering his own microcosm. Believing that when man used his reason to fulfill his designated function in life he could look forward to the ripest fruit of all, that perfect bliss and sole felicity, the sweet fruition of a *heavenly* crown, the orthodox might well have gasped when Tamburlaine builds his speech following traditional concepts, but reaches the climax of "an earthly crown." The traditional scheme of things is undercut; God is ignored and reason is perverted to the role of nature's servant rather than her master.

Because Marlowe did not show the audience how Tamburlaine's character and choice of life evolved, he had to bring the audience to Tamburlaine through the reactions of others to him and his way of life. Most of the characters see Tamburlaine as either entirely glorious or entirely evil, and any audience is, of course, free to choose sides. But to do so would be to fail to react to the total portrait which Marlowe carefully sketched. Of all the characters only Zenocrate maintains the kind of perspective necessary in a choral figure, and it is through her that the audience must come to its final judgment of Tamburlaine.

She appears in Act I mainly for structural reasons: she is taken prisoner in Mycetes' and Cosroe's Persia while enroute from Bajazeth in Turkey to her father, the King of Egypt, and her fiance, the King of Arabia, in order to suggest and reinforce the main tripartite development of the play. But in the second section of the play Marlowe began to give her enough independence so that her points of view are not merely echoes of the hero's, as are the speeches of his friends. On the other hand, she is not forced into a position independent of Tamburlaine by the protagonist's actions, as are Cosroe, Bajazeth, and the opponents in the third section. Tamburlaine never forces his attentions on her, even though he is immediately taken by her beauty. Zenocrate's special independence from the hero is further reinforced by diction and imagery: as Harry Levin has observed, she is always described in earthly terms and in metaphors and similes of Venus and the Moon, while Tamburlaine is described in terms of air and fire and in figures using Mars and the Sun. But this same imagery implies attraction; as a result, Zenocrate's reactions are both objective and subjective. When she reveals in Act III, scene ii, that she has fallen in love with Tamburlaine, and Agydas, in the role of confidant, recalls Zenocrate's initial reactions to the Scythian, the contrast of the speeches projects the change that has come over Zenocrate, a change which reflects the ambivalence of Tamburlaine's "picture in this tragic glass."

We, audience and readers, are like Zenocrate both repulsed by and attracted to Tamburlaine: we can hardly fail to be thrilled by the amazing rise of one from humble obscurity to dazzling prominence, but we would have to be callous not to be appalled by the means of ascent. Fair with his friends he is; but what he does to those whom he takes for opponents and enemies cannot even be called "another question"—it is unspeakable. When in Act IV, scene ii, at the beginning of the last part of the play, Tamburlaine mounts his throne by means of Bajazeth's back, we both see and hear a perfect example of the interwoven appeal and terror of this fortunate scourge of God:

> Now clear the triple region of the air,
> And let the majesty of heaven behold
> Their scourge and terror tread on emperors.
> Smile stars that reigned at my nativity,
> And dim the brightness of their neighbor lamps;
> Disdain to borrow light of Cynthia,
> For I, the chiefest lamp of all the earth,
> First rising in the east with mild aspect,
> But fixèd now in the meridian line,
> Will send up fire to your turning spheres
> And cause the sun to borrow light of you.
>
> .   .   .   .
>
> Then, when the sky shall wax as red as blood,
> It shall be said I made it red myself,
> To make me think of naught but blood and war.
>
>   [Pt. 1, IV. ii. 30–40, 53–55]

These last three lines show us that in spite of his inherent majestic appeal we are watching a sinful man, blood being for the Elizabethan a sign of sin which recalled man's first ethical aberration—the murder of Abel by Cain. But tradition also taught

that man would be forgiven his sins on the day of judgment when
Christ's blood would appear in the firmament, as Faustus recalls
just before his death. Thus lines of Tamburlaine's speech which
may read for us as no more than bragging bombast were calcu-
lated to trigger a complicated response in Marlowe's audience.

Even if this audience, which was forced by law to attend twice
each week services filled with lengthy homiletic disquisition,
missed the rhetorical subtleties of Marlowe's speeches, surely the
action of the last part of the play, the siege of Damascus, must
have startled a good many. When Tamburlaine asks Zenocrate
at the spectacular feast of crowns why she is depressed, she
answers,

> My lord, to see my father's town besieged,
> The country wasted, where myself was born,
> How can it but afflict my very soul?   [Pt. 1, IV. iv. 63–65]

And as she continues, she brings up the point which Marlowe
made the central thematic concern of the last section of the play:

> If any love remain in you, my lord,
> Or if my love unto your majesty
> May merit favor at your highness' hands,
> Then raise your siege from fair Damascus' walls,
> And with my father take a friendly truce.
>
> [Pt. 1, IV. iv. 66–70]

She places all hope for her father's safety in an appeal based on
love, but love is not strong enough to win Tamburlaine from his
ambitious way: he must have his earthly crown.

But Tamburlaine's decision to kill the young emissaries of Damascus and to lay waste the city because his "honour swears it
shall be perform'd" has its effect on him: it makes Tamburlaine
pause to consider the problem Marlowe had been working toward.
Softened by Zenocrate's plea for her father and knowing her sen-
timents concerning Damascus, Tamburlaine reveals in the long
and beautiful soliloquy, "Ah, fair Zenocrate," that he has awak-
ened to the problem of love in juxtaposition with his desire for
reign. In Zenocrate's tear-filled eyes

> . . . angels in their crystal armors fight
> A doubtful battle with my tempted thoughts
> For Egypt's freedom and the Soldan's life,

His life that so consumes Zenocrate,
Whose sorrows lay more siege unto my soul
Than all my army to Damascus' walls;
And neither Persians' sovereign nor the Turk
Troubled my senses with conceit of foil
So much by much as doth Zenocrate.   [Pt. 1, V. ii. 88–96]

After the definition of the problem, Tamburlaine wonders "What is beauty" that it has the power to make him suffer in this way. The thirteen lines that follow offer a stimulating picture of a poet's attempt to project human beauty, but they do not answer the question of the function of beauty. Tamburlaine can only conclude that beauty is something "Which into words no virtue can digest." But the word "virtue" reminds Tamburlaine of his special conception of virtue and suggests an answer to the problem at hand. He turns in disgust from his poetic mood and harshly says:

But how unseemly is it for my sex,
My discipline of arms and chivalry,
My nature, and the terror of my name,
To harbor thoughts effeminate and faint!
                              [Pt. 1, V. ii. 111–14]

After literally finding himself again, he is able to describe forcefully his conception of the function of beauty in human society:

Save only that in beauty's just applause,
With whose instinct the soul of man is touched;
And every warrior that is rapt with love
Of fame, of valor, and of victory,
Must needs have beauty beat on his conceits.
I thus conceiving and subduing both,
. . . .
Shall give the world to note, for all my birth,
That virtue solely is the sum of glory,
And fashions men with true nobility.
                      [Pt. 1, V. ii. 115–120, 125–27]

"Thus conceiving" that the purpose of beauty is only to serve as an approving audience for brave deeds, and "subduing" its power, Tamburlaine concludes that his concept of virtue over-rules all other human attributes. And he is quite right; his idea of virtue does indeed isolate him from all that is moral, all that is human. The whole tradition that beauty is a potential creative force which can be activated through love is alien to Tamburlaine.

Because there is continuous action on stage as the play comes to a climax, the tone of this speech after the virgins' death and the tone of Zenocrate's which follows the suicides of the Turks are both felt in the final statement of the play. Up to this point the plight of Bajazeth and Zabina has been treated as grimly humorous by Tamburlaine, and Marlowe has built Bajazeth as a comic Herod. Here Bajazeth still rants, but the man is far from comic. Utter despair has fallen over him, and his reflections on his low estate are so filled with pathos and anguish that the hand which was to paint the deaths of Faustus and Edward can be seen in the grotesque but profoundly moving deaths of the Turkish King and Queen. When Zenocrate enters and views the carnage, her words have an important place in establishing the final tone and effect of the play because her importance has been strengthened by the fact that Tamburlaine hesitated and began to question his way of life because of her. Within this new aura of dignity, she makes judgments which must have found sympathetic ears in the audience.

The first sixteen lines of Zenocrate's opening speech are a vivid, messenger-like recapitulation of the awfulness of the fall and sacking of Damascus. She then comes to the same kind of problem that troubled Tamburlaine: her reasonable love for humanity conflicts with her private love: "Ah, Tamburlaine, wert thou the cause of this, / That term'st Zenocrate thy dearest love?" (V. ii. 272–73). Although her heart yearns for Tamburlaine, she realizes at last that his ambition is terrible, and she is led to make a moral pronouncement over the Turks. Marlowe's sources make the same kind of traditional *De Casibus* statement with regard to Bajazeth's fall; however, the dramatist broadened the moral statement so that it became a moral judgment of Tamburlaine:

> Those that are proud of fickle empery
> And place their chiefest good in earthly pomp,
> Behold the Turk and his great emperess!
> Ah, Tamburlaine my love, sweet Tamburlaine,

That fights for scepters and for slippery crowns,
Behold the Turk and his great emperess!

. . . .

Ah, mighty Jove and holy Mahomet,
Pardon my love! Oh, pardon his contempt
Of earthly fortune and respect of pity, . . .

[Pt. 1, V. ii. 289–94, 300–302]

Zenocrate understands that she too has sinned and goes on to ask pardon for not having had sympathy for the Turks. This confession heightens the tension and inner anguish she experiences when told that the final battle has been joined between Tamburlaine and the forces of Egypt and Arabia:

Now shame and duty, love and fear presents
A thousand sorrows to my martyred soul.
Whom should I wish the fatal victory,
When my poor pleasures are divided thus,
And racked by duty from my cursèd heart?

[Pt. 1, V. ii. 320–24]

Tamburlaine of course is victorious, and the play, in keeping with an established pattern, ends with a final crowning and a recapitulation of the theme. The crowning, this time of Zenocrate, is the fitting structural and thematic climax to the play, for she has risen from the reluctant captive of a shepherd brigand to the eager wife of the emperor of his world. But the effect is devastatingly ironic: all of her potentially humanizing love has been nullified and objectified by Tamburlaine's realization of his ambition: "The god of war resigns his room to me, / Meaning to make me general of the world" (V. ii. 387–88). The earthly crown has been gained beyond all doubt.

Tamburlaine then recounts his bloody deeds, ending his summary:

And such are objects fit for Tamburlaine,
Wherein, as in a mirror, may be seen
His honor, that consists in shedding blood
When men presume to manage arms with him.

[Pt. 1, V. ii. 412–15]

With the mention of "mirror," we realize that this is more than a concluding summary of the play. It is Marlowe's reminder of the final announcement in the prologue:

> View but his picture in this tragic glass,
> And then applaud his fortunes as you please.

Marlowe consciously projected a "picture in this tragic glass" of rampant ambition which the members of the audience could judge for themselves according to their own particular orientation.

III

Eugene Waith is inclined to believe that the audience was left breathless because Marlowe's portrait is Herculean, is full of characteristics which must evoke admiration.[10] But according to Frank B. Fieler it is just those characteristics which Marlowe gradually erased from his portrait so that the audience would be forced to judge Tamburlaine adversely.[11] The key to this typical critical divergence lies in the observation of Katherine Lever that in the play we see "a consistent picture of a man's rise to power through a rejection of humanity," but receive "the auditory image of a man's quest for divinity." Her conclusion might well have been that of the audience; *1 Tamburlaine* "is not a satisfying play. Our expectations are not fulfilled."[12] But lurking here is the reason for Marlowe's immediate success: the audience came to the theater with established expectations, but Marlowe, instead of invoking old responses, encouraged new, and the audience left prepared for more of this new drama.

That the play made an immediate impact we may assume merely because Marlowe was forced to write a hasty sequel. In 1590 Richard Jones must have felt that these three-year-old plays were enough in the public mind to make an octavo edition of them sell, and we may gather that his estimate was correct because editions continued to appear until 1606. Eight years after their debut, the two plays were still as profitable to the Admiral's Men as any others that they played in 1595.[13] Finally, the number of plays obviously patterned on *1 Tamburlaine* attests that play-

---

[10] *The Herculean Hero* (New York, 1962).
[11] *"Tamburlaine, Part I" and Its Audience* (Gainesville, Florida, 1962).
[12] "The Image of Man in *Tamburlaine, Part I*," *PQ* XXXV (1956):426.
[13] *Henslowe's Diary*, ed. W. W. Greg (London, 1907), pp. 10–14.

wrights competing with Marlowe knew what the public wanted —at least until Shakespeare became the rival poet.[14]

Tucker Brooke has shown the extent to which the magnificent spectacle afforded by Edward Alleyn as the grandiloquent Scythian who had kings as slaves captivated the London playgoers,[15] and Shakespeare's satiric remarks through the ignorant Pistol and the judicious Hamlet would have been pointless had they not referred to fact. Moreover, no one has ever dissented from the view that Marlowe's blank verse dialogue in *Tamburlaine* carried drama a giant-step forward. Still, overwhelming the eyes and ears of an audience may push a dramatist toward success, but will not carry him all the way. Even a Punch and Judy show, a court masque, or a Broadway musical has to have some hint of meaning in it. The novelty of sight and sound soon gives way to natural, human inquisitiveness. Regardless of how much the Elizabethans were entertained by Marlowe's spectacle and rhetoric, they must have come to some judgment of Tamburlaine. But Marlowe did not dictate that judgment; his dramatic technique was to present the viewers with a picture of ambition that was perfectly in keeping with sixteenth century moral thought, then allow them to draw their own conclusions by means of their own knowledge of good and evil. The audience could admire the Scythian conqueror for being the master of his own destiny, or hate him because of his evil nature.

Although the general playgoer may have hissed Tamburlaine and applauded Marlowe, the University Wits hissed both. Whether they got it from Aristotle, Horace, or Ascham, they all agreed out of habit that, as Sidney said, poetry "is an Art of *Imitation.* . . . A speaking *Picture,* with this end to teach and delight." The standard was absolute: no play could ignore decorum and still be a moving picture of nature, or forget to draw a moral and still entertain. The statement was a single measure with which a play either conformed, or did not. *1 Tamburlaine* kept decorum, showed natural ambition in action, and entertained; however, it did not come to any moral conclusion. The Univer-

[14] See John Bakeless, *The Tragicall History of Christopher Marlowe* (Cambridge, Mass., 1942), I, 238–48.

[15] "The Reputation of Christopher Marlowe," *The Transactions of the Connecticut Academy of Arts and Sciences* XXV (1922):347–408.

sity Wits knew from their study of Terence and Seneca that drama should have a moral, but to find one in Marlowe's plays seemed impossible. The natural villain never came to defeat, and the audience was told to judge as it pleased. It was Marlowe's failure to follow convention that led Greene to make his famous statement in 1588: "I could not make my verses iet vpon the stage in tragicall buskins, . . . daring God out of heauen with that Atheist *Tamburlan.* . . .: but let me rather openly pocket vp the Asse at *Diogenes* hand: then wantonlye set out such impious instances in intolerable poetrie: such mad and scoffing poets, that haue propheticall spirits, as bred of *Merlins* race, if there by anye in England that set the end of scollarisme in an English blank verse, I think it is the humor of a nouice that tickles them with selfe-loue."[16] This passage has always been read as an attack on the use of blank verse, but Greene's emphasis is clearly on the absence of "scollarisme." The form of the poetry was not "intolerable"; its "impious" content was wanton. It disregarded the fundamental principle of moral end.[17]

That it was Marlowe who started this new trend in writing is clear from Greene's reference to Tamburlaine and his pun on Marlowe's name. Greene's friend Nashe in 1589 also criticized the novice playwright for initiating the end of a tradition in composition: "I am not ignorant how eloquent our gowned age is grown of late; . . . which I impute, not so much to the perfection of Arts, as to the seruile imitation of vaine glorious Tragedians, who contend not so seriously to excell in action, as to embowell the cloudes in a speech of comparison. . . . But heerein I cannot so fully bequeath them to folly, as their ideot Art-Masters, that intrude themselues to our eares as the Alcumists of eloquence, who (mounted on the stage of arrogance) thinke to out-braue better pennes with the swelling bumbast of bragging blanke verse."[18] Nashe continued his criticism four pages later: "when an irregular Ideot, that was vp to the eares in diunitie, before euer he met with *probable* in the Vniuersitie, shall leaue *pro et*

---

[16] "To the Gentlemen Readers," *Perimedes the Blacke-Smith,* in *Life and Works,* ed. A. B. Grosart (London, 1883), VII, 7–8.

[17] See Madeleine Doran, *Endeavors of Art* (Madison, 1954), pp. 85–100, and throughout, for the clearest analysis of the moral bias of Elizabethan drama.

[18] "To the Gentlemen Stvdents of Both Vniversities" [preface to Greene's *Menaphon*], *Works of Nashe,* ed. R. B. McKerrow (Oxford, 1904–10; reprinted 1958), III, 311.

contra before hee can scarcely pronounce it, and come to correct common-weales, that neuer heard of the name of Magistrate before hee came to *Cambridge,* it is no meruaile if euery Alehouse vaunt the table of the world turned vpside downe, since the child beateth his father, and the Asse whippeth his Master." Nashe wrote this in 1589; later his enmity was to cool, and in 1592 he defended Marlowe against Greene's attack in *A Groats-Worth of Wit.* But Greene's second attack was not on professional grounds, but "pious." By 1592 Marlowe's method of presentation was the method of the new wave of drama.

We should not criticize Greene and Nashe for their indignation in 1588 and 1589, for Marlowe's dramatic method had not yet reached perfection. The Tamburlaine story had no beginning and end outside of birth and natural death; there was no dramatic problem of choice to start the significant part of Tamburlaine's life, and no decisive resolution based on that choice. Still Marlowe placed Zenocrate in the first play as a counter-theme, and tried to show Tamburlaine wavering in his ambitious desires. In *2 Tamburlaine* his study of the progressive mania which came with Tamburlaine's way of life was a masterful departure from his sources. He never again took such unmalleable material, but his efforts with his first two plays brought increasing rewards in his treatments of the plots and themes of *Faustus* and *Edward II,* in which he proved himself a master of his craft.

When the University Wits rushed to copy *1 Tamburlaine,* they used grandiose spectacle and bombastic blank verse, but followed the old Morality method of presentation.[19] Their plays failed and are forgotten; the tools used by Marlowe were taken up by Shakespeare. Although spectacle and sensation were part of drama's native heritage, blank verse was not itself new, and the theme of ambition was as traditional as *A Mirror for Magistrates,* Marlowe in *1 Tamburlaine* put structure and thematic purpose in his pageantry, lively English rhetoric and dramatic decorum into his verse, and treated ambition with objectivity instead of as a sermon *exemplum.* Marlowe's prologue was, indeed, a manifesto of something new.

[19] See Irving Ribner, "Greene's Attack on Marlowe: Some Light on *Alphonsus* and *Selinus,*" *SP* LII (1955):162–71; W. A. Armstrong, " 'Tamburlaine' and 'The Wounds of Civil War,' " *N & Q,* N. S., V (1958):381–83; and Cole, *Suffering and Evil,* pp. 99–100.

SUSAN RICHARDS

Marlowe's *TAMBURLAINE II*
A Drama of Death

In drama which treats a man who deals in death, death has a peculiar role of its own to play. Instead of being the concomitant of action, the precipitator of action, or simply the final cutting off of action, it becomes the enveloping action of the play, the continued and repeated action which has meaning in itself. Such a death-dealing man is Tamburlaine, as Christopher Marlowe conceived him, and such an action is central in Marlowe's second play about Tamburlaine.

Tamburlaine attained what is the ultimate power in terms of human life—the power of giving death, which is the essential power of the warrior-emperor, the cause and result of his position. In the course of *Tamburlaine II,* we see his power of death steadily growing. The action of the play is hung (rather loosely, at times) on a series of battles; there is one battle involved in each of the last four acts: the battle of the Turks and Christians, the siege of Balsera, the battle of Tamburlaine's forces against all the Turkish kings, and the siege of Babylon. The first act (which does not include a battle) presents the two forces of the Turks which will unite against Tamburlaine: Orcanes and the other contributory kings, and their emperor, Callapine, who in Scene ii is released from his captivity under Tamburlaine by his keeper, Almeda.

From these specific actions comes the over-all action of the

First published in *Modern Language Quarterly* XXVI (1965):375–87. Reprinted by permission of the author and the editors.

play, the increase of Tamburlaine's power on the battlefield, of his death-dealing power. Each act reveals this power augmented a little: in Act I, Tamburlaine is rejoined by his viceroy-generals, with their considerable forces; in Act II, the alliance of Christians and Turks formed against Tamburlaine in the first scene of Act I is broken by the treachery of the Christians; in Act III, Balsera is captured; in Act IV Tamburlaine is victorious over his Turkish enemies; and Act V begins with the victory in Babylon.

In his private fortunes, however, the reverse process occurs: Tamburlaine loses his power over death. The loss is first anticipated in Act I with a minor disaffection between Tamburlaine and his eldest son, Calyphas, because Calyphas is not enough of a warrior to suit Tamburlaine. But Zenocrate's death in Act II, Scene iv is the first great blow to Tamburlaine himself, and, as Theodore Spencer has noted, it is this event that first makes Tamburlaine aware of death as his opponent.[1] Zenocrate's funeral in Act III shows the extent of Tamburlaine's grief and allows for another brief altercation between him and Calyphas. The fourth act reveals the consequences of the dissension between Tamburlaine and Calyphas: Calyphas refuses to go to battle against the Turks, and Tamburlaine answers his refusal by killing him. The final act, of course, involves Tamburlaine's own illness and death.

Thus, although Tamburlaine's powers over death on the battlefield increase throughout the play, his subjection to death off the battlefield grows greater and greater and at last culminates in his own death. His quarrel with Calyphas comes over Calyphas' refusal to devote himself to the art of death, and the murder of Calyphas seems an act of sacrifice which Tamburlaine makes to that art. He suggests this view himself in his answer to his younger sons' pleas for mercy to their brother: "Stand up, my boys, and I will teach ye arms, / And what the jealousy of wars must do" (IV. ii. 28–29). That he sees the death of Zenocrate as the same kind of reversal is reflected in his address to death:

> Proud fury and intolerable fit,
> That dares torment the body of my love
> And scourge the scourge of the immortal God!
>
> [Pt. 2, II. iv. 78–80]

---

[1] Theodore Spencer, *Death and Elizabethan Tragedy: A Study of Convention and Opinion in the Elizabethan Drama* (Cambridge, Mass., 1936), p. 224.

The funeral rites which he performs for Zenocrate in Act III can, of course, be viewed as the ancient ritual of sacrifice to death.

But the role of death as conqueror of Tamburlaine becomes explicit only in the last act. In the beginning of Scene iii, when Tamburlaine himself is dying, he speaks thus:

> See where my slave, the ugly monster Death,
> Shaking and quivering, pale and wan for fear,
> Stands aiming at me with his murdering dart,
> Who flies away at every glance I give,
> And when I look away, comes stealing on.
> Villain, away, and hie thee to the field!
> I and mine army come to load thy bark
> With souls of thousand mangled carcasses.
> Look, where he goes! But see, he comes again
> Because I stay. Techelles, let us march
> And weary Death with bearing souls to hell.   [V. iii. 67–77]

Death is revealed at this point as a kind of Mephistopheles to Tamburlaine's Faustus—the servant who gives unlimited power only to become the master.[2]

Tamburlaine goes out to fight, but his enemy runs away, leaving him again to face death, which he finally recognizes as his ruler:

> The monarch of the earth,
> And eyeless monster that torments my soul,
> Cannot behold the tears ye shed for me,
> And therefore still augments his cruelty.   [V. iii. 216–19]

This recognition of the true nature of his relation to death comes to Tamburlaine when, at the pinnacle of his power, his sacrifices to death in the battlefield have increased enormously. In the last significant battle, the battle of Babylon, there is the only real picture of wholesale destruction that we get in *Tamburlaine II,* the shooting of the governor and the drowning of the populace:

---

[2] G. I. Duthie, in "The Dramatic Structure of Marlowe's *Tamburlaine the Great, Parts I and II," English Studies,* n.s., *E&S,* I (1948):117–26, also sees the play as a struggle with death, but considers Tamburlaine partially triumphant, on the basis of Tamburlaine's own notions about his death. Those notions are discussed at the end of this essay.

Thousands of men, drowned in Asphaltis' lake,
Have made the water swell above the banks,
And fishes, fed by human carcasses,
Amazed, swim up and down upon the waves, . . .

[V. i. 202–5]

The structure of the play, then, is based on the incidents which demonstrate Tamburlaine's power over death and the revelation of death power over him, culminating in his final triumphant massacre at Babylon and his own death.

The episodes which somewhat impair this structure are the encounters of Christians and Turks and the Olympia-Theridamas incidents. The problem here is not irrelevance, as has sometimes been charged; these incidents fit in well with the theme of the play. It is the remembrance of the Turks' slaughter of Christians in the past which persuades the Christians to break their truce, and the broken truce results in their deaths—another sacrifice of lives in the name of death which reduces the threat to Tamburlaine's own powers of destruction. The Olympia-Theridamas encounters are, as H. L. Gardner has stated[3] in a way parallel to Zenocrate's death—the lover loses his beloved to death, though in the case of Olympia the death is greatly desired. (There is an echo here of, "But let me die, my love; yet let me die," as in II. iv. 66.)

Olympia's speeches are interesting in the light of the death theme because, in her desire to rejoin her husband and son by dying, she becomes almost a priestess or nun dedicated to death:

My lord and husband's death, with my sweet son's
. . . .
Forbids my mind to entertain a thought
That tends to love, but meditate on death,
A fitter subject for a pensive soul.   [IV. iii. 22–27]

And when Theridamas proposes to spend his life in "sweet discourse of love" with her, she replies,

No such discourse is pleasant in mine ears,
But that where every period ends with death,
And every line begins with death again.   [IV. iii. 46–48]

---

[3] Helen L. Gardner, "The Second Part of 'Tamburlaine the Great,' " *MLR* XXXVII (1942):22.

Theridamas' desire for the ointment with which he thinks to preserve himself from death, and Olympia's demonstration of the ointment's power on her own throat, provide another sacrifice to death, parallel to Tamburlaine's attempt to usurp power from death, only to be foiled by it.

The problem of these scenes is not, then, one of relevance, but of focus: they pull attention away from the main action and actors for too long. More than 500 lines in the Ellis-Fermor text (based on the Huntington Library copy of O_1 [1590]) are devoted to the Olympia-Theridamas and Turkish-Christian encounters; thus a great deal of attention is drawn to the actions of characters not central to the over-all action of the play.[4]

But despite this problem of focus in *Tamburlaine II,* there is no real problem of unity of action. And beyond structural unity, there is another unifying force in the language of the play. In presenting his action of war and death, Marlowe uses a complex system of imagery which reveals Tamburlaine's vision of himself as superhuman and godlike in his involvement with death. As various critics have noted, this is most often done in images of light, heat, and color, Tamburlaine himself usually being pictured as flamelike, sunlike, or sometimes meteor-like.

Marlowe has been criticized for cramming these images in so fast and so thick that they distract the reader from the total progress of the play. Richard L. Hillier, for example, who has precisely analyzed the basic types of imagery Marlowe uses in the play, writes: "The imagery, qua imagery, is too concentrated . . . to permit the leisurely appreciation that contributes so much to the highest esthetic pleasure."[5]

But what Marlowe often achieves with his use and re-use of certain images is a peculiar kind of enforced or double value. He uses a series of images until they become equated, almost identified, with their referent; then he reverses the equation, and the referent itself becomes the image. The effect of this reversal is always a vast expansion of the meaning of the image pattern. For

[4] Clifford Leech, in his essay "The Structure of *Tamburlaine,*" *Tulane Drama Review* VIII, no. 4 (1964):46, says that Marlowe uses a "deliberately casual structure" in Part II because in this play Tamburlaine can no longer impose his pattern on the world, as he could in Part I.

[5] Richard L. Hillier, "The Imagery of Color, Light, and Darkness in the Poetry of Christopher Marlowe," in *Elizabethan Studies and Other Essays: In Honor of George F. Reynolds* (Boulder, 1945), p. 125.

example, as part of his light-imagery system he sets up the meteor image, which is first used at Zenocrate's funeral:

> And kindle heaps of exhalations
> That, being fiery meteors, may presage
> Death and destruction to th' inhabitants!
> Over my zenith hang a blazing star,
> That may endure till heaven be dissolved,
> Fed with the fresh supply of earthly dregs,
> Threatening a dearth and famine to this land! [III. ii. 3–9]

Then, later in the play, when Tamburlaine answers the curses of the Turkish captives, the equation is reversed:

> I will persist a terror to the world,
> Making the meteors, that like armèd men
> Are seen to march upon the towers of heaven,
> Run tilting round about the firmament
> And break their burning lances in the air,
> For honor of my wondrous victories. . . . . [IV. ii. 126–31]

This is the conversion of the meteor image to the original referent. And the reversal enlarges enormously the implications of the image envisioning a warrior as a meteor illuminates the figure of the warrior, but then to reverse the process and image a meteor as a warrior makes all the universe into a kind of cosmic battlefield.

The same thing happens with the imagery of blood. Blood, of course is the natural, vivid image with which the meaning of war can be made concrete, and Marlowe has characters swimming in blood, bathing in blood, marching under bloody flags, dyeing the ocean red with blood—all to represent in concrete form the fact of war. Then, when Tamburlaine gashes his arm to show his sons the insignificance of a wound, he announces, "Blood is the god of war's rich livery" (III. ii. 116), and the circle is completed; the original referent, war, in a transformed state, as a god, appears out of the blood which runs from Tamburlaine's wound. And of course the reversal leaves us with the identification between Tamburlaine and the god of war, thus universalizing the character of the protagonist.

This kind of closed imagery is very like a metaphysical conceit when we isolate its various instances; but the fact is that the open-

ing out into the image and the closing up into the original referent again continue throughout the play. Because of this constant
movement, the effect is not of the concentration of the senses on
one strand of imagery at a time, which would distract from the
action of the play, but of an unbroken web which, for all its in-
tricacy, enriches and encloses the unity of the action without dis-
tracting from it.

The fact that the play can bear this kind of enrichment says
something about it—specifically about its tone. This is a subject
which needs some investigation, because without thorough study
it is too easy to take the view that the dominant tone of *Tamburlaine II* is merely bombastic and rhetorical. The highly figured
language, the formal syntax, the welter of allusions to various
mythologies (Greek, Moslem, and disguised Judaeo-Christian),
the catalogues of sonorous but sometimes obscure place names—
all these add up to what is for many people merely a florid treatment of a flamboyant subject.

But when we examine the events contained in the play, we find
that the main action in every case (with the exception of several
personal acts of persuasion, like Callapine's of Almeda) is based
on various occasions of ritual observance, some of which still
maintain vestiges of ritual even in our deritualized culture today:
"peace talks," deathbed scenes and funerals, victory parades, returns of heads of state, surrenders, punishment of "war crimi-
nals," etc. Then when we consider that the language of drama in
the poetic tradition (which is, of course, intimately connected
with the ritual tradition) is a reflection of the thoughts and feelings of men, and that in the ritual situation these thoughts and
feelings are infused with the formalizing influence of the tradition, it is easier to understand the appropriateness of the tone of
Tamburlaine II. An examination of a specific instance is the best
way to demonstrate this appropriateness.

Let us take for a sample Tamburlaine's speech after the triumph over the entire Turkish force, when the conquest of Babylon is being planned, and Tamburlaine is reflecting on his expected return to his birthplace, Samarcanda, as an emperor. The
ritual nature of the situation is obvious; the classical triumph
was a carefully observed ceremony, it was the exhortation to the
next victory. This passage may stand as a representative or even

an epitome of the language of the play: it contains the place names, the mixture of mythologies, the formal syntax, the extended figures, and the characteristic rhetorical device of hyperbole. But the question is not so much what poetic devices it uses as what use it makes of them: whether they evoke the emotions, or merely ring on the ear; whether they are appropriate to the immediate situation and the total meaning and effect of the play; whether they serve a function or merely, as Una M. Ellis-Fermor has said of the imagery of the play as a whole, decorate the text.[6] Here is the passage (with an apparent borrowing from Spenser omitted):

> Now crouch, ye kings of greatest Asia,
> And tremble when ye hear this scourge will come
> That whips down cities and controlleth crowns,
> Adding their wealth and treasure to my store.
> The Euxine sea, north to Natolia,
> The Terrene, west, the Caspian, north-north-east,
> And on the south, Sinus Arabicus,
> Shall all be loaden with the martial spoils
> We will convey with us to Persia.
> Then shall my native city Samarcanda,
> And crystal waves of fresh Jaertis' stream,
> The pride and beauty of her princely seat,
> Be famous through the furthest continents;
> For there my palace royal shall be placed,
> Whose shining turrets shall dismay the heavens
> And cast the fame of Ilion's tower to hell.
> Thorough the streets, with troops of conquered kings,
> I'll ride in golden armor like the sun,
> And in my helm a triple plume shall spring,
> Spanglèd with diamonds, dancing in the air,
> To note me emperor of the three-fold world;
> . . . .
>
> Then in my coach, like Saturn's royal son
> Mounted his shining chariot gilt with fire,
> And drawn with princely eagles through the path
> Paved with bright crystal and enchased with stars,
> When all the gods stand gazing at his pomp,
> So will I ride through Samarcanda streets,

[6] U. M. Ellis-Fermor, *Christopher Marlowe* (London, 1927), pp. 51–54.

Until my soul, dissevered from this flesh,
Shall mount the milk-white way, and meet Him there.
To Babylon, my lords, to Babylon!   [IV. iv. 98–133]

First, a word about the syntax: whether the usual word order is inverted or not, the general effect is of descriptive passages, stately and slow in movement, building up to the particularizing of Tamburlaine himself. The division of subject and verb, or verb and object, by deliberate measured phrase and clause gives the effect of a piling up of glorious vision, and every time, Tamburlaine—his spoils, or his castle, or his empery, or his soul—is put on top of this mounting glory.

As for the particular devices, we may first notice the pun on the word scourge. The scourge in this case refers both to the wire whips, which Tamburlaine uses to urge his king-horses forward, and to Tamburlaine himself as the Scourge of God, a reference which has been established long before. The pun serves to make the transition from the immediate situation of the departure to the subject of Tamburlaine in his dual-role as the powerful Scourge of God.

Then there is the catalogue of geographic names: "The Euxine sea, north to Natolia; / The Terrene, west; the Caspian, north north-east; / And on the south, Sinus Arabicus; / Shall all be loaden. . . ." The effect Marlowe is trying for here, obviously, is the usual one of the catalogue—the building up of effect, the expansion or piling up of language, to represent the immensity of the burden. Another effect which this catalogue has is the movement in time and space, the dissociation with this particular place and time and a casting loose of the mind by the incantatory effect of the names (a typical device of ritual), a literary way of getting the reader to Samarcanda.

A conventional figure is the personification of the city of Tamburlaine's birth, Samarcanda, as sharing in the glory that he will bring home with him. There, he says, "My palace-royal shall be placed, / Whose shining turrets shall dismay the heavens, / And cast the fame of Ilion's tower to hell." The echo here of the Judaeo-Christian Tower of Babel is subtle and fits in quite neatly with the classical allusion to "Ilion's tower," especially in the notable irony that both of them fell.

Then comes the extended simile, first of all indirectly, out of the "golden armour like the sun," and eventually developing fully to the comparison with Jove, mounted in his chariot, pulled by "princely" eagles, with all the gods admiring him; this, of course, is the imagined moment of supreme triumph, when Tamburlaine envisions himself as almost godlike. Part of the success of the simile depends on what we make of the city of Samarcanda: are we to take it literally here, or is it a kind of mythical city? The element of myth is strongly suggested by the "crystal waves of fresh Jaertis' stream," like a River of Life, with the "shining turrets" that will dismay the heavens, and the connection of its streets with the path paved "with bright crystal and enchas'd with stars," where all the gods stand to gaze at Jove. The suggestion of a kind of heavenly city is too strong to miss, and the mythical element is appropriate, if not essential, in ritual terms.

The hyperbole with which this passage concludes, "So will I ride through Samarcanda streets, / Until my soul, dissevered from this flesh, / Shall mount the milk-white way, and meet him there," signs the final transformation of the streets of Samarcanda into a heavenly street. Again we find the element of mysticism here, a suggestion of Christian resurrection, which is functional in terms of the ritual nature of the situation and also in terms of Tamburlaine's own conception of himself as a kind of god.

The final irony of the passage is in the last cry, which reminds us that, in spite of this vision of Samarcanda as the gateway to the heavens, it is not to Samarcanda that they are going now, but to Babylon, the ancient city of sin, the gateway to Hell. This looks forward to the vision of Babylon in Act V, painted by Tamburlaine as having "pillars, higher than the clouds," where heroes have ridden and queens have danced (V. i. 64). The last cry also anticipates the fact that Tamburlaine will die outside the walls of Babylon, never having returned to Samarcanda.

On the purely literal level the final cry moves us on in the action of the play; and, having discovered the ritual nature of the language, its resonance in the meaning of the play, and its skillful movements from the particular situation to the thoughts and feelings of the speaker and back again, we may find that the language is also a clue to the source of the action, which may, to a modern reader, at first seem arbitrary. The murder of Calyphas for his refusal to join the warriors, the cruelty of Tamburlaine to his captives, the king-drawn chariot, and the shooting of the governor of Babylon as he hangs on the city walls—all these things which, when viewed through the eyes of "civilized man," may seem mere monstrous spectacle, become reasonable if we think of Tamburlaine as, say, the chief of an American Indian tribe.[7] In a hurried world of individualized values, the rituals of coming to manhood, the careful cruelties to the enemy, like the deliberate speeches of antagonists before battle, seem arbitrary; because they have no meaning for us, we refuse to see in them anything but sadism (the personality trait most often charged to Marlowe on the basis of Tamburlaine). This is not to say, of course, that we must become early American Indians or fourteenth-century Mongolians or even Elizabethan Englishmen to grasp the ritual dimensions of Tamburlaine, just as we do not have to become fifth-century Greeks to appreciate Oedipus Rex in its ritual implications. What we must do is cast our minds beyond our time to the no-time of drama, lifting from our own experience those basic desires and experiences which were answered in other times by formalized action.

Having understood the ritual basis of the action, though, we have not yet understood the action fully, because finally we must deal with Tamburlaine II as drama, which, though it may spring from ritual, is a different thing from it. If there is nothing in the action of Tamburlaine II but splendid ritual, those who say that this is a pageant and not a play are correct.[8] If, however, the ritual underlies and intermeshes with individual actions, and if it serves the function of dramatic action in revealing individual character, we cannot classify Tamburlaine II as simple pageantry.

Let us examine the most famous of all spectacular actions in Tamburlaine II, the hauling of Tamburlaine's chariot by the kings. How does this idea come into being? Is it a natural consequence of the action, or is it introduced arbitrarily? It first comes up when Tamburlaine replies to the King of Jerusalem in a vaunting match before battle: the King threatens to chain Tamburlaine in a brigadine and make him row the Turks around

[7] Eugene M. Waith, in The Herculean Hero in Marlowe, Chapman, Shakespeare and Dryden (New York and London, 1962), p. 64, calls Marlowe's Tamburlaine "an early edition of the 'noble savage.' "

[8] For an extended treatment of this view, see Roy W. Battenhouse, Marlowe's Tamburlaine: A Study in Renaissance Moral Philosophy (Nashville, 1941).

when he is captured; Tamburlaine replies in kind, with the boast that he will chain the kings to his chariot, and, as usual, he goes the King one better in his invention of appropriate details (III. v. 92–107). Thus the idea comes into being as part of the concrete action of the play.

When Tamburlaine finally appears in his chariot, with the famous "Holla, ye pampered jades of Asia!" speech (IV. iv. 1), complaining that his steeds can draw only twenty miles a day, the effect is hardly the simple, allegorical one of the pageant. For one thing, this scene dramatizes the final defeat of the Turkish forces, thus advancing the plot. And mounted in his chariot, Tamburlaine reveals thoroughly the peculiarity of his character, with all his pride, his grim humor, and his imagination, which had the instinct for capturing others' imagination, particularly his followers', with the flamboyant act.

From this time on, Tamburlaine's appearances on stage are in his king-drawn chariot. His triumphs are attended in it; his sickness first falls on him in his chariot (and there is irony here, in the vision of the great conqueror suffering the pangs of beginning death but still holding his proud position). In the death scene, the removal of Tamburlaine from the chariot and his replacement by his son Amyras are actions which signal his end as Scourge of God, and his final speech to Amyras is based on the story of Phaëthon, who ran the sun-chariot too close to the earth. (There is certainly irony here, too; Tamburlaine himself has been running his chariot pretty close to the earth, causing devastation and death, and now he is to be cast out.)

Thus Tamburlaine's appearance in his king-drawn chariot, far from being simply a spectacular device of pageantry, operates on four different levels within the play: first, on the ritual level, as the demonstration of Tamburlaine's role within the tradition of the conquering Greco-Roman or Asiatic hero and his simultaneous role as the Christian Scourge of God; second, on the dramatic level, as action which evidences the progression of the plot, Tamburlaine's victory over the Turkish forces; third, as a means of characterization, displaying Tamburlaine's flamboyance, his grim humor, his enormous pride, and his success in the role of the hero-figure who held the imagination of his soldiers and his world; and fourth, as a symbol of the meaning of the play and the figure of Tamburlaine in his universal sense—the human figure who strives to reach godhood by his deeds and is limited by his very nature, his earthliness, who thinks to climb the heavens in a chariot drawn by the symbols of his very earthly power, his captive kings.

This treatment of language and action in terms of ritual makes it obvious that *Tamburlaine II* is within the realm of tragedy. Obviously, man is not being considered here in the context of his relation to society, but in the context of his relation to God or at least godhood. Tamburlaine perceives a moral order in the universe and eventually discovers the implications of this order for himself; though the discovery is not a full one, at one point he does recognize that being the instrument of the execution of this order does not exempt him from its demands. Whether the moral order he discovers is the true one or the right one, the most Christian or pagan or deistic, is not the point; it is real for him, and in it he must work out his rise and fall.

The status of the play within the realm of tragedy depends greatly, of course, on whether Tamburlaine can be considered a tragic hero. He certainly has qualities of the tragic hero: an immense will, a great strength, and courage of a kind which is not merely physical. Though we can hardly call him a "good man," yet his acts, viewed without twentieth-century squeamishness, are not signs of vice or depravity, not monstrous or improbable in the light both of the universal he represents—the man of action, of power—and of his frailty in depending on action and power to accomplish all his ends. The irony of reversal is certainly present in the final defeat of Tamburlaine at the hands of his old ally, death.

If there is a stage of the "tragic rhythm" (as Francis Fergusson has used the term) which is missing in the play, it is certainly not purpose or passion: the purpose is there, hugely so, and the suffering, though periodic, is present and real—Tamburlaine feels grief at Zenocrate's death, shame at Calyphas', and fear at his own. What is missing, it seems, is the perception, and it is not so much missing as refused. Though Tamburlaine at one time acknowledges the conquering role of death and perceives the ironic connection between his own power and that of death, he refuses to accept this realization and seeks to circumvent death, first by

fighting a battle and offering other souls to death, then by deciding he is not so much dying as being translated to a "higher
throne," and finally by having his son take over his old position
in the chariot as the Scourge of God.

Tamburlaine's end, then, is basically melodramatic: he seeks
to conquer death physically by fighting it off; he then considers
himself not as dying but as going to rule in a much better place
(forgetting, as usual, that God or Jove or Allah is the only ruler
in higher spheres); and, finally, he seeks to ignore it by regarding
himself as still living in his sons. All are appealing ideas, certainly, and universal human reactions to death, but they interpret the issue in melodramatic terms, refusing the perception of
man's limitations—even that most irrevocable of his limitations,
his mortality—which is necessary to the achievement of tragedy.
However, if *Tamburlaine II* misses being a real tragedy, it does
not miss by much. Though it has faults—occasional lack of focus,
Tamburlaine's final refusal of self-knowledge—its conception of
Tamburlaine's struggle with death goes far toward the commitment to the inescapable nature of tragedy which Marlowe later
reached in his *Faustus*.

DAVID DAICHES

Language and Action in
Marlowe's TAMBURLAINE[1]

The greatest drama demands poetry rather than prose, and the
reason is not far to seek. In drama the total meaning must be
carried by the speech of the characters; the author cannot, as he
can in the more discursive form of the novel, allow himself to
comment or explain or moralise or in any other way to comment
on or interpret the action. The author disappears behind his
characters, whose speech and action constitute the play. The
novel, which allows of every variety of author's direct and indirect comment and manipulation, does not require a language rich
enough to be capable of satisfying simultaneously both the needs
of the plot and the full range of awareness of the author's imaginative understanding of all its implications and suggestions.
There the author can always speak in his own person. But the
drama needs poetry because it needs an extra dimension of meaning built into the speech of the characters. Modern dramatists of
any stature who have used prose have tended to insert bits of nov-
els under the guise of stage directions, as Bernard Shaw did, giving detailed biographical and psychological information in ex-
planatory prose before allowing any character to come onto the
stage. But we could hardly imagine Shakespeare inserting a long
stage direction before Hamlet's first appearance telling us that he
was a sensitive young man who had recently had a severe shock

From *More Literary Essays* (Edinburgh: Oliver & Boyd Ltd. 1968), pp. 42–69. Reprinted by permission of the author and publisher.
[1] Delivered at the Sorbonne, November 1961.

and discussing the implications of his childhood relations with his dead father, his adored mother, and his smooth and resourceful uncle. In *Hamlet* all this comes out in the speech of the characters, in the language they use, in the overtones, associations, suggestions, and explorations achieved by poetic dialogue and soliloquy.

If, then, drama always tends towards poetic speech—even when, as often in Ibsen, it is formally written in prose—because it is only through poetic speech that the dramatist can make us aware of the full implications of the action, we surely do right to seek for the dramatist's meaning, his personal sense of the significance of the action he is showing us, in patterns of imagery and other characteristically poetical aspects of his use of language. To put it crudely, one might say that it is the way in which the characters talk about the actions in which they are involved that shows us what those actions mean both to the characters and to the author. In Shakespeare we often find a most suggestive counterpointing between those aspects of the language which suggest a character's own view of the significance of his actions and those which suggest if not the author's then at least some more objective or inclusive vision. In Marlowe, especially in the early Marlowe (and though the chronology of Marlowe's plays is largely a matter of inference, there can be little real doubt as to which are the earlier plays), the situation is rather different: the poetry is used not so much to interpret the action as to embody it. In *Tamburlaine* particularly there is a kind of relationship between language and action which is not easily parallelled in other poetic drama and which clearly reflects something of Marlowe's own temperament and approach to the subject. Before developing this point, let me try and illustrate it by some examples.

The Prologue, as has often been noted, shows Marlowe repudiating the more popular modes of drama of his time: he announces that he will eschew equally the "jigging veins of rhyming mother wits" and "such conceits as clownage keeps in pay"—that is, jog-trot rhyming verse and rough-and-tumble comic scenes. Instead

> We'll lead you to the stately tent of war,
> Where you shall hear the Scythian Tamburlaine
> Threat'ning the world with high astounding terms

And scourging kingdoms with his conquering sword.

[Prologue 3–6]

We are going to see Tamburlaine in action, and that action involves, first, his "threat'ning the world in high astounding terms"
and then "scourging kingdoms with his conquering sword." His
action, that is, involves his way of talking, and indeed we might
almost say that in view of the way it is put here language and action are actually equated: threatening with words and scourging
with swords are parallel and even equivalent activities. The high
imagination that leads to the desire for great actions must always
first prove itself in rhetoric. Rhetoric, indeed, is shown in this
play to be itself a form of action. We move immediately from the
Prologue to the opening scene, where we find the weak Persian
king Mycetes expressing to his brother his incapacity to express
in words what the occasion demands:

> Brother Cosroe, I find myself agrieved,
> Yet insufficient to express the same,
> For it requires a great and thund'ring speech.
> Good brother, tell the cause unto my lords;
> I know you have a better wit than I.   [Pt. 1, I. i. 1–5]

It seems clear from these few lines that Marlowe is implying that
the ability to take appropriate action is bound up with the ability
to express forcibly in "a great and thundering speech" the nature
of the action proposed and of the situation which provokes it.
Cosroe, the stronger brother, replies to the weaker in a speech
which attempts to recover in language something of the lost
might and glory of Persia:

> Unhappy Persia, that in former age
> Hast been the seat of mighty conquerors,
> That in their prowess and their policies
> Have triumphed over Afric and the bounds
> Of Europe, where the sun dares scarce appear
> For freezing meteors and congealèd cold, . . .   [I. i. 6–11]

This is Marlowe's first introduction of the vocabulary of power
which so dominates the play. "Might," "conquerors," "prowess,"
"triumphed," "dares"—these potent words rise in the beat of the
blank verse with a martial clang. Their force is feeble compared
to the force of Tamburlaine's own speeches, but at this opening

moment in the play they sufficiently express the difference between the two brothers—just as Tamburlaine's even more soaring speech will express *his* martial superiority to Cosroe.

Now this is not simply a question of Marlowe's realising the
limitations of the stage, as Professor Harry Levin suggests.
"Driven by an impetus towards infinity and faced with the limitations of the stage," Professor Levin writes, "the basic convention of the Marlovian drama is to take the word for the deed."[2]
This is true, and the point is acutely made, yet is seems to me
wrong to suggest that "the limitations of the stage" represent a
significant cause of this characteristic of Marlovian drama. It is
not as though Marlowe were saying, "I cannot show you their
actions, the limitations of the stage being what they are; I shall
therefore have to content myself by letting you listen to them
talking about their actions." It is made clear in innumerable ways
that for Marlowe the proper kind of talk is both the precondition
for and in a sense the equivalent of action. Soaring talk is the
sign of the soaring mind, and only the soaring mind can achieve
spectacularly successful action. I am not altogether happy, either,
about the other cause which Professor Levin gives for Marlowe's
characters taking the word for the deed—"an impetus towards
infinity." One needs to be more specific about what is involved
here. The infinite ambitions which spur on the Marlovian hero
represent the impulse to do something more than can ever be
achieved or even defined, but which at best can only be suggested
by a particular kind of poetic imagery and rhetorical splendour.
There is never an objective correlative in action to the ambitions
of such a hero. When Dr Faustus exclaims

> O what a world of profit and delight,
> Of power, of honor, of omnipotence
> Is promised to the studious artisan!

he is not merely giving expression to the Baconian concept of
knowledge as power, as control over one's environment; both the
abstractness and the variety of the words he chooses—"profit,"
"delight," "power," "honor," "omnipotence"—suggests that he
seeks something greater than could be represented by any prac-

[2] [Harry Levin, *The Overreacher: A Study of Christopher Marlowe* (Cambridge, Mass., 1952; reprinted 1964), p. 43—*Ed.*]

tical example. True, Faustus' trivial use of the power which he gets—playing practical jokes on the Pope and similar pranks—suggests the fatuity which overcomes man once he has achieved power through infernal help, and this is an important moral point: but it is also true that any given example of power in action must be trivial beside the exalted human imagination that aspires after it. The disparity between desire and achievement is for Marlowe part of the human condition, and, this being so, it is in the expression of the desire rather than in accomplishing the achievement that man reveals his most striking qualities.

To return to the opening scene of *Tamburlaine*. The first mention of the hero's name is deliberately reductive: the Persians are trying to diminish him by reducing his stature verbally, by denying his claims to a grand description. The initial description of him is as a highway robber, compared to a fox in harvest time:

> ... that Tamburlaine,
> That, like a fox in midst of harvest-time,
> Doth prey upon my flocks of passengers, ...   [I. i. 30–32]

And Meander follows this up by describing him as

> ... that sturdy Scythian thief
> That robs your merchants of Persepolis,
> Treading by land unto the Western Isles,
> And in your confines with his lawless train
> Daily commits uncivil outrages, ...   [I. i. 36–40]

Marlowe wants to give Tamburlaine a chance to build himself up from the lowest possible position. What could be more lowering than "sturdy Scythian thief" and "lawless train," and what a contemptuous and reductive phrase we have in "uncivil outrages" when applied to Tamburlaine's deeds! When we first see Tamburlaine in the following scene, he does not immediately proceed to build himself up by magnificent rhetoric. When the Medean lords tell him that

> Besides rich presents from the puissant Cham,
> We have his highness' letters to command
> Aid and assistance if we stand in need.   [I. ii. 18–20]

he vaults over all intermediate ranks in a single quiet sentence:

> But now you see these letters and commands
> Are countermanded by a greater man, . . .   [I. ii. 21–22]

Tamburlaine excels in the expression of the consciousness of superiority, and this is in fact one important reason why he *is*
superior.

Consciousness and acceptance of mortality limits both speech
and action. The weak Mycetes charges his captain Theridamas to
destroy Tamburlaine and return swiftly:

> Return with speed; time passeth swift away.
> Our life is frail, and we may die today.   [I. i. 67–68]

Like Tamburlaine, he can imagine destruction, but not with the
intoxicating sense of being the "scourge of God" and acting in
the spirit of divine wrath, rather merely as a more passive ob-
server of his dead enemies:

> I long to see thee back return from thence,
> That I may view these milk-white steeds of mine
> All loaden with the heads of killèd men, . . .   [I. i. 76–78]

No sooner is Mycetes off the stage than his brother Cosroe asserts his power and is crowned king by Ortygius and Ceneus. The
rhetoric begins to rise:

> Magnificent and mighty prince Cosroe,
> We, in the name of other Persian states
> And commons of this mighty monarchy,
> Present thee with th' imperial diadem.   [I. i. 136–39]

This is followed shortly afterwards by the first of many speeches
in which exotic geographical names sound trumpet-like, proclaiming pomp and power:

> We here do crown thee monarch of the East,
> Emperor of Asia and of Persia,
> Great lord of Media and Armenia,
> Duke of Africa and Albania,
> Mesopotamia and of Parthia,
> East India and the late discovered isles,
> Chief lord of all the wide, vast Euxine Sea,
> And of the ever-raging Caspian Lake.
> Long live Cosroe, mighty emperor!   [I. i. 161–69]

Eventually, of course, Tamburlaine's trumpets out-blow all

others; his rhetoric soars to heights unequalled by any other
speaker in the play. But his first appearance, following immediately on Cosroe's magniloquence and Ortygius' cry, "Sound up
the trumpets, then. God save the king!", shows him as relatively
subdued. He is still merely the robber-shepherd, leading in his
captured treasure and his fair captive Zenocrate, to whom he
speaks at first rather as Comus speaks to the Lady in Milton's
Masque:

> Come lady, let not this appall your thoughts;
> The jewels and the treasure we have ta'en
> Shall be reserved, and you in better state
> Than if you were arrived in Syria, . . .   [I. ii. 1–4]

Zenocrate addresses him as "shepherd." Then, after Tamburlaine's second speech to Zenocrate, in which, as I have noted, he
quietly raises himself above the "puissant Cham," Zenocrate addresses him as "my lord," adding significantly "for so you do import." Tamburlaine accepts the title, adding the characteristically
Marlovian remark that it is his deeds rather than his birth that
will prove him so. (It should be noted, in passing, that Marlowe
was a rebel against a hereditary social hierarchy, and though his
imagination revelled in all the ritual of power and rank—he several times makes great play, for example, with subordinate kings
receiving their crowns from the chief of them all—he accepted it
only when it was the reward of achievement rather than merely
of birth. Thus Faustus was born of "parents base of stock" and
Tamburlaine vaunts rather than denies his humble origin. The
poverty of the University Wits bred a special kind of pride, which
in Marlowe's case merged with one current of Renaissance humanism to produce a non-hereditary view of aristocracy.) Zenocrate's third address to Tamburlaine appeals to him as one who

> . . . hop'st to be eternizèd
> By living Asia's mighty emperor.   [I. ii. 72–73]

It is an interesting and rapid progression—from "shepherd," to
"my lord," to "mighty emperor"—and is produced entirely by
Tamburlaine's way of speech.

It is perhaps surprising that Tamburlaine's first appearance
should show him less as the warrior than as the lover. After all,
the chief interest of the play centres on his power, whether of

language or of action, and falling in love is a kind of submission rather than an exercise of power. But it is significant that Tamburlaine regards Zenocrate as someone precious whose possession signifies power. As the daughter of the Soldan of Egypt she represents a high and ancient lineage, as the betrothed of the King of Arabia she represents a challenge, and as having supreme beauty she is, like a supremely precious stone, of inestimable *value*. Tamburlaine manifests his growing power by talking about and by achieving the conquest of inexpressibly rich treasures and of kingdoms. Competitive speeches promising wealth and pomp to your favourites or to those who come over to your side, represent one of the recurring features of the play, one of Marlowe's ways of establishing relative greatness of character. In his wooing of Zenocrate Tamburlaine is outbidding all other kings and princes in the wealth and glory he can promise her and at the same time he is winning for himself something infinitely precious. His first speech of courtship both expresses his sense of Zenocrate's enormous value and promises her the highest possible style of living. Rhetoric is the art of persuasion: in putting a blazing rhetoric into Tamburlaine's mouth Marlowe expressly recognises that one of the roads to power is the ability to *win people over*. Great speech is not only both the guarantor and even the equivalent of great action; it is also in itself a means to power which takes precedence of naked physical aggression. On several occasions Tamburlaine is shown as using it first, as trying to seduce his enemies into his service or into unconditional surrender. Action, we are sometimes made to feel, is only to be resorted to when speech meets with stubbornness or deafness. Or rather, to make the point yet again, speech is presented as being the primary form of action, that form which corresponds most closely to man's actual ambitions.

We first hear the full sound of Tamburlaine's rhetoric when he encounters Theridamas, the Persian captain sent against him by Mycetes. Before Theridamas' arrival, Tamburlaine has his soldiers lay out in public view their captured gold treasure, "that their reflexions may amaze the Persians." Surrounded by this spectacular wealth, he is found by Theridamas and greets him with a huge elemental dignity:

> Whom seek'st thou, Persian? I am Tamburlaine.   [I. ii. 153]

Theridamas is impressed by Tamburlaine's appearance, and takes fire from it to speak in Tamburlaine-like tones:

> His looks do menace heaven and dare the gods.
> His fiery eyes are fixed upon the earth
> As if he now devised some stratagem,
> Or meant to pierce Avernus' darksome vaults
> To pull the triple-headed dog from hell.   [I. ii. 156–60]

Tamburlaine responds at once to this kind of rhetoric: this is his way of talking, and he appreciates it. We may wonder perhaps why he takes it as a sign that Theridamas is "noble and mild," but I should think that we are to regard these adjectives as a general sign of approval of his worthiness on the one hand and his capacity for being won over on the other. Tamburlaine then returns the compliment paid by Theridamas to his appearance:

> With what a majesty he rears his looks!   [I. ii. 164]

He then embarks on the greatest of all the several speeches of competitive promising in the play. The increasing abstractness of Tamburlaine's imagery in the opening lines is the measure of his rapidly soaring imagination. The difference between being "but captain of a thousand horse" and triumphing "over all the world" is more than a difference in degree; it is the difference between the paltriness of a realisable kind of power and the magnificence of an ambition too tremendous to be capable of concrete definition. The contrast is immediate:

> Art thou but captain of a thousand horse,
> That by characters graven in thy brows,
> And by thy martial face and stout aspect,
> Deserv'st to have the leading of an host?
> Forsake thy king and do but join with me,
> And we will triumph over all the world.   [I. ii. 167–72]

From this point—as though he has intoxicated himself with the phrase "And we will triumph over all the world"—Tamburlaine's speech moves into its full grandiloquence:

> I hold the Fates bound fast in iron chains,
> And with my hand turn Fortune's wheel about,
> And sooner shall the sun fall from his sphere
> Then Tamburlaine be slain or overcome.

Draw forth thy sword, thou mighty man-at-arms,
Intending but to raze my charmèd skin,
And Jove himself will stretch his hand from heaven
To ward the blow and shield me safe from harm.
See how he rains down heaps of gold in showers,
As if he meant to give my soldiers pay;
And as a sure and grounded argument
That I shall be the monarch of the East,
He sends this Soldan's daughter, rich and brave,
To be my queen and portly emperess.
If thou wilt stay with me, renownèd man,
And lead thy thousand horse with my conduct,
Besides thy share of this Egyptian prize,
Those thousand horse shall sweat with martial spoil
Of conquered kingdoms and of cities sacked.
Both we will walk upon the lofty clifts,
And Christian merchants, that with Russian stems
Plough up huge furrows in the Caspian Sea,
Shall vail to us as lords of all the lake.
Both we will reign as consuls of the earth,
And mighty kings shall be our senators.
Jove sometimes maskèd in a shepherd's weed,
And by those steps that he hath scaled the heavens,
May we become immortal like the gods.
Join with me now in this my mean estate—
I call it mean because, being yet obscure,
The nations far removed admire me not—
And when my name and honor shall be spread
As far as Boreas claps his brazen wings,
Or fair Boötes sends his cheerful light,
Then shalt thou be competitor with me,
And sit with Tamburlaine in all his majesty.   [I. ii. 173–208]

One has the feeling, here as elsewhere, that when Marlowe uses classical mythology it is not for decorative purposes or to make literary capital out of references to known legends, but in order to give the myths new meaning by showing their usefulness in illustrating the limitless nature of human ambition at its most magnificent:

Jove sometimes maskèd in a shepherd's weed,
And by those steps that he hath scaled the heavens,
May we become immortal like the gods.

It is as though Marlowe is showing us for the first time what classical mythology is all about, what it is *for*: it helps to provide
symbols for the undefinable ambitions of the unfettered human
imagination. Similarly, the monstrous extravagance of

> I hold the Fates bound fast in iron chains,
> And with my hand turn Fortune's wheel about,

is not to be glossed simply by reference to the medieval notion of
Fortune's wheel, though of course Marlowe depends here for his
shock effect on his readers' and hearers' realising that this is a
frontal attack on the common idea of the fickleness of fortune.
That attack is not, however, as it has sometimes been taken to be,
a sign of an almost blasphemous arrogance on Tamburlaine's or
on Marlowe's part; it is a way of expressing what it feels like to
have limitless ambition and limitless self-confidence. Once again
one might say that the use of this kind of language is a kind of
action: to be able to talk that way is half the battle. Marlowe does
not present this kind of talk as *boasting*, and the actual boasting
of lesser figures, such as Bajazeth, is clearly differentiated from
this particular kind of abstract extravagance. Tamburlaine, when
he speaks like this, has gone far beyond boasting: he is in an
almost trance-like condition of relishing the significance of his
own highest imaginings. Such talk carries its own conviction: a
man who can talk like that is the man on whose side we want to
be. Theridamas makes this quite clear:

> Not Hermes, prolocutor to the gods,
> Could use persuasions more pathetical.   [I. ii. 209–10]

This scene ends with Tamburlaine's creating around him an atmosphere of total loyalty and mutual trust. Here Tamburlaine is
at his most attractive. Service on the one hand and protection on
the other are subsumed in a common notion of soldierly friendship and faithfulness which has its own simpler eloquence:

> *Theridamas.*   But shall I prove a traitor to my king?
> *Tamburlaine.*   No, but the trusty friend of Tamburlaine.
> *Theridamas.*   Won with thy words and conquered with thy looks,
>   I yield myself, my men, and horse to thee,
>   To be partaker of thy good or ill,
>   As long as life maintains Theridamas.
> *Tamburlaine.*   Theridamas, my friend, take here my hand,

Which is as much as if I swore by heaven
And called the gods to witness of my vow.
Thus shall my heart be still combined with thine,
Until our bodies turn to elements,
And both our souls aspire celestial thrones.
Techelles and Casane, welcome him.
Techelles.   Welcome, renownèd Persian, to us all.
Usumcasane.   Long may Theridamas remain with us.
Tamburlaine.   These are my friends in whom I more rejoice
Than doth the king of Persia in his crown; . . .   [I. ii. 225–41]

The next scene shows us Cosroe being swung round to Tamburlaine by Menaphon's description of his appearance. Like Shakespeare's Cleopatra, whose beauty is symbolised by its ability to inspire eloquence in hard-bitten military men when they describe it, so Tamburlaine's greatness lies partly in its capacity for being eloquently talked about. The language here has not Tamburlaine's passion of grandeur, his commitment through language to the genuineness of his own enormous ambitions, but it strikes effectively the note of compelled admiration:

Of stature tall, and straightly fashionèd,
Like his desire, lift upwards and divine,
So large of limbs, his joints so strongly knit,
Such breadth of shoulders as might mainly bear
Old Atlas' burden. 'Twixt his manly pitch,
A pearl more worth than all the world is placed,
Wherein by curious sovereignty of art
Are fixed his piercing instruments of sight,
Whose fiery circles bear encompassèd
A heaven of heavenly bodies in their spheres,
That guides his steps and actions to the throne
Where honor sits invested royally.
Pale of complexion, wrought in him with passion,
Thirsting with sovereignty, and love of arms,
His lofty brows in folds do figure death,
And in their smoothness amity and life.
About them hangs a knot of amber hair,
Wrappèd in curls, as fierce Achilles' was,
On which the breath of heaven delights to play,
Making it dance with wanton majesty.
His arms and fingers, long and sinewy,
Betokening valor and excess of strength—

> In every part proportioned like the man
> Should make the world subdued to Tamburlaine.   [II. i. 7–30]

This mediated persuasion does not work as effectively as the words of Tamburlaine himself work directly on Theridamas. Cosroe does not yield to Tamburlaine as a preliminary to gaining his true friendship; he tries to make the best of both worlds by asserting that Tamburlaine will be his regent in Persia. Where Cosroe goes wrong is made abundantly clear in a later scene, where he patronises Tamburlaine and indicates that he is using him to further his own ambitions. He addresses Tamburlaine jovially as 'worthy Tamburlaine' and asks, in the tone of a squire addressing a farm labourer,

> What think'st thou, man, shall come of our attempts? [II. iii. 3]

In answer to Tamburlaine's speech of boundless confidence, Cosroe simply reiterates that he expects that the efforts of Tamburlaine and his friends

> Shall make me solely emperor of Asia,   [II. iii. 39]

and proceeds to dole out promises of advancement in language that sounds very tame beside that of Tamburlaine in his promising mood:

> Then shall your meeds and valors be advanced
> To rooms of honor and nobility.   [40–41]

Tamburlaine replies with an irony of which Cosroe is totally oblivious:

> Then haste, Cosroe, to be king alone, . . .   [42]

We are prepared for Cosroe's ultimate rejection and destruction by Tamburlaine: he has not made the right response to Tamburlaine's language.

The scene in which the timid Mycetes, caught by Tamburlaine in the act of trying to hide the crown, is contemptuously given back the crown by Tamburlaine and then runs away, will be misconstrued by the modern reader if he reads Mycetes' opening line

> Accursed be he that first invented war! [II. iv. 1]

as a serious pacifist argument. Those critics who see Marlowe here as showing a humanitarian feeling and voicing a proper horror of war, or as adding some subtle touches to his portrait of Mycetes, are not reading the play that Marlowe wrote. The point about Mycetes—one is tempted to add, the only relevant point—is that he can find neither language nor gesture to correspond to his royal state, and therefore his royal state is forfeit. A crown is a symbol of human aspiration; in great spirits it provokes to eloquence of speech and magnificence of action, or at least to some behaviour correlative to the symbol's significance. All that Mycetes can think of doing with it is to hide it, to prevent himself from being known as king:

> So shall not I be known, or if I be,
> They cannot take away my crown from me.
> Here will I hide it in this simple hole.   [II. iv. 13–15]

This is anti-rhetoric, one might say. To say of a crown "Here will I hide it in this simple hole" is the ultimate lack of response to the challenge of the symbol. Tamburlaine's words, "The thirst of reign and sweetness of a crown," spoken later, show the approved response. Mycetes tends to speak in monosyllables, "For kings are clouts that every man shoots at," "And far from any man that is a fool," and when he encounters Tamburlaine he is quite incapable of rising to the occasion. Even Tamburlaine in his presence speaks with an unwonted and contemptuous simplicity:

> Well, I mean you shall have it again.
> Here, take it for a while; I lend it thee
> Till I may see thee hemmed with armed men.
> Then shalt thou see me pull it from thy head;
> Thou art no match for mighty Tamburlaine.   [II. iv. 36–40]

And when Mycetes discovers that it was Tamburlaine himself speaking, he records the fact in the most deflating language possible:

> O gods, is this Tamburlaine the thief?
> I marvel much he stole it not away.   [41–42]

Everywhere it is language that provides the clue. Compare, for example, the Persian Meander cheering up his army, with Tamburlaine's speaking to *his* men. Here is Meander:

> Therefore cheer up your minds; prepare to fight.
> He that can take or slaughter Tamburlaine

> Shall rule the province of Albania.
> Who brings that traitor's head, Theridamas,
> Shall have a government in Media,
> Beside the spoil of him and all his train.   [II. ii. 29–34]

The province of Albania or a government in Media is tame indeed beside the vaguer but infinitely more eloquent

> We'll chase the stars from heaven and dim their eyes
> That stand and muse at our admirèd arms.   [II. iii. 23–24]

Again, we find that for Marlowe what is realisable in precise terms cannot be the product of a truly inspired imagination. The greatest ambitions are undefinable save in terms of abstraction, mythology, or cosmic metaphor. The best that Meander can promise his soldiers is that they shall

> Share equally the gold that bought their lives,
> And live like gentlemen in Persia.   [II. ii. 70–71]

Live like gentlemen indeed! Tamburlaine's soldiers will live like gods:

> For fates and oracles of heaven have sworn
> To royalize the deeds of Tamburlaine,
> And make them blessèd that share in his attempts.
>   [II. iii. 7–9]

That Tamburlaine cannot enjoy his power unless he is talking about it or indulging in a gesture symbolical of it is not to be explained simply by the limitations of the stage: it is a paradox inherent in Marlowe's conception of human ambition. It is only after he has crowned Cosroe as emperor that Tamburlaine allows his imagination to batten on the thought of kingship. Menaphon promises Cosroe that he will "ride in triumph through Persepolis," and after he and Cosroe have gone out, leaving Tamburlaine, Theridamas, Techelles, and Usumcasane on the stage—that is, Tamburlaine and his most faithful officers—Tamburlaine repeats and savours the words:

> And ride in triumph through Persepolis!
> Is it not brave to be a king, Techelles?
> Usumcasane and Theridamas,
> Is it not passing brave to be a king,
> And ride in triumph through Persepolis?   [II. v. 50–54]

Here for the first time we hear the note of pure incantation in Tamburlaine's language. What is in fact involved in being a king? If we think of it, limited things—limited functions, limited powers, above all, limited length of life. The idea of kingship as it kindles the aspiring mind is more significant than a king's actual rights and duties. The word suggests power and glory—"for Thine is the kingdom, the power and the glory"—of a kind more absolute than any given example of human power and glory can be. Human beings have the power of responding to this suggestion, and in this lies their especial capacity for tragedy. Macbeth and Lady Macbeth, captivated by the magic of the idea of king-ship, destroyed themselves in order to obtain it and learned at the very moment of obtaining it that their imagination of it had had nothing to do with the reality. *Tamburlaine* however is not a tragedy: Marlowe is not concerned with the disparity between the magic of names and the true nature of things, between the imagination and the reality, or with the corruption of noble minds to which this disparity can lead. To this extent the play lacks a moral pattern, lacks any real core of meaning. There is no sense of the pity of it or the waste of it or even of the ambiguity of it, though Marlowe does show some awareness of some of the paradoxes involved in the relation between words and actions. Tamburlaine is held up to our admiration in the literal Latin sense of *admirari*. His cruelty, which can be appalling, has no real moral significance one way or the other; it is simply a mode of action appropriate to a soaring ambition, and to Marlowe a soaring ambition is a mode of feeling appropriate to man's restless desire to break out of the limiting bounds within which any given actions of his must be confined. The slaughtering of the virgins and the other inhabitants of Damascus is a *gesture,* like the change of Tamburlaine's colours from white to red to black, and gestures are attempts to find actions which, though inevitably limited, are at least symbolic of something larger than themselves. I am not here concerned with Part 2, which raises some different questions, but I would remark that Tamburlaine's insistence on courage to bear wounds and so on, in his discussion with his sons in Part 2, and the somewhat confused picture of Calyphas as part coward, part sensualist, part realist, and part pacifist, lead us into other realms altogether. Part 1 is the original play, and complete in itself: in continuing it Marlowe had to modify the purity of his original conception and introduce elements which if examined closely take us far from the essential play as first conceived and written.

Tamburlaine, then, in repeating the phrase about riding in triumph through Persepolis and building up from it into an incantatory speech on the joys of kingship, is demonstrating his superiority to more mundane imaginations and his capacity for enjoying speech as a mode of action. What a king actually does, how a king actually employs and enjoys his power, is not inquired into. The idea of kingly power is itself intoxicating. When he sounds the names of his followers in a litany of invoked kingship, he is trying to carry them with him in his imaginative conception of the sweets of power. But they are not Tamburlaine. All that Techelles can say is

> O, my lord, 'tis sweet and full of pomp.   [II. v. 55]

Usumcasane tries to go one better with

> To be a king is half to be a god.   [56]

But Tamburlaine[3] brushes these tame expressions away impatiently:

> A god is not so glorious as a king.
> I think the pleasure they enjoy in heaven
> Can not compare with kingly joys in earth:
> To wear a crown enchased with pearl and gold,
> Whose virtues carry with it life and death;
> To ask and have, command and be obeyed;
> When looks breed love, with looks to gain the prize,
> Such power attractive shines in princes' eyes.   [II. v. 57–64]

From now on he is to be chasing his language in his actions, and, in the nature of things, never catching up. I have said that the spectacle is not tragic. Tamburlaine's imagination vents itself in rhetoric which in turn re-kindles his imagination to still greater ambitions, and this process is shown as guaranteeing military success. But it is an amoral process. We get the point about the restless, limitless nature of human ambition and the impossibility of

---

[3] [This speech is usually given to Theridamas—*Ed.*]

its being able to find any single correlative in action. But what does it all add up to in the end?

It is no use saying that it adds up to great poetry, even if not always great dramatic poetry, for the point at issue is just how great is this kind of poetry and why. Consider the speech in which Tamburlaine most fully equates kingship with limitless human aspiration:

> The thirst of reign and sweetness of a crown,
> That caused the eldest son of heavenly Ops
> To thrust his doting father from his chair,
> And place himself in the imperial heaven,
> Moved me to manage arms against thy state.
> What better precedent than mighty Jove?
> Nature, that framed us of four elements
> Warring within our breasts for regiment,
> Doth teach us all to have aspiring minds.
> Our souls, whose faculties can comprehend
> The wondrous architecture of the world
> And measure every wandering planet's course,
> Still climbing after knowledge infinite,
> And always moving as the restless spheres,
> Wills us to wear ourselves and never rest,
> Until we reach the ripest fruit of all,
> That perfect bliss and sole felicity,
> The sweet fruition of an earthly crown.   [II. vii. 12–29]

Critics have differed as to whether the conclusion of this passage is an anti-climax or a supreme climax. At the beginning of the speech, characteristically, Marlowe presses a new meaning on a Greek myth to make it serve as an illustration and an illumination of the inevitability of continuously aspiring ambition among men. The line "What better precedent than mighty Jove?" rings out as an arrogant challenge. He next goes on to say that the four elements of which man's physical nature is composed (according to medieval and Aristotelian physiology), since they are in continual conflict with each other, teach us all to have aspiring minds. We might say that the relation between conflict and aspiration is not made clear and there seems to be no reason why the former should suggest the latter, but there is a suppressed middle term, emulation, which might bridge the logical gap here. In any case the argument is not essentially rational, but rhetorical: Tambur-

laine is seeking mythological, cosmic, and natural sanctions for
human aspiration: human ambition forms part of the total wonder of nature. The Faustian lines

> Our souls, whose faculties can comprehend
> The wondrous architecture of the world
> And measure every wandering planet's course,
> Still climbing after knowledge infinite,

are very impressive in their rising eloquence and the fine, steady
abstraction of "Still climbing after knowledge infinite." We are
made to feel the *insatiable* nature of human curiosity. The search
is never-ending—

> Until we reach the ripest fruit of all,
> That perfect bliss and sole felicity,
> The sweet fruition of an earthly crown.

The play itself, of course, belies this. Tamburlaine collects crowns
as a philatelist collects stamps and remains unsatisfied. The extraordinary force of the abstract words "perfect bliss and sole
felicity," suggesting a theological conception of heavenly beati-
tude, and, reminding us of Milton's "When everything that is sincerely good and perfectly divine," hardly prepares us for what
they are leading up to, "the sweet fruition of an earthly crown."
Yet I do not think the passage ends in anti-climax. The *ripest
fruit* of all, that *perfect bliss* and *sole felicity,* turns out to be the
sweet fruition of an earthly crown. The crown in this context is
made, by its culminating position, into a symbol of ultimate human ambition. *This is what Tamburlaine (and Marlowe) mean,
then, when they talk of a crown.* It is not the usual meaning of
the word "crown" that limits the totality of meaning achieved by
these lines; on the contrary, it is the meaning set up by the preceding lines that determines in what sense we are to take the
word "crown" when we come to it in its climactic position. Con-
templated by the imagination, an earthly crown seems to be the
guarantee of what a heavenly crown is conventionally assumed to
promise—"perfect bliss and sole felicity." It is the imagination
which invests words and objects with symbolic meaning. The
word "crown" literally "means" a circle placed on the head of a
king. But the word, like the word "king," can be used to contain

an idea or an emotion. This is what Shakespeare does with the words in *Richard II*. But with Marlowe the idea and the emotion are larger than any practice of kingship would warrant. Acting out kingship in language or in coronation ceremony thus becomes a way of pointing to the nature of human aspiration. Indeed, language and gesture become the best kind of action because they can bear all that the imagination puts into them and are therefore not limited as even the greatest ordinary actions are bound to be. A coronation ceremony is always more moving than a king giving laws or in any other way exhibiting his power. And in the last resort it is in the ceremony of language that human aspiration finds fullest satisfaction. This is the point so splendidly made by —or rather embodied in—the passage quoted.

What, then, does it all add up to in the end? *Tamburlaine* is a play in which the virtuosity of the actor is more important than the moral nature of his actions. The hero tells us what he is going to do before he does it; tells us what he is doing when he is doing it, and after he has done it tells us what he has done—and all in language whose grandiloquence makes almost every speech a ritual of aspiration. Successful action follows on the speech almost automatically, for speech of this kind can only spring from an irrepressible energy, a perpetual hunger for always going further and doing more, which *must* be satisfied. Those who fail are those with limited aims—contrary to the vulgar view that to limit one's aim is to make success more probable. Tamburlaine's antagonists are not only those with pettier minds; they are also those—like Bajazeth, his most formidable opponent—whose aim is complacently to maintain their achieved power, which they take for granted as part of the permanent state of things. The language of Bajazeth is not unlike that of Tamburlaine: he must be an opponent to challenge Tamburlaine's imagination and also one whose overthrow marks a significant step in Tamburlaine's pursuit of his words by his actions. One difference between the language of Bajazeth and that of Tamburlaine is that Tamburlaine's tends to be directed towards the future—what he wills to do and what he therefore will do, "For Will and Shall best fitteth Tamburlaine"—whereas the language of Bajazeth is more a complacent vaunting of what he is. When Bajazeth does talk of the future, it is in terms of intention—

> —We mean to take his morning's next arise
> For messenger he will not be reclaimed,
> And mean to fetch thee in despite of him.   [III. i. 38–40]

which sounds tentative beside Tamburlaine's

> I that am termed the scourge and wrath of God,
> The only fear and terror of the world,
> Will first subdue the Turk, and then enlarge
> Those Christian captives which you keep as slaves, . . .
>
>   [III. iii. 44–47]

In the verbal duel between Bajazeth and Tamburlaine this difference disappears, and both speak in terms of "will" and "shall." The event shows which is the boaster. It is however worth noting that Bajazeth projects his images of power in terms of number and quantity rather than in the cosmic and mythological imagery characteristic of Tamburlaine.

The scene immediately preceding the exchange of words between Tamburlaine and Bajazeth shows us Zenocrate, now deeply in love with Tamburlaine, being urged by Agydas to give up Tamburlaine in favour of her original Arabian king. Agydas, significantly, has no appreciation of Tamburlaine's language. When Zenocrate looks for "amorous discourse," he tells her, Tamburlaine

> Will rattle forth his facts of war and blood, . . .   [III. ii. 45]

Marlowe is deliberately playing a dangerous game here, allowing us to hear this brilliantly contemptuous description of Tamburlaine's speech in the very middle of the play. But he is confident that once we hear Tamburlaine's voice sounding again we shall dismiss this belittling description. Even before this, he has Zenocrate reply, in language that echoes Tamburlaine's own,

> As looks the sun through Nilus' flowing stream,
> Or when the morning holds him in her arms,
> So looks my lordly love, fair Tamburlaine;
> His talk much sweeter than the Muses' song
> They sung for honor 'gainst Pierides,
> Or when Minerva did with Neptune strive;
> And higher would I rear my estimate
> Than Juno, sister to the highest god,
> If I were matched with mighty Tamburlaine.   [III. ii. 47–55]

Tamburlaine discovers Agydas trying to tempt Zenocrate away
from him, and to this man who belittles his language he addresses
no words but only sends a dagger as an invitation to him to kill
himself. Agydas gets the point:

> He needed not with words confirm my fear,
> For words are vain when working tools present
> The naked action of my threatened end.   [III. ii. 92–94]

There is a fine irony in Tamburlaine's refusal to use words to the
man who cannot appreciate them. One is reminded of a dialogue,
earlier in the play, between Mycetes and Meander.

> *Mycetes.*   Was there such brethren, sweet Meander, say,
>   That sprung of teeth of dragons venomous?
> *Meander.*   So poets say, my lord.
> *Mycetes.*   And 'tis a pretty toy to be a poet.   [II. ii. 51–54]

Miss Ellis-Fermor, in her note on this line in her edition, drew
attention to what she considered its "biting irony," seeing it as a
bitter comment by Marlowe on the reputation and fate of poets.
But surely the irony does not lie here at all, but in the man who
can neither speak nor act both doubting mythology and despising
poetry. Mythology is the very stuff of much of Tamburlaine's
speech, and his poetic utterance is bound up with his aspiration
and thus with his capacity for action. Mycetes, incapable of poetic
utterance and equally of effective action, shows his lack of understanding of the relation between language and action by his contemptuous remark about poets.

The slanging match between Zenocrate and the Turkish empress Zabina is a rather crude acting out of this same correlation
between speech and action that is so important in the play: while
their husbands fight it out on the field, they "manage words" in
mutual taunting. Tamburlaine's humiliation and degradation of
Bajazeth and Zabina and his complete victory over the Turkish
forces is another acting out of his soaring ambition, yet it cannot
be denied that there is an element of sadism in the detailed presentation of this cruel treatment. Bajazeth has counted on Mahomet to save him, and appeals desperately to the prophet for
succour: but none comes. Man stands alone in Marlowe's universe and draws his strength from his own aspiring imagination.
When Tamburlaine uses Bajazeth as a footstool and mounts on

him to his throne, the gesture itself is striking—a gesture of over-weening ambition and aspiration; he is not content, however, to leave it at that, but breaks out into a speech whose rhetorical extravagance gives full meaning to his symbolic act:

> Now clear the triple region of the air,
> And let the majesty of heaven behold
> Their scourge and terror tread on emperors.
> Smile stars that reigned at my nativity,
> And dim the brightness of their neighbor lamps;
> Disdain to borrow light of Cynthia,
> For I, the chiefest lamp of all the earth,
> First rising in the east with mild aspect,
> But fixèd now in the meridian line,
> Will send up fire to your turning spheres
> And cause the sun to borrow light of you.
> My sword struck fire from his coat of steel,
> Even in Bithynia, when I took this Turk,
> As when a fiery exhalation,
> Wrapped in the bowels of a freezing cloud,
> Fighting for passage, makes the welkin crack
> And casts a flash of lightning to the earth.
> But ere I march to wealthy Persia,
> Or leave Damascus and th' Egyptian fields,
> As was the fame of Clymene's brain-sick son
> That almost brent the axle-tree of heaven,
> So shall our swords, our lances, and our shot
> Fill all the air with fiery meteors.
> Then, when the sky shall wax as red as blood,
> It shall be said I made it red myself,
> To make me think of naught but blood and war.
>
> [IV. ii. 30–55]

In any other kind of tragedy such a speech would represent the ultimate *hubris*. But, as I have insisted, Tamburlaine is not a true tragedy and is a wholly amoral play. This is inordinate aspiration in action: it is offered to us for our admiration, not necessarily for our approval.

There is an element not only of sadism but at times of sheer sensationalism in the later scenes with Bajazeth and Zabrina, which are carefully spaced so as to suggest a crescendo of humiliation to its ultimate point. The contrast between what these two were and what they have now become is not pointed, as it would be in a medieval tragedy, with the lesson of the uncertainty of fortune and the other usual accompaniments of accounts of the falls of princes, nor, after a certain stage, does it serve any more to symbolise Tamburlaine's achievement in overcoming the great Turkish emperor. An independent psychological interest comes in, and the scene in which, after Bajazeth has brained himself against his cage, Zabina goes mad and in a whirl of lunatic words follows his example, exist for its own sake; it had many successors in Elizabethan drama.

Meanwhile, we have had the destruction of Damascus, with all its histrionic accompaniments, and the defeat, and liberation for Zenocrate's sake, of Zenocrate's father, the Soldan of Egypt. As I have already argued, Tamburlaine's behaviour at Damascus is to be interpreted as showing him applying the appropriate rituals of destruction which are in turn the appropriate accompaniments of the rituals of his rise to ever increasing power. Zenocrate is unhappy, because these are her fellow Egyptians who have been slaughtered and she has not yet been reassured about her father. But we are not to see a genuine conflict here. Marlowe is not presenting Tamburlaine as torn between desire for military glory on the one hand and love of Zenocrate on the other; there is no suggestion either of any sort of conflict between love and honour. Marlowe was no Corneille, and no Dryden. True, he shows us Zenocrate troubled about her father, and Tamburlaine troubled because Zenocrate is troubled. And Tamburlaine's distress produces one of the most admired speeches in the play. What he says in this speech is that his appreciation of female beauty is one thing which cannot be adequately represented in words. Hitherto, as we know, he has never had any difficulty in giving verbal embodiment to his ambitions, and he has not been able to savour them until he has given them verbal embodiment. Zenocrate, whom he had earlier described in language suggesting her value and preciousness, is now seen to be the possessor of a quality which troubles because the expression of it in words lies beyond "the highest reaches of human wit." The passage is a set piece— I cannot help feeling that it may have been written earlier as a separate poem and then incorporated into the play at this point —and the point it makes is not developed, nor is it related to any

other pattern of meaning in the play. Further, the latter part of
the speech is textually confused and in parts difficult to interpret.
It almost looks as though Marlowe did not know what to do with
his speech on beauty after he had introduced it. Here is the
passage:

> What is beauty, saith my sufferings, then?
> If all the pens that ever poets held
> Had fed the feeling of their masters' thoughts,
> And every sweetness that inspired their hearts,
> Their minds, and muses on admirèd themes;
> If all the heavenly quintessence they still
> From their immortal flowers of poesy,
> Wherein, as in a mirror, we perceive
> The highest reaches of a human wit;
> If these had made one poem's period,
> And all combined in beauty's worthiness,
> Yet should there hover in their restless heads
> One thought, one grace, one wonder, at the least,
> Which into words no virtue can digest.
> But how unseemly is it for my sex,
> My discipline of arms and chivalry,
> My nature, and the terror of my name,
> To harbor thoughts effeminate and faint!
> Save only that in beauty's just applause,
> With whose instinct the soul of man is touched;
> And every warrior that is rapt with love
> Of fame, of valor, and of victory,
> Must needs have beauty beat on his conceits.
> I thus conceiving and subduing both,
> That which hath stopped the tempest of the gods,
> Even from the fiery-spangled veil of heaven,
> To feel the lovely warmth of shepherds' flames
> And march in cottages of strowèd weeds,
> Shall give the world to note, for all my birth,
> That virtue solely is the sum of glory,
> And fashions men with true nobility.   [V. ii. 97–127]

The first fourteen lines constitute a poem on the mystery and in-
expressibility of beauty, very Elizabethan in feeling and imagery
and conventional in movement and diction. Then Tamburlaine
reproaches himself for harbouring effeminate thoughts, but goes
on to defend himself by making the point that it is the working

of beauty on the human imagination which leads men to their highest exploits. He ends by saying that he, who both responds to beauty and knows how to keep it in its proper place—that beauty which has led the gods to assume humble disguises—will announce to the world that it is the proper response to beauty which enables men to achieve true glory and nobility. It is difficult to feel that this speech really belongs to the play. How is this consistent with

> Nature, that framed us of four elements
> Warring within our breast for regiment,
> Doth teach us all to have aspiring minds

and the rest of that great vindication of the perpetually aspiring mind? Further, the conflict suggested here is not developed dramatically at all. Immediately after the speech he briefly baits Bejazeth, announces that for Zenocrate's sake he will spare her father, and goes off to win another victory. Then comes the spectacular scene of the suicide of both Bajazeth and Zabina, followed by a speech by Zenocrate in which we really see her with a divided mind. She is unhappy at the slaughter of the citizens of Damascus, and she is shaken to see the dead bodies of Bajazeth and Zabina. The sight leads her to fear for Tamburlaine: he has defied Fortune, and may in the end come to a sudden fall like "the Turk and his great empress." She asks both Jove and Mahomet to pardon Tamburlaine's "contempt of earthly fortune" and then— and this is the first and only touch of this in the whole play— shows some pity for Bajazeth and Zabina and regret that she "was not moved with ruth," for which she also asks pardon. Her main fear seems to be that Tamburlaine's contempt of fortune threatens them both. Immediately after this, the King of Arabia, mortally wounded, comes in to die at Zenocrate's feet, and Tamburlaine enters bringing in the captured and now liberated Soldan of Egypt, Zenocrate's father. Tamburlaine's worry about beauty and Zenocrate's about her husband's temerity receive no further mention. Indeed, Tamburlaine now breaks into one of his most thundering speeches, abounding in high images of power, in which he sees the multitude of those dead by his hand, including the culminating sight of the dead Bajazeth and Zabina and the dead king of Arabia, as "sights of power to grace my victory." For the first time we feel Tamburlaine's speech almost horrible, in-

deed inhuman, in its expression of limitless lust for power and
his intoxication with the bare notion of triumphing and overcoming:

> The god of war resigns his room to me,
> Meaning to make me general of the world.
> Jove, viewing me in arms, looks pale and wan,
> Fearing my power should pull him from his throne.
> Where'er I come the Fatal Sisters sweat,
> And grisly Death, by running to and fro
> To do their ceaseless homage to my sword.
> And here in Afric, where it seldom rains,
> Since I arrived with my triumphant host,
> Have swelling clouds, drawn from wide-gasping wounds,
> Been oft resolved in bloody purple showers,
> A meteor that might terrify the earth,
> And make it quake at every drop it drinks.
> Millions of souls sit on the banks of Styx,
> Waiting the back-return of Charon's boat;
> Hell and Elysium swarm with ghosts of men
> That I have sent from sundry foughten fields
> To spread my fame through hell and up to heaven.
> And see, my lord, a sight of strange import,
> Emperors and kings lie breathless at my feet.
> The Turk and his great empress, as it seems,
> Left to themselves while we were at the fight,
> Have desperately despatched their slavish lives;
> With them Arabia too hath left his life;
> All sights of power to grace my victory.
> And such are objects fit for Tamburlaine,
> Wherein, as in a mirror, may be seen
> His honor, that consists in shedding blood
> When men presume to manage arms with him.   [V. ii. 387–415]

It is immediately after this speech that the play ends with the
crowning of Zenocrate and promise of her immediate marriage to
Tamburlaine.

Tamburlaine is essentially a play about human aspiration,
which is presented as something admirable, to be wondered at,
and as something which can be fully rendered only in a special
kind of rhetorical poetry in which, and only in which, the proper
vehicle for the expression of this aspiration can be found. Action

takes second place; it is often either perfunctory, or the casual implementation of previous and succeeding speech about it, or stylised into a ritual which removes from it all moral implication. Human nature in its less strenuous aspects breaks in on occasion, but this forms no part of the grand design of the play but is the inevitable consequence of the dramatist's inability to sustain in a state of continuous excitement his vision of man as purely *homo ambitiosus* (in his translation of Ovid's *Elegies,* Marlowe renders *ambitiosus amor* of Elegy IV Book II as "my ambitious ranging mind"). It is indeed impossible to keep going a whole play without paying some attention to the more domestic elements in human nature. The dialogue between Bajazeth and Zabina in their extremity of torment and humiliation has a kind of affectionate sweetness which threatens the whole fabric of the play:

> Sweet Bajazeth, I will prolong thy life
> As long as any blood or spark of breath
> Can quench or cool the torments of my grief.
>
> [V. ii. 220–22]

Zabina, who is here speaking, never falters in her tone of loving courtesy towards her degraded husband, so long as he is alive. This suggests a world of values in the light of which the value of aspiration as such demands to be judged with a moral judgment. But the whole point of *Tamburlaine* is that moral judgments are irrelevant. Aspiring man is for Marlowe man at his most impressive, and impressiveness of this sort has no relation at all to morality: it is *virtù,* not virtue in the present English sense of the word, that matters. But though aspiration does certainly represent an important and captivating aspect of man, and though the picture of the great conqueror as representing one mode of man "still climbing after knowledge infinite" is presented by Marlowe with extraordinary brilliance, the glare of naked and continuous desire for power, however that desire may be presented so as to symbolise a central aspect of the human condition, becomes in the end too unrelieved a light by which to look at human nature. There are moments when we feel that Marlowe himself realised this, but because at such moments Marlowe is deflected away from his grand design, it is difficult to integrate them into the play as a whole. To take up such moments and discuss them as though they represent a genuine psychological sophistication in the presentation of the characters seems to me to be quite unrealistic. To attempt to see subtleties in the development of Zenocrate's character or to find profound moral conflict implied in Tamburlaine's "What is beauty, saith my sufferings then" speech is to try to read the play for something other than it is, and this is not profitable. *Tamburlaine* is a dramatic poem about man as an aspiring animal, and so far as a play can be made out of this limited theme Marlowe has made one. The greatest drama does not, however, push a single viewpoint so relentlessly. However much we call into service our knowledge and appreciation of the way in which Renaissance humanism developed a new and exciting view of the significance of human aspiration, the fact remains that *homo ambitiosus* is in the end a bit of a bore. For all its splendour, *Tamburlaine* tires us before we have done with it.

"I put," wrote Thomas Hobbes in his *Leviathan,* "I put for a general inclination of all mankind, a perpetual and restless desire of power after power, that ceaseth only in death." Hobbes thought that this notion was his own sadly realistic discovery. But Marlowe had been there before him, noting the same fact not with sadness but triumphantly. In spite of the sustained note of triumph, however, even in Marlowe the sadness is there. What in the end is this fury of ambition, this boundless appetite for power, this high frenzy of rhetorical expression of lust for perpetually exceeding? It divides man from his fellows (in spite of Tamburlaine's capacity for loyalty and friendship), damps down the more valuable human responses, and rides roughshod over reason and morality. Marlowe cannot, in spite of all his endeavors, prevent a sense of this from breaking into his play, though it never becomes really part of it. *Tamburlaine* the play, like Tamburlaine the character, exhibits astonishing virtuosity: but in the end we feel that, in plays as in men, virtuosity is not enough.

KENNETH FRIEDENREICH

Directions in TAMBURLAINE Criticism

Critics of Marlowe's *Tamburlaine* inherited from the late nineteenth century a view of the play which was idolatrous and biographical, rooted in the belief that Marlowe was not only the supreme poetic innovater of his time, but also a sacrilegious rebel whose plays were primarily vehicles for his own aspirations and whose heroes were always embodiments of the poet himself. It was a view perpetuated by Algernon Charles Swinburne in his widely influential *The Age of Shakespeare*,[1] where Marlowe is called "the great discoverer, the most daring and inspired pioneer, in all of our poetic literature." Tamburlaine in this view was Marlowe himself, the rebellious deification of a superman, in love with beauty as with conquest, at war with all of the idols of his age, powerful enough to challenge the gods themselves. Tucker Brooke in his *Tudor Drama* of 1911 carried on this notion, calling *Tamburlaine* the finest expression in English of the heroic play, a fusion of drama with chivalric romance. Marlowe and his Tamburlaine were inseparable for this writer, who while he criticized the formlessness and crudity of the two plays could excuse their defects on the grounds that "the bombast and violence of Marlowe's play was transmuted into legitimate dramatic material by the fervency with which the poet expressed his own high aspiring soul in the terms of world-conquest and war-like ruthlessness."

Such notions are slow in dying, and much of twentieth century

---

[1] Full bibliographical data for all critics cited is contained in the bibliography.

criticism of Marlowe's play may be viewed as an attempt to defend this essentially romantic notion of Marlowe's achievement against the reactions which inevitably have set in against it. These countercurrents of criticism have tended to stress the independence of the play as a work of art and thus the irrelevance of our admittedly faulty and often incorrect notions about Marlowe's life. They have pointed to moral and intellectual concerns in the work far more complex than the simple amoral optimism which Swinburne and his followers found in it. They have related it to an older tradition of dramatic literature reaching back to the Middle Ages, and they have closely examined the relation of its parts to one another, unwilling to accept the verdict of formlessness which earlier critics called a special part of the play's character; and they have begun to closely analyze the play's unique and special use of language, specifically the language of poetry. Some recent critics, like David Bevington, have found an "ambiguity of moral impact" quite at variance with the positive kind of affirmation which earlier critics had found in the play, and this moral ambiguity may in fact be borne out by the widely diverse interpretations to which the play is now being subjected. It is likely that out of this very diversity a new synthesis may finally emerge.

Probably the most influential study of Marlowe in our time has been Una M. Ellis-Fermor's *Christopher Marlowe,* first published in 1927, for while this book perpetuated the individualistic rebel Marlowe of Swinburne and Tucker Brooke, it carried this notion in new directions and established attitudes which have profoundly affected the work of later critics. For Ellis-Fermor Tamburlaine was Marlowe's vision of human aspiration and the play a triumph of the will and imagination over all physical limits, the hero a symbol of Marlowe's personal quest for power. The formlessness which she found in the plot she explained as inherent in the very nature of the play, for the themes of aspiration and conquest were themselves without dramatic interest. Ellis-Fermor may have established the persistent later tradition of denigration of the second part of *Tamburlaine,* for she saw in it only a raving oriental despot transformed from the superman of the first play, and she saw this alteration and decline as the inevitable consequence of the kind of play Marlowe was writing. She went far beyond earlier critics in her analysis of Marlowe's poetry, calling it not the "poetry of imagery at all, but the poetry of ideas," and thus reinforcing the notion that the plays were vehicles for the intellectual convictions of their author. Marlowe and Tamburlaine in her view soar after infinite power together; only as Marlowe grows in intellect, moving finally to utter anguish in his last plays, does he come to realize that even a Tamburlaine can not attain his dream of consummate power, knowledge, and will.

But at the very time that Ellis-Fermor was writing, the reaction against her view of Marlowe was already beginning. It came, in part, through such source studies as those of Ethel Seaton whose three articles on the sources of Marlowe demonstrated that he was a voracious reader with a facile imagination who could make dramatic material out of what was essentially undramatic. While earlier critics had argued that Marlowe had infused the historical Tamburlaine with all of his own personal aspirations, writers like Leslie Spence went on to demonstrate that many of the features of Marlowe's plays were virtually dictated by the sources he adapted. She found in Thomas Fortescue and Petrus Perondinus the same kind of superman Marlowe depicted in *Tamburlaine* and she attacked those critics who belittled the dramatist's "ability as a playwright in assuming that he lacked the detachment necessary to create an objective character." Her essays on the sources asserted importantly for perhaps the first time the need to separate Marlowe the man from the characters he created, and the need to see these characters in terms of the historical milieu in which Marlowe found them rather than in terms of his own personality.

Spence's articles are reflections of the spirit of historical criticism which was coming to dominate the study of Elizabethan literature. Carroll Camden in "Tamburlaine: the Choleric Man" (1929) tried to relate Marlowe's protagonist to what an Elizabethan audience might naturally believe about the theory of the humours, just as Spence had tried to relate him to his historical sources. Humours psychology was to be again invoked in the study of Marlowe's play some years later by Johnstone Parr, who in *Tamburlaine's Malady* (1953) sought to prove that *Tamburlaine* was not a tragedy of ambition, but one rather about a hero who is both the beneficiary and the victim of astrological influences and his own choleric disposition. Willard Thorp in "The

Ethical Problem in Marlowe's *Tamburlaine*," tried to relate the play to the normal expectations of an Elizabethan audience, arguing that no dramatist writing for such an audience could dare to outrage the orthodox sense of morality and that in creating *Tamburlaine* Marlowe was forced to cope with this fact. Since, Thorp argues, Marlowe's historical sources generally viewed Tamburlaine as a blasphemous "scourge of God" who had risen from humble origins, Marlowe could present him in such terms without offending the sensibilities of his audience, allowing him to openly flaunt convention upon the stage and blaspheme as freely as he would. Thorp argued also that Marlowe had cast his play within a deliberately Christian framework, a point that was soon to be taken up by other critics.

Most notably it was taken up by Roy W. Battenhouse whose *Marlowe's Tamburlaine: A Study in Renaissance Moral Philosophy*, published in 1941, is the only single book devoted in entirety to the play, and remains one of the most thorough of all studies of *Tamburlaine*. Battenhouse denied the moral ambiguity which most earlier critics had found in the work and instead interpreted it in Christian terms. From this study Marlowe emerges neither an intellectual revolutionary nor a religious heretic, but a consciously Christian creator of "one of the most grandly moral spectacles in the whole realm of English drama." Battenhouse regards the two parts of *Tamburlaine* as, in effect, a single ten-act tragedy in which the protagonist is finally destroyed when he challenges the very deity which had created him as a "scourge of God." This view of *Tamburlaine* as a consistent tragic exemplum depicting the fall of man through pride and ambition represents a polar contrary to the notion of the play as a heroic rather than a tragic spectacle, in which the hero is the subject of Marlowe's admiration, ultimately triumphant, and dying at last only because all men must die, no matter how magnificent. What critics like Ellis-Fermor saw as the far from magnificent ranting tyrant of *Part II*, Battenhouse saw as a consistent deterioration of the tragic protagonist in terms of the larger tragic conception of the play which called for his destruction. Battenhouse is thus one of the first critics to regard *Part II* as a consistent part of Marlowe's design rather than an afterthought prompted by the stage popularity of *Part I*, and thus as a work of art of considerable merit in its own right. In this new appreciation of the importance of *Part II*, he was to be followed by Helen Gardner, G. I. Duthie, and most recently by Susan Richards.

Battenhouse's work was among the first of many attempts to study *Tamburlaine* in the light of Renaissance ideas. Other critics, using similar historical methodology, often came to quite different conclusions. D. C. Allen, for instance, in "Renaissance Remedies for Fortune: Marlowe and the *Fortunati*" (1941), suggested that Marlowe shaped Tamburlaine as one of the *Fortunati* such as were described by Giovanni Pontano in *De Fortuna* (1501), men born to dominate fortune regardless of their own conduct, who thus might act as capriciously and impulsively as they wished, without regard to moral law. Irving Ribner in "The Idea of History in Marlowe's *Tamburlaine*" (1953), came to a similar conclusion by demonstrating the historicity of Marlowe's play and arguing that the plays were informed not by a Christian but rather by a classical idea of history, in which not providence, but fortune and human will became the dominating forces in human affairs, and in which Tamburlaine could be conceived of as the "lawgiver" who might stand outside of all moral standards while he worked the reformation of states which had fallen into corruption. But the most significant of the historical studies which took exception to Battenhouse was that of Paul H. Kocher, whose *Christopher Marlowe: A Study of his Thought, Learning and Character* appeared in 1946 and whose very title may indicate the author's special bias.

Kocher began with the old assumption that Marlowe was a highly "subjective" artist who revealed himself in his plays, and he set out to examine these plays "only secondarily as works of art, and primarily as mirrors of the thought, learning and character of their creator." The creator emerges as a passionate, articulate, and anguished skeptic about religion. Kocher cannot accept the notion of the two parts of *Tamburlaine* as having much relation to one another, for he sees each of the plays to be concerned with a different religious issue. The first part portrays a "scourge of God" in traditional Christian terms, of whom Christians might naturally approve, but whose God is one of naked power. In the second part there is much ironic playing with Christian dogma, an attack upon Christianity combined with an imaginative fascination with it which leads Kocher to conclude that "however bitterly Marlowe may have hated Christian dogma, there were some elements in it, notably in its teaching about God, which could enlist the highest fervor of his imagination." It is thus impossible for him to agree with Battenhouse that the two parts comprise a single ten-act play. The hero's death is not a punishment for sin but a final victory in which "all is sympathy, adoration, and grief." We have in Kocher's work an historical study which attempts to use contemporary documents to illuminate *Tamburlaine,* but which arrives at last at a conception of the play quite different from that of Battenhouse and, in fact, very close to that of Ellis-Fermor.

Battenhouse's reading of *Tamburlaine* as a ten-act play of strong moral import was attacked as "a desperate argument" by F. P. Wilson in his Clark lectures for 1951, published two years later as *Marlowe and the Early Shakespeare.* Wilson held that there was little in the character of Tamburlaine which could not be accounted for by the play's sources, and he ridiculed the notion that this or any other of Marlowe's heroes could be viewed as a mirror of their author. "The danger of reading private allusions into Marlowe's plays," he wrote, "is that we do injury to his dramatic gifts. We are tempted to see him in a false perspective as a frustrated lyric poet instead of the very considerable dramatic poet that he was." Marlowe, for Wilson, was a dramatist who suspended moral judgment, leaving it to his audience to ponder the nature of his hero and draw what conclusions about him they could.

Wilson's consistent historical perspective cannot be said to have had great influence upon other critics of Marlowe. In the very year that he gave his lectures the conception of Tamburlaine as a reflection of Marlowe's own lust for power appeared again, this time in Michel Poirier's *Christopher Marlowe,* where the play is regarded as a formless work and its leading character not as a psychological study, but as "the dramatic expression of a lyrical theme" close to the author's heart, "one of the most perfect symbols of the quest of the infinite that torments the poet's soul." Poirier's Marlowe is exactly the kind of writer that Wilson had argued he was least of all. The distinction between the hero and his creator virtually disappears when Poirier writes that "Tamburlaine-Marlowe proclaims his indomitable will, his need of reaching goals that seem farthest from his reach, as well as his absolute confidence in his own strength, which he deems great enough to enable him to fulfill his idea."

Poirier stressed Marlowe's use of hyperbole in the language and action of *Tamburlaine,* a notion developed further and more effectively by Harry Levin in *The Overreacher* (1952). All of Marlowe's protagonists for Levin are heroic figures who reach beyond their own ability to attain, a belief quite different from Wilson's view of the dramatist as an objective craftsman who could handle whatever materials he found in his sources. Levin regards the language of *Tamburlaine* as a hyperbolic extension of the will to act, for "the basic convention of Marlovian drama is to take the word for the deed." Tamburlaine is the "consummate rhetorician," one whose emotions, expressed in rhetoric, are always externalized, and who thus is incapable of growth or development as a character. Levin sees Marlowe as having begun with a conventional heroic play in *Part I,* but as having been in *Part II* "forced, by the very impact of his creation, to face the genuinely tragic conflict that was bound to destroy the monster he created." He thus, by the use of irony, revealed Tamburlaine's seeming victories to be quite other than what they appeared to be, and all his triumphs finally to be delusions prefiguring his own meteoric fall. Later critics were to continue to explore Marlowe's irony, to which Levin pointed more clearly than ever before. Among the best of such later attempts has been Robert Cockcroft's "Emblematic Irony: Some Possible Significances of Tamburlaine's Chariot" (1968), which argues that the hero's personal degeneration is ironically prefigured in the dramatic emblem of his chariot being drawn by captive kings, an emblem which had ancient symbolic implications.

Levin's probing of Marlowe's use of language, more penetrating than that of any earlier critic, was taken up by many later writers. Donald Peet, for instance, in "The Rhetoric of Tamburlaine" argued that Marlowe was himself an accomplished rhetorician, and analyzed the play in terms of the conventional rhetorical figures studied in Renaissance schools. Peet pointed to Marlowe's use of hyperbole and amplification so as to create in the audience a sense of wonder and admiration at Tamburlaine, and this use of diction, he held, prevented him from writing any play other than one devoted to a single commanding figure. Perhaps the most thorough analysis of Marlowe's language thus far to appear is in David Daiches "Language and Action in Marlowe's *Tamburlaine*," a lecture delivered at the Sorbonne in 1961.

The past decade has seen an amplification and a development in various directions of the basic attitudes of Ellis-Fermor, Battenhouse, Wilson, Kocher, and Levin. The highly personal *Tamburlaine* appears again in Michael Quinn's "The Freedom of Tamburlaine" (1961), where the hero is seen as a self-sufficient figure who is Marlowe's ideal and whose self-sufficiency rests upon a theory of history which Marlowe espoused. *Tamburlaine* is related to Shakespeare's *Henry V* and the developing tradition of the heroic play by Robert Egan in "A Muse of Fire—*Henry V* in the Light of *Tamburlaine*" (1968). Amplifications of Egan's view have recently appeared in Eugene M. Waith's *Ideas of Greatness: Heroic Drama in England* and David Riggs's *Shakespeare's Heroical Histories: Henry VI and Its Literary Tradition,* where Marlowe's *Tamburlaine* plays are considered crucial to the evolution of historical and romantic drama. F. P. Wilson's view of Marlowe as the objective artist concerned with manipulating his audience appears in new form in Frank B. Fieler's *Tamburlaine, Part I and its Audience* (1961). For this writer, Marlowe approached the difficult problem of how to glorify a figure generally regarded by his audience as morally reprehensible by maintaining audience suspense and anticipation, the fall of the hero which was an inevitable part of the story being skillfully held in abeyance throughout the first part of the play. Marlowe for Fieler finally reveals in Tamburlaine a "vision of a magnificent human being who acted in a way unworthy of his own greatness," and this vision of the hero he finds to have been in accord with the conception of him which Marlowe inherited from the humanist historians and philosophers who had transmitted his story.

Three important books on Marlowe appeared in 1962, each revealing a separate approach to *Tamburlaine*. E. M. Waith's *The Herculean Hero,* the earlier of his two lengthy treatments of Marlowe's plays, gives us an heroic Tamburlaine once more, one conceived within the tradition of the Herculean hero, who despite his excesses and brutalities promotes admiration and awe in the audience and in whose tragic fall from greatness there is a sense of wonder. More closely allied to Battenhouse is Douglas Cole's treatment of the play in *Suffering and Evil in the Plays of Christopher Marlowe,* although Cole specifically disagrees with Battenhouse's reading of the play in explicit Christian terms. For Cole the play is Marlowe's stern vision of gratuitous malevolence in the world which manifests itself in human suffering, with Tamburlaine, in spite of what greatness he has, participating inevitably in the evil he looses: "Tamburlaine, in his dynamic drive for superhumanity through martial conquest leads inevitably to inhumanity. The law of strife, not harmony, is the foundation of his aspiration, and it can only be fulfilled in terms of destructive physical violence."

A third position appears in David M. Bevington's *From Mankind to Marlowe.* Like many earlier critics Bevington sees the play as morally ambiguous, and regards this very moral ambiguity, moreover, as the distinctive feature of Marlowe's artistry. He tries to explain it in terms of a tradition of staging which had sprung from the very structure of the old morality plays and which had been developed by the travelling troupes who performed the later moralities and early Tudor interludes. The need for actors to double roles perpetuated a kind of structure in which good and evil forces were constantly being balanced against one another, and of this structure Marlowe's plays were the culminating example. Moral ambiguity resulted in *Tamburlaine* because the sources with which Marlowe worked could not be perfectly reconciled with the dramatic structure he had inherited from tradition, so that "contradictory impressions of divinity and bestiality are never reconciled, and their interplay creates the basic interest of the drama." This stress upon moral ambiguity, the delicate balancing of contrary modes of perception as a basic element of Marlowe's artistry, and indeed of all great drama, has become increasingly more marked in essays written since the publication of Bevington's book. It informs Robert Kimbrough's essay included in the present volume and Sidney R. Homan's "Chapman and Marlowe: The Paradoxical Hero and the Divided Response" (1969). Homan would include Marlowe among those dramatists who create characters "with mutually exclusive qualities, glaring strengths and demeaning vices, in order to produce a divided response," this kind of audience reaction representing the highest achievement of dramatic art. In *Tamburlaine* Homan sees a tension of contraries represented by Tamburlaine's deeds, which are reprehensible, on the one hand, and on the other his thoughts and aspirations which are heroic and admirable.

The four hundredth anniversary of Marlowe's birth was commemorated in 1964 by an all-Marlowe issue of the *Tulane Drama Review*. Included in it were Clifford Leech's important essay on "The Structure of *Tamburlaine*" and Jocelyn Powell's "Marlowe's Spectacle," which returned to the examination of Marlowe's stagecraft, a subject which the author argued had received all too little previous consideration. For Powell, Marlowe was a dramatist who knew how to create dramatic images or "emblems" by the subtle combination and interrelationship of language and action, with the language often serving as a kind of commentary upon the action which had just preceded it. By this device he was able to create dramatic interest and tension in a play whose basic material was essentially episodic and undramatic. Dramatic technique is also Robert Y. Turner's concern in "Shakespeare and the Public Confrontation Scene in Early History Plays," published in the same year. *Tamburlaine,* for Turner, "can be described as a rhythmic alternation between narrative and dramatic scenes. . . . For Marlowe the confrontation was a dramatic aria, sufficient in itself and the momentum of the drama paused for the full display of this experience." Audience manipulation by Marlowe appeared again as the concern of Timothy G. A. Nelson in "Marlowe and his Audience: A Study of *Tamburlaine*" (1969), which argued that by his manipulation of his audience Marlowe rendered them more susceptible to his assault on orthodox beliefs.

The Marlowe quartercentenary prompted also the publication of J. B. Steane's *Marlowe: A Critical Study.* Like Kocher, Steane sees Tamburlaine's world as one where the law of Nature is one of strife and insurrection, ruled over by a God of force and naked power. The structure of *Tamburlaine* rests on the alternation of scenes which present the hero first in a favorable and then in an unfavorable light, the poet compelling us to abandon our more civilized inclinations and submit to our baser impulses which compel us to admire the ruthless conqueror. This results in a moral ambiguity. But, nevertheless, Steane sees *Tamburlaine* "in its extraordinary way fundamentally and deeply a religious work," for it embodies a reverence for beauty, a pride in man, and a creed of aspiration. There is, however, a basic inconsistency in Steane's approach to the play which, while it takes issue with Battenhouse's Christian reading, nevertheless sees Tamburlaine's sudden distemper in *Part II* as an act of divine retribution and a judgment upon the hero's behavior which Marlowe has supposedly exalted. The notion of divine retribution in the play appears also in Peter V. LePage's "The Search for Godhead in Marlowe's *Tamburlaine*" (1965), who sees the work finally as an expression of the inhumanity of such striving as Tamburlaine exemplifies.

Criticism of *Tamburlaine* has tended to reflect most of the preoccupations of current critical theory. C. L. Barber in "The Death of Zenocrate" (1966), for instance, has subjected the play to a currently fashionable kind of mythic-psychological analysis in which Tamburlaine is seen as engaged in "a titanic struggle for manhood" which comes to center upon his relation to Zenocrate, and which reflects a similar struggle on the part of the play's author. Tamburlaine, for Barber, provides an example of "the familiar pattern of striving to supplant the father, conceived as all-powerful." He cannot wed Zenocrate until he has achieved this mastery and thus demonstrated his own manliness. Since she is the final end of all his striving, he is utterly dependent upon Zenocrate, and her death thus becomes an illustration of the final futility of such dependence. He can only react to it in the meaningless bluster of encasing her body in gold and burning the city in which she has died.

There have been more radical departures from conventional criticism of the play, such as John Cutts' "Tamburlaine: 'as fierce as Achilles was'" (1967). Arguing that Marlowe has drawn heavily upon the story in Ovid's *Metamorphoses* of the rescue of Achilles from the bondage of womanhood imposed upon him by his mother, Thetis, so that he may escape death in battle, Cutts holds that Tamburlaine is described by Marlowe in feminine terms, and that he is, in fact, as cowardly as Mycetes, since we never see him in actual battle. The heroic Tamburlaine and the sinful Tamburlaine in this view have given way to the effeminate Tamburlaine.

With this reading of the play it might seem that the possibilities of criticism have been exhausted. But actually the basic questions raised by serious critics of *Tamburlaine* are far from resolved, and the polarities of interpretation are perhaps even more sharply than ever before posed in the most recent interpretations. On whether the play is a heroic celebration of an admirable hero or a tragic portrait of the degeneration of a sacrilegious tyrant, the divergence of opinion remains as wide as ever, and this issue must be linked to the larger question of whether the play was written as a vehicle for Marlowe's own personal heresy, as a traditional moral exemplum, or as a disinterested example of moral ambiguity, designed perhaps to manipulate the feelings of an audience in contrary directions at the same time. Perhaps the most significant contribution of the play's most recent criticism has been in a narrower range. It has done much to explain *Tamburlaine's* dramatic structure and to illustrate Marlowe's own special use of language. It has also begun the long neglected task of relating the two parts of *Tamburlaine* to one another. As the range of opinions described here suggests, Marlowe's *Tamburlaine* plays have not ceased to excite and fascinate readers or spectators.

Selected Bibliography

ALLEN, D. C. "Renaissance Remedies for Fortune: Marlowe and the *Fortunati.*" *Studies in Philology* XXXVIII (1941):188–97.

BAKELESS, JOHN. *The Tragicall History of Christopher Marlowe.* 2 vols. Cambridge, Mass., 1942. Reprinted 1964.

BARBER, C. L. "The Death of Zenocrate." *Literature and Psychoanalysis* XVI (1966):13–24.

BATTENHOUSE, ROY W. *Marlowe's Tamburlaine: A Study in Renaissance Moral Philosophy.* Nashville, Tenn., 1941. Reprinted 1964.

———. "Protestant Apologetics and the Subplot of *2 Tamburlaine.*" *ELR* 3 (1973):30–43.

BEVINGTON, DAVID M. *From Mankind to Marlowe: Growth of Structure in the Popular Drama of Tudor England.* Cambridge, Mass., 1962.

BOAS, FREDERICK S. *Christopher Marlowe: A Biographical and Critical Study.* Oxford, 1940. Rev. ed. 1953.

BROOKE, C. F. TUCKER. *The Tudor Drama.* Boston, 1911.

BRADBROOK, M. C. *Themes and Conventions of Elizabethan Tragedy.* Cambridge, 1935.

BROWN, WILLIAM J. "Marlowe's Debasement of Bajazet: Foxe's *Actes and Monuments* and *Tamburlaine, Part I.*" *Renaissance Quarterly* 24 (1971):38–48.

CAMDEN, CARROLL, JR. "Tamburlaine: The Choleric Man." *Modern Language Notes* XLIV (1929):430–35.

CLEMEN, WOLFGANG. *English Tragedy Before Shakespeare.* Translated by T. S. Dorsch. London, 1961.

COLE, DOUGLAS. *Suffering and Evil in the Plays of Christopher Marlowe.* Princeton, 1962.

COCKCROFT, ROBERT. "Emblematic Irony: Some Possible Significances of Tamburlaine's Chariot." *Renaissance and Modern Studies* XII (1968):33–55.

CUTTS, JOHN. "Tamburlaine: 'as fierce as Achilles was.'" *Comparative Drama* I (1967):105–9.

DICK, HUGH G. "*Tamburlaine* Sources Once More." *Studies in Philology* XLVI (1949):154–66.

EGAN, ROBERT. "A Muse of Fire: *Henry V* in the Light of *Tamburlaine.*" *Modern Language Quarterly* XXIX (1968):15–28.

FANTA, CHRISTOPHER G. *Marlowe's "Agonists": An Approach to the Ambiguity of His Plays.* Cambridge, Mass., 1971.

FIELER, FRANK B. *Tamburlaine, Part I, and its Audience.* Gainesville, Fla., 1961.

FRIEDENREICH, KENNETH. "'Huge Greatnesse' Overthrown: The Fall of the Empire in Marlowe's *Tamburlaine* Plays." *CLIO* I:2 (1972):37–48.

HOMAN, SIDNEY R. "Chapman and Marlowe—The Paradoxical Hero and the Divided Response." *Journal of English and Germanic Philology* LXVIII (1969):391–406.

IZARD, THOMAS C. "The Principal Source for Marlowe's *Tamburlaine.*" *Modern Language Notes* LVIII (1943):411–17.

KOCHER, PAUL H. *Christopher Marlowe, A Study of his Thought, Learning, and Character.* Chapel Hill, N.C., 1946.

KNOLL, ROBERT E. *Christopher Marlowe.* New York, 1969.

LE PAGE, PETER V. "The Search for Godhead in Marlowe's *Tamburlaine.*" *College English* XXVI (1965):604–9.

LEVIN, HARRY. *The Overreacher: A Study of Christopher Marlowe.* Cambridge, Mass., 1952. Reprinted 1964.

MAHOOD, M. M. *Poetry and Humanism*. London, 1950; New York, 1970.

MASINTON, CHARLES G. "Marlowe's Artists: The Failure of Imagination." *Ohio University Review* XI (1969):22–35.

MORRIS, BRIAN, editor. *Christopher Marlowe* (Mermaid Critical Commentaries). London, 1968.

MORRIS, HARRY. "Marlowe's Poetry." *Tulane Drama Review* VIII (1964):134–54.

NELSON, TIMOTHY G. A. "Marlowe and His Audience: A Study of *Tamburlaine*." *Southern Review* III (1969):249–63.

PARR, JOHNSTONE. *Tamburlaine's Malady and other Essays on Astrology in Elizabethan Drama*. Tuscaloosa, Ala., 1953.

PEARCE, T. M. "Tamburlaine's 'Discipline to His Three Sonnes': An Interpretation of *Tamburlaine, Part II*." *Modern Language Quarterly* XV (1954):18–27.

PEET, DONALD. "The Rhetoric of *Tamburlaine*." *ELH* XXVI (1959):137–55.

POIRIER, MICHEL. *Christopher Marlowe*. London, 1951. Reprinted 1968.

POWELL, JOCELYN. "Marlowe's Spectacle." *Tulane Drama Review* VIII (1964):195–210.

QUINN, MICHAEL. "The Freedom of Tamburlaine." *Modern Language Quarterly* XXI (1961):315–20.

RIBNER, IRVING. "The Idea of History in Marlowe's *Tamburlaine*." *ELH* XX (1953):251–66.

——. "Marlowe and Machiavelli." *Comparative Literature* VI (1954):349–56.

——. "*Tamburlaine* and *The Wars of Cyrus*." *Journal of English and Germanic Philology* LIII (1954):569–73.

——. "Marlowe's 'Tragicke Glasse.' " In *Essays on Shakespeare and Elizabethan Drama Presented to Hardin Craig,* edited by Richard Hosley, pp. 91–114. Columbia, Mo., 1962.

RIGGS, DAVID. *Shakespeare's Heroical Histories: Henry VI and Its Literary Tradition*. Cambridge, Mass., 1971.

SEATON, ETHEL. "Marlowe's Light Reading." In *Elizabethan and Jacobean Studies Presented to Frank Percy Wilson*, edited by Herbert Davis and Helen Gardner, pp. 17–35. Oxford, 1960.

———. "Fresh Sources for Marlowe." *Review of English Studies* V (1929):385–401.

SMITH, HALLETT. "*Tamburlaine* and the Renaissance," In *Elizabethan Studies and Other Essays: In Honor of George F. Reynolds*, pp. 126–31. Boulder, Colo., 1945.

SMITH, WARREN D. "Substance and Meaning in *Tamburlaine, Part I.*" *Studies in Philology* 67 (1970):155–66.

SPENCE, LESLIE. "Tamburlaine and Marlowe." *PMLA* XLII (1927):604–22.

———. "The Influence of Marlowe's Sources on *Tamburlaine I.*" *Modern Philology* XXIV (1926):181–99.

STEANE, J. B. *Marlowe: A Critical Study*. Cambridge, 1964.

SWINBURNE, A. C. *The Age of Shakespeare*. London, 1909.

TOMLINSON, T. B. *A Study of Elizabethan and Jacobean Tragedy*. Cambridge, 1964.

THORP, WILLARD. "The Ethical Problem in Marlowe's *Tamburlaine.*" *Journal of English and Germanic Philology* XXIX (1930):385–89.

TURNER, ROBERT Y. "Shakespeare and the Public Confrontation Scene in Early History Plays." *Modern Philology* LXII (1964): 1–12.

WAITH, EUGENE M. *Ideas of Greatness: Heroic Drama in England*. London, 1971.

WILSON, F. P. *Marlowe and the Early Shakespeare*. Oxford, 1953.